Teaching
Narrative
Theory

Modern Language Association of America
Options for Teaching

For a complete listing of titles,
see the last pages of this book

Teaching
Narrative
Theory

Edited by
David Herman,
Brian McHale, and
James Phelan

The Modern Language Association of America
New York   2010

MLA and the MODERN LANGUAGE ASSOCIATION are trademarks
owned by the Modern Language Association of America. For information
about obtaining permission to reprint material from MLA book publications,
send your request by mail (see address below), e-mail (permissions@mla.org),
or fax (646 458-0030).

Library of Congress Cataloging-in-Publication Data

Teaching narrative theory / edited by David Herman, Brian McHale, and James
Phelan.
        p. cm. — (Options for teaching, ISSN 1079-2562 ; 29)
        Includes bibliographical references and index.
        ISBN 978-1-60329-080-7 (hardcover : alk. paper)
        ISBN 978-1-60329-081-4 (pbk. : alk. paper)
    1. Narration (Rhetoric)—Study and teaching.   I. Herman, David, 1962–
II. McHale, Brian.   III. Phelan, James, 1951–
        PN212.T38 2010
        808'.0711—dc22   2010027697

Cover illustration of the paperback edition: *Riddle Me This, Batman.*
By Jean-Michel Basquiat (1987). © The Estate of Jean-Michel Basquiat /
ADAGP, Paris / ARS, New York.

Published by The Modern Language Association of America
26 Broadway, New York, NY 10004-1789
www.mla.org

Contents

David Herman, Brian McHale, and James Phelan

Introduction

Backstory: Why This Book, and Why Now?

The past couple of decades have witnessed an explosion of interest in narrative. As accounts of what happened to particular people in particular circumstances and with specific consequences, stories are now viewed as a basic human strategy for coming to terms with time, process, and change—a strategy that contrasts with but is in no way inferior to "scientific" modes of explanation that characterize phenomena as instances of general covering laws. Concomitantly, the analysis of stories and storytelling has become a key concern in fields ranging from sociolinguistics, discourse analysis, communication studies, history, and philosophy to cognitive and social psychology, ethnography, sociology, media studies, artificial intelligence, medicine, business, and jurisprudence. Martin Kreiswirth and others have written about a "narrative turn," parallel in scope to the linguistic turn in earlier twentieth-century philosophy and culture, to explain this diffusion, or spread, of narrative across disciplinary boundaries (see also Hyvärinen). Whatever the ultimate cause of this narrative turn—whether it is the sense that all knowledge claims are grounded in particular situations best characterized in narrative terms; the need to use stories to negotiate the multiple

1

(sub)cultures, traditions, and ways of seeing being brought into ever-closer proximity by the forces of globalization; or something else—the many fields involved in the turn toward narrative have contributed new ideas and methods to the domain of narrative theory. The result is that classical structuralist narratology has given way to a variety of "postclassical" approaches (Herman, Introduction), encompassing feminist, ethical, cognitive, transmedial, and other frameworks for narrative inquiry. We coeditors have assembled this volume, *Teaching Narrative Theory*, because we believe that the proliferating interest in narrative across disciplines, genres, and media and the attendant proliferation of methods for studying stories have created the need for a comprehensive resource focusing on the pedagogy of narrative and narrative theory at colleges and universities.

Recent years have seen the publication of a spate of critical guides to key issues in narrative theory, each with its own perspective on core aspects of the field.[1] Despite this diversity, contemporary narrative theorists share a consensus about both their object of study and fundamental methods for studying it. Narrative theory investigates what makes narrative a distinctive mode of discourse, regardless of the medium of the telling—whether face-to-face conversation, print, film, or the digital environments used for blogs and interactive fictions. In other words, narrative theory seeks to identify what constitutes narrativity or the properties that mark a text or discourse as a narrative rather than a description, a list, a lyric poem, an argument, or some other text type. To capture the distinctive structure of stories and the specific interpretive challenges they pose, narrative theorists have analyzed narrative into three components: the story, that is, the basic sequence of states, actions, and existents recounted; the text or discourse on the basis of which interpreters reconstruct that story; and the act of narration that produces the text. In this heuristic scheme, elements such as character, setting, and events are aspects of story, while features of narrative time can be discussed in terms of all three components. Flashforwards and flashbacks, for example, can be characterized as a noncorrespondence between story order and discourse order, whereas the distinction between retrospective and simultaneous telling turns on when the act of narration happens in relation to the events of the story. In the process of analyzing stories and storytelling along these lines, narrative theorists have also generated the host of technical terms and concepts for which the field is famous—or infamous, depending on your point of view. While we appreciate the rigor that such technical terminology makes possible, we also recognize that it can create impediments for newcomers to the field.

Hence our discussion below of translation as a key part of the practice of teaching narrative theory. Hence, too, our inclusion of a glossary of some of the most relevant terms at the back of this book and the care taken by our contributors to define technical terms whenever they first use them.

Although the framework for narrative study just outlined harkens back to the classical structuralist narratology that emerged in the sixties, post-classical theorists have built on that framework to develop fresh, envelope-pushing questions. They ask, for instance, how do readers reconstruct a story from the diverse details of narrative discourse, particularly when the discourse in question can consist of anything from verbal language alone to the word-image combinations of movies and graphic novels to the non-verbal sequences of pantomime or dance? What textual cues signal the presence of unreliable narration, and more broadly why do readers tend to treat a third-person (or heterodiegetic) account presented by an impersonal narrative voice as more authoritative than a first-person (or homodiegetic) account delivered by a character who has been involved in the actions and events being recounted? How does genre come into play, and to what degree does it dictate what styles of narration, and what kinds of charac-ters and plots, are normative for a given kind of text, for example, senti-mental novel versus cold-war spy fiction? How might stereotypes about gender, ethnicity, or sexuality affect readers' interpretations of characters and their actions at the level of the story, and conversely in what ways might a narrative, whether through characterization, plot, or narration, contest dominant ideologies about identity?

This last question points toward another important feature of con-temporary narrative theory: it is constantly in dialogue with broader devel-opments in critical and cultural theory. Contemporary narrative theorists turn to other kinds of theoretical inquiry because they regard form and structure as situated within history, ideology, ethical positions, and dis-cursive contexts and as influenced by the subjectivity and positionality of authors and readers. As the "Interfaces" section of this book indicates, in recent years narrative theory has engaged in productive dialogue with work on gender, ethnicity, ethics, and ideology. But there have been significant interfaces with many other important areas of critical theory, including psychoanalysis, deconstruction, postcolonial theory, and queer theory, to name just a few. Thus, Peter Brooks, in developing a theory of plot, maps some of Freud's theorizing of psychic functioning onto textual function-ing as a way to discover "something about how textual dynamics work and something about their psychic equivalents" (90). J. Hillis Miller rereads

Aristotle's *Poetics* and Sophocles's *Oedipus the King* to deconstruct the apparent logic of both Aristotle's conception of tragic plots and the plot of Sophocles's play. Gerald Prince proposes a postcolonial narratology that would be "sensitive to matters commonly, if not uncontroversially, associated with the postcolonial (e.g., hybridity, migrancy, otherness, fragmentation, diversity, power relations)" and that would "envisage" and "incorporate" their "narratological correspondents" ("On a Postcolonial Narratology" 373). Judith Roof examines the strong ideological link between heterosexuality and narrative and then seeks to undo it. The more general point here is that these dialogues and interfaces have an effect on both parties: the encounters alter our understandings of narrative and of the specific branches of critical theory at issue.

What is true of narrative theory's interactions with recent work in critical theory is also true of its interactions with other disciplines. On the one hand, narrative theorists have sought to refine classical structuralist approaches by adapting insights developed in fields ranging from media studies and linguistics to psychology and philosophical ethics. As a result, narrative theorists have reconsidered the extent to which the same story can be presented across different media, the strategies readers use to make sense of fictional minds, and the ways in which narratives both shape and are shaped by broader cultural norms and values. On the other hand, because narrative theorists study not only how people interpret stories but also how stories help us understand and navigate the world, research on narrative has begun to have a major impact on the broader investigation of human sense-making strategies across a variety of institutional and communicative settings. Thus, Rita Charon has explored how incorporating the study of narrative into the medical curriculum can enhance health care by attuning physicians to the rich complexity of individual lives. For her part, Charlotte Linde has investigated the role of storytelling in institutions, while Daniel D. Hutto has built on the work of Jerome Bruner to characterize narrative as a primary resource for folk psychology, or the everyday heuristics on which people rely to make sense of their own and others' actions in terms of reasons for acting.

So narrative theory has over the last fifteen years engaged more fully in intra- as well as interdisciplinary conversations and has as a result become increasingly influential across multiple areas of inquiry. It is striking, however, that there currently exists no other volume that specifically addresses how narrative theory, its questions, and its concepts can be brought into play in the classroom. Although the contributors to this volume draw on early pioneering work as well as state-of-the-art research in narrative studies, they focus their attention elsewhere: namely, on how key concepts from the field can inform pedagogical practice in a variety of disciplinary settings and at different levels of instruction. As the organization of the volume suggests, narrative theory is currently taught across the curriculum: in undergraduate literature courses, where elements of narrative theory are routinely taught as tools for textual analysis and interpretation; in theory courses at the undergraduate and graduate levels; in courses on film, cultural studies, folklore, linguistics, cognitive studies, and history; in rhetoric and composition programs; and in creative writing programs. In short, many instructors, in various disciplines and kinds of classes, introduce elements of narrative theory in their teaching. The present volume is targeted at all these teachers; our hope is that, collectively, the chapters included here will enable instructors in all fields and at all levels to reflect on the pedagogy of narrative theory and learn more about others' teaching practices.

Although the "narrative turn" across the arts and (some of the) sciences has helped create the broad sociodiscursive context—in Foucauldian terms the *episteme*—from which this volume has emerged, other, more local, causes have also shaped the project from the outset. For one thing, through multiple decades of combined experience in the classroom, the coeditors have encountered firsthand many of the challenges of presenting narratological terms and concepts to undergraduates and graduate students. Coupled with our own classroom experiences are those that we have learned about from our fellow participants in the sessions on the teaching of narrative that have now become a regular feature of the annual conference sponsored by the International Society for the Study of Narrative. In the spirit of those meetings, the present volume seeks to carry on the tradition of collaboratively developing practical, nuts-and-bolts strategies for teaching narrative theory.

Another impetus for the volume is the establishment of Project Narrative, an interdisciplinary initiative launched in the fall of 2006 at Ohio State University and designed to promote best practices of teaching as well as research in the field of narrative studies (http://projectnarrative.osu .edu). As it goes forward, Project Narrative intends to develop a number of curricular innovations, including an interdisciplinary undergraduate minor and a graduate specialization. Planning for these initiatives has led the coeditors to consider, more broadly, core issues of pedagogy in this domain: what needs to be taught, and how, in various kinds of classes focusing on narrative and narrative theory.

As part of this same process we have also been led to reflect on the larger instructional goals that, though not necessarily explicitly stated as such, regularly guide teachers as they work both to convey the power of narrative as a form of expression and a way of understanding the world and to teach the richness of the scholarly traditions that have grown up around the study of stories and storytelling. We suggest that three broad goals are especially salient in this connection, and we encourage readers of the volume to consider how the contributors collectively outline strategies for achieving these key pedagogical aims. The three goals can be called translation, justification, and integration. Translation refers to the process by which students at whatever level acquire, first, a basic understanding of the concepts behind terms of art such as *zero focalization, figural narrative situation, deictic shift, actant, extradiegetic-homodiegetic narration, metalepsis,* and *emplotment;* and, second, the ability to implement these and other technical terms and concepts in their own interpretive practice. For example, a fundamental responsibility for teachers of narrative theory is not just to present the nomenclatures that have been developed to describe fluctuations in the perspectival organization of a narrative text but also to enable students to internalize those nomenclatures and make them part of their basic skill set as interpreters, analysts, writers. In this way, students can move from merely labeling differences among the kinds of viewpoints structuring a narrative as it unfolds in time to using the concept of internal focalization, say, to identify the vantage point of a particular center of consciousness or "reflector"—and then to factor into their interpretations the biases attendant on having a specific, situated position in the world evoked by the narrative.[2] Students can also compare how shifts into and out of character-based perspectives function in different narratives, thereby gaining fuller appreciation of narrative as a system of formal possibilities that have different "meaning potentials" in any given case.

Indeed, in describing this second aspect of translation, which involves putting new terms and concepts into practice, we have already started to sketch the second broad pedagogical goal, namely, justification. Here, as in other areas of scholarship and teaching, translation and justification are intertwined aspects of pedagogical practice. Successfully carrying out the process of translation requires that instructors demonstrate to students not just the existence but also the value—the productiveness for interpretation and analysis—of ideas from narrative theory. In other words, it is not sufficient to expose students to the sometimes-dizzying constellations of terms developed by narrative analysts working in different traditions within the field (e.g., Genette on internal focalization vs. Stanzel on figural narration), nor is it sufficient to show that these terms *can* be used to develop interpretations of particular texts. An additional responsibility is to show why the terms *should* be used—how they function as invaluable heuristic tools that can open up insights that would not otherwise be available. Thus, the concept of internal focalization can help students identify part of what makes the experience of reading Henry Fielding's *Tom Jones* and Franz Kafka's *The Trial* so very different. Both texts are told in the third person, that is, narrated heterodiegetically; but in contrast with the synoptic vantage point on the storyworld provided in Fielding's novel, Kafka's text is rigorously internally focalized, resulting in an account refracted through K.'s limited, fragmentary, and inescapably situated perspective on events. This perspective is steeped in uncertainty about even the elementary "facts" of the storyworld, conveying a world that is experienced as fundamentally indeterminate by K. (Herman, *Universal Grammar* 124–34)—and that readers are compelled to experience in the same way, since K.'s perspective is their only means of access to the world of the narrative.

What is more, at the graduate level in particular, the challenge goes beyond translating key terms and concepts and demonstrating their interpretive yield. Instructors also face the task of enabling more advanced students to integrate ideas from narrative theory into their growing repertoire of interpretive approaches, their strategies for professional development, and their ongoing apprenticeship as teachers in their own right.[3] The challenge of integration also applies at the undergraduate level, but in a more generic way; that is, in lower-level classes instructors need to help beginning students think of what they are learning as one aspect of the multiple bodies of knowledge to which they are being introduced through their coursework as a whole. In graduate courses, however, the onus is on instructors to show students how ideas from narrative theory can be made part of their everyday practice as professional scholars in training. In this connection, though many of the contributors to this volume suggest ways to tailor particular aspects of the teaching of narrative theory to the graduate classroom, readers are encouraged to focus on Susan Mooney's essay, which reviews a range of strategies for incorporating narrative theory into a graduate seminar in literature. Also relevant are the essays contained in parts 3 and 4, which discuss how to teach concepts proposed by narrative theorists in concert with ideas developed in other domains relevant for graduate education—for example, theories of popular genres, scholarship in film studies, work on the new electronic media, and research on gender and ethnicity.

The Main Story: Situations, Elements, Media, Interfaces

As noted above, we have aimed to make this volume useful to teachers of narrative theory at all levels and in all corners of the curriculum, and our organization of the essays into four different sections follows from that goal. Part 1 addresses the variety of curricular and disciplinary situations in which narrative theory is commonly taught in United States colleges and universities. Part 2 concentrates on teaching the fundamental conceptual and terminological tools developed to address the basic elements of narrative such as plot, time, space, world, voice, and character. Part 3 moves away from the more literary emphasis of part 2 as it addresses teaching narrative theory in relation to "subliterary genres" and media other than the printed word. Finally, part 4 addresses teaching narrative theory's interfaces, or intersections, with significant issues in contemporary critical theory: gender, ethnicity, ethics, and ideology.

The first three essays of part 1 consider the situations of the undergraduate literature course (Keen), the undergraduate theory course (Barsky), and the graduate literature course (Mooney). The next five essays form a cluster on teaching narrative theory in classrooms devoted to subjects other than literature: rhetoric and composition (Boehm and Journet), creative writing (Evenson), folklore and ethnography (Shuman), history/historiography (Kellner), and image-text studies (Kafalenos).

In her essay Suzanne Keen provides a blueprint for using narrative theory to help undergraduates sharpen their skills as readers of and writers about narrative literature. Keeping her eye on these larger goals, Keen offers an admirable set of practical and portable exercises for distinguishing between actual and implied authors; analyzing characterization by tracing motifs and engaging in scalar descriptions; identifying different modes of representing consciousness; and mapping plots through actantial functions. Robert Barsky begins his essay on the undergraduate theory course by articulating eight principles underlying his pedagogical approach to narrative theory (e.g., some narrative theory is implicit in narrative texts themselves) and then turns to show how these principles can inform the teaching of three significant domains of narrative theory that are also part of the larger history of critical theory: Russian formalism, Bakhtinian dialogism, and structuralist narratology. Susan Mooney presents a model for encouraging (and directing) two-way traffic in the graduate classroom between narrative theory and narrative texts. Her exemplary narrative text is James Joyce's *Ulysses*, and she shows how it can be used both to illuminate and to challenge theoretical accounts of a range of narrative phenomena, including focalization, plot, and speech representation.

Beth Boehm and Debra Journet emphasize three objectives in their teaching of rhetoric and composition to graduate students: helping them understand that narrative is an epistemological and a rhetorical tool, that is, a way of knowing as well as a way of communicating; acquainting them with narrative theory as a research tool, one that can enhance their ability to analyze the diverse texts they work with and to carry out their own case studies and ethnographic projects more productively; and helping them become more effective teachers of the wide variety of narratives they will assign—and encounter—in their own classrooms. For his part, Brian Evenson argues that explicit instruction in narrative theory can reframe and enhance the more common intuitive approach of the creative writing workshop. By learning concepts from narrative theory and using them in the analysis of published fiction, creative writing students become better readers of that fiction and of one another's work, and those enhanced reading skills in turn enable them to become better writers and editors of their own narratives. Amy Shuman focuses on teaching narrative as a situated communicative performance, an approach that leads to fresh considerations of a variety of traditional topics in folklore research: collection, transmission, form, context, genre, repertoire, and interaction. Hans Kellner, anchoring his discussion in examples from Shelby Foote's *The Civil War: A Narrative—Gettysburg to Vicksburg*, shows how teaching basic concepts of narrative theory—the story-discourse distinction, the notion of an event, character, focalization, anachrony, and transmission—also provides a foundation for teaching the nature and methods of historiography. Finally, Emma Kafalenos discusses several concrete exercises that encourage students to explore the interconnections between visual art and storytelling and that help liberal arts students become better critical thinkers and fine art students better artists. These exercises focus students' attention on the selection and distribution of events, perspective, organizing structures or designs, and paratexts.

Part 2 addresses teaching the fundamental elements of narrative that instructors, regardless of their curricular or disciplinary location, will probably want their students to learn; these elements include plot (Richardson); time, space, and world (Herman); authors, narrators, and audiences (Phelan); perspective, or point of view (Matz); and character and characterization (Gorman). Under the rubric of plot, Brian Richardson considers various aspects of narrative progression, ranging from conventional patterns of disequilibrium and restored equilibrium to apparently plotless "unnatural narratives," with examples from Joyce, Alain Robbe-Grillet, and *Sex and the City*. David Herman uses Ernest Hemingway's "Hills like White Elephants" to show how students can be made aware of their own ways of narrative worldmaking—the operations they use to project and imaginatively occupy a storyworld at the prompting of temporal and spatial cues in the text. James Phelan, reflecting on the teaching of voice, walks us through exercises involving Jane Austen's *Pride and Prejudice* and Frank O'Connor's "My Oedipus Complex." In these exercises, students tease apart the voices and positions of implied authors, narrators, and authorial and narrative audiences, gauging the distances among them and thereby enhancing their own appreciation of the rhetorical means and ethical stakes of narrative. Jesse Matz's essay addresses the crucial but vexed concept of focalization, along with related issues of voice, vision, and the representation of consciousness, recapitulating the sequence of theoretical contributions from Norman Friedman and Wayne C. Booth to Dorrit Cohn, Gérard Genette, Mieke Bal, Seymour Chatman, and beyond, all the while grounding his discussion in fine-grained analyses of Russell Banks's "Sarah Cole: A Type of Love Story." Character, as David Gorman observes in the final essay of this part, is one of the most intuitive and readily graspable categories of narrative theory, but its very intuitiveness imposes on us the obligation to defamiliarize it, whether by reconceiving characters in terms of functions, in the manner of the Russian formalists and then the structuralist narratologists, or by emphasizing the historical variability of the very idea of character. In the course of his essay, Gorman also considers the construction of typologies of characters and techniques of characterization.

Part 3 refocuses the teaching of narrative theory in yet another way. The explosion of interest in narrative—the so-called narrative turn—has brought to light new objects of narrative study (or created new perspectives on overly familiar ones). Narrative theory now addresses a wide range of genres and media, including "subliterary" genre fiction, visual media (both still and moving), and digital media, among others. Acknowledging this expanding corpus of stories, part 3 cuts across the curricular and disciplinary categories of part 1 and the theoretical categories of part 2, offering essays on teaching popular narrative genres (McHale), narrative in film (Morrison), narrative in visual culture (Hirsch), and narrative in digital media (Rettberg and Rettberg).

Brian McHale considers three of the most ubiquitous, enduring, familiar, and teachable genres of popular fiction: the Western, the detective story, and science fiction. Freely migrating from medium to medium, each of these popular genres lends itself to the foregrounding of a different area of narrative theory: in the case of the Western, the functional analysis of plot; in the detective story, the opening and filling of narrative gaps; in science fiction, narrative worldmaking. Narrative theory, James Morrison argues in his essay on film, provides the categories through which students can articulate the differences they intuitively grasp between classic Hollywood movies such as *Stella Dallas* or *Touch of Evil* and popular contemporary films such as *Erin Brockovich*, *Training Day*, and *Pulp Fiction*— though narrative theory may also induce them to see the classic films as less "conventional" than they supposed and the contemporary films, conversely, as less "radical." Writing about narrative in visual culture, Marianne Hirsch describes some of the materials she uses in exercises designed to enhance her students' "visual-verbal literacy," ranging from ekphrastic "prose pictures" and texts that juxtapose photographs and verbal narrative (such as those of W. G. Sebald) to photographic archives that seem to solicit narrativization to fully "biocular" visual-verbal texts such as comics and graphic novels. Finally, Scott Rettberg and Jill Walker Rettberg outline a possible course in digital narrative, surveying some of the landmarks in criticism and theory of electronic literature (by George Landow, Jay Bolter, Espen Aarseth, N. Katherine Hayles, and Marie-Laure Ryan) and then introducing a number of digital narratives that have proven fruitful in the classroom, including hypertext fictions such as Michael Joyce's *Afternoon* and Shelley Jackson's *Patchwork Girl*, and Web-based narratives such as Robert Arellano's *Sunshine '69*, Rob Wittig's *Blue Company*, and Rob Bevan and Tim Wright's *Online Caroline*.

Part 4 explores the teaching of narrative theory's interfaces with broader developments in contemporary critical and cultural theory. As noted above, narrative theory, instead of existing in parallel with current trends in the study of literature and culture, both shapes and is shaped by key concepts in these and other areas. The discussions here focus on productive, two-way classroom interactions between narrative theory and gender (Warhol), ethnicity (Aldama), ethics (Newton), and ideology (Elias).

Robyn Warhol demonstrates how the intersection of feminist theory and narrative theory known as feminist narratology provides a framework for teaching students about the impact of gender on our understanding of narrative and, more briefly, the impact of narrative on our understanding of gender. Using examples from nineteenth- and twentieth-century fiction, Warhol shows how directing students' attention to gender can influence their understanding of fundamental elements of narrative (e.g., character, plot, focalization, and the gaze) even as that attention enables them to compare gender attitudes expressed in narrative with their own attitudes. Drawing on his experience of teaching Chicano/a narrative, Frederick Luis Aldama argues for the advantages of teaching ethnic narratives as both a political act and an aesthetic achievement, forms of practice that can be illuminated both through attention to the cultural situations of their authors and through a wide selection of narrative-theoretical concepts, including the story-discourse distinction, the implied author and reader, narrator and voyeur, style and voice, duration, palimpsest, genre, filter and slant, flashback (analepsis), exposure of the device, and cognition and emotion. Conversely, by including a range of indigenous narrative texts and traditions in the classroom, instructors can explore the extent to which these narratological tools may need to be refined or adjusted to accommodate an enriched corpus of stories. Adam Zachary Newton takes the idea of the interface in an uncanny direction, contending that narrative is haunted by ethics and showing how students can explore the consequences of this shadowy interrelation through cases studies of voice and spectacle in Saul Bellow's *Herzog* and John Stuart Mill's *Autobiography* and of Bakhtinian answerability in W. G. Sebald's *Austerlitz* and Haruki Murakami's "The Kidney-Shaped Stone That Moves Every Day." Finally, Amy J. Elias addresses the interface between narrative theory and ideological critique by discussing the principles and practices of her course Worldmaking in Contemporary Literature. This course's three modules— what is a narrative world? what do narrative worlds and actual worlds have in common? who controls the world?—require the students to move from a primary emphasis on narrative theory in the first two modules to a primary emphasis on ideological critique in the third, but each emphasis is altered by the presence of the others.

Denouement: Strategies for Using the Volume

We have designed this volume to accommodate the diverse interests of teachers of narrative theory, and in keeping with that goal we would like to conclude this introduction by indicating alternative routes through its contents. Readers who primarily or exclusively teach courses on literature may wish to focus special attention on the first three essays and parts 2 and 4. Specialists in comparative media studies might wish to concentrate on part 2 in tandem with part 3, considering the extent to which strategies for teaching the elements of narrative might need to be adjusted to take into account the medium-specific properties of the narratives they commonly work with. These same readers may also wish to explore the cross-disciplinary perspectives presented in the first eight essays, since the contributors there explore not only indigenous, field-specific traditions for studying stories but also methods of analysis geared toward print texts, narratives told in face-to-face interaction, stories conveyed through visual art, and so on. These essays are likely to provide a useful point of entry into the volume for readers who are based in fields other than literature, language, or film and media studies and who want to learn more about how to incorporate strategies for teaching narrative and narrative theory into their everyday pedagogical practices. Likewise, both the suggestions for further reading placed after the list of works cited in each essay and the glossary included at the end of the book are designed to make the text simultaneously the basis for a broader exploration of the field and an autonomous, stand-alone resource in its own right.[4]

Our hope, in sum, is that this book has something to offer for everyone interested in teaching narrative in all of its many guises and that the book will also help build even more interest in this rapidly developing area of inquiry. For seasoned instructors as well as those who have not yet incorporated ideas about narrative into their classrooms, the collective insights of the master teachers on whose experience we have fortunately been able to draw should provide a sense of the extraordinarily rich options for teaching narrative theory.

Notes

1. General guides to the field published, in English, just within the past decade include Abbott; Herman and Vervaeck; Jahn; Keen; Lothe; McQuillan; Rimmon-Kenan; and Toolan. Readers can also consult Scholes, Phelan, and Kellogg, as well as a number of other recently published resources: Bamberg; Bamberg and Andrews; Herman, *Narratologies* and *Companion*; Herman, Jahn, and Ryan; Ochs and Capps; Prince, *Dictionary*; Phelan and Rabinowitz; and Richardson.

2. For more information about theories of perspective or focalization and about strategies for teaching those theories, see Matz's essay, in this volume.

3. As this volume was being assembled, a colleague of the coeditors complained that one of the students in her graduate seminar was "shutting down" class discussions by using terms like *autodiegetic narration* without adequately explaining such terms to other students less familiar with scholarship on narrative. This incident points up other issues that fall within the domain of integration: namely, the need to encourage graduate students to help their peers explore the heuristic value of ideas from narrative theory—and to engage in larger debates about the

merits of the ideas themselves—through open, inclusive discussions of the ideas' possibilities and limits.

4. Although contributors suggested some of the items in the lists of further readings provided at the end of each essay, in other cases the additional sources are ones recommended by the coeditors and not the contributors.

Works Cited

Abbott, H. Porter. *The Cambridge Introduction to Narrative*. 2nd ed. Cambridge: Cambridge UP, 2008. Print.

Bamberg, Michael, ed. *Narrative: State of the Art*. Amsterdam: Benjamins, 2007. Print.

Bamberg, Michael, and Molly Andrews, eds. *Considering Counter-Narratives: Narrating, Resisting, Making Sense*. Amsterdam: Benjamins, 2004. Print.

Brooks, Peter. *Reading for the Plot: Design and Intention in Narrative*. New York: Knopf, 1984. Print.

Bruner, Jerome. *Acts of Meaning*. Cambridge: Harvard UP, 1990. Print.

Charon, Rita. "Narrative Medicine: Attention, Representation, Affiliation." *Narrative* 13.3 (2005): 261–70. Print.

Foucault, Michel. *The Order of Things*. 1970. New York: Vintage, 1994. Print.

Herman, David. *The Cambridge Companion to Narrative*. Cambridge: Cambridge UP, 2007. Print.

———. Introduction. Herman, *Narratologies* 1–30.

———, ed. *Narratologies: New Perspectives on Narrative Analysis*. Columbus: Ohio State UP, 1999. Print.

———. *Universal Grammar and Narrative Form*. Durham: Duke UP, 1995. Print.

Herman, David, Manfred Jahn, and Marie-Laure Ryan, eds. *Routledge Encyclopedia of Narrative Theory*. London: Routledge, 2005. Print.

Herman, Luc, and Bart Vervaeck. *Handbook of Narrative Analysis*. Lincoln: U of Nebraska P, 2005. Print.

Hutto, Daniel D. *Folk Psychological Narratives: The Sociocultural Basis of Understanding Reasons*. Cambridge: MIT P, 2008. Print.

Hyvärinen, Matti. "Towards a Conceptual History of Narrative." *The Travelling Concept of Narrative*. Ed. Hyvärinen, Anu Korhonen, and Juri Mykkänen. Helsinki: Helsinki Collegium for Advanced Studies, 2006. 20–41. *Collegium*. Web. 31 Mar. 2010.

Jahn, Manfred. *Narratology: A Guide to the Theory of Narrative*. N. pub., 2005. Web. 10 Aug. 2009.

Keen, Suzanne. *Narrative Form*. London: Palgrave, 2004. Print.

Kreiswirth, Martin. "Narrative Turn in the Humanities." Herman, Jahn, and Ryan 377–82.

Linde, Charlotte. *Working the Past: Narrative and Institutional Memory*. Oxford: Oxford UP, 2008. Print.

Lothe, Jakob. *Narrative in Fiction and Film: An Introduction*. Oxford: Oxford UP, 2000. Print.

McQuillan, Martin, ed. *The Narrative Reader*. London: Routledge, 2000. Print.

Miller, J. Hillis. *Reading Narrative*. Norman: U of Oklahoma P, 1998. Print.

Ochs, Elinor, and Lisa Capps. *Living Narrative: Creating Lives in Everyday Storytelling*. Cambridge: Harvard UP, 2001. Print.

Phelan, James, and Peter J. Rabinowitz, eds. *A Companion to Narrative Theory*. Oxford: Blackwell, 2005. Print.

Prince, Gerald. *A Dictionary of Narratology*. 2nd ed. Lincoln: U of Nebraska P, 2003. Print.

———. "On a Postcolonial Narratology." Phelan and Rabinowitz 372–81.

Richardson, Brian, ed. *Narrative Dynamics: Essays on Time, Plot, Closure, and Frames*. Columbus: Ohio State UP, 2002. Print.

Rimmon-Kenan, Shlomith. *Narrative Fiction: Contemporary Poetics*. 2nd ed. London: Routledge, 2002. Print.

Roof, Judith. *Come as You Are: Sexuality and Narrative*. New York: Columbia UP, 1996. Print.

Ryan, Marie-Laure, ed. *Narrative across Media: The Languages of Storytelling*. Lincoln: U of Nebraska P, 2004. Print.

Scholes, Robert, James Phelan, and Robert Kellogg. "Narrative Theory, 1966–2006: A Narrative." *The Nature of Narrative*. Oxford: Oxford UP, 2006. 283–336. Print.

Toolan, Michael. *Narrative: A Critical Linguistic Introduction*. 2nd ed. London: Routledge, 2001. Print.

Part I

Situations

Suzanne Keen

The Undergraduate Literature Classroom

In the undergraduate classroom the tools of narrative theory can be used in engaging exercises that enhance students' skills as both readers of and writers about literature. A teacher of narrative or the novel can most easily incorporate narrative-theory lessons into a course, but shorter exposures can also be built into other commonly taught undergraduate classes, including the traditional survey course, composition courses with a focus on reading the genres, and period-based courses. Depending on class size, some of the exercises elaborated here could be carried out in fifteen minutes; others could support group work leading into a lengthy follow-up discussion. Experience suggests that making an explicit link from a narrative theoretical concept to a principle of good reading or writing makes the matter relevant to most invested students.

In this essay, I describe four freestanding lesson plans: for distinguishing implied author and actual author, for analyzing character and characterization through motif tracing, for recognizing different modes of the representation of characters' minds, and for mapping plot through actantial functions (of characters and other entities). These plans work with classes on short fiction, novels, and other narratives in prose, film, and verse. In each case, teaching narrative theory addresses a near-universal set of aims of undergraduate literature teachers: to help students move from a synoptic mode of comment to analysis, to avoid the treatment of characters as if they were only portraits of real people, to select textual evidence that illustrates arguments (avoiding simple plot summary), to support observations about themes with accurate discussion of techniques, and to train students in the conventions of literary critical discourse.

Distinguishing Implied Author and Actual Author

Though not all narrative theorists agree with the necessity of distinguishing between the "implied author" and the "real" or "flesh and blood" author, teaching the difference can hone students' abilities to understand biographical figures versus textual personas and also the convention governing the use of the past and present tenses in discussing literature.[1] Diana Hacker states the convention clearly: "When writing about a work of literature, you may be tempted to use the past tense. The convention, however, is to describe fictional [textual] events in the present tense" (*Writer's Reference* 171). More to the point, she elaborates, "When you are quoting, summarizing, or paraphrasing the author . . . use present-tense verbs such as writes, reports, asserts, and so on. This convention is usually followed even when the author is dead" (171). The exception pertains to the writing of literary history, and that brings us right back to the distinction between the implied and actual author.

My understanding of the implied author as an effect of the text relies on Seymour Chatman and Wayne Booth; I explain this concept in *Narrative Form*:

> The author is the actual historical person who wrote the text. For instance, Charles Dickens is the author of *David Copperfield* (1849–50) . . . the *implied author* is the version of the author projected by the text itself and sometimes also conditioned by our knowledge about the actual author's life and career. Thus we can speak of the Dickens of *The Pickwick Papers* (1836–37), as contrasted with the Dickens of *Our Mutual Friend* (1864–65). (Keen 33)

The real author gets past-tense references in literary history (a form undergraduate literature teachers are relatively unlikely to ask students to write), while the implied author, in the literary analysis they write in literature courses, gets the present tense.

A ten-minute review of the group's knowledge about a specific author (preferably one they've been studying) sorts out implied and actual author. I ask all the students to stand. The privilege of sitting down is earned by a spoken sentence about the real author using a past tense verb and one about the implied author using a present tense verb. I exemplify the difference in *Narrative Form*:

> Thus the historical Dickens *lived*, *suffered* the indignity of the blacking factory, *wrote*, *made* loads of money, *left* his wife, *went* on reading tours, and *died* exhausted, whereas the implied author, "The Dickens of *Bleak House* (1852–53)," perpetually *experiments* with a mixture of first and third person, *continues* to employ characters to do his bidding, and permanently *abides* in the realm of the present tense. (34)

This fast-paced performative exercise can also be used as strong-verb practice if the professor bans "is" and "was" at the outset. Pressure mounts as the obvious statements get used up and students resort to humorous speculations about the real author's experiences and ingenious synonyms for the implied author's continuing influence on readers. (Dickens *writes, composes, implies, shapes, disorders, repeats, leaves out, overemphasizes*: they get the picture.) In a large class, a small group of volunteers can demonstrate the difference for their peers, with shout-out assistance. By the time they are all seated, they will have acquired the convention, and they can be held responsible for getting their tenses right (and keeping them consistent) in their written work.

When working with beginning writers in freshman composition courses, I emphasize the variety of strong verbs they might attribute (in present tense!) to the implied authors they discover through reading, and discussion helps them frame sharper analytic comments about textual effects. As students discover different qualities in the implied author, they begin to channel their responses and their opinions into more precise observations about the text. They even discover the beginnings of arguments: the implied author condenses/expands/omits/repeats_____ in order to create/achieve/emphasize/suppress _____. I have used the preceding Mad Lib sentence as a classroom exercise in the composition classroom, where I've taught students to avoid tautological arguments even as they practice present-tense references and the use of strong verbs.

Analyzing Characterization: Motifs and Scalar Description

That English professors agree fictional characters should be regarded as "paper beings" (Barthes 261), "word masses" (Forster 44), or nonexistent "nobodies" (Gallagher) is not a safe assumption. Many effective teachers elide the difference between fictional characters and human beings. If one begins with the assumption that characters are not *only* imitations of possible people or personlike entities designed to make readers forget their fictiveness, the trained reader also goes on to understand characters as constructs whose artifice repays our attention.

To help students achieve some critical purchase on the characters that interest them, I teach them to trace motifs through texts, paying special attention to the repetitive details that cluster around fictional characters. Several rules govern the students' motif tracing. A motif must appear at least three times. It may contribute to a sense of theme, but it must be something particular, a textual detail that can be underlined and located in a passage, not a diffuse topic that arises from the text. I affirm that the collection of details will lead to better analysis and fresher argumentation than a paper process that begins with a broad topic of, for instance, mortality, coming of age, or sexuality. Getting students to attend to hair in Thomas Hardy's fiction or hands in Dickens or scars in Toni Morrison leads more surely, in my experience, to rich arguments about sexuality, agency, and trauma than papers that start with a broad theme. Often I dedicate a whole class period to motif tracing before I even give my first paper assignment.

The leap between motif tracing as a critical practice, which involves marking up a narrative, and making richer arguments about fictional characters can be daunting. Students appreciate a bridge between their personalizing approach to character and a professor's demand for analytic commentary. Teachers in large survey courses know that some students capable of very good explication of a poem may struggle to break free from less analytic reading habits that take over when studying narrative. Motif tracing provides a bridge to an analytic mode for character-focused readers.

I prepare for the exercise described below by practicing motif tracing with students and asking them to identify the words, colors, phrases, items of clothing, style of speech (and thoughts), physical locations, and small-scale actions associated repeatedly with the characters in a narrative text. With these details, I try to persuade them, the implied author provides the prompts that invite our busy brains to project believable, three-dimensional personlike entities. Thus I offer them another recipe sentence:

> The author associates _____ (identify the motif) with the character in order to _____ (suggest a meaning, motive, or consequence).

In short order even first-year undergraduates make analytic statements about characterization.

To get at the way narrative artists use characters in patterns that contribute to the formal architecture of the narrative, I introduce multiple scales by which an individual character might be evaluated and placed in relation with other characters and entities in the fictional world. This exercise, which I derive from the work of Baruch Hochman on character (89–140), helps students practice writing and thinking about characters as constructions made out of words. My handout leaves space for jotting textual evidence to support their judgments about characters' qualities. Students can spend a full class period working in groups, and small groups can be assigned different characters from a text and Hochman's rubric (slightly altered to make the vocabulary more accessible). Because this exercise strains the space on a typical classroom blackboard, I create a sheet presenting the following opposed terms in columns:

Character traits for _____ (name of character)

Supply quotations from the text to justify your choice between the options.

stylization	naturalism
coherence	incoherence
wholeness	fragmentariness
literalness	symbolism
complexity	simplicity
transparency	opacity
dynamism	inertness

When spread out on a single sheet, the options allow space for students to jot down textual evidence and page-number citations. One could of course develop a *PowerPoint* presentation with illustrative quotations for a "stylized" or "naturalistic" character (and so forth), but I always seek quick and practical lesson plans that do not require the luxury of teaching in a smart classroom.

Once the students have the handout, I choose a fictional character from a work we have finished discussing and run through the terms, defining them and seeking students' opinion on where that character would fall on each of the scales. Is J. R. R. Tolkien's Aragorn presented naturalistically or in a stylized fashion? The students opt for stylization and point to the appropriate descriptive passages. Before long more debatable items on the scale come up. When students disagree, as for instance in a discussion of whether Gollum is a whole or fragmented character, I elicit evidence from both sides and praise them for discovering a debatable proposition.

I warn my students that the columns of terms do not represent pre-fabricated sets of qualities: that is, a particular fictional character may well be judged stylized, coherent, symbolic, and opaque or naturalistic, literal, simple, and inert. Though certain qualities often travel together, such as stylization and symbolic value, writers may surprise us by making a complex character—such as Faramir—relatively unchanging (and thus inert). When we think about fictional characters, I remind my students, the dynamic of the reading experience alters our insights: a rereading or concluded reading differs from an assessment made midway through a narrative. I thus urge students to consider whether the novelist changes the characterization of a particular figure during the course of the novel, taking an apparently whole and coherent character apart or drawing together fragments into a dynamic whole.

A second warning, that the alternatives on the scales do not imply value judgments about the characters, would hardly seem necessary, except that many students arrive in the college classroom with the idea that "round" characters are good and "flat" ones bad. Reminding students that flat characters (according to Forster) performed necessary functions in their fictional worlds helps, but the substitution of *dynamism* and *inertness* (or *complexity* and *simplicity*) for *round* and *flat* works best to free students from the notion that a character who changes must inevitably be a better, and better-written, character. A subsidiary goal of this exercise focuses students' attention on the alternatives available to writers as they craft fictional worlds and their inhabitants.

In an hour-long class, I assign small groups to work with different individual characters from a narrative all the students have read. Each group conducts a text search for the words and phrases that justify placing the character under the left or right heading in each pairing. Students who have prepared by underlining their texts as they read and noticing motifs that contribute to characterization can accomplish the task in thirty minutes. Their presentation, through a designated spokesperson or group report, takes the form of oral commentary about their character, with the (implied) author as active agent: "Zadie Smith presents Hortense in a (stylized or naturalistic) fashion, when she writes 'quote evidence.'" Each sentence represents a critical judgment on the part of students and depends for its persuasiveness on the deftly chosen textual evidence presented in support of their judgment. I point out to the students that all their commentary, including their judgments about the placement of characters on each of the scales and their production of appropriate evidence, achieves the goal of being analytic.

The accessibility of the terms involved in Hochman's paradigm varies quite a lot, and inexperienced readers may struggle even to imagine what may be meant by an "incoherent" or a "fragmentary" character. Students immediately see the difference between a "stylized" and "naturalistic" character, however, and a "complex" and "simple" one. Some of the more difficult terms present teaching opportunities, as for instance the juxtaposition of "transparency" and "opacity." One way to assess a character's relative transparency is to attend to the mode of representation of inner thoughts and feelings, if the narrator provides them.

Recognizing Modes for the Representation of Fictional Minds

A matter of technique that remains nearly invisible to students until they have been trained to recognize it, representation of fictional consciousness contributes immeasurably to readers' experiences of "knowing" characters. One need only have students read a story (or play) such as Ernest Hemingway's "The Killers" in which no commentary at all about characters' minds appears to establish how vital the representation of mind stuff can be. In her book *Transparent Minds,* Dorrit Cohn names three predominant modes of representing consciousness in fictional characters, and although these categories have since been augmented and contested by other narrative theorists,[2] I find that in the undergraduate literature classroom, her terms provide more than enough for cultivating students' awareness of how novelists bring readers into contact with the thoughts, feelings, and internal states of fictional characters.

To grasp the point of this exercise, students need to have a basic understanding of narrative situation, including the grammatical person of the narration, and the relationships among narrator(s), reflector(s)/focalizer(s), and other characters. I use this exercise when I am teaching a third-person (or heterodiegetic) narrative. Using examples from their reading, I introduce Cohn's three modes of representation of consciousness: psychonarration, narrated monologue (also called free indirect discourse), and quoted monologue (in certain cases called interior monologue).

Psychonarration consists of the narrator's discourse about a character's consciousness, preserving the tense and person of the narration. Smoothly following the narrator's reports on external features, quoted speech, and characters' actions without any shift in the norms of the narration, psychonarration allows the narrator to generalize about what a character has thought about for a long time, as well as reporting in the narrator's language on the gist of characters' thoughts and feelings. So, for instance, Iris Murdoch's narrator observes of her character George's mental state, in *The Philosopher's Pupil*, "George felt that in another moment he would suffocate; all his blood seemed to have rushed up into his head and to be bursting out there into a blazing bleeding wet flower" (13). Psychonarration can be used effectively to convey what a character has *not* thought or felt. Psychonarration can be spread around, when the narrator explains what a host of characters think or feel, but it can also be useful in figural narrative situations, for it can be used to report on subverbal states and dreams of a central consciousness or reflector.

Narrated monologue, also known as free indirect discourse when it omits tagging (with words such as "she thought"), presents the character's mental discourse in the guise of the narrator's discourse. Most theorists thus consider it a double-voiced kind of discourse.[3] In other words, reading narrated monologue gives the impression of the words and modes of expression of the character while retaining the tense and person of the narrator's language. Harriet, the mother of the monstrous Ben in Doris Lessing's *The Fifth Child*, is "afflicted with remorse" (the narrator reports): "poor Ben, whom no one could love. She certainly could not!" (56). The diction and tone of the character's inner speech to herself come through and so do the tense and person of the narrator. Because narrated monologue retains the tense and person of the narration, it can be smoothly combined with psychonarration, sometimes even in the same passage about a character's thoughts. So, for instance, Alan Hollinghurst moves from narrated monologue into psychonarration of Nick Guest's thoughts in *The Line of Beauty*:

> He wanted to be with him, as he had been, more or less, for the past ten days, in the thoughtless luxury of top-class hotels; but he felt the relief of being alone as well: the usual relief of a guest who has closed his door, and a deeper thing, the forgotten solitude which measures and verifies the strength of an affair, and which, being temporary, is a kind of pleasure. (267)

Even Nick's self-consciously Jamesian voice cannot plausibly speak the words from "thoughtless luxury" onward, but he can be imagined saying

"I want to be with him" to himself. Neither psychonarration nor thoughts rendered in narrated monologue could plausibly be spoken aloud by the character without significant revisions into present tense and first person (the standard modes for speech and dialogue).

Quoted monologue, by way of contrast to the other two modes, presents the character's mental discourse by shifting from the past tense of narration to present tense and from the third person of narration to the first person of thoughts.[4] So, for instance, in Pat Barker's *The Ghost Road*, the narrator represents Billy Prior's thoughts as follows: "It's my embarkation leave, he wanted to howl. We're engaged" (70). In present tense narrations, such as those in Keri Hulme's *The Bone People*, quoted monologue still shifts, from third to first person: "Kerewin sits smoking, cross-legged by the fire, watching her smokerings dissolve over the still spread form of the boy, who is thinking, not half so much asleep as he seems, It looks as if someone tried to cut her throat" (39). This reported thought, though unspoken, is written so that it could plausibly be spoken aloud without violating the reader's sense of grammatical speech. By Cohn's nomenclature, this sort of thought is "quoted," not told, as in "narrated monologue."

Having taught these terms with sample sentences (illustrations can be found in my *Narrative Form* 60–63), I then ask students to free write for ten minutes and to attempt to capture their thoughts and feelings on paper as fully as possible. I warn them ahead of time that the materials will be shared, so they can engage in self-censorship if they wish. I usually move around the room and make noise so that some students will record a reaction to an external event. Once they have completed ten minutes of writing, I lead a brief discussion of the exercise, focusing on the extreme difficulty of capturing even a fragment of one's thoughts on paper. Through discussion of their notes, the students observe that they have made decisions about what to include and ignore, whether to incorporate bodily sensations, background mood, and worries or only top-level, narratable thoughts. All students will have noticed the incompatibility of speedy thoughts to the laborious paper-and-pen method of capturing thinking in prose, so they will be receptive to the idea that any and all representations of consciousness claiming to seem "real" must be subject to a high degree of manipulation by the writer. The task of learning how novelists manipulate thought stuff into the three modes can be undertaken using the freewriting transcripts.

I ask students to exchange their consciousness transcripts so each student has a thought transcript not his or her own. This procedure puts each student in the position of a contriving author manipulating another's thought stream. I ask them to rewrite (and label) a passage of their exchanged transcripts into quoted monologue, that is, into the first-person, present-tense form resembling speech. This task sometimes requires no rewriting at all, since most students capture their thoughts in first person, present tense. (In discussion, I emphasize that quoted monologue gets its reputation of naturalness and authenticity from its resemblance to our habitual autobiographical mode of discourse.) Next, I ask students to rewrite a passage into narrated monologue in third-person, past-tense narration. I ask students to surround this passage with invented narration of their own, also written in third person, past tense, suggesting the context in which the narrated thoughts occur. Finally, I ask the students to write summary sentences of psychonarration in third person, past tense, based on the remaining thoughts in the transcript provided by their classmates. I invite students who feel especially creative to add analogies or metaphors for feeling states or to assert in psychonarration what their "character" does *not* think about.

In the discussion that follows, I ask for volunteers to read their recasting of their classmates' thoughts. As we discuss examples, I reinforce the formal traits for each mode of representation of consciousness. This exercise not only emphasizes the gap between our experiences of our own minds and any written version of mind stuff—all three modes show compression, omission, gaps—but also makes it easy for students to recognize the combinations of modes that present themselves in most narrative fiction after 1800. I finish with a page of a text from the course reading (see, e.g., the treatment of Virginia Woolf's "Mrs Dalloway in Bond Street" in my *Narrative Form* 63) in which all three modes of representation of consciousness appear. This final step allows students to practice identifying the modes and (importantly) to discover the limit cases, such as sentence fragments, in which too little information about tense and person appears to permit certain identification, or passages where differentiation of psychonarration and narrated monologue poses interpretive challenges.

For the teacher of narrative who wishes to emphasize the difference between film fiction and prose narrative or for the novel teacher who wants to bring students to awareness of the craft of fiction, teaching the distinctions among modes of representation of fictional consciousness lays bare devices that ordinarily go unnoticed by students. Empowered to identify the modes with confidence, students can then go on to interpret the allocation of that representation, its withholding or withdrawal, and its contribution to character identification. Like the prior exercise on characterization, this exercise assists students in seeing the techniques by which narrative artists make word masses into personlike beings.

Mapping Plot through Actantial Functions

A final exercise stems from discussion of character and opens up a way for students to analyze plot without falling into the trap of recounting the story in synoptic form. A. J. Greimas's actantial model for the analysis of "actants," including but not limited to character, provides a rubric for a fast, fun group-work exercise. Where space permits, I handle this exercise by having students work in groups to fill in the rubric on the board, with separate groups working side by side, but in a larger class where board space is limited, the same effect can be achieved through an in-class writing exercise using a handout. On the board, I write out the six actants with space below each one:

Sender	Object	Receiver
Helper	Subject	Opponent

I gloss the "object" as the goal and begin the class by having students brainstorm about alternative plot goals. Recently, a group of students who had read Roddy Doyle's *The Commitments* came up with four plot goals, including bringing soul to Dublin, keeping the band together, protecting Dean from the influence of jazz, and getting together with Imelda. These goals I transcribed directly onto the board under the actantial category object, in four separate sections of the board. Students working in groups with a handout could be assigned one of the objects as a starting point. Brainstorming objects of the plot immediately clarifies that most narratives, even apparently simple ones, have multiple objects.

Before beginning the group work, I clarify that not all actants will be represented by a single personlike character. Other actantial qualities will be "existents" of the fictional world, including elements of setting; objects; and natural, social, or economic forces. An actantial role can be performed by a combination of existents, so the opponent(s) to bringing soul to Dublin could include poverty, lack of musical skill, and the limitations of the performance spaces.

Having several students work on the board using different objects from the same narrative rapidly results in analytic commentary and markedly different perspectives on the story they have read. The exercise works best if the students work together in small groups, filling out the subject(s), sender(s), receiver(s), helper(s), and opponent(s) for their object. Group work brings out the richest responses to the challenge, as students discover that aspects of the setting, the social context, or inanimate forces may share space with human agents in the rubric. Quickly students discern that a single existent may both send and receive or may alternately help and oppose a narrative's goal.[5] When they present their discoveries to their classmates in oral presentations, they articulate these discoveries and the reasons for assigning actantial roles to particular existents. If time permits, a whole class can be dedicated to discussing alternative actantial interpretations of a single narrative work. With an alert teacher participating to emphasize the differences, paradoxes, and surprising discoveries made possible by the analytic method, students gain confidence in making arguments about the plots of novels, short stories, films, and other narrative works. Virtually everything students say in such presentations qualifies as analytic commentary on plot, and their dependence on plot synopsis drops away. A teacher who can show students how to think about plot analytically does more to help them master the conventions of literary discourse than one who simply tells them, "don't summarize" or, "don't retell the story." Having spent many years fruitlessly admonishing students in precisely that way, I can attest to the effect of using Greimas's actantial model: it achieves positively what no amount of warning can do.

The descriptive language and analytic tools of narratology point to debates that may seem remote from the concerns of the undergraduate literature and composition teacher. My experience (and those of my students who are now classroom teachers) suggests that small doses of narrative theory, used with dynamic classroom exercises (emphasizing group work, board work, oral presentations, and peer-to-peer interactive writing), support good writing pedagogy. I do not insist that my general-education literature students absorb a large amount of narratological jargon, but I do hope that they will leave my classroom equipped to write with strong verbs in the appropriate tense, to respond analytically and argumentatively to literature, to treat fictional characters and their stories as artifacts of language, and to recognize the way that fictional discourse gains power through narrative techniques.

Notes

The author extends grateful thanks to Randall Cluff, of Southern Virginia University, for his thoughtful comments and suggestions on this essay.

1. See Nünning's account of critical dissents to the concept.

2. See, e.g., Fludernik; Palmer.

3. For an influential alternative view, see Banfield.

4. In Cohn's version quoted monologue conflates two modes, mental speech with and without quotation marks and tagging, such as "he thought." Some teachers may wish to distinguish these subcategories of quoted monologue or treat them as independent modes of representation.

5. That Greimas thought it a problem that his actantial model could be used in this fashion does not prevent us from reading the discursive level of a narrative for multiple and overlapping matches of actantial role and characters.

Works Cited

Banfield, Ann. *Unspeakable Sentences: Narration and Representation in the Language of Fiction*. Boston: Routledge, 1982. Print.

Barker, Pat. *The Ghost Road*. 1995. New York: Dutton, 1996. Print.

Barthes, Roland. "An Introduction to the Structural Analysis of Narrative." 1966. *New Literary History* 6.2 (1975): 237–72. Print.

Booth, Wayne. *The Rhetoric of Fiction*. 2nd ed. Chicago: U of Chicago P, 1983. Print.

Chatman, Seymour. *Story and Discourse: Narrative Structure in Fiction and Film*. Ithaca: Cornell UP, 1978. Print.

Cohn, Dorrit. *Transparent Minds: Narrative Modes for Presenting Consciousness in Fiction*. Princeton: Princeton UP, 1978. Print.

Doyle, Roddy. *The Commitments*. Dublin: Farouk, 1987. Print.

Fludernik, Monika. *The Fictions of Language and the Languages of Fiction: The Linguistic Representation of Speech and Consciousness*. London: Routledge, 1993. Print.

Forster, E. M. *Aspects of the Novel*. 1927. New York: Harcourt, 1954. Print.

Gallagher, Catherine. *Nobody's Story: The Vanishing Acts of Women Writers in the Marketplace, 1670–1920*. Berkeley: U of California P, 1995. Print.

Greimas, A. J. "Actants, Actors, and Figures." 1973. *On Meaning: Selected Writings in Semiotic Theory*. Trans. Paul J. Perron and Frank H. Collins. Minneapolis: U of Minnesota P, 1987. 106–20. Print.

Hacker, Diana. *A Writer's Reference*. 5th ed. Boston: Bedford, 2003. Print.

———. *Writing about Literature: A Supplement to Accompany* A Writer's Reference. Boston: Bedford, 1999. Print.

Hochman, Baruch. *Character in Literature*. Ithaca: Cornell UP, 1985. Print.

Hollinghurst, Alan. *The Line of Beauty*. New York: Bloomsbury, 2004. Print.

Hulme, Keri. *The Bone People*. Baton Rouge: Louisiana State UP, 1983. Print.

Keen, Suzanne. *Narrative Form*. Houndmills: Palgrave, 2003. Print.

Lessing, Doris. 1988. *The Fifth Child*. New York: Vintage, 1989. Print.

Murdoch, Iris. *The Philosopher's Pupil.* London: Chatto, 1983. Print.

Nünning, Ansgar. "Implied Author." *Encyclopedia of the Novel.* Ed. Paul Schellinger et al. Vol. 1. Chicago: Dearborn, 1998. 589–91. Print.

Palmer, Alan. *Fictional Minds.* Lincoln: U of Nebraska P, 2004. Print.

Further Reading

Abbott, H. Porter. *The Cambridge Introduction to Narrative.* 2nd ed. Cambridge: Cambridge UP, 2008. Print.

Cobley, Paul. *Narrative.* London: Routledge, 2001. Print.

Herman, David, ed. *The Cambridge Companion to Narrative.* Cambridge: Cambridge UP, 2007. Print.

Lothe, Jakob. *Narrative in Fiction and Film: An Introduction.* Oxford: Oxford UP, 2000. Print.

Scholes, Robert, James Phelan, and Robert Kellogg. *The Nature of Narrative.* 2nd ed. Oxford: Oxford UP, 2006. Print.

Robert F. Barsky

The Undergraduate
Theory Course

The goal of this essay is to provide background information and pedagogical tools to help teachers present narrative theory in an undergraduate theory course. I focus on teaching three approaches to theorizing narrative—Russian formalism, classical narratology, and Bakhtin's dialogism—and draw larger lessons that follow from this particular focus. I begin just as I do when teaching the narrative-theory unit to my students, namely, by presenting eight foundational principles of my pedagogical approach (see also Barsky, *Introduction*). The first two principles provide my point of departure. The third principle builds on the demonstration of the first two.

    1. I explain that the apparently naive questions people ask about narratives are often not only valid and illuminating but also the basis for narrative theory itself.

    2. Much of what is known as narrative theory can be productively understood as the institutionalized form of a practice that occurs every minute of every day, in every society. People respond to narratives; they summarize, recap, recall, recount, and analyze what they hear or read using intuition or some situation-specific frame of reference. I illustrate these

principles by giving students a short text such as a provocative op-ed article that uses narrative to make its point and asking them whether they like it and why. Typically some will like it and some won't, and after pressing the students to articulate their reasons for a while, I call a halt to the discussion and ask them to reflect on the kind of reasoning they have used. Once they do that, I inform them that they are now budding narrative theorists, and to illustrate the point I note connections between some of their comments and the approaches we will discuss in more detail later in the course.

3. Interpreting narratives with the aid of narrative theory is not about learning esoteric terms and mechanically applying them to texts but rather about starting with one's own perceptions and responses to narratives and then using some well-honed tools—or fashioning some new ones—to sharpen, deepen, and where necessary revise those perceptions and responses.

4. Some narrative theory is implicit in narratives themselves. To illustrate this principle, I read short passages from (say) Marcel Proust and ask the students to identify what he is teaching us about temporality. I follow up by reading passages from Dostoevsky and asking what he is teaching us about voice and style. For instance, in a passage from a short story entitled "Easter Holidays," which could be viewed as theory couched in imaginative prose, Proust writes:

> Novelists are fools who reckon time by days and years. Days may, for a clock, be of equal length, but not for men. One day is steep and wearisome and takes infinity to climb: another has a gentle gradient down which we sing our way full speed. There are some natures, high-strung, sensitive natures in particular, that need an equipment of changeable gears, like motorcars, if they are to face their journey through the years with confidence. There are days, too, that come out of due order, that seem to have been interpolated in the calendar, to have strayed from their proper season with weather not their own. (278)

At the outset of this passage, Proust offers a window on the concept of *durée*, duration, a critical point in Gérard Genette's approach. In the last sentence, Proust offers a window on the concept of order, another critical point in Genette's approach.

5. The genre of the text in question often influences the analyst's focus on some narrative elements and not others—and even the analyst's choice of methodologies—because different genres foreground some elements and background others. The detective story, for example, foregrounds the relation between two series of events—the one leading up to the crime,

and the other leading up to the discovery of the criminal's identity, whereas the psychological novel foregrounds the revelation of consciousness. Consequently, in the first case the analyst will focus on issues of plotting (in multiple senses), and in the second case focus on techniques for the direct and indirect representation of thought. (For further discussion of detective stories, see Brian McHale's essay in this volume.)

6. Just as genre matters, so too does historical context, and the relation between text and context is a two-way street. We can enhance our understanding of a narrative by placing it in its context and by asking how it might have altered the context for subsequent narratives.

7. Narrative theory in the twentieth and twenty-first centuries has unfolded less as a single, grand conversation than as a series of different movements that have sometimes interacted and sometimes not. When it is possible to trace threads of inquiry from one theory to the next and when the intersection between different approaches is made clear, we can better identify both the value and limitations of individual approaches.

8. Narrative theory, like critical theory more generally, can be mapped according to the emphasis of individual approaches on four main elements: text, author, audience, and context, though, as M. H. Abrams, who introduced this approach to mapping theory, reminds us, each approach will have a role for all four elements. Text-based approaches such as Russian formalism and structuralist narratology focus rigorous attention on formal elements of narrative such as plot, character, voice, and focalization. Author-based approaches attend not just to biography but also to the author's cultural status, and they include psychoanalysis and some versions of feminist narratology. Audience-based approaches include some versions of rhetorical theory, reception theory, and the theory of interpretive communities proposed by Stanley Fish. Context-based approaches include dialogism, Marxism, and feminist narratology.

With these principles in place we are ready to turn to our more detailed look at formalism; structuralist, or classical, narratology; and dialogism as alternatives to the ideas associated with both formalism and structuralism.

Russian Formalist Approaches to Narrative

Russian formalist theory is a good place to start because, in its approaches to the manifestations and dimensions of literariness, it emphasizes close reading rather than extratextual dimensions, such as the relation between psychological or sociohistorical factors in the production or interpretation of stories. I begin by placing formalism in its historical context. The movement began in two related centers, Moscow and Petrograd, in the first decades of the twentieth century. The burgeoning interest in new methodologies, especially scientific-linguistic ones, arose in response to Ferdinand de Saussure's influence in the linguistic community. Formalist theorists at times drew ire from ruling Bolsheviks who took from Marxism the idea that art is contingent on social and historical events. In response, some language theorists emphasized "disinterested" textual analysis, couching their work in paradigms less overtly political or historical, while others advocated some version of Marxist language studies.

We begin with the formalists' attempt to understand literariness, those qualities of a text that mark it as literary rather than nonliterary. One important effect of literature, the formalists observed, is to sharpen perception. Literary works, they noted, produce an effect of defamiliarization (остранение, in Russian, literally translated as "estrangement") that renders the ordinary world "strange" and thus heightens the reader's powers of observation. Classroom discussion can be enlivened by demonstrating that this defamiliarization is similar to the freshness of perception prized by the Romantics, as, for example, in Lord Byron's devotion to the sublime, William Wordsworth's celebration of children's innocence, or Samuel Taylor Coleridge's concept of genius. I call the students' attention to the oft-cited lines from the 1817 text of Coleridge's *Biographia Literaria*:

> To carry on the feelings of childhood into the powers of manhood; to combine the child's sense of wonder and novelty with the appearances which every day for perhaps forty years had rendered familiar . . . this is the character and privilege of genius, and one of the marks which distinguish genius from talents. (80–81)

Narrative is one route into this re-viewing of the familiar. The basic stuff of narrative is its "material," the events and the ideas it contains, and the transformation of this material into a particular narrative provides the opportunity for defamiliarization. Viktor Shklovsky provided concepts to describe this transformation by distinguishing between the story, or fabula, the set of events underlying a narrative in their chronological order, and the plot, or *sjužet*, the artistic arrangement of this fabula into a narrative. More generally, formalist analysis seeks to uncover and analyze the devices by which an author transforms fabula into *sjužet* and to consider the defamiliarizing effects of those devices.

Formalism has different variants depending on the historical moment and the particular theorist studied, but in all its articulations it encourages readers to pay attention to what is really there, on the page. Students enjoy learning the formalist method because it helps them learn how narrative is consciously constructed with specific devices. For instance, a secondary character may appear in the text not because the author wants to make a thematic point about people like that character but because the author needs that character to disclose some information. Focusing on techniques helps students recognize the devices that contribute to the making of a work of art.

Students can tune in to the techniques of defamiliarization in various ways, especially when they encounter a text that itself lays bare the devices of other texts. Although most Russian formalist examples came from literature, I have found it effective to look at different rhetorical or creative techniques used to digress from, disrupt, displace, or violate the expected formal arrangements of incidents, as in the famous example of Horace Mitchell Miner's "Body Ritual amongst the Nacirema." This satire of anthropological papers, published in *American Anthropologist* in 1956, sets out the traits of the Nacirema (American, spelled backward) people as though they are members of an exotic tribe. The advantage of fictional examples flows from the fact that artificiality is at the heart of the writer's craft, whereas nonfictional work, including Miner's article, is bound by the references made in the text to the "real," no matter how it is presented. Jan Mukařovský, a theorist of the Prague stucturalist circle that built on the ideas of the Russian formalists, adds further focus to a study of techniques when he discusses the use of foreshadowing, which takes away the suspense that the reader generally expects to feel as she or he reads through a text. How something is described comes to be more important than the story being told, an interesting spin on the idea of defamiliarizing the narrative experience.

The most prevalent critique of formalism is that it's ahistorical, that is, it doesn't meaningfully address the context within which the work was written and then read. This is only partially valid, because literariness and strangeness must be evaluated with regard to the "everyday" language spoken in the society and to the history of literary form itself—what is new and strange to one generation becomes old and familiar to the next. If within a given community everyone spoke in iambic pentameter, then what we call ordinary discourse would be strange or poetic, and

Shakespeare's writings wouldn't. Formalists are also challenged on the basis of their claim to scientific objectivity, a challenge that opens the door to many useful questions. First, if formalist analysis is "scientific" according to some use of the word that implies repeatability, predictability, and the consistency of results, then one would have to assume that anybody who learned its technique for exhaustive accumulation and cataloging of formal elements would undertake the exact same analysis as any other formalist. But it is very difficult to believe that the assumption would hold up to empirical testing. The quest for systematization also suggests that formalist interpreters should eventually become expendable; there is no reason why a machine could not be taught to follow the system.

All this leads to a crucial generalization that I underline for my students: no single approach will be satisfactory except within clearly delimited ends set out in advance. Consequently, I explain, we need to look at some other approaches and to question each in its own terms and in those afforded by the others.

Structuralism and Classical Narratology

When I turn to structuralism, I identify it as the broader movement that led to narratology, and I situate it in relation to both formalism and semiotics. Structuralism and semiotics are based on similar underlying (formalist) assumptions, and they use the kinds of analytic tools favored by the formalists. Both movements are dedicated to the study of signs, but they position language differently within that broader study. Structuralism regards language as the paradigm of all sign systems, whereas semiotics regards it as one of many possible sign systems.

Genette's influential work provides a particularly convenient illustration of the link between structural linguistics and classical narratology. Genette refers to the "figures" that, like "figures of speech," encompass both the rhetoric and the process of writing. These figures are fundamental properties of literature, sources for the "surplus of meaning" offered to both the writer and the reader. To illuminate narrative strategies and discursive practices, Genette applies a nomenclature as well as a few techniques that he borrows from classical rhetoric. In *Narrative Discourse* he also establishes a grammar of the text based on the categories of the verb: *temps* (i.e., the order, duration, frequency that express the relation between the time of the story and the time of the discourse), *mode* ("mood," the distance and perspective of the narration), and *voix* ("voice"). For

Genette, "point of view" falls under the general heading of "mood" (*Figures* 84), but he unpacks the concept by distinguishing its two main elements, voice and vision, that is, who speaks versus who sees, narration versus focalization.

Genette's central application is to Marcel Proust's *À la recherche du temps perdu*, which, he suggests, can be understood as the radical expansion of a single sentence: "Marcel becomes a writer" (*Narrative Discourse* 6). Teachers of narrative theory can use the same procedure in the classroom, although it's not necessary to dive into a text as complex as Proust's. Instead, we can choose a short narrative, such as Fyodor Dostoevsky's short story "Bobok," which is narrated by an aspiring but disheveled narrator, who has had too much to drink. This is a good example to start with in a class because events unfold in a linear fashion, but something seems to happen to the time of the narrative the moment the inebriated narrator drifts off. To that point time has proceeded faster in the discourse than it does in the story, but suddenly the duration of events increases, and we are led to linger in this underground setting. The effect of this slowing down of the narrative recounting is that the reader is drawn into this world headlong, listening to the voices and being seduced or entertained by the zany world below.

Virtually any narrative reveals its workings through the application of these narratological categories, allowing for fine-grained analysis of the techniques used in the story by the author. Indeed, once students are made aware of narrative elements, they generally realize that these components are on the one hand easy to discern but are on the other so obvious and central to any text that they can be overlooked. For this reason, students, already armed with tools from Russian formalism, find considerable additional payoff in the narrative approach taken by Genette, and they can almost immediately undertake sophisticated analyses of texts, using precise terminology, which allows them to recognize the structuring elements that make a text signify.

In the end, structuralist narratology, like all "scientific" approaches to language studies, has lost some of its currency in the light of more political or aesthetic approaches, and even Tzvetan Todorov now suggests that early structuralist work may have actually turned many students away from the study of narrative and literature. Genette's work, inspired and influenced by classical traditions of rhetoric, avoids the scientism evident in early work by Roland Barthes, Todorov, A. J. Greimas, or Claude Lévi-Strauss, while still insisting on the system of narrative possibilities in a text versus the interpretation of particular narrative messages. In this regard, the works of Genette and also of Seymour Chatman or even Michel Meyer (in his work on argumentation and rhetoric) and Chaim Perelman (on rhetorics and the law) provide links between narrative theory and models for understanding discourse that derive from ancient Greek and Roman commentators.

In my experience, the best counterbalance to both formalism and structuralism is dialogism, partly because of the different assumptions made by Mikhail Bakhtin in his assessments of narratives. Indeed, much of what Bakhtin wrote was a contemporary challenge to the school of formalist studies as it was being elaborated in the former Soviet Union and a prescient challenge to later work by structuralists of different types. At the same time, Bakhtin's attention to the social and rhetorical dimensions of discourse, while not inspiring the formation of a full-fledged Bakhtinian narratology, has been enormously productive for narrative theory's efforts to offer an adequate account of narrative discourse.

Dialogism

Bakhtin is a wide-ranging thinker whose work bears on almost all areas of contemporary discourse theory, and some historical information helps situate his work. The fundamental points of the dialogic approach, its emphasis on how any given utterance or text both responds to prior texts and anticipates later ones, can be gleaned from most of the texts in Bakhtin's diverse corpus, notably the 1929 *Problems of Dostoevsky's Poetics*. His (re)discovery in the Soviet Union occurred in the sixties, and his introduction to the West occurred in Paris through the writings of Julia Kristeva and Todorov shortly thereafter. As such, even though Bakhtin's work should chronologically follow the discussion of formalism, he came to be introduced to the West by theorists who at that time were working in the structuralist enterprises that had such a hold on Paris in that era. Both Kristeva and Todorov harnessed Bakhtin's work for their efforts at undertaking systematic and rigorous studies of utterances, with the belief that the dialogic approach, despite its avowed refusal of formalists' claims to scientificity, would help explain how intertextuality helps create meaning across hybrid texts (such as novels, which incorporate elements from different genres) or in texts that make obvious reference to other texts or utterances.

Dialogism migrated westward when Michael Holquist began to translate, edit, and write English-language introductions to Bakhtin's work in the eighties. At that point, it became clear that much of Bakhtin's work was specifically articulated to undermine the assumptions of the two prevailing approaches to discourse in his lifetime, Marxism and formalism. In so doing, he undermined a significant portion of structuralist analysis to boot because it couldn't account for the social nature of texts and their consumption, an accomplishment for which he now seems prophetic. Bakhtin states unequivocally in "Discourse in the Novel" that "the principal idea" of his work

> is that the study of verbal art can and must overcome the divorce between an abstract "formal" approach and an equally abstract "ideological" approach. Form and content in discourse are one, once we understand that verbal discourse is a social phenomenon—social throughout its entire range and in each and every one of its factors, from the sound image to the furthest reaches of abstract meaning. (259)

From our present perspective it's valuable to talk about the carnivalesque, the dialogic, and heteroglossia, because each of these terms focuses our reading on the intensely social and ideological nature of discourse, which makes it resistant to Saussure-inspired approaches that privilege langue over parole, that is, closed formal structures over living dialogue. For Bakhtin, language itself is a part of material reality, so the sign system cannot be dissociated from social construction, and each utterance made in a given context is saturated by situation-specific ideological markers.

An effective strategy for helping students grasp these points is to return to Dostoevsky's "Bobok," which in its details is a window to the compendium of basic tools offered by Bakhtin. While meandering about, the narrator comes across a funeral of a distant relative of his. From a distance he describes the scene, noting that the overwhelming smell of rotting corpses makes him "dream," contributing to the many other factors that put him into a liminal space between life and death, summer and winter, sober and stoned. In this state he sits down on a gravestone and falls into a dreamlike half sleep, during which time, most unexpectedly, he begins to hear different voices that seem to emanate from the recently deceased bodies that lie beneath the surface of the earth. At one point, the Baron Klinevitch, the "king" of the corpses, implores everyone there to "tell the truth." Klinevitch says:

> I don't want us to be telling lies. That's all I care about, for that is one thing that matters. One cannot exist on the surface without lying, for life and lying are synonymous, but here we will amuse ourselves by not lying. Hang it all, the grave has some value after all! We'll all tell our

stories aloud, and we won't be ashamed of anything. First of all I'll tell you about myself. I am one of the predatory kind, you know. All that was bound and held in check by rotten cords up there on the surface. Away with cords and let us spend these two months in shameless truthfulness! Let us strip and be naked!

This utterance itself combines a range of voices from the formal philosophical register of "for life and lying are synonymous" to the direct exhortation of "[l]et us strip and be naked." The utterances that follow from the other corpses, truthful or not, are raucous, inflammatory, and unrestrained, peppered with insults, vulgarity, and frequent mention of the lower bodily stratum. This setting has no boundaries, no hierarchy, and no punishment for speaking inappropriately, and all of the corpses are swept up in the wake of the uncensored enthusiasm it generates: "'Let us be naked, let us be naked!' cried all the voices. 'I long to be naked, I long to be,' Avdotya Ignatyevna shrilled."

This whole carnivalesque uproar ceases when the narrator is brought back to consciousness, to his own situated self, and henceforth the dreamlike state that allowed for free and unfettered heteroglossia and dialogism disappears forever. What remains is the narrator's wakeful state and his relatively monologic discourse:

> And here I suddenly sneezed. It happened suddenly and unintentionally, but the effect was striking: all became as silent as one expects it to be in a churchyard, it all vanished like a dream. A real silence of the tomb set in. I don't believe they were ashamed on account of my presence: they had made up their minds to cast off all shame! I waited five minutes—not a word, not a sound. It cannot be supposed that they were afraid of my informing the police; for what could the police do to them? I must conclude that they had some secret unknown to the living, which they carefully concealed from every mortal.

Like the carnival itself, this dreamlike state occurs in a parallel reality, a second life that is outside the normal pressures and constraints of discourse in the world. In this alternative world we have access to voices that lie below the surface of normal existence. By engaging with these voices, we make it possible for narratives to take form in our minds and for "dead" characters to be "revitalized." Eventually in Dostoevsky's story, the narrator, like any reader, cannot distinguish between the people among whom he lives and the people who are created through his interaction with the ghostly voices.

A story like this one situates narratives and utterances in the realm of the creative, the unexpected, the context specific, and the spontaneous. Our world, constituted as it is of memories and voices that speak to us through words and utterances, produces moments of dialogic vitality that are the product of a huge number of variable circumstances. So if I read a particular narrative or hear a given utterance at a given moment and in a given space, which I always do because I'm a "situated" self, that narrative speaks to me, and I to it, in ways that are both limited and expanded by that moment and that place. Bakhtin's concept of the utterance recalls Saussure's concept of parole, but the utterance is thoroughly social, historical, concrete, and ideological. Furthermore, the concept resists Saussure's idea of langue, the abstract formal system of a language. For Bakhtin any linguistic system encompasses multiple sociolects and idiolects; consequently, he regards it as counterproductive to draw sharp lines between system and utterance, competence and performance, langue and parole. From Bakhtin's perspective, what is interesting in the aesthetic verbal act that we call narrative, therefore, is not the sometimes complex relations between fabula and *sjužet* but the living dialogic interactions among its multiple utterances and how this interaction relates to the precise context within which it occurs.

Reading Bakhtin alongside the formalists and the narratologists helps students realize that dialogic interaction includes not just the perspectives and situations of individual speakers but also the way that their dialogue combines to produce unexpected utterances and ideas that are not typical of either speaker. One person directs his or her discourse toward the perceived other, who understands it according to a particular set of contextual elements and then responds, taking for granted certain kinds of constants but adding to what was just said. This way, the conversation creatively constructs dialogue in the space that exists between the two speakers. In such a model, no single speaker is complete because she needs the other to fill in the spaces that she cannot see, and she becomes answerable for the utterances of the other. What emerges is a complex dialogue between the author, the characters, and the reader, wherein the reader becomes another character whose own situated point of view gives particular meaning to the interaction that is unique not only to the text at hand but to the particular context within which the text is read. The next time, the reader will be differently situated, if only because she's familiar with the text from the first reading.

Bakhtin's approach, which has been picked up by an array of scholars in various domains, should be attended to by students concerned with the sociohistorical moment of utterances because it touches on such fundamental human concerns as creativity, originality, repeatability, devalorization (of "privileged discourses"), and answerability. It also speaks to the attempts undertaken in society to isolate, vilify, or consecrate certain narratives or otherwise to demarcate some narratives from others by showing that speech is a social act that addresses particular situations and that uses materials drawn from previous speech acts and speakers.

This approach to teaching narrative equips students to go on to read the wide variety of postclassical narratologies (feminist, rhetorical, cognitive, etc.) in two related ways: the unit gives students a valuable knowledge base, one important to virtually all postclassical narratologies, and the unit gives the students a valuable intellectual habit of asking questions designed to identify both the power and the limits of any approach, a habit that serves them well not just for postclassical narratology but for any theoretical paradigm. In other words, consistent with what was suggested at the outset of this chapter, narrative studies evolve and respond to the exigencies of the moment and the perceived weaknesses or insufficiencies of earlier work, and students can be called on to explain how they themselves might work to develop a theory better suited for the texts they hope to understand. An assignment of this kind can make their work more pertinent to them and may even lay the groundwork for rethinking existing narratological paradigms.

Works Cited

Abrams, M. H. *The Mirror and the Lamp: Romantic Theory and the Critical Tradition*. New York: Oxford UP, 1953. Print.

Bakhtin, Mikhail M. "Discourse in the Novel." *The Dialogic Imagination: Four Essays by M. M. Bakhtin*. Ed. Michael Holquist. Trans. Caryl Emerson and Holquist. Austin: U of Texas P, 1981. 259–422. Print.

Barsky, Robert. *Introduction à la théorie littéraire*. St. Foy: PU du Québec, 1997. Print.

Chatman, Seymour. *Story and Discourse: Narrative Structure in Fiction and Film*. Ithaca: Cornell UP, 1978. Print.

Coleridge, Samuel. *Biographia Literaria*. Ed. W. Jackson Bate and James Engell. Princeton: Princeton UP, 1985. Print. Vol. 7 of *Collected Works*.

Dostoevsky, Fyodor. "Bobok." *Somebody's Diary*. 1873. Trans. Constance Garrnett. Arthurs Classic Novels. 10 Dec. 2004. Web. 11 Aug. 2009.

Fish, Stanley. *Is There a Text in This Class?* Cambridge: Harvard UP, 1980. Print.

Genette, Gérard. *Figures III*. Paris: Tel Quel, 1972. Print.

———. *Narrative Discourse: An Essay in Method*. Trans. Jane E. Lewin. Ithaca: Cornell UP, 1980. Print.

Meyer, Michel. *Meaning and Reading*. Amsterdam: Benjamins, 1984. Print.

Miner, Horace Mitchell. "Body Ritual among the Nacirema." *American Anthropologist* 58 (1956): 503–07. *Wikisource*. Web. 11 Aug. 2009.

Mukařovský, Jan. "Standard Language and Poetic Language." *A Prague School Reader on Esthetics, Literary Structure, and Style*. Ed. and trans. Paul L. Garvin. Washington: Georgetown UP, 1964. 17–30. Print.

Perelman, Chaim. *The New Rhetoric: A Treatise on Argumentation*. Trans. John Wilkinson and Purcell Weaver. Notre Dame: U of Notre Dame P, 1969. Print.

Proust, Marcel. *Pleasures and Days*. Ed. F. W. Dupee. Trans. Louise Verese, Gerard Hopkins, and Barbara Dupee. New York: Doubleday, 1957. Print.

Shklovsky, Viktor. *Theory of Prose*. Trans. Benjamin Sher. Normal: Dalkey, 1991. Print.

Todorov, Tzvetan. *La littérature en péril*. Paris: Flammarion, 2007. Print.

Further Reading

Bakhtin, Mikhail M. *Problems of Dostoevsky's Poetics*. Ed. and trans. Caryl Emerson. Minneapolis: U of Minnesota P, 1984. Print.

Barthes, Roland. Writing Degree Zero *and* Elements of Semiology. Trans. Annette Lavers and Colin Smith. Boston: Beacon, 1968. Print.

Coleridge, Samuel Taylor. *The Works of Samuel Taylor Coleridge*. London: Crissy, 1853. Print.

Greimas, A. J. *Structural Semantics: An Attempt at a Method*. Trans. Danielle McDowell, Ronald Schleifer, and Alan Velie. Lincoln: U of Nebraska P, 1983. Print.

Holquist, Michael. *Dialogism*. 1991. New York: Routledge, 2002. Print.

Jakobson, Roman, and Claude Lévi-Strauss. "Les chats de Baudelaire." *Selected Writings of Roman Jakobson*. The Hague: Mouton de Gruyter, 1984. Print.

Kristeva, Julia. "Le mot, le dialogue et le roman." *Critique* 239 (1966): 438–65. Print.

Lévi-Strauss, Claude. *Structural Anthropology*. Trans. Claire Jacobson. New York: Basic, 1963. Print.

Saussure, Ferdinand de. *Course in General Linguistics*. Ed. Charles Bally and Albert Sechehaye. Trans. Roy Harris. La Salle: Open Court, 1983. Print.

Susan Mooney

The Graduate Classroom

My experience teaching a graduate seminar on narrative and narrative theory—*Ulysses* and Theories of Narrative—can address the broader issue of teaching narrative theory at the graduate level. My objectives can be readily adapted by other graduate teachers to their own situations and choices of primary texts. I sought to develop a two-way inquiry that unfolded in two main stages. In the first half of the course, we explored—by means of close reading, attention to relevant contexts, and some introductory work on narrative theory—how James Joyce uses the resources of narrative in constructing his remarkable novel. Students read *Ulysses* (1922) in its entirety, while I highlighted certain narrative elements that we would be returning to. Then in the second half of the course, we investigated narrative theory's capacity to yield a deeper understanding of *Ulysses*. We also analyzed this novel's potential to contest some received ideas in narrative theory.

Laying Foundations: Characterization and Perspective

Joyce's experimentation with narrative forms and coherence stimulates study of narrative and narrative theories. To lay the basis for our subsequent discussions, the course first focused on two especially salient narrative elements in *Ulysses*: characterization and perspective. Students read the chapters on these two narrative elements in Shlomith Rimmon-Kenan's *Narrative Fiction*. Rimmon-Kenan integrates the work of other theorists into a reflective and coherent discussion of fundamental elements of narrative theory. H. Porter Abbott or Wallace Martin would be equally fine and were listed in my syllabus. My idea here was to provide a kind of textbook, or "go to" book to answer questions involving narrative elements and who theorizes what.

At least since the bildungsroman, modern characters have been a complex site for the representation of both metamorphosis and innate attributes. In modernist narratives like Joyce's, character is paradoxically stable and unstable. Given *Ulysses*'s setting of one day in Dublin, it is difficult to determine how the three main characters—Stephen Dedalus, Leopold Bloom, and Molly Bloom—have altered, if at all; the short time span of the narrative seems to preclude transformation. Or does it? The narrative begins in media res; perhaps we are observing a special day in which change may develop. We also become aware of how characters have developed over time; Molly remembers her childhood, early adulthood, and previous years in her marriage, and both she and Leopold note how the death of their infant son Rudy eleven years earlier marks a change in their sexual relations. Through characters' imagination and memory, and also in their interactions, *Ulysses* offers fragments of narratives of becoming and ending, creating and censoring, desiring and repressing.

Rimmon-Kenan's discussion of characterization helps students think about these issues analytically. (See also David Gorman's essay in this volume.) Her catalog of means of characterization ("character-indicators") reminds students that narratives construct character. In my class, we focused on how this process works in selected episodes of *Ulysses*. Other character-foregrounding novels could be substituted, ranging from eighteenth-century staples such as *Moll Flanders* (1722) and *Tristram Shandy* (1760–67) to works by Charles Dickens, Honoré de Balzac, and Fyodor Dostoevsky in the nineteenth century and to Virginia Woolf's *To the Lighthouse* (1927), Samuel Beckett's trilogy (1951–53), and Toni Morrison's *Beloved* (1987). In Rimmon-Kenan's account, character indicators can be divided into two categories: direct definition or indirect presentation. Indirect presentation includes action, speech, external appearance, and environment, as well as reinforcement by analogy (setting, other characters, etc). Later in the course, when we considered David

Lodge, we revisited modernism's investment in mimetic representations of character. With advances in science and the rise of psychoanalysis and phenomenology, modernist writers were aware of competing theories of representation and perception, and they offered accounts of human experience that differed from nineteenth-century realism. Works like *Ulysses* and *To the Lighthouse* attempt to capture grains of life lived, often focusing on daily minutiae and on the inner consciousness and unconscious of human subjects.

Not long after *Ulysses*'s opening sentence, which directly defines character ("Stately, plump Buck Mulligan . . ."), Joyce resorts to a myriad of indirect presentations that students can be asked to identify. For example, while Buck comments theatrically on Stephen's appearance and character ("Kinch," "Jesuit"), we follow a competing inner commentary by Stephen, which reveals an unhappy young man, still mourning his mother and lamenting his faltering friendship with Buck.

With Rimmon-Kenan's discussion of focalization (a subject treated at greater length in Jesse Matz's and James Phelan's contributions to this volume), we turned to the thorny question of the relations between voice (who speaks?) and vision (who sees?). Is the narrator intradiegetic (inside the primary level of action) or extradiegetic (outside that level)? How does the focalizer (the vehicle of focalization) influence the text? Centering on Stephen's and Bloom's focalizations, *Ulysses*'s first six episodes consist of a third-person narration of the external action, free indirect style, and an interior monologue or stream-of-consciousness processing, in which Joyce presents the focalizer's thoughts, associations, comparisons, and questions in an abbreviated thought language (e.g., Bloom reflects, "Wonder what I look like to her [the cat]. Height of a tower? No, she can jump me" [45]).

The students' first writing assignment asked them to select one of the novel's initial six episodes and analyze its techniques of either characterization or focalization. This exercise prepared them for the detailed close readings and applications of theory that I would be looking for in their presentations and research papers in the second half of the semester.

Rereading *Ulysses*, Discovering Theory

After the first half of the course, we shifted to the task of rereading *Ulysses* in conjunction with reading additional narrative theory and other relevant theoretical frameworks. The students worked through several theoretical readings (three or so a week); each reading was discussed in class, accompanied by student presentations and critical responses. Each student was assigned a theorist's work. The presentations (15–20 minutes) had five objectives: to explore critically ideas discussed in the reading; to consider the implications of the theory in terms of any episode from *Ulysses*; to lay possible groundwork for the final research paper; to simulate a conference paper; to provide the source for another student's critical response. The critical response (8–10 minutes) corresponded to the practice of having a respondent at a conference panel; the response ideally provoked more discussion and debate.

To engage the audience as active readers, I required each student in the audience to write down three questions and to ask one or two during the discussion. I then collected the questions and handed them back with encouraging comments in the next class. This two-staged method prompted students to think critically about the theory. Suddenly *Ulysses* became the "easy" text in the room: the common referent in our conversations and the source of concrete examples for illustrating or countering points in our discussions (among other literary texts).

Among the theorists we discussed were Madame de Staël, Émile Zola, E. M. Forster, Mikhail Bakhtin, Peter Brooks, Hayden White, Homi Bhabha, Chinua Achebe, Patrick Colm Hogan, Sigmund Freud, Jacques Lacan,[1] Seymour Chatman, David Lodge, Susan Winnett, Susan Lanser, Nancy K. Miller,[2] and Rachel Blau DuPlessis.[3] The first three provided "old school" texts, which helped historicize narratological inquiry (theories of fiction, theories of the novel) and to set up debate over such topics as narrative structure and characterization. De Staël provides a comparatist perspective of the modern European novel and its relation to history, while Zola's treatise on the experimental novel can be compared with Joyce's laboratory, which draws in part on the scrupulous observation of realia. Forster's classification of characters into "round" and "flat" types retains a classic if faded charm, and in class it contrasted well with our more multifaceted exploration of characterization in Rimmon-Kenan and, later, with our consideration of feminist and postcolonial arguments about characterization, narrative voice, and emplotment.

Moving on to Bakhtin, Brooks, and White, we became immersed in some recent narratological concerns to build on our prior considerations of characterization and perspective, as well as plot and style. With Bakhtin, I wanted to explore *dialogism* and *heteroglossia*, terms that he developed to account for, respectively, the double-voiced quality of the modern novel and the novel's use of many languages that pertain to different social and cultural practices and strata. These discussions of Bakhtin were further continued in our consideration of Brooks, and, in the final unit of the course, of Lodge's work on speech representation in narrative. Thus, the readings were arranged to create points of reemphasis, reconsideration, and return. The feminist narratologists and scholars of postcolonialism and psychoanalysis invited us to think about how narrative relates to corporeal, mental, historical, socioeconomic, and political human experiences and some of the ideologies that inform these.

For Bakhtin, dialogism functions on two levels: on a general linguistic level, all language is dialogic because it is primed for communication and exchange; on a novelistic level, dialogic or double-voiced utterances (in which two distinct sociolects are present in a single phrase or sentence) can be deployed. It is this second definition that was important for our class discussions. Bakhtin explains that the modern novel often uses language that seems to carry quotation marks or a kind of scaffolding of discourses. Stephen and Buck in the opening episode "Telemachus" have a conversation loaded with passages shot through with competing meanings. For example, Buck's urging Stephen to perform for Haines and Buck's own Irish prancing before the Englishman open up a colonially inflected dialogic arena. At times, characters like Buck and Stephen play with high and low culture through their utterances. As a hybrid character, Bloom uses a language, especially in his mental sphere of expression, that is heteroglot in social aspiration and bricolaged learning.

Narrative Theories in Contest: Brooks, Feminist Narratology, and *Ulysses*

Our attention to Brooks's conception of plot proved productive in two ways: it provided an example of a well-articulated theoretical position that then gets contested by other theorists, in this case, feminists; it provided a way to consider the fit between theory and narrative, since *Ulysses* does not initially seem to conform to Brooks's model. One of the attractions of Brooks's approach to plot is that it trains the tools of psychoanalysis not on authors, characters, or readers but on the narrative text itself, as Brooks argues that psychic functioning can be mapped onto textual functioning. More specifically, he draws on Freud's *Beyond the Pleasure Principle*, particularly the notion of desire as motorized Eros, to develop a theory of narrative that sees desire emplotted in the text and in our reading experiences. Brooks asserts, "Desire is always there at the start of a narrative, often in a state of initial arousal, often having reached a state of intensity such that movement must be created, action undertaken, change begun" (*Reading* 38).

Feminist narratologists such as Winnett, Lanser, DuPlessis, and Miller enabled us to consider problems with Brooks's account and with other male theorists' approaches to narrative. Winnett argues that Brooks's model takes for granted that the appropriate paradigm to describe the movement of the ambition plot is male sexual experience (i.e., moving toward one climax and then detumescence). Winnett notes how some narratives, often written by women, may map better onto diverse aspects of female sexual experience, such as giving birth, breast-feeding, and reaching multiple climaxes. DuPlessis, Lanser, and Miller add other layers to the debate. DuPlessis offers a feminist critique of the "romance plot," which,

> [a]s a narrative pattern, . . . muffles the main female character, represses quest, valorizes heterosexual ties, incorporates individuals within couples as a sign of their personal and narrative success. The romance plot separates love and quest, values sexual asymmetry, including the division of labor by gender, is based on extremes of sexual difference, and evokes an aura around the couple itself. (5)

Lanser and Miller both link plot and power. Lanser notes that many men conceive of plot by thinking of power and notes further that in patriarchal culture men have typically been given the privilege of exercising power ("Narratology" 356). Miller proposes a conception of a feminist plot, whose repressed content consists of

> not erotic impulses but an impulse to power: a fantasy of power that would revise the social grammar in which women are never defined as subjects; a fantasy of power that disdains a sexual exchange in which women can participate only as objects of circulation. (35)

We moved from these comparisons to focus on the underlying questions they raise about narrative and narrative theory. To what extent, if any, are elements of narrative gendered? If they are gendered, how can we best differentiate between, say, male plots and female plots? If the elements of narrative are not gendered, then how do we best account for the relation between gender and narrative? What are the advantages and disadvantages of Brooks's and Winnett's shared starting point, namely, that human sexual experience should be the basis for a theory of plot?

We added yet another dimension to our discussions by bringing in *Ulysses*. When Joyce ends the novel with Molly Bloom's interior monologue, which seems to flow from a woman's corporeal experience, how much was Joyce incorporating a feminist agenda into the very form of his narrative? *Ulysses* deflates both romance and quest plots, revealing through Molly and Leopold the fraught ideologies that support such lines of action. Because their marriage is neither beginning nor ending and because their infidelities will not lead, at least in the near future, to actual or symbolic death and thus condemnation, Joyce opens narrative structure and endings to new possibilities. What is gained or perhaps obscured by labeling Joyce's deflation of quest and romance feminist? *Finnegans Wake* celebrates another elision of plot and joins the ending to the beginning; it, along with *Ulysses*, questions the "social and ideological organization of gender" that DuPlessis skewers (5). Beckett takes the destruction of plot one step further by creating narratives that revel in repetition and circularity and resist empowerment, especially that of men. Students could debate the degree to which such modernist and postmodernist narratives are feminist. After all, for all of Molly's alterity and command of the conclusion, many of her reflections return to the "romance plot," albeit with amendments and deconstructions. The class certainly noticed how Molly's power seemed to derive, at least in part, from her participation in heterosexual exchange in an updated marriage contract that allowed for her to be shared with other men, resulting in different erotic pleasures for the married couple. On the other hand, she is not contained solely by these relations. Alternative (female-authored) texts that could be used to consider the deconstruction or transgressive permutation of romance and marriage plots would be Kate Chopin's *The Awakening*, Eliot's *The Mill on the Floss*, Woolf's *To the Lighthouse* and *Orlando*, and Margaret Atwood's *The Handmaid's Tale*.

Narrative Contesting Theory: *Ulysses* versus Brooks (inter alia)

Brooks defines plot as

> the principle of interconnectedness and intention which we cannot do without in moving through the discrete elements—incidents, episodes, actions—of a narrative: even such loosely articulated forms as the picaresque novel display devices of interconnectedness, structural repetition that allow us to construct a whole. ("Reading" 328)

Juxtaposing that definition against Joyce's practice again raised some fundamental questions: What is the purpose of plot, as opposed to character?

What is the effect of reducing plot to a few master strokes of beginning, middle, and end, as explored in creation and eschatological myths and stories?

A narrative like *Ulysses* both supports and challenges some of Brooks's assertions. Joyce uses the narrative element of the episode—eighteen of them—and fastens them to the hours of the clock in the period stretching from the morning of 16 June to the dawn of 17 June 1904. The narrative's formal dependence on durational time of one or two hours per episode emphasizes *chronos* over *kairos*, or critical time, that is, the chronological sequence over the rich and opportune moment. Stephen and Bloom mostly delay, wait, meditate, and indulge. Meanwhile, Brooks goes on to (re)define plot not as a series of actions but rather as the "logic of narrative discourses" ("Reading" 330); this position actually allows for the kinds of diversity that feminist and postcolonial narratologists seek. The refinement boosts the usability of the concept of plot for a text like *Ulysses*, by shifting emphasis to the logic Joyce develops for the narrative discourses in the various episodes as well as the overarching narrative of the day's experiences. But could we still call this "logic" plot? Would we give a more adequate account of *Ulysses* if we substituted "character" for Brooks's "plot," given that he further qualifies plot as "the dynamic shaping force of the narrative discourse" (335)? DuPlessis asserts that the romance plot is dependent on dominant ideologies or social scripts, and we could debate how this concept of plot compares with Brooks's emphasis on the "logic." Are not both theorists making similar claims?

We used Brooks's attention to the growing secularization of culture in the nineteenth and twentieth centuries as a way into discussions of the historical transformation of narrative. Given that secularization, have we increasingly looked for fictional plots that can explain our lives? However, we also noted that, despite the secular orientation of much fiction of the past two hundred years, these novels are not without consideration of sacred or spiritual plots, stories of becoming, falling, dying, redeeming. The plot of Eliot's *The Mill on the Floss* (1860) resists a conservative Christian interpretation; nonetheless the two proud Tulliver children, Maggie and Tom, die in each other's arms, destroyed by a flood. Surely Eliot is offering a complex cautionary tale of sorts while unraveling marriage and quest plots. For their part, *Ulysses* and *To the Lighthouse* are both hospitable to eschatological and typological readings. Indeed, Brooks's text, paired with Frank Kermode's *The Sense of an Ending* and Walter Benjamin's "The Storyteller," would be fruitful for students to consider, particularly to reflect on how much plot (and narrative) depends on beginnings and endings and how our understanding of these relates to the beginning and end of the world and of our lives. With this pairing, I suggested ways to connect theories of narrative and theories of fiction, especially the novel.

Narratology Meets Historiography, Postcolonial Theory, Psychoanalysis

This part of the course considered how historical and literary narratives can be comparatively theorized, explored postcolonial criticism embedded in narrative fiction, and questioned possible connections between psychoanalytic narratives and concepts and literary narratives. These theories were prompted by my selection of *Ulysses* and my interest in extending our discussions beyond the usual boundaries of narrative theory. The issues raised in this section of the course are too numerous and too complex to treat adequately here, but I can sketch the main lines of our discussion.

White rigorously examines narratives that structure different periods of historical writing and contends that our understanding of history is ideologically loaded. He also suggests the links between the construction of fictional plots and the emplotment of events in historical narrative. I referred to his arguments to question *Ulysses*'s complex historicism. (Morrison's *Beloved* and other postmodernist narratives that question received history could also be explored.) Joyce does not romanticize the past; rather, his narrative shows how history can be "recovered" and either represented in a realist manner (as in its references to the Gold Cup race that actually took place that day) or reframed in diverse critical ways (e.g., Stephen's "nightmare" of history or the text's presentation of competing Irish nationalist and pro-British histories).

In a kind of *histoire totale*, Joyce uses actual historical detail to build his narrative: the pages of *Ulysses* teem with names of streets, hotels, pubs, restaurants, businesses, monuments, and schools as well as with documentary texts of all sorts, from songs to newspaper pieces. We reflected on Joyce's deployments of history: What kinds of competing national, imperial, and cosmopolitan plots, settings, characters, or allegories does he convey? How do the Citizen, Stephen, Bloom, Deasy, and Haines think of Irish history, and what discourses does the Citizen combine to create?

White's text raised students' awareness of the political circumstances structuring our ideas and writing and helped us put Joyce's text into dialogue with work by commentators such as Achebe, Bhabha, and Hogan, who focus in various and sometimes conflicting ways on the experiences of colonial subjects. A key question we considered is whether Western theorists and narrative artists can adequately address the situations and experiences of colonized and postcolonial people. Indeed, in grappling with this question, we found *Ulysses* to be an especially productive text. Because the Irish were so often considered in popular and political discourses as racially inferior to Britons, the Irish could be seen as historical counterparts to the colonial subjects discussed in Achebe, Bhabha, and Hogan. In this sense, Joyce's novel offers a kind of layered postcolonial criticism, for Joyce writes from multiple perspectives and uses many voices, capturing the views and discourses of a pro-British flunkey like Deasy and of virulent nationalist essentialists like the Citizen, as well as more moderate positions. Joyce's insider-outsider status allows these perspectives; his political rejection of both Irish and British nationalist positions and his self-exile from both British-ruled and free Ireland establish him as a postcolonial critic in his own right.

For its part, psychoanalysis has allowed us to think about narrative in ways related to theories of the conscious, unconscious, desire, trauma, identity, and subjectivity. As Joyce is sensitive to the whole human subject, incorporating into his narratives stream-of-consciousness technique and other ways of reflecting the unconscious, the symptom, and the irrational, I wanted to sensitize students to Freudian, Lacanian, and other contributions to psychoanalytic thought that would help them interrogate not only aspects of subjectivity, but also features of the narrative text itself. This section of the course returned to our earlier discussions of characterization and focalization, but now from a psychoanalytic vantage point.

Narration and Speech Presentation

In the final unit of the course, we returned to a focus on narrative discourse, taking up the relation between direct and mediated presentations of speech by considering theoretical work on narrators—both the classical model proposed by Chatman and the feminist model proposed by Lanser—and on mimesis and diegesis, particularly Lodge's development of Bakhtin's typology of narrative discourse. By drawing on work influenced by Bakhin, I was able to connect this research on speech presentation to the broader issues of discourse, heteroglossia, and intertextuality that we had previously considered in our discussions of the relevance of feminism, psychoanalysis, historiography, and postcolonial theory to questions about narrative form and narrative meaning.

In Joyce's novel, certain episodes, or parts of them, get told without an apparent teller. In "Oxen of the Sun," the narrator emulates or parodies the style and form of successive literary eras. But in other episodes, such as "Circe" (dialogue with stage directions) and "Penelope" (stream of consciousness), the narrator seems to disappear. Chatman argues that not all narratives *need* an actual narrator; an implied author is sufficient. He contends that a diegetic text has a narrator whereas a prominently mimetic text or a "direct witnessing of action" creates the illusion of "showing" without a narrator (247).[4] Lanser's writings give us the tools to examine the gender of narrators (and implied authors) and how that inflects the narrative.

Additionally, Chatman's article prompted us to explore divided loyalties among narrators and characters. Chatman concisely lays out the agents of narrative transmission and reception: real author, implied author, narrator, real reader, implied reader, and narratee, with references to earlier theorists of these roles. In *Ulysses*, after the sixth episode, each episode assumes a different style and orientation, so the novel has no unified narrator. Instead, Joyceans have resorted to an elegant concept, "the Arranger" (proposed by David Hayman), to account for the overall narrative design of the work. The Arranger's function does not entirely cohere with Chatman's account of nonnarrated narration. The class could debate the possibility that the Arranger is located between the implied author and the narrator.

We then examined how Lodge reconceives the terms mimesis and diegesis. In modernist and postmodernist works, there is a heightened attention to the depiction of reality in its jagged, only partially apprehended forms; writers like Joyce seek a kind of mimesis of speech by presenting dialogue and inner thoughts complete with pauses, stammers, interruptions, changes in address and tone, digressions and associations. Joyce tends to reject, except in parody, overly heavy, dogmatic diegesis, which can produce what Lodge calls a "linguistic homogeneity" or, what Vološinov calls "linear style" (qtd. in Lodge 354). Lodge uses *Ulysses* to explore the analytic potential of Bakhtin's typology of literary discourse. First Lodge lays out three types of narrative speech:

> *The direct speech of the author.* This corresponds to Plato's diegesis.
>
> *Represented speech.* This includes Plato's mimesis—i.e., the quoted direct speech of the characters; but also reported speech in the pictorial style.
>
> *Doubly oriented speech,* that is, speech which not only refers to something in the world but refers to another speech act by another addresser. (358)

Regarding direct authorial speech, Lodge notes how Joyce, with his aesthetic of godlike artistic removal from the narrated events, works to elude or minimize authorial speech. Teachers could also turn to other texts such as Eliot's *The Mill on the Floss* and *Middlemarch* or works by D. H. Lawrence. Students debated the advantages and disadvantages of sometimes conflating a fictional narrator with the author. The term *authorial speech* invites such conflation, as we could see explicitly in Vološinov and in Lodge's analysis. Chatman, feminist narratologists, and postcolonial theorists can be enlisted for such debates.

Represented speech is an easier category for Lodge to apply to *Ulysses*, and Molly Bloom's monologue in the ultimate episode, "Penelope," is the most sustained example. He explains how Stephen's and Bloom's thoughts combine "interior monologue with free indirect speech and focalized narration—in short, a mixture of mimesis and diegesis, in which mimesis dominates" (359). The students liked how Lodge models applications of the concepts of mimesis and diegesis to the text at the syntactic level. What we originally discussed in the course as characterization and focalization now returned at the end of the course with linguistically oriented approaches to speech representation and how these relate directly to narrative. "Doubly oriented speech" (similar to Bakhtin's double-voiced speech) applies well to certain later episodes of *Ulysses*, such as "Nausicaa," "Aeolus," and "Cyclops." Lodge notes how, in the first half of "Nausicaa," the narrative is doubly oriented toward the characterization of Gerty (along with language and terms she would use) and toward the "original discursive context" (of women's magazines and novels of the turn of the century) (361).

He sees more of an evolution in narrative methods or styles than I do. Nonetheless, students could benefit from a heightened awareness of possible trajectories of change in narrative over time. Lodge proposes a historical sequence of classic realism, modernism, and postmodernism, based on the discourse typologies of Plato, Vološinov, and Bakhtin. He contends:

> The classic realist text . . . was characterized by a balanced and harmonized combination of mimesis and diegesis, reported speech and reporting context, authorial speech and represented speech. The modern novel evolved through an increasing dominance of mimesis over diegesis. (362–63)

We discussed the idea of evolution in narrative prose by debating Lodge's assertions, returning to Joyce's "Oxen of the Sun," an episode in which Mina Purefoy endures labor and gives birth to a son while the narrative moves through the ages of writing, from classical Latin and ancient Irish invocations and Latin prose styles of Roman historians through to modern turn-of-the-century slang and dialect. Joyce clearly suggests transformations over time in language and narrative discourse while also throwing his contemporary era's supposedly "evolved" mastery of language into doubt, pointing to both diversity and disintegration. This doubt is of course made comic when the episode ends with the discordant dissolution of a drinking party.

Cultivating Writing and Applied Theory

This course emphasized applied theory and methods of inquiry over a particular doxology or epistemic mastery of a canon of theoretical and literary texts, with an aim to prepare students for the task of writing future conference papers and articles. I guided students' writing and critical thought and research throughout the semester. The first short writing assignment was followed by a self-evaluation by the students to prompt them to reflect on their work. The final research paper involved stages of in-class development: first, a thesis workshop (I had students work in groups of two or three; they also had to send me their thesis statement or paper proposal for approval and possible guidance); then, three to four weeks before the due date, two in-class, sixty-minute sessions, one on research methods and another on scholarly writing, in which I demonstrated how to develop their research ideas as part of a scholarly dialogue; and finally an in-class peer review a week before the due date.

Narrative theory arises from a negotiation of previous theories of fiction and the novel, and, as my approach shows, should not be divorced from other theoretical considerations such as feminism, postcolonialism, historiography, and psychoanalysis. Rather, such bodies of thought (among others) can be shown to question narratological presuppositions and claims and can contribute to the continued growth and refinement of approaches to the study of stories.

Notes

1. From *The Four Fundamental Concepts of Psycho-analysis*, I used for this class the seminars "From Love to the Libido" (187–200) and "From Interpretation to the Transference" (244–60).

2. From *Subject to Change*, I used for this class the chapter "Emphasis Added: Plots and Plausibilities in Women's Fiction" (25–46).

3. From *Writing beyond the Ending*, I used for this class the chapter "Endings and Contradictions" (1–19 and 198–202).

4. Students could compare this approach with Rimmon-Kenan's. For Chatman a narrative need not have a narrator or narratee, while Rimmon-Kenan contends that "there is always a teller in the tale. . . . Even when a narrative text presents passages of pure dialogue . . . , there is . . . a 'higher narratorial authority responsible for quoting' . . ." (89). See Keen's and Phelan's contributions to the present volume for further discussion.

Works Cited

Abbott, H. Porter. *The Cambridge Introduction to Narrative*. 2nd ed. Cambridge: Cambridge UP, 2008. Print.

Achebe, Chinua. "An Image of Africa: Racism in Conrad's *Heart of Darkness.*" *Hopes and Impediments: Selected Essays*. New York: Doubleday, 1989. 1–20. Print.

Bakhtin, Mikhail M. "Discourse in the Novel." *The Dialogic Imagination: Four Essays by M. M. Bakhtin*. Ed. Michael Holquist. Trans. Caryl Emerson and Holquist. Austin: U of Texas P, 1981. 259–422. Print.

Benjamin, Walter. "The Storyteller." *Illuminations*. Ed. Hannah Arendt. Trans. Harry Zohn. New York: Schocken, 1968. 83–109. Print.

Bhabha, Homi K. "DessemiNation: Time, Narrative, and the Margins of the Modern Nation." *Nation and Narration*. London: Routledge, 1990. 291–322. Print.

Brooks, Peter. *Reading for the Plot: Design and Intention in Narrative*. New York: Knopf, 1984. Print.

———. "Reading for the Plot." Hoffman and Murphy 326–47.

Chatman, Seymour. "Discourse: Nonnarrated Stories." Hoffman and Murphy 246–57.

DuPlessis, Rachel Blau. *Writing beyond the Ending: Narrative Strategies of Twentieth-Century Women Writers*. Bloomington: Indiana UP, 1985. Print.

Forster, E. M. *Aspects of the Novel*. 1927. New York: Harcourt, 1954. Print.

Freud, Sigmund. "On Narcissism: An Introduction." Trans. James Strachey. *The Standard Edition of the Complete Works of Sigmund Freud*. Vol. 14. London: Hogarth, 1957. 67–102. Print.

Hayman, David. Ulysses: *The Mechanics of Meaning*. Englewood Cliffs: Prentice, 1970. Print.

Hoffman, Michael J., and Patrick D. Murphy, eds. *Essentials of the Theory of Fiction*. Durham: Duke UP, 1996. Print.

Hogan, Patrick Colm. *Colonialism and Cultural Identity: Crises of Tradition in the Anglophone Literatures of India, Africa, and the Caribbean*. Albany: State U of New York P, 2000. Print.

Joyce, James. *Ulysses*. Ed. Hans Walter Gabler. New York: Vintage, 1986. Print.

Kermode, Frank. *The Sense of an Ending*. Oxford: Oxford UP, 1967. Print.

Lacan, Jacques. *The Four Fundamental Concepts of Psycho-analysis*. Ed. Jacques-Alain Miller. Trans. Alan Sheridan. New York: Norton, 1978. Print.

Lanser, Susan S. "Toward a Feminist Narratology." *Style* 20.3 (1986): 341–63. Print.

———. "Toward a Feminist Poetics of Narrative Voice." *Fictions of Authority: Women Writers and Narrative Voice.* Ithaca: Cornell UP, 1992. 3–24. Print.

Lodge, David. "Mimesis and Diegesis in Modern Fiction." Hoffman and Murphy 347–71.

Martin, Wallace. *Recent Theories of Narrative.* Ithaca: Cornell UP, 1986. Print.

Miller, Nancy K. *Subject to Change: Reading Feminist Writing.* New York: Columbia UP, 1988. Print.

Rimmon-Kenan, Shlomith. *Narrative Fiction.* New York: Routledge, 2002. Print.

Staël, Madame de [Anne-Louise-Germaine]. "Essays on Fictions." *An Extraordinary Woman: Selected Writings of Germaine de Staël.* Ed. and trans. Vivian Folkenflik. New York: Columbia UP, 1987. 60–78. Print.

White, Hayden. "The Politics of Historical Interpretation: Discipline and De-sublimation." *The Content of the Form: Narrative Discourse and Historical Representation.* Baltimore: Johns Hopkins UP, 1987. 58–82. Print.

Winnett, Susan. "Coming Unstrung: Women, Men, Narrative, and Principles of Pleasure." *PMLA* 105.3 (1990): 505–18. Print.

Zola, Émile. *"The Experimental Novel" and Other Essays.* Trans. Belle M. Sherman. New York: Haskell, 1964. 1–54. Print.

Further Reading

Herman, David, ed. *The Cambridge Companion to Narrative.* Cambridge: Cambridge UP, 2007. Print.

Herman, David, Manfred Jahn, and Marie-Laure Ryan, eds. *Routledge Encyclopedia of Narrative Theory.* London: Routledge, 2005. Print.

Herman, Luc, and Bart Vervaeck. *Handbook of Narrative Analysis.* Lincoln: U of Nebraska P, 2005. Print.

Jahn, Manfred. *Narratology: A Guide to the Theory of Narrative.* 2005. Web. 10 Aug. 2009.

Phelan, James, and Peter J. Rabinowitz, eds. *A Companion to Narrative Theory.* Oxford: Blackwell, 2005. Print.

Beth Boehm and Debra Journet

Across the Curriculum: Rhetoric and Composition

Narrative is a primary way of making and communicating meaning in the interdisciplinary field of rhetoric and composition. We teach in an English department that is home to one of the oldest doctoral programs in rhetoric and composition in the country, and, perhaps more important, we offer the doctorate only in rhetoric and composition. While some of our students come from undergraduate and masters programs in literature and creative writing, others come from programs in communications, education, linguistics, history, even social work. Although we do require literature courses and a course in contemporary literary theory as part of their doctoral training, our students generally arrive with little or no experience in narrative theory. In this essay, then, we focus on why and how we teach narrative theory to these doctoral students. Whether we teach narrative analysis as part of a graduate seminar on rhetorical and textual analysis or in a seminar dedicated to narrative and composition studies, we continually ask students to consider how narrative theory from literary studies and the human sciences will strengthen and enhance teaching and research in composition. More specifically, our questions arise from three related objectives. First, we hope to provide students with a broad theoretical foundation that understands narrative as both epistemological and rhetorical; that is, we teach narrative as a way of both constructing and communicating knowledge. Second, we want students to understand narrative as a useful research tool; we want them to be able to use methods of narrative analysis for textual and discourse analysis, as well as use empirical research methodologies (such as case studies and ethnographies) that create narrative knowledge. Finally, as we prepare future university composition teachers and writing program administrators, we focus on pedagogy—considering how to teach and analyze narrative modes of discourse in the writing classroom and across the curriculum.

Establishing the Theoretical Foundation

Although the students in our seminar on rhetorical and textual analysis are well versed in composition theory and contemporary critical theory (and many are particularly interested in the intersections of composition and cultural studies), they do not have much experience with narrative theory. Indeed, most come to the class with an expectation that narrative analysis is akin to New Critical analysis. We begin with a quick tour of reception theory to encourage students to start thinking of narrative as communicative—as rhetorical. By beginning with critics who examine the role of the reader in making meaning from the text (e.g., Fish, Bleich, Prince, Fetterley, and Iser), we immediately start to distinguish narrative analysis from New Criticism and its strictures against the "affective fallacy." As we read selections by these theorists, we attempt to categorize the kinds of readers and the types of analytic methods implied by each. We then apply each method to short narrative texts (Hemingway's "My Old Man," Glaspell's "A Jury of Her Peers," and Morrison's "Recitatif" are literary texts to which we continually return), asking, for instance, How would Iser's reader respond? or, How would Fetterley's reader resist? As we collaboratively construct analyses of fictional narratives using reader-response methods, we not only discuss the strengths and weaknesses of a given method but also consider the implications that paying attention to the reader has for composition research and pedagogy. Students are asked to seek out composition theorists who have drawn on reception theory in their work and to bring in studies they believe have been influenced by this work.

After this focus on readers, we turn to "classical" narratology (e.g., Genette, Chatman). While students sometimes find this structuralist approach to narrative alien, we try to get students to examine both narratology and rhetoric and composition as disciplines in which practice and theory are intertwined in interestingly similar ways. What Monika Fludernik has recently suggested about narratology's "difficult relation between theory and practice" could apply equally to rhetoric and composition: "On the one hand, narratology claims to deliver a set of instruments for analyzing texts . . . ; on the other hand, narratology focuses on the why and the wherefore, the semiotics and grammar of narrative. In other words, narratology is both an applied science and a theory of narrative texts in its own right" (38–39). Our brief (and selective) introduction to narratology thus provides students with both a theory about the dynamic nature of narrative interaction and tools for analysis—including a vocabulary (e.g., *story/discourse, focalization, homodiegesis, heterodiegesis, duration, voice*), a taxonomy, and fairly explicit methods for dealing with specific narrative texts. At this point in the semester, we apply the narratological methods to the short stories we've been working with throughout the course and begin to look at nonfiction texts to see how the tools of narratology help us understand historical narratives and case studies (e.g., Freud's *Dora* or case studies by researchers in rhetoric and composition selected by students). Again, our approach is to analyze the strengths and weaknesses of the methods and to consider whether such methods emphasize the continuities or differences between fictional and nonfictional narratives. Finally, we ask what compelling questions narratological analysis does not help us answer, including questions about race, class, or gender or about the ethics of telling another's story.

These questions, of course, bring us to the rhetorical, ideological, and ethical turns in literary theories of narrative. We read selections from Wayne Booth (*Company, Rhetoric*), Peter Rabinowitz, James Phelan, Mikhail Bakhtin, Susan Lanser, and Robyn Warhol. These readings add to our growing analytic vocabulary (e.g., *implied authors, unreliable and naive narrators, authorial and narrative audiences, progression, tensions, instabilities, engaging narrators, dialogism, heteroglossia*). But, more important, with their focus on the rhetorical nature of narrative—on the dynamic relation between authors and readers and texts and cultural contexts—these theories provide warrants and methods for analyzing the ethical and ideological implications of reading and writing and for conducting research.

As students read a narrative like "Recitatif," for example, in which the character-narrator draws attention to racial issues without ever naming her own race or that of the other main character, they move from uncomfortable reader-response analysis in which they examine their own raced responses to the story to a narratological analysis of the narrator's *paralipsis* and finally to a rhetorical analysis that traces the dynamic relations among authors, narrators, and readers (authorial, narrative, and real; see Phelan's essay in this volume for more on these readers) and their various cultural contexts. Such layered reading experiences of fictional narratives help students use narrative analysis to frame some of our discipline's most important ethical issues: how narrative can enable students to organize and evaluate their own experiences and how an understanding of narrative can help students resist dominant cultural narratives of race, gender, and class (Mortensen and Kirsch).

Narrative Theory and the Human Sciences

When we teach the seminar devoted to narrative theory and composition, we continue to pursue questions about the relation between theory and analysis, but we also turn to the robust theoretical discussion located in the human sciences that examines narrative as a form of action as well as a mode of discourse or representation. This work is based on the assumption that human beings organize experience through narrative, endowing their lives with such narrative qualities as sequence, causality, direction, coherence, and purpose. Because rhetoric and composition is a highly interdisciplinary field, we draw on theory and scholarship from a variety of related areas, such as psychology, philosophy, history, and anthropology.[1] Narrative is thus understood as a way of linking actions and events, evaluating the significance of those actions and events, and configuring them into a coherent whole. That is, people narrativize their lives, and the process of constructing these lived stories is related to the processes they engage in when they read, view, or compose other kinds of stories, such as novels. These narratives of human action take a variety of forms, such as everyday stories, descriptions of individual lives, family and social histories, and other cultural forms of meaning making. And they are constructed and represented in a variety of semiotic domains, including oral, visual, and written modes of communication.

This work thus has immediate relevance for our students as future teachers and researchers in rhetoric and composition. First, it helps us frame key disciplinary concepts—such as identity, agency, and literacy—that are important to teaching and learning. After we read work on the self as a narrative construct and on the narrative quality of human experience, we reflect on how these ideas shape our understanding of the goals of a composition class. We consider, for example, what kinds of selves students and teachers are narrating in the classroom; how these acts of self-narration shape processes of composing or rhetorical action; how available stories are constrained by or made possible through other cultural forces, such as race, class, or gender. The work our students have produced in response to these questions has encompassed such topics as narrative, identity, and literacy in video and role-playing games; master tropes and grand narratives in student-authored literacy narratives; stories of displacement by Katrina survivors; or narrative ethics in the composition classroom.

There has also been a significant rhetorical turn in the human sciences, and consequently a considerable body of scholarship from within human-science disciplines about strategies and practices of representation (Nelson, Megill, and McCloskey). We introduce our students to this work, specifically focusing on work that addresses how narrative is used to produce disciplinary knowledge. In response, many of our students analyze the "textual dynamics" (Bazerman and Paradis) of disciplinary narrative genres, using the methods they've learned from both narratology and the human sciences. Typical of this work are analyses of the narrative elements of such texts as Supreme Court opinions, school mission statements, encyclopedic accounts of African expeditions from the nineteenth century, environmental-impact statements, as well as published research in rhetoric and composition.

Additionally, we introduce our students to empirical research methodologies that construct narrative knowledge—including historical accounts, case studies, and ethnographies. These research methodologies use narrative in a variety of ways. Qualitative researchers, for example, collect and analyze narrative data (Cortazzi; Emerson, Fretz, and Shaw) and report their findings in narrative form (Mortensen and Kirsch); teachers write and publish classroom narratives (Trimmer). Inherent in these research genres are complex rhetorical and epistemological as well as methodological issues. Students in our seminars thus consider such questions as, What are the differences between narrative and other, more generalized forms of knowledge? What are the canonical research narratives in our field? What constitutes an effective and persuasive narrative within a research context? What ethical issues are raised in narrative representations of research? Many of our students will themselves do empirical, narrative-based research, including case studies and ethnographies of composing within school and university composition classes, writing centers, programs in writing across the curriculum, out-of-school literacies, and the workplace. Consequently, we address how narrative informs the work they will do: the object of their research, their practice as researchers, and the written texts they will themselves produce.

Narrative and Pedagogy in Rhetoric and Composition

As we train future teachers and writing-program administrators, we ask our students to consider the roles of narrative in the classes they will teach. Narrative enters the undergraduate composition classroom in a number of ways. There is a long-standing tradition of personal writing in first-year composition (see, e.g., Hindman). Seminar participants thus consider ways to implement narrative assignments in undergraduate composition syllabi, such as literacy narratives in which students reflect on their own processes and histories as writers and readers. We also talk about the role of narrative in undergraduate research: students regu-larly confront narrative in science and history courses, and we often ask them to produce historical narratives and ethnographic narratives in their college research courses. Additionally, students in creative nonfiction classes compose narratives in many genres (see Hindman on this topic). Narrative is also important in new digital media productions that are increasingly the focus of composition programs. Additionally, there is a growing recognition of the role of narrative in the professional writing curriculum (Perkins and Blyler) and in medical and legal education (Charon and Montello). In our graduate seminars, we raise questions about how we teach and assess these narratives. In particular, we consider what kinds of stories we value as teachers, how we can promote stories that resist dominant narratives, and how we can help students use narrative as argument as well as personal exploration. We offer a specific example in our final section.

Toward a Conclusion

Our classes focus on theoretical research that sometimes appears to our students to be overly abstract or only tangentially related to the work they envision they will do. In particular, because the theory we read generally comes from disciplines outside rhetoric and composition, its relevance is not always readily apparent. We thus see one of our primary jobs as helping students find connections between that theory and the concerns we share with them as teachers and scholars. One way we try to make connections is to read scholarship within rhetoric and composition that engages with the theoretical issues we are exploring. We also spend a good deal of time in our classes reflecting on how these theories of narrative can or should shape our own teaching. Indeed, the most productive conversations generally come back to how the theory we have just read illuminates something that happened in our own teaching lives.

In 2005, for example, when one of us (Journet) taught this class, Hurricane Katrina was insistently in the news. Throughout that semester, we kept returning to how we made sense of—and how we assessed—the stories we saw and heard on television, on the Internet, and in the newspapers about Katrina survivors, a process of interpretation and evaluation that was also going on in many of the first-year writing classes that seminar participants were then teaching. Narrative theory became a lens through which we tried to frame the stories of disaster and displacement, both in the graduate seminar and in our undergraduate classrooms. We considered how the stories of Katrina were framed by particular media, how individual examples grew into canonical stories of rescue or abandonment, how narratives of race and poverty in New Orleans were both suppressed and reconstructed in national discourse, and how the meanings of Katrina narratives were the product of complex, multilayered historical and ideological processes. That is, in Katrina, the relevance of narrative theory to human experience was immediately clear. One cannot ever expect (and certainly never hopes) to repeat that experience. But it does provide a salient example of narrative theory's capacity to illuminate an enormous range of meaning-making activities.

Note

1. A good selection of representative work is the volume edited by Hinchman and Hinchman; the earlier volume edited by Mitchell also offers influential work from a variety of disciplines. Of particular value for our classes has also been work by Burke and by Bruner. For a good overview of related theory and research, see Polkinghorne.

Works Cited

Bakhtin, Mikhail M. *The Dialogic Imagination: Four Essays by M. M. Bakhtin*. Ed. Michael Holquist. Trans. Caryl Emerson and Holquist. Austin: U of Texas P, 1981. Print.

Bazerman, Charles, and James Paradis, eds. *Textual Dynamics of the Professions: Historical and Contemporary Studies of Writing in Professional Communities*. Madison: U of Wisconsin P, 1991. Print.

Bleich, David. "Epistemological Assumptions in the Study of Response." Tompkins 134–63.

Booth, Wayne C. *The Company We Keep: An Ethics of Fiction*. Berkeley: U of California P, 1988. Print.

———. *The Rhetoric of Fiction*. 2nd ed. Chicago: U of Chicago P, 1983. Print.

Bruner, Jerome. *Acts of Meaning: Four Lectures on Mind and Culture*. Cambridge: Harvard UP, 1990. Print.

Burke, Kenneth. *A Grammar of Motives*. Berkeley: U of California P, 1945. Print.

Charon, Rita, and Martha Montello, eds. *Stories Matter: The Role of Narrative in Medical Ethics*. London: Routledge, 2002. Print.

Chatman, Seymour. *Story and Discourse: Narrative Structure in Fiction and Film*. Ithaca: Cornell UP, 1978. Print.

Cortazzi, M. *Narrative Analysis*. London: Falmer, 1993. Print.

Emerson, Robert M., Rachel I. Fretz, and Linda L. Shaw. *Writing Ethnographic Fieldnotes*. Chicago: U of Chicago P, 1995. Print.

Fetterley, Judith. *The Resisting Reader: A Feminist Approach to American Fiction*. Bloomington: Indiana UP, 1981. Print.

Fish, Stanley. *Is There a Text in This Class? The Authority of Interpretive Communities*. Cambridge: Harvard UP, 1982. Print.

Fludernik, Monika. "Histories of Narrative Theory (II): From Structuralism to the Present." *A Companion to Narrative Theory*. Ed. James Phelan and Peter J. Rabinowitz. Oxford: Blackwell, 2005. 36–59. Print.

Genette, Gérard. *Narrative Discourse: An Essay in Method*. Trans. Jane E. Lewin. Ithaca: Cornell UP, 1980. Print.

Hinchman, Lewis P., and Sandra K. Hinchman, eds. *Memory, Identity, Community: The Idea of Narrative in the Human Sciences*. Albany: State U of New York P, 1997. Print.

Hindman, Jane E., ed. *Personal Writing*. Spec. issue of *College English* 64.1 (2001): 34–108. Print.

Iser, Wolfgang. "The Reading Process: A Phenomenological Approach." Tompkins 50–69.

Lanser, Susan Sniader. "Shifting the Paradigm: Feminism and Narratology." *Style* 22.1 (1988): 52–60. Print.

Mitchell, W. J. T., ed. *On Narrative*. Chicago: U of Chicago P, 1981. Print.

Mortensen, Peter, and Gesa Kirsch, eds. *Ethics and Representation in Qualitative Studies of Literacy*. Urbana: Natl. Council of Teachers, 1996. Print.

Nelson, John S., Allan Megill, and Donald N. McCloskey, eds. *The Rhetoric of the Human Sciences: Language and Argument in Scholarship and Public Affairs*. Madison: U of Wisconsin P, 1987. Print.

Perkins, Jane, and Nancy Blyler, eds. *Narrative and Professional Communication*. Greenwich: Ablex, 1999. Print.

Phelan, James. *Narrative as Rhetoric: Technique, Audiences, Ethics, Ideology*. Columbus: Ohio State UP, 1996. Print.

Polkinghorne, Donald E. *Narrative Knowing and the Human Sciences*. Albany: State U of New York P, 1988. Print.

Prince, Gerald. "Introduction to the Study of the Narratee." Tompkins 7–25.

Rabinowitz, Peter J. *Before Reading: Narrative Conventions and the Politics of Interpretation.* 2nd ed. Columbus: Ohio State UP, 1998. Print.

Tompkins, Jane, ed. *Reader Response Criticism: From Formalism to Post-structuralism.* Baltimore: Johns Hopkins UP, 1980. Print

Trimmer, Joseph. *Narration as Knowledge: Tales of the Teaching Life.* Portsmouth: Boynton, 1997. Print.

Warhol, Robyn. *Gendered Interventions: Narrative Discourse in the Victorian Novel.* New Brunswick: Rutgers UP, 1989. Print.

Further Reading

Gergen, Kenneth J., and Mary M. Gergen. "Narrative Form and the Construction of Psychological Science." *Narrative Psychology: The Storied Nature of Human Conduct.* Ed. Theodore R. Sarbin. New York: Praeger, 1986. 22–44. Print.

MacIntyre, Alasdair. *After Virtue: A Study in Moral Theory.* 3rd ed. South Bend: U of Notre Dame P, 2007. Print.

McCloskey, Donald N. *If You're So Smart: The Narrative of Economic Expertise.* Chicago: U of Chicago P, 1992. Print.

White, Hayden. *The Content of the Form: Narrative Discourse and Historical Representation.* Baltimore: Johns Hopkins UP, 1990. Print.

Brian Evenson

Across the Curriculum: Creative Writing

Mieke Bal's suggestion that "the aim of textual analysis is not to account for the process of writing, but for the conditions of the process of reception" (78) underscores some of the initial difficulties faced in bringing narrative theory into a creative writing workshop. Generally such workshops focus on the generation and critique of student work and on helping individual students establish their own set of stylistic gestures and their own aesthetic sensibility while improving the work's quality. Evaluation and self-evaluation are key to this process of the writer's development in a way that they are not for most students seeking to acquire mastery of narrative theory. Yet I have found that teaching narrative theory in the creative writing workshop enables students to become better writers and better evaluators of their own and others' work.

In the traditional fiction-writing workshop (often called the Iowa model, after University of Iowa's groundbreaking MFA program), a writer composes a story that is read before class by all students. In the next class session, the student sits silently as his or her professor and fellow students "critique" the story. What is meant by "critique" changes from classroom to classroom, but one of the more common interpretations involves describing what is happening in the story, evaluating whether the story accomplishes what it sets out to do, and then determining if the story is finished, needs more revision, or should be abandoned. Generally each student is allowed to have a say, responding both to the story and to others' comments, as the instructor directs discussion.

Traditionally, the creative writing workshop has tended to operate on intuitive rather than theoretical principles. Consider for instance some quotations from Anne Lamott's *Bird by Bird*, the most widely read creative writing handbook: "And then the miracle happens" (9); "You are going to love some of your characters, because they are you or some facet of you" (45); "You get your confidence and intuition back by trusting yourself, by being militantly on your own side" (112); "The rational mind doesn't nourish you" (112). Likewise, evaluation of student work often relies on intuition ("It didn't feel right") or vague notions of belief ("I didn't *believe* in this character" or "I didn't 'buy' that he would do that"). This intuitive approach is often augmented by Aristotelian and New Critical ideas—for instance, instructors might offer units on plot and character—but rarely does creative writing pedagogy actively draw on contemporary narrative theory. And yet, treating the creative writing classroom as a practicum for narrative theory leads to a more rigorous workshop at all levels and to a more precise understanding both of well-known short stories and of student work. Narrative theory gives aspiring writers a terminology that allows them to understand how contemporary writers create particular narrative effects. This understanding in turn allows student writers to use the techniques that bring about these effects in their own fiction. Indeed, a shared understanding of narrative theory helps establish a common set of terms and concepts that will strengthen students' reading ability, improve their fiction, and hone their abilities to critique the work of others and to self-critique and revise their own work. In the remainder of this essay, I describe strategies I've used in my own workshops to bring about a rapprochement between ideas from narrative theory and those traditionally used to support the teaching of creative writing. Overall, this approach can help students realize that narrative theories provide excellent tools for understanding the range of possibilities for individual elements within fictional works, that effective fictions are built on a wide range of aesthetic and stylistic principles, and that evaluation of individual narrative elements must be based on their function within a given story structure.

Reading

The key to using narrative theory in the creative writing workshop comes in making students gradually aware of its practical relevance. In beginning and intermediate undergraduate courses, I start by reading a variety of published stories, considering them as models of different kinds of narrative practice and as tools for introducing ideas from narrative theory. Discussion will likely begin with traditional thematic readings of the stories—such as students are often taught to perform in literature courses—but should quickly be steered toward craft issues: How does a particular story manage to achieve its effects? Where does the author spend her time? Why does she choose to break a scene where she does?

One cannot underestimate the importance of choosing stories that both effectively reveal the range of available narrative techniques and remain appealing to students on an aesthetic level. I start by mixing traditional workshop favorites such as Raymond Carver, Flannery O'Connor, William Trevor, and Tim O'Brien with innovative but still eminently readable writers such as Donald Barthelme, Kelly Link, Bruno Schulz, Gary Lutz, George Saunders, and Shelley Jackson. Discussion can begin with the strategies for interpretation that students have absorbed and are used to using. It's worth acknowledging, for instance, that there is something to the statement "I didn't believe in this character" but that this will only take us so far in our understanding of either the character or the narrative. Some students will offer more considered notions, such as the Aristotelian idea that a character should be consistent, or at least consistently inconsistent. These ideas deserve to be acknowledged; they in fact function adequately for many stories. But it should be made clear that elements and techniques are better understood not in relation to intuitive expressivist standards but in relation to their function in bringing about certain effects in the work as a whole. "Intuition" is not an end point but an initial response to be tested with the tools of narrative theory and the idea of means-ends relations between techniques and effects—so that we can offer clearer reasons for our intuitions or come to a new evaluation.

Intuitive theories are less useful as a beginning point when it comes to nonstandard characters in avant-garde texts. For instance, what about characters who take on the author's name (e.g., Jonathan Safran Foer's *Everything Is Illuminated* and Ben Marcus's *Notable American Women*), who take the names of real people (David Foster Wallace's use of Lyndon Johnson in *Girl with Curious Hair*), or who undergo inexplicable transformations (the protean eponymous hero of Eric Chevillard's *Palafox*)? In exposing students to characters who are difficult to account for through their usual ways of looking at fiction, we open the door to narrative theory. Possible-worlds theory, for instance, allows us to think about the textual inclusion of authors and real people in a way that Aristotelian notions do not. Similarly, Brian McHale's idea that postmodernist fiction engages in ontological rather than epistemological interrogation can give students more productive ways of thinking about a protean character than the idea of "consistent inconsistency."

At this point, it strikes me as important to circle back: What else can possible-worlds theory tell us about characters in those stories that "consistently inconsistent" seemed sufficient to address? Since in general "fictional worlds don't have to conform to the structures of the actual world" (Doležel 19) and since both realistic and fantastic fictions cue readers to construct alternative possible worlds, albeit in different ways, the distinction between realistic and nonrealistic characters needs to be rethought. Both realistic and nonrealistic characters emerge from the interaction between the logic stated or implied in a given fictional world and readers' real-world "encyclopedias"—or rather, their use of what Marie-Laure Ryan calls the principle of minimal departure, which allows the fictional world to be "filled out" with experiential reality except at moments when the text explicitly overrules this move. By demonstrating how all stories, realistic or otherwise, blend real-world and textual knowledge in various ratios, one helps students see that realistic and nonrealistic characters have more in common than they might initially believe, thereby challenging the relevance of the traditional divide between the mimetic and the nonmimetic.

From here, one could easily move into discussion of Roman Ingarden's work and, from there, into the nuances of reader-response theory, and indeed for the right group of students this sequence makes perfect sense. For beginners, it is more important to establish a limited series of terms and several clear ways of thinking about texts that can be built on later.

One can approach notions of duration, narrative rhythm, focalization, and so on in similar ways, by building on the student's commonsensical and received knowledge, illustrating its potential strengths and limitations, complicating it, and moving beyond it. Indeed, ideas of duration, order, and frequency, as explained by Gérard Genette (and later by Bal, Chatman, and others), are likely to meet less resistance than more complex theories of character—which, tied as they are to our notion of what it means to be human, people tend to be more passionate about. Generally speaking, it is most productive to pair stories that operate very differently and have students compare them in detail—for example, a story with large differences in scene duration with a story with relatively consistent shifts, a story told chronologically with a story told through prolepses or other disruptions of chronology. From there, one might compare similar stories, gauging slighter differences. Students should explicitly be told that the purpose in comparing one device in two stories is not to designate one as better but instead to reveal a range of available possibilities for generating different desirable effects and that what is desirable in one story may be less desirable in another. As with character, students often think they know what perspective is; in introducing a term such as "focalization" one must be prepared to show how new terminology allows one to see a story (and ultimately one's own work) differently and more productively.

In advanced fiction-writing classes in which I can assume some prior familiarity with fictional techniques and a background in reading, I offer a more eccentric range of texts and focus on stories that pose difficult narrative problems. Whereas in beginning classes I generally teach only excerpts of narrative theory, here I often teach at least one full-length theoretical work, usually Bal's *Narratology* or Seymour Chatman's *Story and Discourse*, though other works are equally productive. Recent pairings of Bal or Chatman with anthologies of theoretical essays have also been productive.

In graduate classes, I expose students to increasingly challenging work, introducing them formally to possible-worlds theory (Ryan and Doležel in particular), Ursula Heise and Brian McHale's approaches to postmodernism, William Gass's exploration of the sentence as architecture, and Gaston Bachelard's phenomenological examination of spatiality. We discuss stories that raise complicated problems, such as Antoine Volodine's use of what he calls the "narract" (a complex term used to break down the wall between the real and the imaginary and to question the boundary between representation and creation), Rick Moody's deliberate and jarring shift from external to internal focalization at the end of *The Ice Storm*, Robert Coover's use of contradictory and mutually exclusive narrative lines, Marie Redonnet's and Laird Hunt's appropriations of the detective genre, and Ben Marcus's use of peculiar noun-noun fusions as a means of short-circuiting the principle of minimal departure.

In all these cases, the focus is on how narrative theory allows writers to notice things about stories that other sorts of approaches do not.

Writing and Revision

Once students have a familiarity with narrative theory and have recognized its usefulness for understanding the craft of published stories, it is a short step to get them thinking about it in regard to their own fiction. I find it useful to start with exercises focusing on form and style, such as those found in Brian Kiteley's *The 3 A.M. Epiphany: Uncommon Writing Exercises That Transform Your Fiction*. Exercises that focus on rhythm, sequencing, duration, differences between different types of narrators, and so on or exercises that ask one to write a short scene in one way and then rework it formally (rearranging it, changing the narration, etc.) are ideal for helping students use concepts from narrative theory to rethink their own craft. It also leads them to understand how theories of narrative, while not denying the importance of the intuitive stage of the creative process, can accelerate the composition and revision processes by making them more aware of their choices and these choices' impact and by allowing their choices to establish a text whose effects are less prone to be working at cross-purposes. Beginning with exercises allows students to become comfortable talking about narrative theory in relation to their own writing without feeling threatened and becoming defensive: exercises feel less personal to them than do their full-length stories.

In a beginning class, as much as the first half of each class session might be devoted to reading and to exercises, with the second half focusing on workshopping. As students become more comfortable with narrative theory at the intermediate, advanced, and graduate level, I dedicate increasingly more time to workshopping.

Once workshopping has begun, narrative theory is largely a matter of praxis, something that informs the discussion of student stories in the same way that it has informed the discussion of published work. It makes discussions more precise and more useful to the writer, more exactly describing the story and its effects. Some students adapt easily to narrative theory, others tend to move back and forth between narrative theory and the more intuitive and expressive ideas exemplified by Lamott. Later in the course the sorts of stories we look at tend to change as well, with the class discussing work that illustrates specific narrative techniques or poses unusual narrative problems. I tend, particularly in graduate courses, to choose these stories according to the needs of particular students: work that either reassures them about the risks they are taking or poses problems intended to encourage them to take more risks. For instance, for students struggling with foreshadowing, we might examine Muriel Spark's use of anticipation and achrony in a few pages of *The Prime of Miss Jean Brodie*. For a student whose work is becoming increasingly oblique, we might explore the multilayered use of ellipsis in Amy Hempel's enigmatic "Daylight Come" and discuss what Wolfgang Iser says about gaps stimulating meanings into existence. For a student who insists that a realistic story should be linear, we might look, aided by Genette's notions of duration and order, at how countless "realistic" narratives are in fact told nonchronologically.

Narrative theory keeps writers from taking as gospel truth the untheorized ideas that have come to characterize the discourse of the creative writing workshop; even if students continue to draw from those ideas, they do so in a more considered way. Narrative theory allows them to look at well-known stories differently, unveiling the craft that has gone into a story's construction and how each narrative whole has been constructed from numerous parts and effects. This, in turn, allows them to think about their own work differently, gives them a catalog of techniques to draw on, and emphasizes the techniques that all writers share rather than keying on value-laden distinctions such as realistic versus experimental. Ultimately, I would argue that, after having been sufficiently metabolized, narrative theory has an effect on the conception of the work as well, providing different conscious and unconscious structures for organizing the sources from which writers draw.

In my experience, the biggest danger in teaching narrative theory in the creative writing workshop is not that students will reject it but that one or two students accept it too enthusiastically. I try to keep in mind Bal's caution that "the issue of chronology is not a tool to decide literary quality. Narratology helps understanding, not evaluation" (83). For most students, the realization that they can construct stories in countless ways is remarkably liberating and will lead to a flowering of possibility. The occasional student, however, will fixate on one idea from narrative theory and use it as a replacement for a proper aesthetic, deciding for instance that all the scenes within all his stories should have equal duration without a clear sense of why this works for some stories and not for others. There is an important place for arbitrary constraints, such as those used by the Oulipo group or by collage artists, as a means of liberating the way we approach material for fiction—especially since, as Rosmarie Waldrop suggests in speaking about collage, "Our concerns and obsessions will surface no matter what we do" (155). However, the idea that one can find a "right" form or that a formal arrangement should be used repeatedly like a cookie cutter should be discouraged. Teaching a good cross-section of stories largely mitigates this danger: by exposing students to quite different narrative strategies, one makes clear that there are many paths to a successful story. And a better understanding of the dynamics of the story encourages better evaluation. As should be clear from the discussion above, however, one of the effects of introducing narrative theory into the creative writing classroom is to bring increased weight to the process of describing and understanding the work, taking at least some of the emphasis off evaluation. When used deftly, narrative theory can help make the workshop into a place where students do their most productive work.

Works Cited

Bachelard, Gaston. *La poétique de l'espace*. Paris: PUF, 1958. Print.

Bal, Mieke. *Narratology: Introduction to the Theory of Narrative*. 2nd ed. Toronto: U of Toronto P, 1997. Print.

Chatman, Seymour. *Story and Discourse: Narrative Structure in Fiction and Film*. Ithaca: Cornell UP, 1978. Print.

Coover, Robert. "The Babysitter." *Pricksongs and Descants*. New York: Dutton, 1969. 206–39. Print.

Doležel, Lubomír. *Heterocosmica: Fiction and Possible Worlds*. Baltimore: Johns Hopkins UP, 2000. Print.

Gass, William H. *The World within the Word: Essays*. New York: Knopf, 1978. Print.

Genette, Gérard. *Narrative Discourse: An Essay in Method*. Trans. Jane E. Lewin. Ithaca: Cornell UP, 1980. Print.

Heise, Ursula K. *Chronoschisms: Time, Narrative, and Postmodernism*. Cambridge: Cambridge UP, 1997. Print.

Hempel, Amy. "Daylight Come." *The Collected Stories of Amy Hempel*. New York: Scribner's, 2007. 101–02. Print.

Hunt, Laird. *The Impossibly*. Minneapolis: Coffee House, 2001. Print.

Iser, Wolfgang. *The Implied Reader: Patterns of Communication in Prose Fiction from Bunyan to Beckett*. Baltimore: Johns Hopkins UP, 1974. Print.

Kiteley, Brian. *The 3 a.m. Epiphany: Uncommon Writing Exercises that Transform Your Fiction*. Cincinnati: Writer's Digest, 2005. Print.

Lamott, Anne. *Bird by Bird: Some Instructions on Writing and Life*. New York: Anchor, 1995. Print.

Marcus, Ben. *The Age of Wire and String*. New York: Knopf, 1998. Print.

McHale, Brian. *Postmodernist Fiction*. London: Methuen, 1987. Print.

Moody, Rick. *The Ice Storm*. Boston: Little, 1994. Print.

Redonnet, Marie. *Nevermore*. Paris: POL, 1994. Print.

Ryan, Marie-Laure. "Possible-Worlds Theory." *Routledge Encyclopedia of Narrative Theory*. Ed. David Herman, Manfred Jahn, and Ryan. London: Routledge, 2005. 446–50. Print.

Spark, Muriel. *The Prime of Miss Jean Brodie*. New York: Harper, 1961. Print.

Volodine, Antoine. *Minor Angels*. Trans. Jordan Stump. Lincoln: U of Nebraska P, 2004. Print.

Waldrop, Rosmarie. "Collage or the Splice of Life." *Encyclopedia*. Vol. 1. Providence: Encyclomedia, 2006. 155–58. Print.

Further Reading

Berry, R. M., and Jeffrey R. Di Leo. *Fiction's Present: Situating Contemporary Narrative Innovation*. Albany: State U of New York P, 2007. Print.

Federman, Raymond. *Critifiction: Postmodern Essays*. Albany: State U of New York P, 1993. Print.

Motte, Warren F., Jr., trans. and ed. *Oulipo: A Primer of Potential Literature*. Lincoln: U of Nebraska P, 1986. Print.

Richardson, Brian. *Unnatural Voices: Extreme Narration in Modern Contemporary Fiction*. Columbus: Ohio State UP, 1996. Print.

Sukenick, Ronald. *Narralogues: Truth in Fiction*. Albany: State U of New York P, 2000. Print.

Amy Shuman

Across the Curriculum: Folklore and Ethnography

Ethnographers and folklorists approach narrative as a dimension of cultural communication to be studied as a performance, often in face-to-face interaction. This focus on the production of narrative in specific cultural contexts is a defining feature of ethnographic studies of narrative, differentiated from literary approaches. The teaching strategies described in this essay are designed to introduce students to methods and theories of fieldwork, collection, and transcription and to analytic description and theory. All the issues discussed, including form, meaning, and ethics, are studied with regard to relations among tellers, listeners, and other participants engaged in cultural communication.

Historically, folk-narrative courses focused on the comparison of texts from a particular group or in a particular genre (e.g., traditional tales, epics, or contemporary legends). The teaching strategies discussed here draw on this research but focus on narrative as performance, communication, and interaction. A central premise is that narratives (texts) and contexts (cultural, situational, intertextual) are interdependent. In lectures, class discussions, assignments, and exercises, I encourage students to question what counts as context. We discuss the narratives that they have collected in relation to a variety of contexts, including interaction, structures of language, and political ideologies.

For both undergraduate and graduate classes, students collect a narrative (or group of narratives) to examine throughout the course. To make optimal use of the units outlined here, I prefer to have students collect the narrative in performance (either face-to-face or using other media). I treat some portion of each class session as a workshop in which small groups closely discuss the topic of the day in terms of one student's materials.

In an undergraduate class, our focus is on how to describe a narrative performance; theoretical issues arise directly out of the challenges students face in undertaking their projects. The course provides tools for fieldwork, including ethical principles governing the relation between the field-worker and members of the community, and methods of narrative analysis (such as identifying the formal dimensions of a narrative and understanding genre). I encourage students to pay attention to their own cultural perspectives as both important and limiting.

Students in a graduate course work on their own fieldwork-based projects, and they are also introduced to the larger scope of ethnographic narrative research, especially in folklore and sociolinguistics. Some areas of ethnographic narrative work, such as thematically based collections, are undertheorized, and we identify these and discuss possibilities for new areas of research. The course is structured as a seminar with in-depth discussions of readings and workshops to discuss the materials collected by the students.

In what follows, I describe several units that could be tailored to fit the different needs of undergraduates and graduate students, could serve as the basis for an entire course, or could instead be used as a module in a class surveying key issues in ethnography. The sequence of units presented is designed both to familiarize students with the range of approaches to ethnographic narrative research and to suggest theoretical challenges that remain to be addressed in future scholarship in this area.

Collecting / Fieldwork

This unit places two topics often considered separately (collections of texts and fieldwork-based research on narrative performances) in conversation with each other. A collection/corpus can represent a historical period, one person's repertoire, a dominant or minority perspective, and it can be based more on structural properties than on content. Also, collections can be organized according to types of situations rather than narrative genres. In this unit, folkloric and sociolinguistic narrative theories merge in the study of narratives in the situational contexts of ordinary life.

Topics for this unit include the following:

The conditions that warrant considering narratives as part of a corpus.

The role of the collector, including ethical considerations (especially obligations to the people who tell the stories or the people described in the stories) and methods of collection.

Categories and subcategories for organizing, selecting, and excluding material, whether by theme (birth narratives), occasion (narratives told during a wake), or repertoire (told by a particular performer).

Collecting as part of an ethnographic study of everyday life (Linde; Briggs).

Additional topic for graduate students: Narrative collections and fieldwork-based research on narrative performance may seem to be diametrically opposed, and indeed represent different threads of folkloric narrative research. To some extent, the focus on collection has been replaced by the focus on production (Stewart). Collection is seen to destroy context, performance to restore it. However, this proposed course of study attempts to demonstrate the interdependence of collection and performance in narrative analysis.

For a workshop topic, the class could be asked to use one student's example to consider how the narrative was collected and to discuss possible ethical concerns and how this narrative would be classified in a collection (by the scholar and the performer).

Transmission

The study of narrative transmission begins with the simple assertion that narratives travel from one person, generation, or cultural group to another. Transmission has been studied both intertextually, as a comparison of written versions of tales, and interactionally, to understand how people learn and pass on stories. This unit is included because it is central to folk narrative research. Dan Ben-Amos's work provides a historical survey of the concept of motif ("Concept"); our goal is to learn to use this concept critically rather than casually. John Miles Foley introduces students to oral-formulaic theories of memory and performance. Undergraduate class discussion explores ways that transmission is not linear; we challenge the idea that by tracing a lineage retrospectively we arrive at an explanatory chronology. To some extent, terms like *networking* avoid the assumptions of linearity. Additional graduate readings integrate interdisciplinary discussions of other dimensions of transmission, including memory, literacy, and social networking. This unit offers students ideas for considering the folkloric concept of transmission as connected to other theoretical discussions, for example, Jacques Derrida's critique of origins, Michel Foucault's concepts of archaeologies and genealogies, Walter Benjamin's distinctions between relics and ruins, and Gilles Deleuze and Félix Guattari's concept of the rhizome.

For this unit, a workshop topic could ask students what they need to know to understand the circumstances in which this narrative is learned, told, and retold and instruct them to include questions about who has the right to tell it.

Form

Formal models or grammars provide students with helpful descriptive tools. Formal studies of narrative have been criticized as applicable only to the particular genres or collections for which they were designed rather than being universally applicable. But that is exactly the point: these grammars are useful for identifying the properties of a particular set of narratives within a cultural context. This unit introduces students to two classic formal models: Valdimir Propp's study of the structure of the Russian folktale and William Labov and Joshua Waletzky's proposal for understanding the fundamental structure of conversational narrative. Both of these models rely on texts considered independently of their performance contexts; several scholars (Norrick; Ochs and Capps) have identified these limitations and provided models that take interaction into account. Graduate students work with a greater variety of models and additionally discuss the limitations of formal models to account for narrative performance or interaction.

An assignment or workshop discussion for this unit might ask students to use one of the models to describe the formal elements of a class member's narrative and to discuss the merits and limitations of this model.

Context

The goal of this section is to introduce students to the skills needed for doing research on narrative as communication and to explore the limits of contextual understanding. Context locates narratives in social interaction, including norms, ideas, time, and space (observable dimensions) and emotions, memories, and agendas (less observable but equally significant). Context is never sufficient to fully unravel or unpack the meaning of a story, and context is limited not only by the researcher's access to information but also by the storytelling participants' perspectives.

Ethnographers have provided several models for distinguishing among contexts, but the key differentiation is between contexts of culture and of situation (Ben-Amos, "'Context'"). Context is not background information but instead involves the complex relations between narrative and multiple realities in time and space (Young). Several folklorists have investigated what Donald Brenneis describes as the "doubly anchored character of narrative" (42): the relation between the events in a story and the situation in which a narrative is performed (Bauman; Ben-Amos, "'Context'"; Shuman, *Storytelling Rights*; Young).

We explore research that describes narrative in situations and cultural contexts and as a form of communicative activity that creates situational contexts. The goal for both undergraduates and graduates is to understand context not as something that stands still or exists wholly outside the narrative but as something partially created by the narrative and as unstable.

For an assignment or workshop discussion, the instructor can have students describe the context for the narrative they have collected and distinguish among, for example, contexts of time, space, physical settings, the emotional climate, cultural norms of speaking, and shared knowledge and belief systems. Students can also be advised to bear in mind that context is never a laundry list and asked to add a paragraph explaining their selection of what they consider the salient elements of context for the chosen narrative.

Repertoire and Style

Repertoire is a relatively naturalized (and thus less theorized) aspect of narrative collection. Folklorists/ethnographers often develop long-standing relationships with particular tellers and understand their repertoires as performances and cultural productions inseparable from the tales them-selves (Glassie; Mills; Pentikainen; Toelken). Although students cannot do extended, longitudinal research in a single course, many of them begin with familiarity with the performers and the repertoires, so this unit has direct application for their work.

Repertoire is neither fixed nor stable but instead involves ongoing stylistic appropriations and constraints at play in the performance of par-ticular narratives in particular occasions by particular performers. Whereas collections constitute a defined set of narratives, a repertoire points to the possibilities of narratives imagined by the teller or audience but not neces-sarily named or performed. The occasion or audience, rather than form or theme, can become the criterion for a repertoire. Graduate students, by addressing questions of style in this section, can interrogate some of the fundamental assumptions about subjectivity in narrative. When we introduce questions of style (local aesthetics), we shift our focus away from fixed subjects and toward discourse and situation; in Mikhail Bakhtin's terms, styles do not merely represent particular realities but rather are a site for negotiating contested realities (Hirschkop).

For undergraduates, an assignment or workshop discussion could ask students to describe a performer's repertoire as comprehensively as possible. Graduate students could be asked to use any repertoire-based narrative study to discuss how attention to issues of repertoire and style decenter the subject.

Genre

This unit is a core component of folkloric narrative research; in fact, it is a fundamental dimension of folklore studies generally. It is by now accepted that genre classification is a culturally specific practice, and the study of genre is one of the most useful ways to understand cultural expectations and norms in the production, performance, and reception of narrative. The European genres of folktale, legend, myth, proverb, and riddle have been studied most systematically. Research on each of these genres is ex-tensive and ongoing. However, like the motif and the collection, genre was, until the 1970s, a relatively undertheorized area of narrative research (Ben-Amos, "Concept" 17–20). Dan Ben-Amos proposed a differentia-tion between analytic, European-based categories (folktale, legend, and myth) and ethnic genres (defined by local tradition bearers). Ethnic genres are not necessarily more stable or fixed than are analytic categories (Ryan). Genre in the context of performance refers to expectations or conventions; genres are best defined in relation to one another (Bauman; Briggs).

Peter Seitel, building on work by Bakhtin, rejects the idea that genre is taxonomy and instead explores genres as part of emergent processes in which style, composition, and theme come together to fulfill (or overturn) expectations and to create situated meaning.

In an assignment or workshop discussion for this unit, undergraduates might discuss the problem of genre in legends and attempt to differentiate among historical, hagiographic, contemporary, and supernatural legends. Graduate students could analyze and assess Seitel's use of Bakhtin's work.

Performance and Interaction

Performance theory takes into account the situation, delivery, speakers, audiences, other participants, genre, repertoire, gesture, modes of communication, norms of interaction, framing, and occasion. I find it useful to introduce students to the now-classical essays that developed this approach, from the early approaches of Bakhtin, Propp, and Roman Jakobson to the ethnography of communication and performance approaches of Dell Hymes, Erving Goffman, and Harvey Sacks. Roger Abrahams's conception of narrative as enactment and Richard Bauman's discussion of verbal art as a continuum of more or less staged, formalized, or ritualized performances have become foundational for folklorists studying narrative performance (whether traditional or conversational) in cultural contexts of everyday life. These investigations often focus on metadiscursive practices, whether about genre and repertoire or about ethical questions of tellability (what gets told to whom and when) and entitlement (who can tell what to whom).

This unit combines all the tools introduced in the other units to provide students with the means to understand how narratives work in cultural settings. For each of the units, I identify areas that have been undertheorized and suggest directions for further theoretical work. This unit builds on the others as we attempt to understand how narratives do the political and social work of negotiating realities. Studying narratives in their cultural and intertextual contexts provides an opportunity to understand collections, repertoires, forms, and genres as emergent, as a dimension of narrative production. Recent work in this area includes Charles L. Briggs, Amy Shuman (*Other*), and Susan Stewart.

An assignment or workshop discussion might ask the class to examine one student's account/analysis of a narrative performance.

Many students, especially graduate students, find their way to a narrative course oriented toward ethnography because they plan to collect narratives as part of their research. In many fields, narrative collection has emerged as a way to identify personal, local, cultural, or countercultural ways of thinking about experience in contrast to mainstream or dominant ideologies. But whereas students are quick to identify their interest in narrative themes, the focus on cultural production, performance, and cultural conventions of style, genre, and repertoire provides them with new analytic tools. Studying performance highlights the emergent dimension of narrative; narrative is produced by the communicative event. Reciprocally, the ethnographic narrative turn brings into focus the emergent cultural production of shared and contested ideas through narrative. Equipping students with concepts and methods reviewed in this essay can provide them with new ways of understanding narrative as negotiating instead of as transparently representing realities.

Works Cited

Abrahams, Roger. "Toward an Enactment-Centered Theory of Folklore." *Frontiers of Folklore*. Ed. William Bascom. Boulder: Westview, 1977. 79–120. Print.

Bakhtin, Mikhail M. "The Problem of Speech Genres." Trans. V. W. McGee. 1953. *"Speech Genres" and Other Late Essays*. Ed. Caryl Emerson and Michael Holquist. Austin: U of Texas P, 1986. 60–102. Print.

Bauman, Richard. *Verbal Art as Performance*. Prospect Heights: Waveland, 1977. Print.

Bauman, Richard, and Charles Briggs. "Genre, Intertextuality, and Social Power." *Journal of Linguistic Anthropology* 2 (1992): 131–73. Print.

Ben-Amos, Dan. "The Concept of Motif in Folklore." *Folklore Studies in the Twentieth Century*. Ed. V. J. Newell. Totowa: Rowman, 1980. 17–36. Print.

———. "'Context' in Context." *Theorizing Folklore: Toward New Perspectives on the Politics of Culture*. Ed. Charles L. Briggs and Amy Shuman. Spec. issue of *Western Folklore* 52.2-4 (1993): 209–26. Print.

Benjamin, Walter. *Illuminations*. Trans. Harry Zohn. Ed. Hannah Arendt. New York: Schocken, 1968. Print.

Brenneis, Donald. "Telling Troubles: Narrative, Conflict, and Experience." *Disorderly Discourse: Narrative, Conflict, and Inequality*. Ed. Charles L. Briggs. Oxford: Oxford UP, 1996. 41–52. Print.

Briggs, Charles L. "Metadiscursive Practices and Scholarly Authority in Folkloristics." *Journal of American Folklore* 106 (1993): 387–434. Print.

Deleuze, Gilles, and Félix Guattari. *A Thousand Plateaus: Capitalism and Schizophrenia*. Trans. Brian Massumi. Minneapolis: U of Minnesota P, 1987. Print.

Derrida, Jacques. *Of Grammatology*. Trans. Gayatri Chakravorty Spivak. Baltimore: Johns Hopkins UP, 1976. Print.

Foley, John Miles. *The Singer of Tales in Performance*. Bloomington: Indiana UP, 1995. Print.

Foucault, Michel. The Archaeology of Knowledge *and* The Discourse on Language. 1969. Trans. A. M. Sheridan Smith. New York: Pantheon, 1970. Print.

———. "Nietzsche, Genealogy, History." *Language, Countermemory, Practice: Selected Essays and Interviews*. Ed. Donald. F. Bouchard. Ithaca: Cornell UP, 1977. 139–64. Print.

Glassie, Henry. *The Stars of Ballymenone*. Bloomington: Indiana UP, 2006. Print.

Goffman, Erving. "The Frame Analysis of Talk." *Frame Analysis: An Essay on the Organization of Experience*. New York: Harper, 1974. 496–559. Print.

Hirschkop, Ken. *Mikhail Bakhtin: An Aesthetic for Democracy*. Oxford: Oxford UP, 1999. Print.

Hymes, Dell. *Ethnography, Linguistics, Narrative Inequality: Toward an Understanding of Voice*. London: Taylor, 1996. Print.

Jakobson, Roman. "Linguistics and Poetics." *Style in Language*. Ed. Thomas A. Sebeok. Cambridge: MIT P, 1960. 350–77. Print.

Labov, William, and Joshua Waletzky. "Narrative Analysis." *Essays on the Verbal and Visual Arts*. Ed. June Helm. Seattle: U of Washington P, 1967. 12–44. Print.

Linde, Charlotte. "Methods and Data for Studying the Life Story." *Life Stories: The Creation of Coherence*. New York: Oxford UP, 1993. 51–97. Print.

Mills, Margaret. *Rhetorics and Politics in Afghan Traditional Storytelling*. Philadelphia: U of Pennsylvania P, 1991. Print.

Norrick, Neal R. *Conversational Narrative: Storytelling in Everyday Talk*. Amsterdam: Benjamins, 2000. Print.

Ochs, Elinor, and Lisa Capps. *Living Narrative: Creating Lives in Everyday Storytelling*. Cambridge: Harvard UP, 2001. Print.

Pentikainen, Juha. *Oral Repertoire and World View: An Anthropological Study of Marina Takalo's Life History*. Helsinki: Suomalainen Tiedeakatemia, 1978. Print.

Propp, Vladimir. *The Morphology of the Folktale*. 1928. Trans. Laurence Scott. Austin: U of Texas P, 1968. Print.

Ryan, Marie-Laure. "On the Why, What, and How of Generic Taxonomy." *Poetics* 10.2-3 (1981): 517–39. Print.

Sacks, Harvey. *Lectures on Conversation*. Ed. Gail Jefferson. Oxford: Blackwell, 1992. Print.

Seitel, Peter. "Theorizing Genres—Interpreting Works." *New Literary History* 34 (2003): 275–97. Print.

Shuman, Amy. *Other People's Stories: Entitlement and the Critique of Empathy*. Urbana: U of Illinois P, 2005. Print.

———. *Storytelling Rights: The Uses of Oral and Written Traditions among Urban Adolescents*. Cambridge: Cambridge UP, 1986. Print.

Stewart, Susan. *On Longing: Narratives of the Miniature, the Gigantic, the Souvenir, the Collection*. Baltimore: Johns Hopkins UP, 1984. Print.

Toelken, Barre. "From Entertainment to Realization in Navajo Fieldwork." *The World Observed: Reflections on the Fieldwork Process*. Ed. Bruce Jackson and Edward D. Ives. Urbana: U of Illinois P, 1996. 1–17. Print.

Young, Katharine. *Taleworlds and Storyrealms: The Phenomenology of Narrative*. Dordrecht: Nijhoff, 1987. Print.

Further Reading

Bateson, Gregory. "A Theory of Play and Fantasy." 1955. *Steps to an Ecology of Mind*. New York: Ballantine, 1972. 177–93. Print.

Briggs, Charles L. "Ethnographic Approaches to Narrative." *Routledge Encyclopedia of Narrative Theory*. Ed. David Herman, Manfred Jahn, and Marie-Laure Ryan. London: Routledge, 2005. 146–51. Print.

Cashman, Ray. *Storytelling on the Northen Irish Border: Characters and Community*. Bloomington: Indiana UP, 2008. Print.

Kapchan, Deborah. "Performance." *Journal of American Folklore* 108. 430 (1995): 430, 479–508. Print.

Labov, William. "Narrative Pre-construction." *Narrative—State of the Art*. Ed. Michael Bamberg. Amsterdam: Benjamins, 2007. 47–56. Print.

Shuman, Amy. "Folklore." *Routledge Encyclopedia of Narrative Theory*. Ed. David Herman, Manfred Jahn, and Marie-Laure Ryan. London: Routledge, 2005. 177–79. Print.

Hans Kellner

Across the Curriculum:
History/Historiography

This brief essay touches on a few of the narratological issues found in historical discourse and how to address those issues in the classroom. These questions illustrate how narrative theory illuminates the work of history. Without an awareness of how narratives function, one might think that histories are found things, waiting in the past to be discovered, and that events narrate themselves. This is not the case, and narrative theory is the ideal way to demonstrate the constructed nature of historical discourse and to clarify the different principles of construction operating in historiography versus fiction, for example.

Teaching Historiography through
the Story-Discourse Distinction

At the most basic level, the ordering of happenings, history is different from fiction. As with any narrative, history is manifestly a *sjužet*, that is, a discourse composed in such a way as to contain a meaning. Although there will likely be a chronological movement, the discourse will move forward and backward in time, choosing such happenings to present as are compatible and useful in the creation of the historical argument. The fabula, or story, a bare sequence of happenings in time, must be reconstructed from the discourse; it can be presented there only in coded form. This Russian formalist notion of story, however, which is never to be found explicitly in literary or historical texts, has, in fact, a nonliterary discourse form—the chronicle (although it can always be imitated in literature). Chronicles, sequences of facts governed by the calendar, are not, for narratological reasons, to be confused with histories.

With these points in mind consider the following paragraph from Shelby Foote's celebrated history of the Civil War; here, the Confederate general James Longstreet has proposed that the planned invasion of the North, a campaign that will end at Gettysburg, be conducted using his favored defensive tactics:

> Lee heard him out with the courtesy which he was accustomed to extend to all subordinates, but which in this case was mistaken for a commitment. He intended no such thing, of course, and when he was told years later that Longstreet had said he so understood him, he refused to believe that his former lieutenant had made the statement. But Old Peter had said it, and he had indeed received that impression at the time, whereby trouble was stored up for all involved. (116)

Creating a chronicle of even this brief excerpt would involve at least four different historical moments: the meeting of Robert E. Lee and Longstreet, a subsequent time when Longstreet revealed his assumptions, and a still later time when Lee was informed of Longstreet's stated assumptions. If we take the word "troubles" to refer to the loss at Gettysburg, that fourth moment also plays a role in this passage. These departures from chronicle order are a consequence of Foote's interest in explaining the events. To put this point another way, the closer a history is to chronicle, the less it will claim to explain the happenings that it presents. Explanation entails departure from chronicle form.

The story can and will be reconstituted by the competent reader of both fiction and history. In history, however, this story is presumed to be a subset of a vast thing that cannot be fully reconstituted. It is called the past. Where are we to find it? How can we reconstruct it, except as a gathering of facts, always radically incomplete and never really historical or even followable? The answer to these questions is found in the discourse of history, the assembled texts that make up our only entry into the past (unless we experience a personal vision) (Ankersmit). The past was, however, invoked in the first place to validate these texts. Constructing a chronology from a passage of history is an important exercise that shows how far narrative must depart from the simple recounting of events and how much of the past and future any event contains. To refer to a war or a reign or an administration entails many unmentioned happenings—rising tensions, declaration of hostilities, royal succession, election campaigns, and much else.

To help these issues come alive in the classroom, students should be asked to consider the similarities and differences between the concept of *story* proposed by narrative theorists and the *past* as it is posited by history. Is the past assumed to consist of a constellation of true stories? Does the accumulated meaning of these stories help explain the past? Is there, ultimately, one story or many? Can stories be merged, or not? Examining a text like Foote's encourages students to extrapolate from a specific historical account to the broader issues raised by how any such account is grounded in narrative as a form of representation and way of knowing.

Teaching Narrative Events

If we stipulate that the past is a vast fabula and that any historical narrative will have its own form, beginning and end, and plot, then it will be impossible to synthesize historical accounts into a unified whole. Jules Michelet's French Revolution is not the same as Simon Schama's. These two accounts cannot be combined in a larger, more inclusive, narrative because, although they may seem to mention the same events, they will construct these events for different narrative purposes.

The passage from Foote apparently concerns a simple event, a meeting and a misunderstanding. If *fabula* "designates the [reconstructed] narrated events," how do we know an event when we see one? (Rimmon-Kenan 3). From the standpoint of European history, the French Revolution was an event; from the standpoint of the French Revolution, the Reign of Terror was an event; from the standpoint of the Terror, the execution of Danton was an event; from the standpoint of Danton, the final days contained a multitude of events. Gérard Genette shrewdly identifies the narrative of events with "an illusion of mimesis, depending like every illusion on a highly variable relationship between the sender and the receiver" (Genette 165). Students grasp the innumerable ways of dividing stretches of time into events when they are asked, Is this class an event? How many events have taken place since the beginning of this class? Are the professor's comments events, and, if so, one or many? Are the students' thoughts events (as they would be in Henry James, for instance)? Are there limits to what may be an event? Who sets these limits?

In what sense was the happening recounted above by Foote an event? Foote might have written, "Longstreet mistakenly believed that Lee agreed with his defensive strategy." Here, no event is implied, only a belief. The event structure is missing. Practically speaking, an event requires a beginning, middle, and end (that is, some duration in time, however large or small) and a name or description. If we accept that this is as close as we can come to defining an event, we must conclude that events are at the services of narrative purposes, rather than the reverse. Although our sample passage bears no formal name, as a battle or a conference might, we understand it as signifying "crucial misunderstanding" or something like that. As presented, this "crucial misunderstanding" event cannot be taken as a single unit found in the records of the war. Simple as it seems, it is intricately constructed. And each of the events implicit in Foote's account—the Battle of Gettysburg, for example—can in turn be subdivided into innumerable events.

Events are human inventions for a purpose, either as part of an argument (rhetoric) or as part of a sequence (narrative). There is no unprocessed world of events (or happenings); historical events are created from the flow of the past, which I have called the advent (Kellner). The selection of certain things as parts of larger things called events is conventional; we are culturally predisposed to consider an attack like 9/11 as part of an event that might be called a war (or something else, but it *will* have a name). Students should be asked whether they feel themselves to be living a story or whether their lives can be cast in the form of a narrative only in hindsight. If a story in this sense involves knowing what comes next, what are the limits of such knowledge? College courses may lead to graduation, which may lead to employment, to family life, to financial and social success. Is an awareness of this conventional or innate? Do literary or historical characters have a sense that they are part of a story with preestablished parameters, or do they perceive the future as open? Lee was part of a war, which would certainly be won or lost. Does this mean he was aware of living a story? These questions are contested; students should use narrative notions of event to frame their responses. If events are made, not found, can we live a story?

Teaching the Construction of Character

Our sample passage of historical narrative illustrates how in historical accounts characters like Lee and Longstreet must be linked in specific ways with real persons. In Foote's narrative, the seme (basic unit of meaning) of good manners ("the courtesy which he was accustomed to extend to all subordinates") attaches itself to the proper name Lee. His interlocutor, Longstreet, then assumes the status of an embedded reader who fails to interpret properly, possibly for reasons that are clarified by other semes belonging to Longstreet, such as his military preferences and his sense of what has been successful for him. Such semes, as bits of character information, whether derived from words spoken, actions taken, or commentary from other characters, may have been established earlier in the story. For example, the seme of command will have attached itself to Lee throughout the volumes of the work.

On the basis of these ideas, students can be asked to compare a historical character with a literary character in a short story. What are the similarities in how they are presented? If the literary character has more direct discourse (i.e., utterances by him or her reported directly by a narrator), how does this affect the reader's sense of the character? Does the relative absence of direct discourse make historical characters less vivid? Along the same lines, students can be asked to rewrite a historical passage using direct discourse.

Teaching Narrative Anachronisms

Historical anachronisms, such as using Scott Joplin's music to accompany the Depression-era movie *The Sting*, are usually condemned; narrative anachronisms, however, are vital to the construction of events and are a key aspect of our passage. Lee's courtesy, although shown at the point of the meeting with Longstreet, is established by implied analepsis, a flashback revealing Lee's behavior over time before the meeting; all who knew Lee, including, now, the implied reader of the history, had become "accustomed" to his courtesy. If Lee had been brusque or rude, it would have taken on its meaning as a departure from his earlier behavior; some meaning would likely emerge, such as stress, irritation, or illness. (It would become a small event.) Next in the text, Lee is whisked proleptically into the future, where he looks back, an analepsis within the prolepsis (which has reset the narrative clock to create a new, temporary present), and refuses to believe that Longstreet could have mistaken him (another character seme for Lee—loyalty, unwillingness to think ill of someone). In the last sentence, we are back in the meeting, but there the future is being envisioned by someone who is different from "all involved" in the meeting itself.

Teaching Focalization

The semes that establish the character of Robert E. Lee clearly express someone's view of him: "Lee heard him out with the courtesy which he was accustomed to extend to all subordinates, but which in this case was mistaken for a commitment." The courtesy, Foote implies, would have been registered by anyone present at the meeting; the misunderstanding, however, is understood only by someone aware of later developments (surviving officers, for example, or the historian). Two different focalizers are at work in this sentence (Foote and Longstreet), and the focalizer who has the benefit of hindsight comments on the focalizer who mistakes courtesy for commitment. The whole miniscene is finally focalized by the use of the phrase "Old Peter" instead of General Longstreet's proper name. The affectionate "Old Peter" assumes the perspective of the Confederate officer corps, more generally of the South, and more particularly of the narrator.

As these remarks suggest, students may rewrite a brief passage in several ways to appreciate how compactly prose narrative does its work. One possibility is to wrest control from the narrator, inventing words for the characters. Alternatively, the scene may be refocalized from the perspective of different figures. A narrator may be supposed more hostile to Lee or more friendly. Students can thus be asked, What statements might have presented semes that change the image of Lee's character?

The Transmission of Historical Narrative

It might appear that the familiar communicative chain—from real author to implied author to narrator to narratee to implied reader to real reader—does not apply to history. Indeed, Émile Benveniste wrote of historical discourse: "No one speaks here; the events seem to narrate themselves" (208). As we have seen, however, in the passage from Foote, the narrator is busily apparent throughout. He establishes the character semes of command, courtesy, and loyalty in Lee and focalizes Longstreet from within the Confederate world as "Old Peter." He sets in motion the play of anachronisms that allow Lee to look forward in the form of intention ("He intended no such thing") and backward in the form of disbelief ("when he was told . . . he refused to believe"). The adverbial "of course" is perhaps the point at which the narrator most explicitly reveals his presence, but it also reminds the implied reader that this is a special form of narrator, a historical narrator, one who possesses a knowledge of past and future that is of a different sort from the narrator in fiction. The knowledge of the historical narrator is by no means greater than that of the fictional narrator—on the contrary, it is far more constrained by documentation. The outcome of events ("trouble for all involved" at Gettysburg) is also known. Of course! The fictional narrator may (or may not) know intentions and outcomes, but for different reasons. This knowledge of Lee's intentions only reinforces the limits of the historical narrator, because the troubles in store are not of his invention.

An explicit narrator and narratee are rare in histories, with two exceptions. Romantic historians like Thomas Carlyle and Jules Michelet occasionally address a reader, who is thus embedded and no longer implied. Thus, Michelet on the French Old Regime:

> A worn-out society, in this crisis of resurrection, affords us a spectacle of the origins of things. The civilians were musing over the cradle of infant nations. Wherefore muse? You have it before you. (433)

This sort of personal appearance is no longer usual, at least in academic history. It seems to signify Michelet's sense that he is a homodiegetic narrator, actually part of events in the past as he relives them. "The Revolution lives in ourselves,—in our souls; it has no outward monument" (3). The second exception to the convention that the historical narrator be absent is the marginal text of introductions, prefaces, acknowledgments, and so forth. Or one may express a personal interest, even passion, for the topic of the history, although usually in less mystical terms than Michelet's. Fernand Braudel, for example, begins his magnum opus as follows (in the preface to the first edition):

> I have loved the Mediterranean with passion, no doubt because I am a northerner like so many others in whose footsteps I have followed. I have joyfully dedicated long years of study to it—much more than all my youth. (3)

In open societies, the implied author and the real author of historical narratives are presumed to be the same; the real author is responsible for the words of the text. I have spoken with Polish historians whose work under Communism had to go through a government censor and who did not express their personal views. The real reader may often differ from the implied reader. The implied reader of Foote's text, for example, is clearly not without sympathy for the Confederate cause.

In this context, students can be asked, what does the implied reader have to know or believe about the past, about the nation or group, or about the values held by the protagonists? And, can you describe this reader? Students must be aware that the implied reader is a creation of the narrative and that their own response to the historical work will be in tension with this implied reader. Without some imaginative ability to identify with that role or persona, the real reader will miss the point of the work and simply be an incompetent reader. Yet each real reader will also retain his or her own knowledge of the world and ethical compass. Students should discuss how they become two persons when they read history: on the one hand, one who can follow any story and understand the motivations of a historical actor and the intentions of the implied author, however distant or ethically repugnant to the present point of view; on the other, a historical individual with his or her own viewpoint on past events.

Works Cited

Ankersmit, Frank R. *Sublime Historical Experience*. Stanford: Stanford UP, 2005. Print.

Benveniste, Émile. "The Correlations of Tense in the French Verb." *Problems in General Linguistics*. Trans. Elizabeth Meek. Coral Gables: U of Miami P, 1971. 205–15. Print.

Braudel, Fernand. *The Mediterranean and the Mediterranean World in the Age of Philip II*. Trans. Siân Reynolds. New York: Harper, 1972. Print.

Foote, Shelby. *The Civil War: A Narrative—Gettysburg to Vicksburg*. New York: Random, 1963. Print.

Genette, Gérard. *Narrative Discourse: An Essay in Method*. Trans. Jane E. Lewin. Ithaca: Cornell UP, 1980. Print.

Kellner, Hans. "Naïve and Sentimental Realism: From Advent to Event." *Storia della storiografia* 22 (1992): 117–23. Print.

Michelet, Jules. *History of the French Revolution*. Trans. Charles Cocks. Ed. Gordon Wright. Chicago: U of Chicago P, 1967. Print.

Rimmon-Kenan, Shlomith. *Narrative Fiction: Contemporary Poetics*. London: Methuen, 1983. Print.

Further Reading

Ankersmit, Frank. "Historiography." *Routledge Encyclopedia of Narrative Theory*. Ed. David Herman, Manfred Jahn, and Marie-Laure Ryan. London: Routledge, 2005. 217–21. Print.

Ankersmit, Frank, and Hans Kellner, eds. *A New Philosophy of History.* Chicago: U of Chicago P, 1995. Print.

Carr, David. *Time, Narrative, and History.* Bloomington: Indiana UP, 1991. Print.

Danto, Arthur, Frank Ankersmit, and Lydia Goehr. *Narration and Knowledge.* 3rd ed. New York: Columbia UP, 2007. Print.

Kellner, Hans. *Language and Historical Representation: Getting the Story Crooked.* Madison: U of Wisconsin P, 1989. Print.

White, Hayden. *The Content of the Form: Narrative and Historical Representation.* Baltimore: Johns Hopkins UP, 1987. Print.

Emma Kafalenos

Across the Curriculum: Image-Text Studies

At colleges and universities that encourage and facilitate interdisciplinary exploration, literature courses often attract fine arts majors who are training to become professional artists and art history majors who are planning careers as curators or scholars. Similarly, art history courses and studio courses in drawing, painting, and sculpture often include students majoring in literature. The result is that students with broad experience viewing, and even making, visual artworks and students who are sophisticated readers of novels and stories sit next to one another in classrooms in literature and art history and in studios where the making of art is taught. My experience is in teaching comparative literature and comparative arts courses that attract majors in the fine arts and in art history as well as in literature. Early on I developed strategies to enable talented artists to express visually their understanding of the narrative techniques exhibited in the novels and stories I was teaching. When I discovered that the same strategies often helped literature majors become more aware of narrative techniques, I began to incorporate these strategies, along with comparisons to the visual arts, in all my literature courses. As we now know from pedagogical studies of how young children learn, no one approach is best for every child. Teachers everywhere are encouraged to offer multiple experiences—even multiple sensory data—to teach children to read. In my classes, comparisons to the visual arts and strategies that encourage visualizing narrative shapes seem to help many of my students, whatever their major, to grasp narrative structures and their effects. In addition, the artists and the art history majors often tell me that the understanding of narrative shapes that they acquire enriches their response to visual artworks. The artists even sometimes report that they are exploring in their own work ideas about narrative structures and their effects.

All the assignments I describe below I have used in one course or another, but not all in any one course. Any one or two of these assignments can be adopted and tried in a course or a segment of a course where they seem pertinent. Here I present the assignments in four categories, according to the aspect of narrative theory they are designed to illuminate, and for each assignment I offer a few suggestions for discussing students' responses in the classroom. For grading, if I give grades at all for assignments of this sort, I avoid the precision of As and Bs and use instead S, S+, and occasionally S++, making sure that the most interesting responses are recognized as such and shared with everyone in the class.

Selection and Distribution of Events

The most obvious difference between a narrative and a discrete visual image is that the image represents one selected situation or event, with its elements distributed spatially, and the narrative represents a number of selected events and situations that are distributed sequentially.[1] To explore that difference I offer two complementary assignments, scheduled on different days. In the first I ask students to narrativize a represented isolated moment and in the second to illustrate a narrative.

> Assignment 1: Write a short account of what is happening, has happened, and is about to happen in an assigned visual representation.[2]

> Assignment 2: Draw or describe the scene you think best represents an assigned story.

For the first assignment I choose a representational painting that includes one or more people or anthropomorphic beings doing something but that is not a representation of a known story—to eliminate the possibility that there is a single "right answer." One can give students postcard reproductions from the local museum or specify an image available online.

Either way, it is important to arrange access that allows the student to look at the image repeatedly before responding.

For both these assignments each member of the class should read everyone else's response. The assignment to narrativize an image can be expected to generate a variety of different responses; a depiction of an isolated moment leaves more decisions to the perceiver about what is happening (and why and where it will lead) than a narrative does. In addition to pointing out to students that the interpretive freedom the visual representation allows can be aesthetically pleasing, one may want to ask students to analyze the differences between the two modes of communication by considering which purposes each most successfully fulfills.

After students draw or describe a scene in an assigned story, the instructor can ask them to explain why they each chose the scene they did. The class might then revisit the responses to the first assignment, this time considering the relation between the depicted scene and the narratives students wrote. The two assignments provide, for each student in the class, two examples of an image representing one moment and a related narrative representing a sequence of moments. Discussion can fall into two broad categories: the details of the representation, a topic to which I will return, and the temporal relations between the depicted scene and the events of the narrative it illustrates or has inspired. To explore the latter I offer the following assignment:

> Depict the chronological sequence of events reported in the narrative
> as a horizontal line, conceived as moving from left to right, and label
> a few points along the line to indicate where major events occur. Then
> draw a vertical line that crosses the horizontal line to indicate the tem-
> poral position of the depicted scene.

Famously, the eighteenth-century playwright Gotthold Ephraim Lessing argued that "painting, [because it] can use but a single moment of an action . . . must therefore choose the most pregnant one, the one most suggestive of what has gone before and what is to follow" (92). But in the student examples one may find scenes that depict the final event (rather than the "pregnant" moment that immediately precedes it), the initial event, or some event or situation somewhere between. Discussion can focus on the effects of the selection of which scene to depict.

Correlations that students may draw between the choice of scene and the attitudes conveyed about the events being illustrated will prepare students to consider the effects of narrative shapes explored in the following assignment:

> Depict the chronological sequence of events reported in an assigned narrative (or each of several assigned narratives) as a horizontal line, conceived as moving from left to right, and label a few points along the line to indicate where major events occur. Then draw a vertical line that crosses the first line to indicate the temporal position of the initial event that is given scenic treatment (as if in a play, rather than merely summarized).

Narrative shapes can vary according to the temporal sequence in which events are distributed in the telling. In some narratives the telling is chronological; the first event told is also the earliest event that will be reported. More often, however, the first event that is recounted will coincide with the beginning of a central action; as one reads on, one learns about earlier events as well as subsequent events. In some narratives (the detective story, for instance), the first event that is told is near the end of the chronological sequence of reported events. (For more on temporal relations in the detective story, see McHale's essay in this volume.) Thus, like the visually depicted scene in relation to the narratives it inspires or illustrates, the first event given scenic treatment in a narrative can represent a variety of temporal positions in relation to the chronological account to which it is linked.

Discussion can center first on the effect of the selection of the initial event scenically treated in a narrative. In narratives, Meir Sternberg points out, the selection of the initial event scenically treated governs the questions a reader will ask. If the initial event is at or near the beginning of a series of events, readers read on, motivated by suspense, to discover what will happen. If the initial event is near the end of a series of events that has led up to it (as, for instance, in a detective story), readers read on, motivated by curiosity, to find out how the present situation has come about.[3] One can then consider the effect of the single scene selected by the artist for visual representation. In what ways does the selection of the scene influence viewers' responses?

In addition to the selection of the scene to be portrayed visually and the selection and distribution of events in a narrative, other aspects of selection and distribution can be considered. In "Introduction to the Structural Analysis of Narratives," Roland Barthes distinguishes between two types of elements in narratives, both of which can be found in visual representations: functions, typically events and their consequences (a number of which are distributed in a meaningful chronological sequence in a narrative and one of which is selected for representation in a visual artwork), and indices, or indexical units, which serve to identify a time or place or person or to convey an atmosphere or provide information about a character's appearance or psychological state.

We have looked at the effect of the selection and distribution of functions. One can explore the effect of indices in visual representations by asking students which visual details they took into consideration (in the first assignment described in this essay) in writing stories inspired by a visual artwork. Typically both viewers and readers vary more in the indexical details they pay attention to and in their interpretation of those details than they do in the functions they identify. To investigate the extent to which readers vary in interpreting indices, one can use an assignment based on an experiment conducted by Marie-Laure Ryan (223–31), who asked students to map Gabriel García Márquez's *Chronicle of a Death Foretold*:

> Assignment: Draw a map of the places where events occur in the assigned story.

If one wants to encourage students to investigate how scenes are distributed in a narrative (or in a sequence of visual representations), one can provide Scott McCloud's illustrated list of types of panel-to-panel transitions in comics (70–72) and a few pages from a novel or story or newspaper article.

> Assignment: Using the six types of transitions Scott McCloud identifies and names (moment to moment, action to action, subject to subject, scene to scene, aspect to aspect, and non sequitur), categorize the types of transitions between paragraphs in the assigned pages.

This assignment will provide different results depending on the type of narrative and the segment of the particular narrative selected for analysis. In conjunction, these last two assignments draw attention to two broad types of transitions in narratives: within the narrative world (from place to place) and in the telling (from topic to topic).

Perspective

Narrative theory draws attention to the effects of focalization, the practice of limiting the information provided about the narrative world to what a specific character perceives and thinks about in response to those perceptions. The focalizer can be a character narrator or, as in Henry James's late novels, a character whose perceptions and thoughts are reported by an unidentified narrator. Metaphorically, the focalizing character serves as a lens through which readers see the events and the other characters in the narrative world. Drawing a focalization diagram guides students to consider the source of the information the narrative is reporting.

> Assignment (focalization diagram): Following the pattern "*Perceiver* looks through *lens* at *object*," sketch a diagram that identifies the lens in an assigned story.

In a novel, the perceiver is the reader and the object is the narrative world. The lens may be single or compound or may shift from one section to another. Often the lens is itself more interesting than the narrative world that we see through it. As an anthropomorphic being, the focalizing character is necessarily selective in what he or she perceives (everyone's perceptions are spatially and temporally restricted); in addition, what the character perceives is colored by her or his interests, mental state, quality of mind, and so forth. The correlation to visual representations is not limited to perspective but also includes such stylistic variables as how identifiable the represented objects are, use of color, quality of line, and so on.

In visual representations as well as in narratives, the lens through which perceivers see the world may be doubled or extended. In a narrative, a focalizer may describe a painting, which gives readers the focalizer's perception of the painter's perception of whatever the painting depicts. This double lens is comparable to the painting within a painting that gives viewers one painter's perception of another painter's perception of whatever the contained painting depicts. Similarly, just as a focalizing character's perceptions are extended by information she or he hears reported by another character, what a painter can record seeing from a given vantage can be extended by a properly placed mirror. In both visual images and narratives, strategies such as these provide ways to exceed the spatial and temporal limitations of what a given individual can perceive.

Shape

A contained element (painting, mirror, story) is not the only similar shape that visual artworks and narratives can share. Both may focus on a single character (a portrait) or the interactions of many characters (a history painting, for instance). Both can portray the creative process and its result (a painter and her or his painting, a writer and the text she or he writes). There can also be similarities in how the material is portrayed. A collage in visual art resembles in its shape a collection of pieces of previously published texts or of several characters' stories that they each tell in their own words (Chaucer's *Canterbury Tales*). A discussion of similar shapes in the two modes could include, on the one hand, a painting or lithograph that reproduces in the artist's hand the kinds of materials typically found in a collage and, on the other hand, a narrative containing stories from various sources retold by one narrating character (Scheherazade in the *Arabian Nights*). To explore these and similar relations I suggest this assignment:

> What is the shape of an assigned narrative (or of an assigned visual artwork)? Choose—or imagine and describe—a visual artwork (or a narrative) that seems to you similar in shape.

If one wishes to extend the category of similar shapes to include multiple treatments of similar or related materials, then one can consider series paintings—Claude Monet's many paintings of water lilies, for instance, or Francis Bacon's series of portraits of popes—as parallel forms to sequels in novels and films.

Paratext

Gérard Genette defines the *paratext* of a literary work as everything other than the primary text (novel, stories, etc.) for which "the author or one of his associates accepts responsibility" (9): the information on the title page (the title itself, the author's name, the publisher, any indication of genre), the preface, typographic choices, notes, illustrations, the author's letters and diary entries, interviews with the author—but not the information that an author cannot control, such as the reviews that other people write or the word-of-mouth recommendations that other people pass on to their friends and colleagues. Genette's focus is on literature. He considers the variety of paratextual information that readers will have acquired by the time they begin to read the text itself and the effects of that information. For visual artworks an analysis of paratexts and their effects is equally pertinent. These two assignments will help students understand the effects of paratext:

> (1) List the paratextual elements that came to your attention before and during your reading of an assigned story and consider their influence on your process of reading and on your thoughts about the story now that you have read it. (2) List the paratextual elements that came to your attention before and during viewing an assigned visual art-

work and consider their influence on your viewing process and on your thoughts about the artwork as you remember it.

Despite the strong similarity between the types of paratextual elements through which perceivers approach narratives and visual artworks, discussion will reveal differences in the effects, probably most clearly in situations where visual representation and language are juxtaposed. One can consider the effect of illustrations in novels in relation to the effect of titles of visual representations. Certainly illustrations can influence readers' mental portraits of characters. Words attached to an image, however, as Barthes perceived, "anchor" the meaning of the image: even literally identifying it as well as guiding responses to whatever is depicted ("Rhetoric" 39–40). As for titles of paintings, A. Kibédi Varga suggests that some painters may choose generic titles like "landscape" or "composition" to avoid restricting what a viewer, looking at their work, is able to perceive (43).

But there are also a number of nearly parallel paratextual elements that affect perceivers' responses in similar ways. Compare the book cover with the artwork frame, the academic press with the museum, the commercial publisher with the gallery, self-publication with the artist's studio. Students will discern other parallels from their own experience. By becoming increasingly aware of these and other similarities and differences between narratives and discrete visual images, generalists may become better readers and better viewers, while specialists, whether in literature or the visual arts, may hone their competence in their primary discipline.

Notes

1. In "Pictorial Narrativity," Wendy Steiner analyzes pre-Renaissance multi-episodic paintings that are narratives because they portray, on one canvas, several situations or events and indicate the sequence in which they occur. In contrast, the visual artwork I am primarily concerned with in this essay is the discrete image that represents a single moment cut from the continuum and thus is not a narrative.

2. This assignment asks students to engage in ekphrasis, the rerepresentation in words of a prior visual representation.

3. The third situation Sternberg discerns occurs in a seemingly chronological telling when a significant event is omitted without any indication that an omission has occurred. When the event is later revealed, the effect produced is surprise.

Works Cited

Barthes, Roland. *Image-Music-Text*. Trans. Stephen Heath. New York: Hill, 1977. Print.

———. "Introduction to the Structural Analysis of Narratives." 1966. Barthes, *Image-Music-Text* 79–124.

———. "Rhetoric of the Image." 1964. Barthes, *Image-Music-Text* 32–51.

Genette, Gérard. *Paratexts: Thresholds of Interpretation.* Trans. Jane E. Lewin. Cambridge: Cambridge UP, 1997. Print.

Kibédi Varga, A. "Criteria for Describing Word-and-Image Relations." *Poetics Today* 10.1 (1989): 31–53. Print.

Lessing, Gotthold Ephraim. *Laocoon: An Essay upon the Limits of Painting and Poetry.* Trans. Ellen Frothingham. New York: Noonday, 1957. Print.

McCloud, Scott. *Understanding Comics: The Invisible Art.* New York: Harper, 1993. Print.

Ryan, Marie-Laure. "Cognitive Maps and the Construction of Narrative Space." *Narrative Theory and the Cognitive Sciences.* Ed. David Herman. Stanford: Center for the Study of Lang. and Information, 2003. 214–42. Print.

Steiner, Wendy. "Pictorial Narrativity." *Narrative across Media: The Languages of Storytelling.* Ed. Marie-Laure Ryan. Lincoln: U of Nebraska P, 2004. 145–77. Print.

Sternberg, Meir. "How Narrativity Makes a Difference." *Narrative* 9.2 (2001): 115–22. Print.

Further Reading

Bal, Mieke. *Reading "Rembrandt": Beyond the Word-Image Opposition. The Northrop Frye Lectures in Literary Theory.* Cambridge: Cambridge UP, 1991. Print.

Spolsky, Ellen. *Word vs. Image: Cognitive Hunger in Shakespeare's England.* New York: Palgrave, 2007. Print.

Yacobi, Tamar. "Interart Narrative: (Un)Reliability and Ekphrasis." *Poetics Today* 21.4 (2000): 711–49. Print.

———. "Pictorial Models and Narrative Ekphrasis." *Poetics Today* 16.4 (1995): 599–649. Print.

Part II

Elements

Brian Richardson

Story, Plot, and Narrative Progression

I regularly include discussions of narrative theory in undergraduate classes on the modern novel, modernism, and twentieth-century literature, as well as in more theory-oriented classes. In this essay, I focus on how I teach plot and related concepts such as fabula, *sjužet*, and narrative progression, moving among the theoretical concepts, interpretations that employ those concepts, and practical pedagogy.

The Fabula-*Sjužet* Distinction

I establish the foundation for our discussions of plot by explaining the crucial distinction introduced by the Russian formalists in the early part of the twentieth century: that between fabula and *sjužet*, or what I term "story" and "text," that is, the difference between the full story that we are able to reconstitute in its chronological sequence and the way that the events are actually set out page by page.[1] I give the students a simple sequence like,

(1) John died today. (2) He fell sick a year ago. (3) In his youth, he seemed to have much promise. (4) He was often sick as a child. (5) He was born in 1961.

The text presents the events in a reverse chronological order; we rearrange them to get the sequence of the story, that is, starting with number 5, then moving to 4, 3, 2, and 1. I mention that many kinds of works like folktales, myths, histories, traditional plays, expressionist fiction, and thrillers tend to be told in a linear fashion where story and text follow the same general trajectory. I note that even in these cases there are always differences between the two due to the "duration" or pacing of the events in the text; I encourage the students to identify which ones are compressed, stretched out, or left largely untold. Such differences are particularly noticeable in works that contain a large temporal ellipsis, such as Father Time's announcement that ". . . I slide / O'er sixteen years and leave the growth untried / Of that wide gap . . ." in *The Winter's Tale* (4.1.5–7) or the gap of several years that signals closure at the end of a novel like Gustave Flaubert's *A Sentimental Education*. It is important to mention that nonlinear works, in which the sequence of the story and the text don't match up, are common from Homer's epics to daily accounts of professional competitions described in the sports section of the newspaper, where the ending is usually presented first, especially if it is a dramatic one. (For more on teaching time in narrative, see David Herman's essay in this volume.)

Students are often intrigued to learn that some works of experimental fiction, following the lead of Vladimir Nabokov's *Pale Fire*, present an ostensibly nonnarrative text from which a compelling story can be derived; Michèle Roberts's "Une glossaire / A Glossary" is an eminently teachable example of this form, which also raises interesting questions about whether and how stories might be gendered (see Page). I historicize the practice by noting that some extensive divergences between story and text sequences can be found in Romantic narratives (Wordsworth's *The Prelude*) and modernist and postmodern fiction and film (Proust, Faulkner, Kurosawa). Passages of counterchronological narrative (Amis's *Time's Arrow*) or films that use reverse linear sequencing (Pinter's *Betrayal*, Nolan's *Memento*) are great to display at this point since they help show how "unnatural" or defamiliarizing this kind of narrative sequencing is as well as how much causal connection is already present in most sequences of events.

Plot: Standard Patterns and Their Alternatives

At this point we are ready to move on to plot proper. I suggest some basic questions for students to ask of each text: What are the primary and secondary stories (or main plots and subplots) being told? How many are there? How are they connected to one another? In what sequence are they arranged? Do the subplots mirror the main plot? Are there miniature sequences that mirror the whole (*mise en abyme*)? Are there seemingly unnecessary parts or sequences that could be deleted or that don't fit the overall pattern of the text? Is the presentation of the events linear or does it move back and forth in time? Are there any temporal oddities in the text?

We go on to some working definitions: Aristotle considered plot (*mythos*), by which he meant the imitation of a coherent set of events in the service of an overall effect, to be the most important aspect of a narrative, more important than character, language, or spectacle, and many subsequent critics have tended to agree with this assessment. In its most general sense, *plot* refers to the way a group of related events are organized together. (Handouts of material from Prince's *Dictionary*, Martin's survey, or recent introductory volumes by Keen or Abbott provide sound definitions, well-chosen examples, and clarifications of differing usages.) According to many accounts, the organization of events generally follows a basic pattern of a state of harmony, a disruption of that harmony, and an attempt to restore the original harmony. Plot emanates from what D. A. Miller calls a condition of "disequilibrium, suspense, and general insufficiency from which a given narrative appears to rise" (ix) or, more simply, a problem appears at the beginning of the story: Odysseus wants to return to his home; a plague is ravaging Thebes; a ghost tells Hamlet to avenge his father's murder. Even before the characters are introduced or the setting is established, the general trajectory of the events of *Pride and Prejudice* is suggested by its first sentence: "It is a truth universally acknowledged that a single man in possession of a good fortune must be in want of a wife" (1).

The initial disequilibrium leads to a desire to rectify the situation; for most of the narrative the protagonist seeks to alter the problematic situation, an effort that typically produce further complications in that situation; the end is signaled when the problem is resolved (or, in some cases, shown to be unresolvable). This basic pattern is found in many works, as popular formulas attest: the classic synopsis for a Broadway musical comedy is often described as "boy meets girl, boy loses girl, boy gets girl." Peter Brooks states that plot is "the dynamic shaping force of the narrative discourse" and "the organizing line and intention of narrative" (13, 37); he suggests that its basic trajectory is a stimulation out of quiescence that seeks to regain equilibrium through a discharge of its accumulated energy. I ask the students whether they can think of any exceptions to this general position as a way of preparing them for some of the texts to come.

Brooks also draws on the work of Vladimir Propp, who devised a "morphology" of the Russian folktale by analyzing basic structural components or "functions" common to seemingly disparate tales. Students love speculation about the putatively limited number of possible plot types. I mention the widespread claim that there are only two basic plots: a stranger comes to town, and someone goes on a voyage. We then discuss other such claims, including ones widely available on the Web concerning the so-called seven basic plots (according to Christopher Booker's version: overcoming the monster, quest, journey and return, rags to riches, comedy, tragedy, and rebirth). Then we are ready to discuss Propp's particular morphology. For Propp, "The king sends Ivan after some marvel; Ivan departs" and "The stepmother sends her daughter for fire; she departs" have the same structure ("Fairy-Tale Transformations" 74): the dispatch and the departure on a quest are constants. In later stages of the quest, obstacles impede the protagonist's progress; these too are, in terms of structure, the same, though the form they take may be very different. This general model of plot was expanded by a number of French structuralists in the sixties and seventies to try to embrace all narratives; it is now widely used in the cognitive sciences. Students find it especially useful and even illuminating to analyze short stories, Hollywood films, television shows, genre fiction, and the homiletic narratives told by their parents. (For more on teaching functional approaches to plot, see Brian McHale's essay in this volume.)

Of course, many stories don't quite resemble the tightly connected Oedipus Rex model favored by theorists like Aristotle, E. M. Forster, R. S. Crane, and Brooks. "Marcel becomes dissatisfied with his life; he then decides to become a writer" is not a very useful description of the plot of *In Search of Lost Time*. Aristotle was fully aware of alternative methods of story construction and condemned the episodic plot, "in which the episodes or acts succeed one another without probable or necessary sequence" (54). Many modernist novels, as will be discussed further below, eschew conventional notions of plot and scorn suspense; they have an attenuated trajectory of events that frequently dispenses with causal connection in favor of connections provided by symbolic descriptions, thematic associations, or a parallelism of situations and events. A plot summary of *Ulysses* or *To the Lighthouse* will not even begin to capture the extraordinary richness of the actions, events, and perceptions in each work.

I take care to point out that there are also many works that draw on non-plot-based orders to arrange events. Novelists may use many different kinds of scaffolding that complements or even supersedes and replaces a conventional, plot-driven arrangement (see Richardson, "Beyond"). There is a wide range of alternative ordering principles: a work may follow the order of an antecedent text but eschew causality as the main link among its episodes (Joyce's *Ulysses*); it may be ordered in the form of a musical composition (the sirens episode of *Ulysses*); it may present events to illustrate a thesis (Johnson's *Rasselas*), or be designed to produce a geometric shape or numerical pattern such as a circle (Wittig's *Les guérillères*), a triad (Dante's *Commedia*), or an hourglass (James's *The Ambassadors*). The extent to which narratives organized by shape are also organized by their arrangement of events can be a matter for productive classroom discussion—do the principles of organization peacefully coexist or compete? Should one take precedence over the other? More concretely, is plot sacrificed to geometry or vice versa, and, if either sacrifice takes place, what is gained and what is lost in this exchange?

More radical are the pictures that precede and seem to generate the subsequent events in a work like Johann Wolfgang von Goethe's "Novelle" or the alphabetical ordering of texts like Walter Abish's *Alphabetical Africa*. Then there are the words or concepts that generate the events of many *nouveaux romans*: thus, the title page of Jean Ricardou's *La prise de Constantinople* displays the name of the publisher, Les Éditions de Minuit. These words in turn produce the characters, Ed and Edith, and the spacial setting—the hill of Sion. The temporal setting of the first episode, naturally, is during the night. And about that most famous of antinovels, Alain Robbe-Grillet's *La jalousie*, the author indicated that his method of composition was first to write a single scene and then to construct a series of variations on that scene, variations that taken together simultaneously suggest and rule out a single, consistent story line. Hypertexts provide still other possibilities. Useful for extra credit is to invite students to trace out the pattern of one of these alternative orderings in an unconventional text.

Traditional Plot, Progression, Antiplot, and Masterplot

The instructor may choose to establish a general pedagogical arc by moving from the more straightforward cases to the seemingly plotless works of modernism, going on to contradictory narrative possibilities, and concluding with the dynamics of serial narrative. In what follows, I offer descriptions of four such pedagogical applications of the theory of plot and narrative progression to two stories by James Joyce, one by Alain Robbe-Grillet, and the final episodes of a popular television series, *Sex and the City*.

Joyce's "Araby" is a fairly straightforward narrative, indeed, a naturalistic version of a traditional quest narrative, which begins with a basic disharmony, the youthful narrator's unexpressed infatuation with his neighbor, identified only as Mangan's sister. When the two finally speak, the narrator promises to bring her back a present from the bazaar, Araby. Here we have a decision to alleviate the disequilibrium, a plan to enable its achievement, and the initial act to set the plan in motion.

The "test" ensues. Unfortunately, the boy is delayed, and by the time he gets to Araby the hour is late, he has too little money, and the saleswoman is more interested in flirting with two Englishmen than in serving him. He realizes his quest will end in failure; gazing up into the darkness, he sees himself "as a creature driven and derided by vanity" (35). By paying close attention to the narrative's themes and images, we can also infer other social and ideological narratives at work: the fact that the boy is ultimately stymied by the immovable presence of the Englishmen is a miniature allegory of the disempowerment of the Irish under the British occupation and sets this narrative within the larger patterns of Irish history. Furthermore, symbolic and imagistic associations equate unrealistic childish infatuation with the fictitious nature of the progressions common to the genre of romance and with the illusory beliefs of Christianity. Each is an idealistic fiction that has no application in the real world. Finally, it is a narrative of desire and a narrative driven by desire, the object of whose quest is almost entirely deindividualized, little more than the object of a young male gaze.

"The Dead," by contrast, is a much more elusive narrative. I encourage students to apply James Phelan's account of narrative progression to help clarify the dynamics at work in this piece. Phelan's is a rhetorical approach and is concerned with the ways in which authors generate, sustain, develop, and resolve readers' interest in a narrative. Phelan differentiates between instabilities and tensions. The former arise within the unfolding of the story in the text and include instabilities between characters; created by situations and complicated through actions, these include the familiar disharmonies described above by Miller. The other class of instabilities, which Phelan calls "tensions," are located in the discourse of the work;

they arise between authors and narrators, on the one hand, and readers on the other. Phelan identifies tensions as instabilities of value, belief, opinion, knowledge, and expectation. If two characters desire the same object, we have an instability; if the narrator cryptically alludes to his greater knowledge of the outcome of the events, we have a tension.

As the text of "The Dead" begins to unfold, the reader is quickly presented with an instability: his aunts' annual party is well under way, but Gabriel has not yet arrived. His presence is especially important for the supervision of another guest, Freddy Malins, who is notorious for turning up drunk. Gabriel soon arrives, however, and the aunts are relieved. Malins appears in passable shape, is handed a glass of lemonade, and behaves himself the rest of the evening. The anticipated instability proves to be a nonissue. Gabriel has a failed conversation with Lily, the caretaker's daughter, who is helping out at the event; this encounter looks forward to Molly Ivors's later castigation of Gabriel for writing book reviews for a conservative newspaper that is opposed to Irish home rule. This is a genuine instability in the story. Gabriel is annoyed and flustered and can come up with no satisfactory answer to Molly's accusations. Although Molly parts from him on friendly terms, Gabriel keenly feels the sting of her remark. In his interactions with both Lily and Molly, Gabriel is much more affected than the text suggests is appropriate; this pattern in turn sets up an interpretative tension: why is Gabriel's judgment of himself so much more severe than Joyce's seems to be?

With the exception of Gabriel's private resentment of Miss Ivors's words, there is no significant instability until the point where the text is two-thirds complete. This fact in turn provokes the work's most important tension (one that has been present for some time): why are we being given such a detailed account of an inconsequential chronicle of minor events? Many first-time readers legitimately wonder, Where is the plot? The final section of the text dramatizes a series of misunderstandings and suspicions in Gabriel's mind as his wife narrates the story of a young man, Michael Furey, who loved her many years before and, seriously ill, had sung to her in a cold rain; he died a few days later. Gabriel is miserable; he feels his affection is pathetic compared with a death-defying love. He questions the basis of their marriage, the pattern of his life, and his sense of self.

This discussion reveals that, in a modernist work like "The Dead," an analysis based on plot or instabilities alone is inadequate to explain the dynamics of narrative progression. Explaining those dynamics must also take into account the tensions in the text as well as other forms of progression, including the sequence of three parallel scenes that depict Gabriel's unsuccessful encounters with women associated with the west of Ireland, the area least affected by English conquest and, by implication, Ireland itself. Though not connected by the succession of events, these scenes form a structural design that helps explain the totality of the work and its movement toward ever-more-powerful and ever-more-personal expressions of repressed Irish culture and history. This movement in turn underscores and clarifies the mythological trajectory of the vengeance of the Eumenides (the Furies) in the form of Michael Furey, who enacts it on the man who would deny or evade the history and culture that his death represents. Architecturally, allegorically, and thematically, all sequences come together in Gabriel's final act of recognition.

One could say that Gabriel discovers that the story of his life is inflected by the stories of others much more than he had ever imagined. Specifically, his wife has an independent life story of her own that is not merely a component of his own narrative; furthermore, his own life story is in many significant ways the opposite of Michael Furey's. Most important, he has not been able to see how his life story is imbricated with the larger narrative of Irish colonial history. These issues in turn lead to discussions of double or multiple plots and how they are braided together or kept apart. Though fairly rare in short stories, they abound in drama (*King Lear*), the modern novel (*Daniel Deronda*), the romance (*The Faerie Queen*), and the serial narrative, including television serials. Students quickly perceive how double or multiple plots can provide a foil for one another, clarify the motives of one set of characters by juxtaposing them to another, produce an aesthetic effect through the arrangement of compositional symmetries, and point to the compelling power of a single plot by seeming to stray from it (see Garrett).

It is also important to show how the material of the story can be inflected by and even stretch beyond the text of "The Dead." This novella concludes *Dubliners*, a series of stories that collectively reflect and echo one another. The "death in life" that Dubliners suffer is given a final resonant image in the snow that lies on all the living and the dead, while the swooning of Gabriel's soul is the final variation on the theme of paralysis that figures in the stories. The coin that Gabriel tries to give to Lily recalls the gold coin that the predatory Corley extracts from another servant girl (who might even be Lily) in "Two Gallants"; Lily's statement that "the men that is now is only all palaver and what they can get out of you" is an effective summary of nearly all the male-female relations depicted in the collection (178)—with the one between Michael and Gretta being a conspicuous exception. Gabriel's story also echoes that of the narrator in "Araby" since both end as amorous failures, impeded by British rule, their harsh epiphanies coming at night, causing tears and excessive self-recrimination. I also inform the students of the later mention of Gretta Conroy in *Ulysses*, set several months after the events depicted in "The Dead," which suggests that no major transformation has occurred in the Conroy household, while simultaneously showing how a story can continue across texts. In my graduate classes, I encourage the students to speculate on the theoretical implications of such expandable stories, transtextual characters, and the persistence of a single storyworld from work to work.

Robbe-Grillet's "The Secret Room" is an illuminating example of an "unnatural narrative" that requires a different kind of analysis and helps reveal the fundamental elements of all narratives. The reader is presented with several depictions of what superficially appears to be the same scene at different times. I ask the students what is being represented. Some say a series of actions, scrambled in time; others suggest the story shows several visual images, presumably paintings, that either can form a narrative or else are merely variations on a theme. Both interpretations are right and wrong: characters are described as moving, which indicates the presence of a narrative, though other images are depicted as painted. We then trace the apparent temporal sequence of the images. The reader is invited to construct from the pieces of the text a narrative of a gothic murder and the escape of the killer. However, because of contradictions in the descriptions of the setting, it remains a pseudostory that ultimately parodies rather than embodies the fabula-*sjužet* distinction.

I then ask the class what pattern is described by the strange sequence of events. They are usually stumped at this point. I next ask whether any of the many descriptions in the text can act as a mirror of this sequence of events and whether there is any geometric shape we might use to describe this pattern. If necessary, I go on to add that these two questions have the same answer. The governing (or generating) figure is the spiral, which is manifested in numerous spatial patterns as well as in the work's temporality. It becomes clear that the text we have been reading is not a realistic representation of a series of events that could occur in the world but rather a uniquely fictional creation that can only exist as literature. How does Robbe-Grillet achieve closure in such an antimimetic text? The answer is surprisingly simple: the final image is largely static: the wound has congealed, the killer has vanished, the only sign of motion is the complicated spirals of smoke from the incense burner. Finally, I ask whether this text transgressively disrupts or unwittingly embodies familiar cultural stereotypes of the pattern of male aggressor / female victim and note that Robbe-Grillet has asserted that pornography demands a linear chronology.

We go on to examine in depth stories that extend across several works or independent episodes and discuss the interconnected dynamics of story, closure, and culture. As I begin this unit, I build on the work we have done with the interconnections among the stories in *Dubliners*. We explore the similarities and differences between a coherent story collection, where we see various characters deal with particular instabilities even as their stories share a setting or themes and a serial narrative, where we follow the same principal characters attempting to address the instabilities in their situations from installment to installment. I remind students that the ending is where we look to find the moral of the story, explain the traditional critical valuation of closure in literary studies from Aristotle to Brooks, and note that closure is also the site where ideological issues are most forcibly present. I ask the students to note whether endings are open or closed, expected or surprising, credible or contrived, and tightly connected or arbitrarily conjoined to the rest of the narrative. I also ask whether a given ending embodies or contests culturally sanctioned resolutions. Here instructors can draw on Russell Reising's argument that many works that dramatize unresolved social contradictions seem compelled to leave the fates of the protagonists similarly unresolved and can note that the ending is the point where an ideological closure may require a resolution in conformity with official social doctrine. Totalitarian regimes demand compliance with national myths, and masculinist societies insist on a limited range of options for female protagonists, as Rachel Blau DuPlessis has documented in her important study, *Writing beyond the Ending*. Virginia Woolf praised unresolved endings in the name of realism ("The Russian Point of View"), and for many years it was postulated that an open, inconclusive ending was more socially progressive than a fixed, closed conclusion, but it is now widely accepted that no narrative form has any inherent ideological valence—especially now that open endings have become rather conventional, at least in literary fiction (see Richardson, "Linearity").

These theoretical tools prepare us to analyze several types of stories, including those presented in serial form. If possible, I ask the class to analyze critically the plot developments and narrative trajectories of a popular serial on television. One semester I was teaching a class on critical and narrative theory as the final episodes of *Sex and the City* were being aired. I asked the class to predict the fates of the various principals, and we discussed what would be most likely, most appropriate, and most satisfying. I also discussed the narratological and ideological implications of different possible endings, beginning with Forster's quip, "If it was not for death and marriage I do not know how the average novelist would conclude" (95). Would the show's writers dare to present a largely open ending without resolving the central characters' dilemmas, as would seem appropriate to the general logic of the show? And how much would it resist cultural master narratives?

Here we spend some time discussing narrative and ideology, starting with Judith Roof's observation that "rather than imitating or responding to life, narrative might determine our notion of the shape of life and what is important in it—birth, love, reproduction, achievement, death" (8). I discuss how feminist theorists have examined the ways female novelists eluded society's master narratives, in particular, the ubiquitous marriage plot that leads many writers to provide only a limited range of possible endings for their female protagonists: marriage, death, or painful isolation. A powerful classroom strategy is to ask the students to name central female characters in narratives before the sixties who are somehow able to elude the typical fate of the marriage plot. The few such examples the class can produce are invariably illuminating (Euripides's Medea, Chaucer's Wife of Bath, Woolf's Lily Briscoe). While on this subject, we also note how other related social plots have historically produced comparable conclusions, such as the frequent deaths of homosexual characters at the end of works by heterosexual authors or the ultimate sacrificial status of many working class or minority characters in white bourgeois fiction (what we might call the "Gunga Din" effect). Scrutiny of the ways narratives embody existing social scripts can help students see how and why they progress to a given ending and why a text that eludes the expected development can be so affecting.

With these conceptual tools in place, we were ready to analyze the final episode of *Sex and the City*. The show's conventional concluding episode, with its glorification of the marriage plot in the ultimate reunion of Carrie Bradshaw and Mr. Big, proved a disappointment to most—though a very instructive one. The class was especially annoyed at the "taming" of Samantha. She had been one of commercial television's most transgressive characters, a successful upper-middle-class woman who had plenty of sex with numerous partners without any negative consequences. Late in the series, when it was determined that one of the four women would develop a serious illness, it came as no surprise to those attuned to the cultural master narrative that Samantha would be the one stricken with breast cancer. Her uncharacteristic conversion to a monogamous lifestyle was solidified in the final episode, which further heightened the ideological closure that was made to contain the story line. Students participating in this class felt they learned a considerable amount about the poetics and ideology of narrative progression.

All students enter the class with some idea of plot; outlining its theory and practices gives them an important overview of its functions and effects and reveals its operation in all narrative forms: popular, classic, and avant-garde. Students perceive how narrative sequencing readily discloses the power of plot as a way of shaping and transmitting experience, and this explains in part the annoyance they feel when they encounter a poorly plotted narrative. Similarly, all experience the disruptive force of modernist authors who refuse to follow the conventions of plot; many will also appreciate and comprehend the bracing shock of estrangement that is produced when these conventions are overthrown and replaced by alternative orderings. The study of plot and progression discloses the shifting dynamics of narrative beginnings, middles, and endings; their respective relations in different works; and the ideological forces they can be harnessed to. Through such analysis students enrich their understanding of the narratives that circulate around them and acquire useful theoretical frameworks that they can successfully apply in their other classes in literature and the humanities—and in their interpretative practices more generally.

Note

1. I am following Rimmon-Kenan's usage (3–4). Not all theorists, however, use the same terminology. Readers interested in fuller discussion of these terms and their synonyms, cognates, and implications should consult Abbott (16–20) and Bordwell (49–61).

Works Cited

Abbott, H. Porter. *The Cambridge Introduction to Narrative*. 2nd ed. Cambridge: Cambridge UP, 2008. Print.

Aristotle. *Poetics*. Trans. S. H. Butcher. *Critical Theory Since Plato*. Ed. Hazard Adams. New York: Harcourt, 1971. 44–66. Print.

Austen, Jane. *Pride and Prejudice*. Oxford: Oxford UP, 1990. Print.

Booker, Christopher. *The Seven Basic Plots: Why We Tell Stories*. New York: Continuum, 2005. Print.

Bordwell, David. *Narration in the Fiction Film*. Madison: U of Wisconsin P, 1985. Print.

Brooks, Peter. *Reading for the Plot: Design and Intention in Narrative*. New York: Knopf, 1984. Print.

Crane, R. S. "The Concept of Plot and the Plot of *Tom Jones*." *Critics and Criticism*. Chicago: U of Chicago P, 1952. Print.

DuPlessis, Rachel Blau. *Writing beyond the Ending: Narrative Strategies of Twentieth-Century Women Writers*. Bloomington: Indiana UP, 1985. Print.

Forster, E. M. *Aspects of the Novel*. New York: Harcourt, 1927. Print.

Garrett, Peter. *The Victorian Multiplot Novel*. New Haven: Yale UP, 1980. Print.

Joyce, James. *Dubliners*. 1914. Ed. Robert Scholes and A. Walton Litz. New York: Penguin, 1996. Print.

Keen, Suzanne. *Narrative Form*. New York: Palgrave, 2003. Print.

Martin, Wallace. *Recent Theories of Narrative*. Ithaca: Cornell UP, 1986. Print.

Miller, D. A. *Narrative and Its Discontents: Problems of Closure in the Traditional Novel*. Princeton: Princeton UP, 1981. Print.

Page, Ruth E. "Feminist Narratology? Literary and Linguistic Perspectives on Gender and Narrativity." *Language and Literature: Journal of the Poetics and Linguistics Association* 12.1 (2003): 43–56. Print.

Phelan, James. *Reading People, Reading Plots: Character, Progression, and the Interpretation of Narrative*. Chicago: U of Chicago P, 1989. Print.

Prince, Gerald. *A Dictionary of Narratology*. 2nd ed. Lincoln: U of Nebraska P, 2003. Print.

Propp, Vladimir. "Fairy-Tale Transformations." *Narrative Dynamics: Essays on Time, Plot, Closure, and Frames*. Ed. Brian Richardson. Columbus: Ohio State UP, 2002. 73–93. Print.

———. *The Morphology of the Folktale*. Trans. Laurence Scott. Rev. Louis A. Wagner. Austin: U of Texas P, 1968. Print.

Reising, Russell. *Loose Ends: Closure and Crisis in the American Social Text*. Durham: Duke UP, 1996. Print.

Richardson, Brian. "Beyond the Poetics of Plot: Alternative Forms of Narrative Sequencing and the Multiple Trajectories of *Ulysses*." *A Companion to Narrative Theory*. Ed. James Phelan and Peter J. Rabinowitz. Malden: Blackwell, 2005. 167–80. Print.

———. "Linearity and Its Discontents." *College English* 62.6 (2000): 685–95. Print.

Rimmon-Kenan, Shlomith. *Narrative Fiction: Contemporary Poetics*. 2nd ed. London: Routledge, 2002. Print.

Robbe-Grillet, Alain. 1957. *La jalousie*. Paris: Éditions de Minuit, 1975. Print.

Roberts, Michèle. "Une Glossaire / A Glossary." *During Mother's Absence*. London: Virago, 1993. 131–81. Print.

Roof, Judith. *Come As You Are: Sexuality and Narrative*. New York Columbia UP, 1996. Print.

Sex and the City. HBO. 22 Feb. 2004. Television.

Shakespeare, William. *The Winter's Tale*. *The Riverside Shakespeare*. Ed. G. Blakemore Evans et al. Vol. 2. Boston: Houghton, 1974. 1569–605. Print.

Woolf, Virginia. 1927. "The Russian Point of View." *The Common Reader: First Series*. New York: Harcourt, 1984. 173–82. Print.

———. *To the Lighthouse*. New York: Harcourt, 1981. Print.

Further Reading

Abbott, H. Porter. "Story, Plot, and Narration." *The Cambridge Companion to Narrative*. Ed. David Herman. Cambridge: Cambridge UP, 2007. 39–51. Print.

Dannenberg, Hilary. *Plotting Coincidence and Counterfactuality in Narrative Fiction*. Lincoln: U of Nebraska P, 2008. Print.

Heise, Ursula K. *Chronoschisms: Time, Narrative, and Postmodernism*. Cambridge: Cambridge UP, 1997. Print.

Kafalenos, Emma. *Narrative Causalities*. Columbus: Ohio State UP, 2006. Print.

Lohafer, Susan. *Reading for Storyness: Preclosure Theory, Empirical Poetics, and Culture in the Short Story*. Baltimore: Johns Hopkins UP, 2003. Print.

Phelan, James. *Experiencing Fiction: Judgments, Progressions, and the Rhetorical Theory of Narrative*. Columbus: Ohio State UP, 2007. Print.

Richardson, Brian, ed. *Narrative Beginnings: Theories and Analyses*. Lincoln: U of Nebraska P, 2009. Print.

David Herman

Time, Space, and Narrative Worlds

Consider the first eight sentences of Ernest Hemingway's 1927 story "Hills like White Elephants":

> [1] The hills across the valley of the Ebro were long and white. [2] On this side there was no shade and no trees and the station was between two lines of rails in the sun. [3] Close against the side of the station there was the warm shadow of the building and a curtain, made of strings of bamboo beads, hung across the open door into the bar, to keep out flies. [4] The American and the girl with him sat at a table in the shade, outside the building. [5] It was very hot and the express from Barcelona would come in forty minutes. [6] It stopped at this junction for two minutes and went to Madrid.
>
> [7] "What should we drink?" the girl asked. [8] She had taken off her hat and put it on the table. (211)

How do these eight sentences evoke (a fragment of) a narrative world? What specific textual cues allow readers to draw inferences about the structure, inhabitants, and spatiotemporal situation of this world? How does the worldmaking process operate in connection with this story opening as compared with, say, the opening of a science fiction novel or the lead paragraphs of a news report? In other words, how can we sift out generically narrative from story-specific worldmaking procedures?

In this essay, drawing on work in narrative theory (and other fields) that attempts to frame answers to these and related questions, I explore in more detail the world-creating power of Hemingway's text, using it to illustrate how ideas about time, space, and narrative worlds can be put into play in a variety of classroom settings. More than this, my essay suggests that processes of worldmaking can provide a point of entry into the core issues of narrative theory; using questions about narrative worlds as a guiding thread, students can get their initial bearings within—grasp the broader relevance of—what may seem like a forbiddingly complex area of inquiry, replete with difficult-to-master sets of technical terms that are (to add insult to injury) sometimes in conflict with one another. Indeed, whereas structuralist narratologists failed to account for the referential properties of narrative, partly because of the exclusion of the referent in favor of signifier and signified in Saussurean language theory, over the past couple of decades one of the most basic and abiding concerns of narrative theory has been how interpreters of stories reconstruct narrative worlds—how readers of print narratives, interlocutors in face-to-face discourse, and viewers of films use textual cues to build up representations of the worlds evoked by stories, or *storyworlds*. Such worldmaking practices are of central importance to narrative scholars of all sorts, ranging from feminist narratologists exploring representations of male and female characters in the light of cultural stereotypes about gender roles to students of the reflexive, self-conscious modes of world building used in historiographic metafictions to analysts (and designers) of digital narratives interested in how interactive systems can remediate the experience of being immersed in a storyworld.

But though strategies for worldmaking have become a focal concern for scholars of narrative and moreover afford a way to navigate the large and growing body of work in the field, it can be a pedagogical challenge to convince students of the need to slow down and deautomatize the rapid, apparently effortless interpretive processes involved in experiencing narrative worlds. Mapping words onto worlds is a fundamental—perhaps *the* fundamental—requirement for narrative sense making; yet this mapping operation may seem so natural and normal that no "theory," no specialized nomenclature or framework of concepts, is necessary to describe and explain the specific procedures involved. Thus, to pick back up with remarks included in the introduction to this volume, instructors using narrative theory to explore aspects of worldmaking in the undergraduate classroom need to engage in the practice of translation and justification; in the present instance, the task is both to fix the scope of terms like *deictic shift, textual actual world, analepsis,* and *scene* (vs. *summary*) and to demonstrate their value as heuristic tools for studying how narrative texts prompt their interpreters to reconstruct (and immerse themselves in) storyworlds. At the graduate level, the challenge goes beyond translation and justification and includes integration—that is, the challenge becomes one of helping more advanced students integrate ideas from narrative theory into their growing repertoire of interpretive approaches, their strategies for professional development, and their ongoing apprenticeship as teachers in their own right. Arguably, by using the process of world creation as the ground on which to test out the analytic relevance of terms and concepts developed under the auspices of narrative theory, instructors can accomplish any or all of these three pedagogical goals—translation, justification, integration—to the extent needed in a given classroom context.

In what follows I outline strategies for teaching ideas about time and space vis-à-vis processes of narrative worldmaking—strategies that can be tailored to different classroom scenarios. Possible scenarios include undergraduate and graduate courses on literature in which ideas from narrative theory are used in a relatively limited, targeted way, as well as undergraduate and graduate courses focusing on narrative theory itself, in which illustrative texts are used to flesh out the theoretical concepts and methods under discussion. I begin with the foundational concept of "narrative world," showing how models designed to explicate that concept provide a framework for discussing the spatial and temporal factors that shape storyworlds. I then sketch how specific narratological approaches to time and space can be presented to students as a necessary part of this broader inquiry into worldmaking processes.

Narrative Ways of Worldmaking: Establishing a Framework for Discussion

As the beginning of my essay suggests, one way to introduce students to the concept of narrative worlds is to focus on how story openings prompt interpreters to take up residence (more or less comfortably) in the world being evoked by a given text. In courses on narrative theory, openings from different story genres can be compared and contrasted to underscore how part of the meaning of "genre" consists of distinctive protocols for world making; discussions and assignments can then use theoretical frameworks to explore the extent to which a common core of worldmaking procedures cuts across such generic differences. In courses examining aspects of narrative across media, the focus can be broadened to include processes of world creation in movies or television shows versus print narratives or graphic novels. Meanwhile, in an introduction to fiction course or for that matter an advanced seminar focusing on a particular genre or subgenre (autobiography or memoir, eighteenth-century epistolary novel, modernist novel of consciousness, etc.), the theoretical accounts can be used to highlight what is distinctive about the focal genre vis-à-vis texts from earlier periods, as well as contemporaneous narratives written in accordance with other generic templates.

Because undergraduates and even many graduate students may not have previously encountered the conceptual distinctions and technical terms of theories of worldmaking, it is often beneficial for teachers at both levels to use handouts and lectures to explain this material. Teachers can also use a series of specific questions about narratives such as "Hills like White Elephants" as a means to help students recognize the underlying logic of world creation. In this discussion, I will sometimes model the lecture method as I explain the theoretical material, and at other times I formulate questions about Hemingway's story that lead to central theoretical concepts—questions that can be transformed into exercises or assignments. Further, instructors may wish to follow the general order of the discussion that follows, beginning with accounts that characterize the experience of narrative worlds in a relatively macrostructural or gestalt way and then moving toward more microstructural approaches that seek to anchor types of inferences about storyworlds (including their temporal and spatial dimensions) in particular kinds of textual designs. On this model, students would focus first on the creation or constitution of narrative worlds and then examine how those worlds can be inhabited and navigated.

Creating Worlds: Transportation and Fictional Recentering

A good starting point for a course or course unit on narrative worldmaking is Richard Gerrig's 1993 study, *Experiencing Narrative Worlds*. Gerrig uses the metaphor of transportation to characterize how readers make sense of the storyworlds evoked through print texts, whether fictional or nonfictional. He identifies six key elements of the source concept of transportation and discusses how each element can be projected onto corresponding features of the target domain, namely, the process by which readers interpret representations of narrative worlds:

1. Someone ("the traveler") is transported
2. by some means of transportation
3. as a result of performing certain actions.
4. The traveler goes some distance from his or her world of origin,
5. which makes some aspects of the world of origin inaccessible.
6. The traveler returns to the world of origin, somewhat changed by the journey. (10–11)

In contrast with models for narrative analysis such as William Labov's, which purport to find direct, fixed mappings from particular kinds of formal structures to specific narrative functions,[1] Gerrig's cognitive-psychological account emphasizes the mental operations that enable worldmaking rather than the specific textual triggers that induce interpreters to perform those operations. In this respect, Gerrig's approach bears a family resemblance to Kendall Walton's work on fiction as a game of make-believe, according to which written texts, images on screen, physical objects, and other sorts of triggers of fictional experiences can all be assimilated to the category of "props" in the game that enables and sustains the make-believe world. In this part of the course, students can be asked to compare different kinds of stories to test out Gerrig's premise that worldmaking processes are the same across fictional and nonfictional texts. Undergraduates might also be asked to perform a skit, complete with props, to see whether their intuitions about fictional experiences match Walton's claim that the process of getting caught up in make-believe worlds is the same irrespective of medium.

Complementing Gerrig's metaphor of transportation is the account of "fictional recentering" developed by Marie-Laure Ryan under the auspices of a possible-worlds approach to narrative—an approach that helps specify the relation between the world of origin and the target world and also the structure of the target world itself. Thus, in concert with Lubomír Doležel, Thomas Pavel, and other theorists, Ryan draws on ideas from analytic philosophy and modal logic to argue that narrative universes are recognizable because of a shared modal structure; this structure consists of a central world that counts as actual and various satellite worlds that can be accessed through counterfactual constructions voiced by a narrator or by the characters and also through what the characters say, think, dream, read, and so on. Of course, not every narrative faithfully exemplifies this structure; indeed, as Brian McHale has shown, a hallmark of postmodern fiction is its refusal to adhere to ontological boundaries and hierarchies of precisely this sort. Yet in metaleptic narratives such as Jorge Luis Borges's

"Tlön, Uqbar, Orbis Tertius," where a world initially construed as a far-flung satellite ultimately merges with the baseline reality of the story, the ontological subversiveness of such texts can be registered because of how they deviate from the default template for worldmaking. By contrast, Hemingway's story conforms to that standard template. The current scene of interaction between Jig and the unnamed male character constitutes the base structure or point of reference for this narrative universe, with the man momentarily opening a window onto a satellite world when (for example) he uses a counterfactual construction to frame an angry rejoinder to Jig's dismissive comment that he is someone who would never have seen a white elephant: "I might have [seen a white elephant]. . . . Just because you say I wouldn't have doesn't prove anything" (211).

In this context, students might be asked to compare representative modernist and postmodernist fictions (e.g., Hemingway's versus Borges's) by charting out the base worlds and satellite worlds in each case and by trying to capture the changing relations among these worlds as the story unfolds in time. At issue are the possible worlds that orbit around what is presented as what Ryan calls the "textual actual world" (TAW), or world assumed as actual within the narrative. Narratives typically feature a range of private worlds or subworlds (see Werth 210–58) inhabited or at least imagined by characters; these satellite worlds include knowledge worlds, obligation worlds, wish worlds, pretend worlds, and so on. Further, the plot of any narrative can be redefined as

> the trace left by the movement of these worlds within the textual universe. [For] participants, the goal of the narrative game . . . is to make TAW coincide with as many as possible of their [private worlds]. . . . The moves of the game are the actions through which characters attempt to alter relations between worlds. (Ryan, *Possible Worlds* 119–20)

Thus, in Hemingway's story, it is not just that satellite worlds come into view as Jig and the male character discuss possible courses of action in response to the unstated "given" of Jig's pregnancy. Rather, the conflict that drives the plot emerges from the two characters' different strategies for bringing the TAW into alignment with their private worlds, particularly their wish worlds and intention worlds—the male character seeking to do so by encouraging Jig to go through with an abortion, Jig by gaining some recognition from the man that having the child would not necessarily be inimical to their relationship. In a lower-level class, a useful assignment in this context would be to have groups of students map out how the characters' private worlds relate to the TAW at a given point in the narrative and how those relations change from moment to moment. Groups could compare their maps and discuss how any differences among them correspond to different interpretations of the story.

More globally, the storyworld evoked by a fictional narrative can be described as an alternative possible world to which interpreters are openly prompted to relocate, such that, for the duration of the fictional experience, "the realm of possibilities is . . . recentered around the sphere which the narrator presents as the actual world" (Ryan, *Possible Worlds* 22). The world evoked by the text may be more or less accessible to the world(s) in which that narrative is produced and interpreted, providing the basis for a typology of genres (31–47). As compared with the reference world of a news report, for instance, the storyworld evoked by a science fiction novel about a superrace with telekinetic powers is less accessible to (less compatible with the defining properties of) the world of the here and now. Yet if no textual or paratextual indicators block their default interpretive stance, readers or film viewers will abide by what Ryan terms the principle of minimal departure, which states that "when readers construct fictional worlds, they fill in the gaps . . . in the text by assuming the similarity of the fictional worlds to their own experiential reality" ("Possible-Worlds Theory" 447). Thus readers of Hemingway's story assume that the interlocutors are human beings rather than murderous aliens who have body snatched male and female earthlings in order to dupe the waitress and the other people at the bar. Even more crucially, perhaps, readers assume that the Ebro in the story is the same Ebro that exists in the actual world and runs through a particular valley in Spain. In this connection, students might be assigned the task of determining the extent to which default assumptions about the actual world can be carried over to their interpretation of Hemingway's storyworld—and conversely which assumptions are disallowed (and why) for worldmaking purposes in this context.

Inhabiting and Navigating Worlds: Deictic Shifts and Contextual Frames

Other research provides the basis for still-finer-grained analyses of how specific textual cues afford resources for world creation. One relevant framework is deictic-shift theory, which seeks to illuminate the cognitive reorientation required to take up imaginary residence in a storyworld. This theory holds that a "location within the world of the narrative serves as the center from which [sentences with deictic expressions such as *here* and *now*] are interpreted" and that to access this location readers must shift "from the environmental situation in which the text is encountered, to a locus within a mental model representing the world of the discourse" (Segal 15). The theory also suggests that over longer, more sustained experiences of narrative worlds, interpreters may need to make successive adjustments in their position relative to the situations and events being recounted—if they are attentive to the blueprint for world building included in the narrative's verbal texture. A useful assignment would have the students identify when and how a text like Hemingway's marks shifts from one deictic center to another and with what consequences for world construction.

Students can be prompted to scan Hemingway's text for cues indicating shifts among spatial vantage points as well as time frames within the narrated world. Thus, an initial deictic shift is required for the reader to take up the perspective in terms of which the preposition "across," in sentence 1, and the prepositional phrase "On this side," in sentence 2, can be parsed. Then, immediately after the opening paragraph, the deictic center shifts again, this time to the vantage point of the male character as he observes Jig from up close; this is the cognitive stance from which sentence 8 must be interpreted. Note that here the use of the past perfect tense ("had taken off her hat") implies a return of the male character's focus of attention to Jig's position within the current scene, as well as a perception of how her appearance has altered over time—that is, since the last time the male character observed Jig closely. An assignment that requires students first to list and then to explicate the function of world-building cues of this sort will help them slow down and monitor the complex inferential processes that support comprehension of—and immersion within—storyworlds such as Hemingway's.

Another microstructural approach to narrative worlds is developed by Catherine Emmott, who focuses on how readers use textual cues to bind characters into or out of mentally constructed contexts, which thereby underpin subsequent interpretations of character-indexing pronouns. Thus in the opening of Hemingway's story, a noun phrase ("the girl") binds Jig into what Emmott would term a *primed* contextual frame—first in sentence 4 and then again in sentence 7. Her presence in that frame allows readers to assign a referent to the pronoun "She" in sentence 8. Similarly, a noun phrase in sentence 5, "the express from Barcelona," allows readers to identify the referent of "It" in sentence 6, differentiating this referent-marking token of the pronoun from the referentially vacuous token in the existential construction "It was very hot" in sentence 7. Assignments or exercises could once again be used to familiarize students with the process of identifying contexts (in Emmott's sense), as well as the specific textual cues that prompt readers to engage in the binding, priming, recalling, switching, and other processing operations that involve such contexts. The assignments could also explore how Emmott's language-based account might be adapted for the study of nonverbal or multimodal storytelling (see Bridgeman).

Configuring Narrative Worlds: Story, Discourse, and the Nexus of WHAT, WHERE, and WHEN

As indicated in my previous section, approaches such as deictic-shift theory, possible-worlds theory, and contextual-frame theory already take into account how temporal and spatial factors affect the process of world creation, that is, the WHERE and the WHEN dimensions of narrative worlds. Accordingly, starting with theories of worldmaking and then moving to ideas about narrative time and narrative space allows instructors to motivate frameworks for inquiry—to show why they are worth learning about in the first place—that might otherwise strike students as overly abstract, formalistic, and without any real bearing on the phenomenology of reading.

An approach based on shifting deictic centers suggests how narrative worlds are structured around cognitive vantage points that may change over the course of an unfolding story. The approach also allows for comparison between narratives in which the orienting perspective point remains relatively stable and fixed and those marked by more or less rapid shifts of cognitive stance. Similarly, accounts based on possible worlds are intrinsically concerned with time and space: characters' situation vis-à-vis the spatial layout of the TAW (and proximity to or distance from other characters) affects their ability to bring that world into conformity with their wishes, intentions, and felt obligations, even as the shifting relations among such subworlds and the TAW provide a way to measure time's passing as events become etched into the history of the narrated domain. Likewise, based on the assumption that characters will be bound into and out of particular contexts over time, as well as the assumption that such contexts will be distributed spatially as well as temporally, Emmott's contextual frame theory points to the nexus of the WHAT, WHERE, and WHEN factors in narrative worldmaking.

Given this general background, scholarship focusing on time and space can be presented to students as a tool for exploring how these factors intersect in representations of a given narrative world. Gérard Genette's influential account of time in narrative, for example, can be motivated as a heuristic framework for studying the WHEN component of world creation. When Genette distinguished between simultaneous, retrospective, prospective, and "intercalated" modes of narration (as in the epistolary novel, where the act of narration postdates some events but precedes others), these narrative modes can now be interpreted in the light of the different kinds of structure that they afford for worldmaking. Retrospective narration accommodates the full scope of a storyworld's history, allowing a narrator to signal connections between earlier and later events through proleptic foreshadowings of the eventual impact of a character's actions on his or her cohorts. Simultaneous narration, in which events are presented in tandem with the interpreter's effort to comprehend the contours and boundaries of the narrated domain, does not allow for such anticipations in hindsight; rather, inferences about the impact of events on the storyworld remain tentative, probablistic, open-ended. Hemingway's text interestingly combines features of these two modes insofar as the dearth of narratorial commentary inhibits prospection into the future of this narrative world—with the tip-of-the-iceberg technique prompting the inference that the world shared by these two characters may not in fact *have* a future.

Likewise, Genette's categories of duration, order (on which I have already begun to comment), and frequency can be explicated more productively if they are linked to the broader issue of narrative worldmaking. Duration can be computed as a ratio between how long events take to unfold in the world of the story and how much text is devoted to their narration, with speeds ranging from descriptive pause to scene to summary to ellipsis. This aspect of the temporal system thus constitutes a metric of value or at least attentional prominence: in extended narratives the shift from rapidly surveyed backstory or expositional material to a slower, scenic mode of presentation can signal aspects of the storyworld valued (or at any rate noticed) by a narrator. Meanwhile, as suggested by my discussion of retrospective versus simultaneous narration above, order can be analyzed by matching the sequence in which events are narrated against the sequence in which they can be assumed to have occurred, yielding chronological narration, analepses or flashbacks, and prolepses or flash-forwards, together with various subcategories of these nonchronological modes. Here students can be posed the following question: How does the story-world evoked by a narrative with a richly analeptic or proleptic structure (*The Sound and the Fury* or *The Prime of Miss Jean Brodie*, respectively) contrast with that evoked by a narrative that largely confines itself to the present, as Hemingway's text does? How is a narrative world "thickened" by forays backward and forward in time, and what processing strategies are triggered by such temporal agglutination? Finally, frequency can be calculated by measuring how many times an event is narrated against how many times it can be assumed to have occurred in the storyworld. Again, more than just a range of formal possibilities, frequency affords ways of allocating attention to and evaluating events in narrative worlds—with repetitive narration foregrounding some event or set of events, iterative narration providing a summative gloss on multiple storyworld incidents, and singulative narration being the baseline metric in this context.

Though their concern with space is less long-standing than their interest in temporality, narrative theorists have in recent years increasingly studied where-related factors of world creation. This work was given impetus by Mikhail Bakhtin's concept of the chronotope, defined as "a formally constitutive category of literature . . . [in which] spatial and temporal indicators are fused" into a gestalt representational structure that is originally associated with a particular genre but that is subsequently taken up in later texts in ways that lead to generic intermixing and the copresence of phenomena hailing from different phases of "the historico-literary process" (84–85). Gabriel Zoran built on Bakhtin's account to develop a three-level framework for studying the space-time nexus in narrative, consisting of the topological level (a map of the narrated world that can be reconstructed from all the elements of the text), the chronotopic level (a domain in which space and time jointly constitute vectors of movement, broadly defined), and the textual level (where space is structured by the semiotic medium of the narrative text, as when the linear nature of verbal language organizes spatial relationships into a temporal continuum). Still more recently, theorists of space in narrative have borrowed from psychological and psycholinguistic work on spatial cognition, as well as cognitive-linguistic research on how abilities and dispositions bound up with embodied human experience find reflexes in the structure and interpretation of language. Sabine Buchholz and Manfred Jahn have suggested that this recent work harmonizes with Iurii Lotman's earlier account of the value-saturation of spatial oppositions (554), whereby distinctions such as near/far, high/low, and so forth are correlated with judgments such as good/bad and valuable/worthless.

In classroom contexts, these and other developments can again be harnessed for students' explorations of narrative worldmaking, in this case its "where" dimension. In my own work, for example, I draw on some of the relevant research to suggest how particular textual cues prompt interpreters to spatialize storyworlds, that is, to build up mental representations of narrated domains as evolving configurations of participants, objects, and places. Working with a text like Hemingway's, students can use this approach to examine how shifts between foregrounded and backgrounded objects and regions in the text, as well as the directions of movement traced by the main participants in the scene (Jig, the man, and the waitress), enable readers to segment the narrative into smaller episodes, each situated in a particular space-time region of the narrative world. Students can then explore other, related questions, such as how Hemingway uses particular subspaces (the hills across the valley, the bar, Jig and the man's table) to stage aspects of the characters' conflict and also how this constellation of subspaces coheres into a world—what net effect the process of moving from one space to the next generates.

The overarching claim of this essay is that by starting with the larger issue of world construction in narrative contexts, students at all levels can better appreciate the models proposed to account for how specific kinds of textual cues afford scaffolding for that worldmaking process. Both beginning and advanced students are often left with the So what? question when faced with something like Genette's account of time in narrative in the absence of any larger concern with the world-thickening functions of analepses or flashbacks or the way the contrast between scene and summary provides a basis for distinguishing between focal and backgrounded elements of narrative worlds. By starting with world creation as a basic cognitive and communicative function served by storytelling and then working backward to the formal structures that support this root function of narrative, teachers can convey to students why fine-grained analyses of narrative texts are worth the effort.

Notes

A different version of material included in this essay was published in chapter 5 of *Basic Elements of Narrative*, by David Herman (Chichester: Wiley-Blackwell, 2009; print).

1. For example, in Labov's model, clauses with past tense verbs in the indicative mood correlate with the complicating action of a narrative, whereas evaluation, or the signaling of the point of a story, is marked by departures from this baseline narrative syntax.

Works Cited

Bakhtin, Mikhail M. "Forms of Time and of the Chronotope in the Novel." *The Dialogic Imagination: Four Essays by M. M. Bakhtin.* Ed. Michael Holquist. Trans. Caryl Emerson and Holquist. Austin: U of Texas P, 1981. 84–258. Print.

Bridgeman, Teresa. "Figuration and Configuration: Mapping Imaginary Worlds in Bande Dessinée." *The Francophone Bande Dessinée.* Ed. Charles Forsdick, Laurence Grove, and Libbie McQuillan. Amsterdam: Rodopi, 2005. 115–36. Print.

Buchholz, Sabine, and Manfred Jahn. "Space in Narrative." Herman, Jahn, and Ryan 551–55.

Doležel, Lubomír. *Heterocosmica: Fiction and Possible Worlds.* Baltimore: Johns Hopkins UP, 1998. Print.

Emmott, Catherine. *Narrative Comprehension: A Discourse Perspective.* Oxford: Oxford UP, 1997. Print.

Genette, Gérard. *Narrative Discourse: An Essay in Method.* Trans. Jane E. Lewin. Ithaca: Cornell UP, 1980. Print.

Gerrig, Richard J. *Experiencing Narrative Worlds: On the Psychological Activities of Reading.* New Haven: Yale UP, 1993. Print.

Hemingway, Ernest. "Hills like White Elephants." 1927. *The Complete Short Stories of Ernest Hemingway.* New York: Scribner's, 1987. 211–14. Print.

Herman, David. *Story Logic: Problems and Possibilities of Narrative.* Lincoln: U of Nebraska P, 2002. Print.

Herman, David, Manfred Jahn, and Marie-Laure Ryan, eds. *Routledge Encyclopedia of Narrative Theory.* London: Routledge, 2005. Print.

Labov, William. "The Transformation of Experience in Narrative Syntax." *Language in the Inner City.* Philadelphia: U of Pennsylvania P, 1972. 354–96. Print.

McHale, Brian. *Postmodernist Fiction.* London: Methuen, 1987. Print.

Pavel, Thomas G. *Fictional Worlds.* Cambridge: Harvard UP, 1986. Print.

Ryan, Marie-Laure. *Possible Worlds, Artificial Intelligence, and Narrative Theory.* Bloomington: Indiana UP, 1991. Print.

———. "Possible-Worlds Theory." Herman, Jahn, and Ryan 446–50.

Segal, Erwin M. "Narrative Comprehension and the Role of Deictic Shift Theory." *Deixis in Narrative: A Cognitive Science Perspective.* Ed. Judith F. Duchan, Gail A. Bruder, and Lynne E. Hewitt. Hillsdale: Erlbaum, 1995. 3–17. Print.

Walton, Kendall. *Mimesis as Make-Believe: On the Foundations of the Representational Arts.* Cambridge: Harvard UP, 1990. Print.

Werth, Paul. *Text Worlds: Representing Conceptual Space in Discourse.* Sussex: Longman, 1999. Print.

Zoran, Gabriel. "Towards a Theory of Space in Narrative." *Poetics Today* 5.2 (1984): 309–35. Print.

Further Reading

Bridgeman, Teresa. "Time and Space." *The Cambridge Companion to Narrative.* Ed. David Herman. Cambridge: Cambridge UP, 2007. 52–65. Print.

Gavins, Joanna. *Text World Theory: An Introduction.* Edinburgh: Edinburgh UP, 2007. Print.

Gibson, John, Wolfgang Huemer, and Luca Pocci, eds. *A Sense of the World: Essays on Fiction, Narrative, and Knowledge.* London: Routledge, 2007. Print.

Goodman, Nelson. *Ways of Worldmaking.* Indianapolis: Hackett, 1978. Print.

Ryan, Marie-Laure. "Cognitive Maps and the Construction of Narrative Space." *Narrative Theory and the Cognitive Sciences.* Ed. David Herman. Stanford: Center for the Study of Lang. and Information, 2003. 214–42. Print.

James Phelan

Voice; or, Authors, Narrators, and Audiences

Teaching voice means engaging with several fundamental concepts of narrative theory: the question, Who speaks (or tells)? not only has the obvious double answer "the author and the narrator" but also entails the complementary question, Who hears (or listens)?, which has the less obvious answer "multiple audiences." In addition, Who speaks? entails the questions, What values are implied in that way of speaking? and What is the significance of this voice speaking with those values in this context? Thus, teaching voice also means examining the interrelations of form with ideology, politics, and ethics. Indeed, my main purpose in teaching voice is to explore with students the nature and consequences of those interrelations. My secondary purpose is one that remains constant across my teaching of narrative theory, and it significantly influences my way of teaching voice. I start by asking the students to listen to a variety of voices. We then move from that experience toward theoretical concepts that can help us hear those voices more clearly and discern their effects more fully. In other words, we move from narrative to theory and then back to narrative in a continuous loop. My purpose is to give students a sense of narrative theory as a dynamic, evolving activity, responsive to the practice of narrative artists, rather than as a set of fixed doctrines to be plopped on top of narrative texts.

In this essay, I present one way of entering the "voice loop" in the undergraduate classroom by focusing on two narratives that use voice in different ways, Jane Austen's *Pride and Prejudice* and Frank O'Connor's "My Oedipus Complex." At the graduate level, I proceed in much the same way, though we spend more time on the theory segments of the loop. Austen's novel provides a bridge to my larger rhetorical approach to voice, an approach that draws on Mikhail M. Bakhtin's concepts of double-voiced discourse and dialogism; Wayne C. Booth's and Peter J. Rabinowitz's respective work on authors and audiences; and Susan S. Lanser's ideas about the politics of narrative authority. O'Connor's short story offers a route to Gérard Genette's distinction between voice and vision (or perspective; see Jesse Matz's essay in this volume for a full-scale treatment of teaching perspective) as well as to my own efforts to extend the rhetorical approach to the issues of unreliable narration and of the ethical dimensions of voice (that is, its connection with moral values underlying the narrative). In the conclusion, I will touch on other ways of entering the voice loop.

Voice as Learnable Synesthesia

I start with a handout containing passages from my two main texts and from numerous other narratives drawn from different historical periods and subgenres (e.g., the gothic novel, the hard-boiled detective story, the New Journalism). I make sure that the handout includes narrative statements and dialogue as well as the first sentences of my two main examples:

> It is a truth universally acknowledged, that a single man in possesion of a good fortune must be in want of a wife. (Austen 3)

> Father was in the army all through the war—the first war, I mean—so, up to the age of five, I never saw much of him, and what I saw did not worry me. (O'Connor 282)

I read several of the selections aloud one right after the other, emphasizing the differences in syntax, diction, cadence, and tone. I then use a mixture of lecture and discussion to establish our points of entry into the voice loop: (1) Converting words on the page into distinctive audible speech can be a source of narrative pleasure. (2) The concept of voice involves not just a metaphor, in which writing gets treated as speech, but also a learnable kind of synesthesia: as we see words on a page we can hear sounds.

(3) This synesthesia applies across the distinction between voice as written (as in the two examples above) and voice as transcribed (as in another example planted on the handout such as Ring Lardner's "Haircut," where the narrator is clearly speaking instead of writing). I then ask the students to practice the synesthesia of voice by calling for volunteers to read some of the other extracts on the handout. As the course continues, we reserve a little time each week for similar practice.

Pride and Prejudice: Double Voicing, Dialogism, Audiences, and Authority

I frame our return to the main texts by saying that our goal will be to get at the sources of their power and our pleasure. With *Pride and Prejudice*, undergraduates will typically be able to identify Austen's famous first sentence as ironic. This ability opens the door to a discussion of one aspect of Bakhtin's concept of dialogism, double-voiced discourse or the combination of two distinct voices in a single utterance. In an ironic statement such as Austen's, one voice utters the literal meaning, and the other voice covertly subverts that meaning. ("Yeah, right" provides a more familiar example.) After we've read the rest of Austen's first chapter, I ask whether we can map the literal and ironic meanings of the first sentence onto the voices we've heard, and the students readily assign the literal meaning to Mrs. Bennet's voice and the ironic meaning not just to the narrator's voice but also to Mr. Bennet's.

This step leads to Bakhtin's valuable point about the interconnection between voice and ideology. We note that each voice carries with it a set of values and attitudes toward marriage: the literal voice sees it solely as an economic transaction, and the ironizing one undercuts that view without providing a positive alternative. Thus to listen to voice in that first sentence is to listen to a synthesis of style (the diction and syntax signaling a significant revelation—not just "A universally acknowledged truth is" but the more sententious "It is a truth universally acknowledged"), tone (the irony signaled in part by the anticlimax of this specific revelation), and values (marriage is all about money and the critique of that view).

I then begin to supplement Bakhtin with Booth by asking about the consciousness behind the construction of the double-voiced discourse, the designer who chooses to open her novel this way. In other words, I introduce Booth's concept of the implied author and suggest that the implied Austen is at the top of the Bakhtinian hierarchy of voices. Although many impressive mansions could have been built and furnished from the trees sacrificed to debates about the necessity and efficacy of Booth's concept, I delve into the details of those debates only at the graduate level.[1] With undergraduates, I find it more productive to offer a clear definition and an illuminating example. I define the concept as the streamlined version of the author's actual or purported self that the author inevitably communicates in constructing the narrative. I then illustrate the concept by asking the group to discuss the relation between their self-understandings and the versions of themselves they construct in various online environments such as *Facebook* or *MySpace*. Students soon recognize that their profiles in these environments imply not just streamlined but also idealized versions of themselves. Often the students will also point out that some people construct false versions of themselves. This observation can lead to a useful discussion of how the concept of the implied author can illuminate the phenomenon of hoaxes and vice versa. In a hoax such as Konrad Kujau's forgery of the Hitler diaries, the actual author constructs an implied self purporting to be a streamlined version of some other person, and the hoax will succeed only as long as the gap between actual and implied author remains unknown.

This discussion supplies a link to the concept of distance. Here I ask the students to help me develop two lists: pairs of narrative agents (of either the transmission or the action) between whom the question of distance matters and kinds of distance. In addition to actual and implied author, the first list will include implied authors and narrators, implied authors and characters, narrators and characters, and all of these agents and audiences. The second list will include the following kinds of distance: spatial, temporal, intellectual, emotional, physical, psychological, ideological, and ethical. I stress that different narratives will make different relationships and different kinds of distance more or less salient. As we loop back to *Pride and Prejudice*, we note the proximity of implied author and narrator (for example, both figures intend the double voicing of the first sentence), the relative closeness between both of them and Mr. Bennet in the first chapter, and the relative distance between them and Mrs. Bennet. If time allows, we look at other kinds of distance and other pairs of agents.

The concept of distance in turn leads to the question of audience. One way to highlight the importance of asking, Who listens? is to ask, From whose perspective are we making these judgments of ideological distance? If Mrs. Bennet were to read the first chapter, would she reach the same conclusions? Students often believe that readers should have a lot of interpretive freedom, and I seek both to reinforce that belief and to complicate it. I suggest that if we can agree that Mrs. Bennet would hear only the literal meaning of the first sentence, then we can distinguish between Austen's hypothetical ideal audience that hears that double voicing—what Rabinowitz calls the authorial audience—and members of an *actual* or flesh-and-blood audience that may not. Furthermore, the very question about Mrs. Bennet as potential audience points toward another audience, one that takes up an observer position in the storyworld and responds to the characters as if they were real people. Rabinowitz calls this position the narrative audience and points out that it is crucial to our affective responses to narrative.

Following Rabinowitz, I stress that both the authorial audience and the narrative audience are roles that actual readers can choose to take on. We have the interpretive freedom not to take on these roles—if we want to read Austen's first sentence as Mrs. Bennet would, we can do so—but sometimes we can choose to surrender some of our interpretive freedom by entering the authorial audience. We typically make such a choice when we believe the experience of being guided by the implied author will yield an experience at least as valuable as the one we are likely to have without attending to that guidance. Furthermore, once we have experienced the narrative from within the authorial audience, we should complete our act of reading by evaluating that experience.

By emphasizing that the authorial and narrative audiences are roles that actual readers may choose to take on, I distinguish them from the textual audience implicitly or explicitly addressed by the narrator, what Gerald Prince has called the narratee. As Prince notes, the narratee can be more or less characterized. Students will recognize the narratee of *Pride and Prejudice* as minimally characterized (he or she has no name, occupation, or identifiable gender, for example), but they can learn more about both that minimal characterization and the theoretical concept by considering what the narratee does and does not know before the narrative begins. Items in the first category include both the narrator and the characters, and items in the second include the class structure and social mores of British society at the time of the action as well as the geography of England.

With these ideas of audience in place, I loop back to the first chapter and our brief sketch of the ideological hierarchy among its voices. In the course of teasing Mrs. Bennet about her expectation that Mr. Bingley, the single man of large fortune, will marry one of their five daughters, Mr. Bennet says that he will write and let Mr. Bingley know that he can marry any one he wishes, "though I must throw in a good word for my little Lizzy" (4). If time allows, students can have a profitable discussion of how the authorial audience knows that Mr. Bennet is not being ironic about his special affection for Elizabeth. The larger point is that Mr. Bennet's remarks have the potential to add another voice to the top of the hierarchy, Elizabeth's, a potential that soon gets realized by Elizabeth's own playfully ironic utterances.

A productive next move is to ask the students, either in discussion or in a short writing assignment, to trace the evolution of the relationships among the voices of the narrator, Mr. Bennet, and Elizabeth over the course of the novel. The loop here is to another aspect of Bakhtin's concept of dialogism, the overall orchestration of the interrelationship of voices throughout a narrative. There are many scenes to draw on, but especially significant developments include the strong reinforcement of the three-way alignment when Elizabeth rejects Mr. Collins's marriage proposal and Mr. Bennet wittily supports her; the introduction of significant ideological distance between Elizabeth and the narrator on one side and her father on the other, when she unsuccessfully tries to persuade him to reject Lydia's request to accompany the regiment to Brighton; and the narrowing of that gap in the final stages of the novel, even as those stages portray a new and stronger alignment among Elizabeth, the narrator, and Mr. Darcy.

All this analysis establishes good ground from which to consider the implicit claims to authority advanced by Austen and her narrator. Returning to the narrator's statements in the first chapter—from the double-voiced opening to the unironic summary of Mr. and Mrs. Bennet's characters at the end—helps establish that both author and narrator claim a great deal of authority. Lanser's work offers a helpful way to understand those claims. Lanser proposes one fundamental distinction based on the relation between narrator and narratee and then a taxonomy of three kinds of voice. A narrator who addresses a narratee external to the storyworld uses a public voice, while a narrator who addresses a narratee internal to the storyworld uses a private voice. An authorial voice is public and heterodiegetic; a personal voice may be public or private, but it will always be homodiegetic; a communal voice may also be public or private, and it belongs either to a spokesperson for a group or to a group who collaborates in the narration. Authority arises out of both the rhetorical and social properties of the specific deployments of these voices. Austen's narrator speaks with an authorial voice that makes an explicit claim for authority. That Austen adopts this voice in the early nineteenth century, when women had less power in the social hierarchy than men, helps underline the boldness of her claim. That boldness is also enhanced because the first sentence is what Lanser calls an extrarepresentational statement—that is, the expression of a maxim that applies beyond the particular situation of the narrative to the wider world—and an ironic one at that. By claiming so much authority, Austen is in effect adopting a "high risk, high reward" strategy. The greater the claim she makes in a situation in which she is lower in the hierarchy, the more likely that claim will be resisted. But if she overcomes that resistance, her assertion of authority is all the more impressive.

All this work establishes the ground for writing prompts, asking students to investigate other dimensions of Austen's deployments of voice. Here's one example:

> Analyze the hierarchy among the voices of the narrator, Elizabeth, and Darcy during the two proposal scenes. For each scene, identify the salient features of the characters' voices, the dialogic relations between them, the authorial audience's assessments of them, and the overall communication the implied Austen seeks to make.

"My Oedipus Complex": Voice, Vision, Unreliability, and Ethics

The first sentence of "My Oedipus Complex" illustrates the value of Genette's insight that the term *point of view* conflates the concept of voice (Who speaks or tells?) and the concept of vision (Who sees or perceives?). Students can easily recognize that the voice belongs to a mature figure engaging in retrospection and that the vision belongs to that figure's childhood self. I continue with Genette's unpacking of *point of view* by describing what I call the diegetic family tree, with its criss-crossing branches of narrative level and participation in the action. The level at which the main action takes place is the diegetic; narration at that level (e.g., Darcy's letter to Elizabeth) is intradiegetic; narration above (about) that level (e.g., from Austen's narrator to the narratee) is extradiegetic; and narration embedded within the diegetic level (a character narrating a story told by a different character) is hypodiegetic. When narrators are participants in the actions they tell about, they are homodiegetic. When they are not participants in that action, they are heterodiegetic. Thus, different combinations of participation and level are possible: Austen's narrator is heterodiegetic-extradiegetic, while O'Connor's narrator's clear retrospection marks him as homodiegetic-extradiegetic. A character who narrates a story about others (e.g., any of Chaucer's pilgrims) is heterodiegetic-intradiegetic, while one who narrates a story about oneself (e.g., the Man of the Hill in *Tom Jones*) is homodiegetic-intradiegetic.

We then return to O'Connor's first sentence—and more specifically to its final clause, "what I saw did not worry me"—to consider the relation between Genette's structuralist separation of voice and vision and the rhetorical conception of voice. While Genette would emphasize that intriguing split between the voice of the mature character narrator and the vision of his childhood self, the Bakhtin-inflected rhetorical conception would include that vision in its description of the voice because that vision conveys some of the utterance's implicit values. More generally, the rhetorical approach would describe the clause as a triple-voiced utterance containing a dialogue among the assertion of no worry in the mature narrator's diction and syntax; the confident tone attached to the child's vision; and the implied O'Connor's orchestration of the comic interplay between the assertion, the tone, and an alternative view that the first two voices are heavily influenced by the Oedipus complex.

The larger theoretical point is that the rhetorical conception endorses Genette's unpacking of the term *point of view* but then transforms his insight by noting that sometimes vision can be an element of voice. This finding has the potential to open up a broader discussion about the interrelations among different approaches to narrative in general and voice in particular. At the graduate level, I would add a layer to this discussion by bringing in F. K. Stanzel's taxonomy of authorial, figural, and first-person narration (e.g., *Middlemarch*, *The Ambassadors*, and "My Oedipus Complex" respectively) that cannot be simply mapped onto either Genette's approach (figural narration joins together what Genette has torn asunder—vision and voice) or the rhetorical approach (which finds Bakhtin's emphasis on the link between language and ideology more important than Stanzel does). In this discussion, the teacher has to decide whether to take sides or to lay out the differences and let the students choose—or indeed do both. My strategy is a version of that third option. In case there's any lingering doubt, I confess to being a partisan for the rhetorical conception, but I stress that the students need not share my partisanship. Instead I ask them to examine the principles and consequences of the conception and then decide whether to accept, reject, or revise it.

The voice loop is now ready to engage with that subset of double-voiced discourse called unreliable narration by returning to such textual voices as these:

> I got up and sat on the floor and played—for hours, it seemed to me. Then I got my chair and looked out the attic window for more hours. (288)

> Every time I had pointed out to her [Mother] the waste of making two beds when we could both sleep in one, she had told me it was healthier like that, and now here was this man, this stranger, sleeping with her without the least regard for her health! (287)

> And there stood Mother in her nightdress, looking as if her heart was broken between us. I hoped she felt as she looked. It seemed to me that she deserved it all. (289)

In each passage, we have one text, two tellers (Larry and the implied O'Connor), two main audiences (the narratee and the authorial audience), and two different purposes (Larry's and the implied O'Connor's). The success of the double voicing depends on the implied O'Connor's ability to use Larry's direct communication to the narratee as the means to communicate something quite different to the authorial audience.[2] With the first passage, once Larry reports a few sentences later that he wakes up his parents when he goes to join them in their bed, the implied O'Connor signals that Larry's "hours" and "hours" are actually minutes and seconds and thus that Larry *misreports* what happens. In the second passage, Larry reports the events accurately—his mother and father are sleeping together—but the implied O'Connor draws on the gap between the child's ignorance about adult sexuality and his authorial audience's understanding of it and of the Oedipus complex to communicate that Larry comically *misreads* or *misinterprets* the events. In the third passage, the implied O'Connor uses Larry's reliable reading of his mother's emotional state as the ground from which to communicate that Larry *misregards* or *misevaluates* his mother in judging her as deserving to have her heart broken.

These cases also invite a discussion about the possible connections and overlaps of these types of unreliability. Is Larry simply misreporting minutes as hours, or is he misinterpreting the duration of his delay before going to his parents' room? Or is it better to describe the first case as Larry misreporting because he is misreading? Similarly, the better way to describe the third case is that Larry misregards because his Oedipus complex leads him to misread the situation as one in which his mother must choose between him and his father. The larger point here again is that theory needs to follow narrative practice: distinguishing among kinds of unreliability does not mean that any unreliable utterance must be a pure example of only one kind.

I return to the third passage and bring in another short story with an unreliable character narrator such as Poe's "The Cask of Amontillado." When Poe's narrator Montresor begins by saying, "The thousand injuries of Fortunato I had borne as I best could; but when he ventured upon insult, I vowed revenge," the effect is to maximize the ethical distance between him and the authorial audience (848). Montresor's moral reasoning is simultaneously perverse and chilling: it ranks insult not only as worse than injury (personal pride seems to be his supreme value) but as warranting revenge—which for him means murder. By contrast, when Larry says that he thinks his mother deserved to have her heart broken, the authorial audience remains sympathetic to him because, as noted above, it recognizes that the misregarding follows from his oedipally induced misreadings. Moreover, the effect of Larry's misreadings is to close the affective distance between Larry and the authorial audience. This contrast between Montresor's and Larry's misregarding points to a wider spectrum of unreliability's possible effects on the relation between the narrator and the authorial audience. At Montresor's end of the spectrum, we have estranging unreliability, which increases one or more kinds of distance, and at Larry's end we have bonding unreliability, which decreases one or more kinds of distance.[3]

Since one kind of bonding or estranging can be ethical, this distinction provides a segue to a discussion of the ethical dimension of voice. (For a fuller discussion of teaching narrative ethics, see Adam Zachary Newton's essay in this volume.) Since the distinction calls attention to the connections between unreliability and ethical distance, it helps establish the point that both characters' actions and authorial and narratorial tellings have an ethical dimension. In other words, the ethical dimension of narrative involves both an ethics of the told and an ethics of the telling. More generally, that ethical dimension arises from the dynamic interaction among four ethical positions: that of the characters (the ethics of the told); that of the narrator in relation to the characters and to the narratee (part 1 of the ethics of the telling); that of the implied author in relation to the narrator, the characters, and the authorial audience (part 2 of the ethics of the telling); and that of the actual audience in relation to the values operating in the first three positions.

Again it is helpful to turn to textual voices:

> At teatime, "talking to Daddy" began again, complicated this time by the fact that he had an evening paper, and every few minutes he put it down and told Mother something new out of it. I felt this was foul play. Man for man, I was prepared to compete with him any time for Mother's attention, but when he had it all made up for him by other people it left me no chance. (285)

The passage shows the interaction between the ethics of the told and the ethics of the telling, since Larry unreliably claims that his father is cheating in the competition for his mother's attention. I ask the students to identify the various misreadings in Larry's narration (is there actually a competition? what is the authorial audience's understanding of his father's motives for sharing the news with Larry's mother?); the way those misreadings influence his misregarding of his father; the ethics of Larry's relation to the narratee, especially Larry's assumption that the narratee will share his readings and regardings; and the ethics of the implied O'Connor's management of all that communication. Does the implied author use the passage to guide the authorial audience to bond with or become estranged from Larry? What are the ethical values underlying the implied O'Connor's communication to his authorial audience? How do you as an individual reader respond to the interaction among the other three ethical positions? Why?

We then make two more turns in the voice loop by returning to *Pride and Prejudice* to analyze its ethical dimension and by drawing on our work on authority in Austen to analyze authority in "My Oedipus Complex." One worthwhile issue for the discussion of *Pride and Prejudice* is the ethics of the implied Austen's treatment of Mrs. Bennet. Should the implied Austen be faulted for inviting the authorial audience to take such a superior attitude toward her? Or does the implied Austen eventually guide us to view Mrs. Bennet more sympathetically? If so, what does that do to our understanding of the double voicing of the first sentence? With authority in "My Oedipus Complex," one worthwhile issue involves the gap between Larry's lack of authority, stemming from his unreliability, and the implied O'Connor's indirect but powerful claim of authority both in his double voicing of Larry's narration and in his appropriation of Freud for humorous purposes. Would we view O'Connor's authority differently if he were not Frank but Frances O'Connor?

The discussion of "My Oedipus Complex" sets up two kinds of writing assignments, the first of which asks the students to do more analysis of the story itself. Here is one possible prompt:

> In the story's conclusion, Larry reports that he and his father bond against his mother's preoccupation with her new child Sonny. How does Larry's unreliability shift in this part of the story, how does that shift affect the ethics of the telling, and what larger effects does that shift produce?

The second kind of assignment asks students to engage with the story's voices in a different way:

> Retell a segment of the story in the voice of Larry's mother or Larry's father and make that voice occasionally unreliable. Add a short analysis of your retelling, explaining the relation between your deployment of voice and your narrative purposes.

Putting Other Voices in the Loop

If time in the classroom allows what space in this essay forbids, one can add other texts and theoretical concepts to the voice loop. Especially noteworthy theoretical concepts include the following: Robyn Warhol's explorations of engaging and distancing direct address by heterodiegetic narrators to their narratees in the nineteenth-century British novel, and her finding that female writers tend to use engaging addresses while male writers tend to use distancing ones; Alison Case's demonstrations of the relation between a narrator's control of a narrative's design and gender in the eighteenth- and nineteenth-century British novel (narrators without such control, whether male or female, are marked as feminine); Brian Richardson's analyses of what he calls "unnatural voices," including "we" narration and second-person narration.

More generally, I find that teaching voice makes me self-conscious about the ethics of my own effort to orchestrate the play of voices among narratives, theories, students, and me. I have learned from experience that I am a better teacher of voice when I make sure that the utterance "I do" is only sometimes the answer to the question, Who speaks in your classroom? but always the answer to the question, Who listens?

Notes

1. The key issues are whether the concept equivocates between designating a global textual effect and an agent who constructs the text and whether it is an unnecessary synonym for the actual author. My position is that the concept designates an agent and adds precision to an account of narrative communication. For more on the debate, see Chatman; Genette (*Revisited*); Nünning; and Phelan (*Living*).

2. For an alternative to this way of describing unreliability, see Nünning.

3. For more on this distinction, including a discussion of six subtypes of bonding unreliability, see Phelan ("Estranging").

Works Cited

Austen, Jane. *Pride and Prejudice.* 1813. New York: Oxford UP, 1988. Print.

Bakhtin, Mikhail M. *The Dialogic Imagination: Four Essays by M. M. Bakhtin.* Ed. Michael Holquist. Trans. Caryl Emerson and Holquist. Austin: U of Texas P, 1981. Print.

Booth, Wayne C. *The Rhetoric of Fiction.* 2nd ed. Chicago: U of Chicago P, 1983. Print.

Case, Alison. *Plotting Women.* Charlottesville: UP of Virginia, 1999. Print.

Chatman, Seymour. "In Defense of the Implied Author." *Coming to Terms.* Ithaca: Cornell UP, 1990. 74–89. Print.

Genette, Gérard. *Narrative Discourse.* Trans. Jane E. Lewin. Ithaca: Cornell UP, 1981. Print.

———. *Narrative Discourse Revisited.* Trans. Jane E. Lewin. Ithaca: Cornell UP, 1988. Print.

Lanser, Susan S. *Fictions of Authority.* Ithaca: Cornell UP, 1992. Print.

Nünning, Ansgar. "Reconceptualizing Unreliable Narration: Synthesizing Cognitive and Rhetorical Approaches." *A Companion to Narrative Theory.* Ed. James Phelan and Peter J. Rabinowitz. Oxford: Blackwell, 2005. 89–107. Print.

O'Connor, Frank. "My Oedipus Complex." *Collected Stories.* New York: Knopf, 1981. 282–92. Print.

Phelan, James. "Estranging Unreliability, Bonding Unreliability, and the Ethics of *Lolita.*" *Narrative* 15 (2007): 222–38. Print.

———. *Living to Tell about It.* Ithaca: Cornell UP, 2005. Print.

Poe, Edgar Allan. "The Cask of Amontillado." *Poetry, Tales, and Selected Essays.* By Poe. Notes by Patrick Quinn and G. R. Thompson. New York: Lib. of Amer., 1996. 848–54. Print.

Prince, Gerald. "Introduction a l'étude du narrataire." *Poétique* 14 (1973): 178–96. Print.

Rabinowitz, Peter J. "Truth in Fiction: A Re-examination of Audiences." *Critical Inquiry* 4 (1976): 121–41. Print.

Richardson, Brian. *Unnatural Voices: Extreme Narration in Modern and Contemporary Fiction.* Columbus: Ohio State UP, 2006. Print.

Stanzel, F. K. *Narrative Situations in the Novel.* Trans. James P. Pusack. Bloomington: Indiana UP, 1971. Print.

Warhol, Robyn. *Gendered Interventions.* New Brunswick: Rutgers UP, 1989. Print.

Further Reading

Cohn, Dorrit. *Transparent Minds: Narrative Modes for Representing Consciousness in Fiction.* Princeton: Princeton UP, 1978. Print.

Grice, H. P. *Studies in the Way of Words.* Cambridge: Harvard UP, 1989. Print.

Kindt, Tom, and Harold Müller. *The Implied Author: Concept and Controversy.* Berlin: de Gruyter, 2006. Print.

Lanser, Susan S. "The 'I' of the Beholder: (Non)Narrative Attachments and Other Equivocal Acts." *A Companion to Narrative Theory.* Ed. James Phelan and Peter J. Rabinowitz. Oxford: Blackwell, 2005. 206–19. Print.

Rabinowitz, Peter J. *Before Reading: Narrative Conventions and the Politics of Interpretation.* 1987. Columbus: Ohio State UP, 1998. Print.

Zunshine, Lisa. *Why We Read Fiction: Theory of Mind and the Novel.* Columbus: Ohio State UP, 2006. Print.

Jesse Matz

Perspective

Middlemarch looks askance at Mr. Casaubon, but in chapter 10, George Eliot's narrator suggests seeing things from his vantage point: "Suppose we turn from outside estimates of a man to wonder, with keener interest, what is the report of his own consciousness of his doings or capacity?" (84). Shifting to Casaubon, Eliot stresses how much depends on perspective: truth varies according to it, sympathy follows from it, and real ethical insight relies on it. Henry James, who held that the "house of fiction" must have many windows if its prospects are to be truly advantageous (*Art of the Novel* 46), cultivated limited perspective to achieve the psychological precision (the "personal, distinct impression") that has become central to novelistic individuality ("Art of Fiction" 170). James's successors have further cultivated *multiple* perspectives to explore the relativity of human understanding, even to make narrative fiction model communal interests; hence Erich Auerbach's famous study of Virginia Woolf's perspectivalism in *To the Lighthouse*, where "the reflection of multiple consciousness" amounts to a model for democratic progress (Auerbach 549).

A sketch of these early theories can help raise fundamental questions about perspective: Why and how do writers try for different points of view? What are the perspectival choices available to them and how do those choices enrich fiction, enhance human insight, and enable ethical understanding? Perhaps the best first question pertains to certain funda-mental expectations students bring to literary study: If we value literature for its power to show us other points of view, how do we account for that power and its effects?

Because the basic theoretical language on perspective has long been part of the vernacular, students may arrive ready to make rudimentary distinctions between third- and first-person narration, between showing and telling, omniscient and limited points of view, single and multiple per-spectives. How to handle that conversation and where to go next depend on the nature and level of the course. Any treatment of the theory of perspective should ultimately center on focalization, the concept that now dominates narrative theory on this subject. But an undergraduate course might lead slowly to focalization and end there, whereas more advanced courses and graduate seminars might get to it immediately and then spend more time on controversies surrounding the concept and further ques-tions about historical contexts, politics, psychology, and new-media ap-plications. The approach will also vary depending on the focus and subject of the course. What follows here is a guide to teaching perspective in un-dergraduate classes generally dedicated to the study of narrative—classes in which perspective would be a discrete topic taking up about one week's attention. But because other kinds of classes—not just more advanced or graduate classes but those geared toward particular writers, genres, or thematic concerns—might take different views of perspective, I also indi-cate ways to condense or expand, to hone or diversify your approach as circumstances demand.

I try to dramatize the importance of perspective by stressing how one's position relative to information conditions perception and understanding. I therefore cover those theories that best expose the effects of narrative's sight situations—or, more precisely, perception situations—on its claims to insight. And I survey those theories (rather than choosing one or two) because perspective, even now, is an open field of inquiry. Even if most theorists now use the term *focalization* to refer to narrative's perception situations, there is still no consensus about that term's exact definition or proper scope. Since the chance to make a vital new contribution might inspire students, I like to survey the unfinished development from early work on perspective to later structuralist accounts of focalization and on to still more recent attempts to talk about the way a story's views shape its meaning.

Theories about Point of View

Rudimentary distinctions in the undergraduate classroom might benefit from reference to *Understanding Fiction,* by Cleanth Brooks and Robert Penn Warren. Time permitting, students might be asked to read the book's two short sections on perspective and point of view (145–50, 659–64) along with the two examples: Ring Lardner's "Haircut" and William Faulkner's "A Rose for Emily." Brooks and Warren discuss differences between first- and third-person narrators who are internal or external to stories and who are given either to analysis or to simpler observation; they also usefully predict the turn to focalization with their theory of the "focus of narration" ("who sees the story," as distinct from who tells it or who is its main character [659]).

With these fundamentals on the table, I turn to short stories that thematize perspective. (More advanced courses might simply begin with such texts.) I use some of the stories in *The Scribner Anthology of Contemporary Short Fiction*—an appealing, flexible companion to any general course in narrative theory (Williford and Martone). As I indicate below, many of the anthology's entries—including Joyce Carol Oates's "Ghost Girls" and Annie Proulx's "Brokeback Mountain"—usefully illustrate different perspectival dynamics. But I focus on one profoundly metaperspectival story: "Sarah Cole: A Type of Love Story," by Russell Banks.

Banks's narrator shifts between first- and third-person perspectives, explicitly discussing and even theorizing his use for each. He tells a story in which he himself is the protagonist—a story about his cruel treatment of a woman he loved but also loathed for her extreme ugliness. Because he regrets his cruelty and because he does not truly understand what motivated it, he tries to tell his story from a third-person perspective: "a man enters a bar," he tells us; "call him Ronald," he continues, and then he goes on to narrate the story objectively (54). He tells us why: "I'm telling it this way because what I have to tell you now confuses me, embarrasses me, and makes me sad, and consequently, I'm likely to tell it falsely" (59). The story vacillates between third- and first-person perspectives, until it ends in a starkly distant description of the narrator's most regrettable act. The point, it seems, is that third-person narration enables neutrality and objectivity and, therefore, better accuracy and understanding. Had the narrator told his story from a first-person point of view, he would have lost himself in emotional confusion; speaking objectively, he is able to construct a rational, complete, precise account. But of course this distinction is incomplete. In the end, rational precision is the problem, for it repeats the detachment that made the narrator behave badly. What then are the uses and effects of these different narratorial perspectives? How does Banks's story finally dramatize the special reasons for each? What might have been other alternatives? Any attempt to answer these questions quickly proves that the term *persons* only gets us so far and that more is needed to explain what Banks's perspectival shifts do for his protagonist's progress toward recognition.

Norman Friedman's "Point of View in Fiction" offers explanations and categories that take things to the next level, whether students read the article or you present Friedman's terms in a handout. Assigning the article can help students get the benefit of Friedman's useful summary of the critical heritage: graduate students in particular might be glad for the preliminary discussion of contributions by Henry James, Percy Lubbock, Mark Schorer, and others. Friedman arrays perspectival modes according to their "progress toward direct presentation" (124), from "telling" to "showing," or according to their degree of "objectification." He distinguishes the following points of view: editorial omniscience, neutral omniscience, "I" as witness, "I" as protagonist, multiple selective omniscience, selective omniscience, the dramatic mode, and the camera (118–31). The "camera" point of view presents things most fully, directly, and with most neutral immediacy; "editorial omniscience" removes narration to the furthest degree of detached, speculative telling. "Persons" are still involved, but they are sidelined in favor of a more systematic progression of possible relationships between subject and object of narration.

Which of these categories best describes Banks's narrator? What combination best explains his variations, and how might Friedman's terms help us recognize the value of his perspectival complexities?

Students might find that Banks uses each of Friedman's styles, exploiting the potential insight of each as he tries for full understanding of his conduct and its consequences. Anchored mainly in the I as protagonist, he sometimes gives us the camera's immediacy and sometimes puts on editorial omniscience, depending on the ethical, psychological, or perceptual problems he faces. Perhaps he only neglects multiple selective omniscience, not taking his lover's point of view—a blindness that is in fact the story's key motivation. If students can say when and why Banks's narrator takes up each of Friedman's positions, they might develop an important first theoretical appreciation for the difference perspectives can make.

Limitations will emerge as well. Still restricted by *persons* and the inadequate distinction between *showing* and *telling*, Friedman's typology fails to account for some of Banks's crucial motivations and effects. For example, Friedman's categories do not help us talk about the distance between Banks's narrator's current and former selves, which has much to do with the story's overall point of view. Because such problems are symptomatic of the limitations that demanded the innovation of focalization theory and its related analytic terms, they are worth stressing; they will enable students to appreciate the difference narrative theory has made and the way its terms enable us to reckon with fiction's more complex associations of perspective and perception.

Wayne C. Booth's *The Rhetoric of Fiction*

Key advances begin in Wayne C. Booth's *The Rhetoric of Fiction*. Booth was one of the first to note the inadequacies in standard accounts of point of view, to decenter distinctions by person, and to consider the way relations among perspectives within a text might construct a larger perspectival effect. Booth stresses the importance of the degrees to which narrators are dramatized or undramatized, self-conscious or unaware, privileged or limited. His chapter, "Types of Narration" (149–65), is well worth assigning for its incisive explanations of these and other distinctions. Each helps substantially toward an understanding of perspectival choices like those Banks has made. Banks's narrator heavily dramatizes his perspective and is quite self-conscious but labors to convert his limitations into perceptual privilege. Moreover, the severe limitations of his past self account for much of the story's moral point, creating the opportunity to discuss the notorious ethical and aesthetic advantages of strictly limited perspectives. The effects of unreliable narration, although mainly a matter of "voice" (see James Phelan's essay in this volume), can come up here, as well as the peculiar benefit of the restricted points of view enabled by perceptually narrow protagonists—children, for example, as in Oates's "Ghost Girls," which might provide a useful comparison at this point.

Booth also stresses the effects of distance: distinguishing among the variations of distance that separate narrator from author, reader, and other characters in the story (156–59), Booth goes a long way toward explaining the way relationships within a narrative compose its point of view (again see Phelan's chapter for distance in relation to voice). In Banks's case, the great gaps between the protagonist and the story's authorial perspective, between the protagonist as narrator and as character, between him and the object of his affection as well as the gap between him and the perceived norms of his audience all contribute to the story's overall viewpoint and its unique take on the information central to it. Booth's identification of these distances proves that perspective concerns a whole array of locations and not just the concern of the person who sees the story's events.

Booth's characteristic evaluation of the ethics of perspectival modes is also critical. Booth notes that critics have tended to favor impersonal narration—the kind with no apparent perspective or the kind that radically locates its source of information in the point of view of one or more characters. We have tended to think that these styles are more artful and more realistic, he notes, and we therefore forget that their "objectivity" creates a problematic moral vacuum. Without authorial points of view to guide us, without explicit or implicit evaluations of character-based perspectives, a story might devolve into "confusion and unintentional ambiguity" (377). Inversely, proper "sympathy" depends on strict and authoritative perspectival "control" (243–66). Here we arrive at a central question: Do certain perspectival choices necessarily entail certain ethical results, and do they conduce directly to better human judgment? Are omniscient narrators more or less ethical—more or less artful? Are strictly fixed, limited points of view more realistic? In the case of Banks's narrator, for example, does ethical evaluation falter when impersonal objectivity takes over, despite the narrator's hope to achieve better understanding through that mode? When he self-consciously adopts a subjective, first-person point of view, does he lose the benefit of objective evaluation or gain the benefit of experiential truth? And which mode feels most real, or most pleasurably artistic? Should Banks himself make his evaluations more explicit? Booth's critique of the ethics of impersonality affords the opportunity to explore the links between formal technique and the ethical dimension of fiction.

Booth also notes that perspective is as much about depth as position. A point of view limited to a particular character's perceptions varies considerably depending on the depth of the plunge into them. If asked when perspectives are deepest, students might respond that the most subjective narrations have the greatest depth, but in fact depth is often the luxury of third-person objectivity, for it depends less on the particular perspective taken than on the narration's approach to the representation of consciousness. Modes of representing consciousness vary widely; "interior" perspectives cut across distinctions of "person." Moreover, they range from deliberate self-narrations to inchoate streams of consciousness.

Dorrit Cohn's Account of Representations of Consciousness

Dorrit Cohn's survey of the "modes for representing consciousness in fiction" abandons "stream of consciousness" and related designations for terminology that better accounts for the diverse narrative situations in which fiction locates its perspectives in the human mind. Cohn distinguishes three third-person modes: "psychonarration," "quoted monologue," and "narrated monologue." In first-person narration she identifies "autonomous monologue," "retrospective" techniques, and combinations of narration and monologue. These are also largely distinctions of "voice," but they make it clear that the extreme, restricted perspective of the individual mind may involve an array of subtly different perspectives—some that proceed from just a part of the self (immediate feeling, for example, without rational judgment), some that combine authorial and character-based modes, and some that mix past and present selves (11–14). The relevance to a story like "Sarah Cole" is clear: Banks's first-person perspective sometimes involves retrospective techniques, and only once we distinguish retrospective and present representations of consciousness can we appreciate the degree to which "dissonance" between them generates the message of the story.

"Narrated monologue" is Cohn's term for free indirect discourse (FID), another mixed mode worthy of special attention in this context (see 143–265). Combining a character's thoughts with the objective, omniscient voice of a third-person narrator, this mode has drawn a great deal of theoretical attention for the way it involves both experiential immediacy and evaluative distance, often with the effect of dissonance and irony. Banks makes some use of free indirect discourse—when, for example, his protagonist considers Sarah Cole's ugliness and "wonders about her husband" (57). "What kind of man would fall in love with Sarah Cole?": this question is spoken by the narrator-protagonist but thought by his past self. The statement combines two different perspectives, laying bare the character's subjective consciousness while also implying an objective judgment of his arrogance. But because this example is complicated by the first-person context (FID appears more typically in third-person narrative) it would be best to give another example—perhaps a classic one from chapter 36 of *Pride and Prejudice*, which features Elizabeth Bennet's self-reproaches upon reading Darcy's letter. For advanced students, Brian McHale's article on the subject is helpful not only for its survey of theories of FID but also for its clarifications of the style's implications for perspective specifically. McHale's concluding pages on the various possible "naturalizations" of FID—the reasons for it, implied by writers and imputed by readers—chart the different points of view that this style can entail. Irony and empathy, stream-of-consciousness through third-person narration, and polyvocality are the motivations that make FID a matter of perspectival complexity (274–81).

Study of mixed perspectives presents a good opportunity to think about texts that take multiple points of view. "Sarah Cole: A Type of Love Story" decidedly does not: we never see things from Sarah's point of view, and you might ask students how the story would be different had Banks divided his narration between his characters (rather than between the past and present selves of his narrator-protagonist). To dramatize alternative possibilities, discuss the effect of changing perspectives in Annie Proulx's "Brokeback Mountain," which focuses mainly on the elegiac recollections of one character but momentarily shifts to represent the love he has lost from the point of view of the character who vainly felt it for him. Consider having the class turn to a film for a striking example of the technique taken to extremes: Mike Figgis's *Timecode* presents many perspectives at once on a split screen, so that the viewer experiences the film's climactic moment as a truly collective event. Advanced students might read the first forty pages of *To the Lighthouse*, along with the last chapter of Auerbach's *Mimesis*, which is still the most powerful appreciation of the various perspectives writers like Woolf dramatize through shifting representations of consciousness. These examples get to the essence of the question: perhaps more than any other style of narration, the use of multiple perspectives stresses the strong connection between angles of vision and beliefs about what is true and therefore best exemplifies the interconnection between point of view and values.

The Concept of Focalization

By this point, students may have raised questions about a certain confusion in these approaches to perspective. In the Banks story, for example, we have a narrator who tells the story and a character who takes part in it—the present and past selves of Banks's protagonist. Should there not be some categorical distinction between the perspective of the one who "speaks" the story and that of the one who "sees" it? And indeed the need for such a distinction has led to the critical turning point in the theory of perspective: the turn to focalization, first in Gérard Genette and then, in subsequent elaborations and complications, Mieke Bal, Seymour Chatman, and others. One useful way into a first discussion of focalization, beyond the initial observation of the need to distinguish between "who sees" (or perceives) and "who speaks" (or tells) is F. K. Stanzel's theory of the *reflector*. In his discussion of the "figural narrative situation"—that which narrates through the point of view of a character—Stanzel makes a pertinent distinction between the mediating voice of any narration and the point of view that voice mediates (186–200). Alternatively, you might have advanced students begin by reading Wallace Martin's *Recent Theories of Narrative* for its survey of theories leading up to and through focalization (130–51), or James Phelan's critical sketch in *Living to Tell about It* (110–14).

Genette's watershed account of focalization begins with a useful summary of previous approaches to the subject of perspective and point of view. Genette then makes his crucial observation, in a statement well worth pausing over:

> [T]o my mind, most of the theoretical works on this subject . . . suffer from a regrettable confusion between what I here call *mood* and *voice*, a confusion between the question *who is the character whose point of view orients the narrative perspective?* and the very different question, *who is the narrator?*—or more simply, the question *who sees?* and the question *who speaks?* (186)

Focalization clears up this confusion by making "perspective" more exclusively a matter of "who sees." Genette distinguishes three kinds of focalization: "zero" focalization, the equivalent of "omniscient" narration, in which all is seen from the nonspecific (or, to cite William Nelles's helpful correction, "free" [81]) point of view of the external narrator; "internal" focalization, in which all is seen from the point of view of a character—whether a single character ("fixed" internal focalization), more than one ("variable"), or many characters presenting alternative views of the same objects and events ("multiple"); and "external" focalization, in which "the hero performs in front of us without us ever being allowed to know his thoughts and feelings" (190)—in other words, in which we are deprived of any insight into what the character perceives.

Perspective has always been confusing for the way it connotes both "point of view" and "opinion"—both the position from which one sees something and "how one sees it." By dealing more exclusively with the first aspect of perspective, focalization not only distinguishes between "who sees" and "who speaks" but also clears up this confusion between rigorously formal aspects of perspective and related concerns that are more essentially thematic. The advantages are clear if we consider the ways focalization clarifies the perspectives in play in "Sarah Cole: A Type of Love Story." The narrator's past self can only speculate about his lover's thoughts and feelings. Internal focalization limits the story's perspective and provides the misperceptions that, later, contrast so powerfully with the narrator-protagonist's ultimate ethical discoveries. But precisely because there is a difference between the past self's presumptions and the narrator's current understanding, there must not only be a categorical difference between what the past self "saw" and what the narrator now "says" but some way to distinguish between the modes of focalization at work in the story's different styles of narration. For when the narration shifts between "zero" and "internal" focalization, it creates a far subtler variation of its shifts between first- and third-person report. Critical attention to these subtle shifts in perspective allows students to contrast more incisively the narrator-protagonist's alternating forms of understanding.

Debates about Focalization

This very difference raises further questions about focalization—demanding further analysis and provoking certain challenges to the validity of the concept. Is Banks's narrator in fact the story's focalizer? Or must focalizers be characters, and, if so, does the term exclude too much of what happens in the production and interpretation of narrative discourse? And do Genette's terms yet confuse distinct aspects of a narrative's perspectival orientations?

Important critiques of focalization include those advanced by Bal, who criticizes Genette's confusion of "perspectival subject and object" and his failure to distinguish "focalization on" and "focalization through" (84); by Monika Fludernik, who questions the metaphor of "seeing" stories, noting that it seems especially inappropriate in cases of "zero focalization," since a narrator in an authorial position really "produces" rather than sees that which he or she speaks (345); and by Shlomith Rimmon-Kenan, whose broader approach restores ideological "facets" to purely perceptual focalizations (72–86). Surely Banks's narrator cannot be said to "see" anything;

surely his attitudes condition his viewpoints; and surely the lack of any distinction between focalization "on" and "through" Banks's protagonist only confuses and does not clarify the subtle variations of point of view accomplished in the telling of his story. It might not be possible, after all, to make a clean distinction between who sees and who speaks, even if theorists try for such distinctions in order to make *focalization* a more precisely serviceable term. As Phelan, following Genette, notes in his account (in this volume) of the way a Bakhtinian rhetorical model would preserve focalization while helpfully encouraging us to include vision in voice when interpreting what a narrator says, simple "vision" sometimes bespeaks narratorial complexity and cannot be purely optical.

At the same time, there has been a backlash against these critiques of Genette's original account—a backlash that accuses revisionist approaches of failing to respect the fundamental narratological distinction between "story" and "discourse." As Phelan puts it, some theorists, most prominently, Gerald Prince and Seymour Chatman,

> resist the idea that both characters and narrators can be focalizers because that idea violates the logic of the story/discourse distinction, which locates characters in story and narrators in discourse and stipulates that never the twain shall meet . . . that characters perceive, think, act, and feel but narrators only report. (*Living* 112)

Prince and Phelan debate the question of whether focalization ought to be restricted to "the perception of the narrated by . . . an entity in that narrated" (*Living* 74), Prince arguing that such restriction is essential and Phelan arguing that narrators can indeed be focalizers. For Prince, only the past self of Banks's narrator could be the story's focalizer. Phelan, who argues that narrators "perform acts of *perception* that ought to be called 'focalization'" ("Why" 52), would note that the narrator himself participates in the story's variable focalization and that the story's unique insights into the demands of human self-understanding in fact depend upon its particular "vision/voice relationships" ("Why" 59) and its shifts between the past and present focalizations.

Focalization might best be tested and evaluated through reference to the alternative scheme proposed by Chatman, who maintains that focalization confuses the very different functions performed by characters and narrators; "identifying the narrative process with that of focalization confuses fundamental narrative distinctions" ("Characters and Narrators" 195). "Only a character may be said to see" (197): this distinction leads Chatman to propose different terms. "Filter" and "slant" are his main categories, referring respectively to the character-based point of view within a story and the narratorial attitude external to it. Chatman persuasively argues that clarifications follow from his revision to Genette's terminology. Banks's story specifically works well with Chatman's approach, helping us see that Banks's narration is peculiar for the way it only selectively filters past events. Only when Banks's narrator needs to review those events does he filter them through the perceptions of his past self—and the relationship between his narratorial slant and his filtered narrative strikingly shows us how these two aspects of narration might align, part, and dialectically reshape each other.

Additional Questions

Further complexities emerge when we pursue the question of focalization beyond the realm of contemporary narrative fiction. The longer historical development of narrative perspective suggests that particular tendencies align with particular cultural needs and priorities (Watt); the varied developments featured in film and new-media narratives indicate that different narrative technologies very differently inflect points of view (Chatman, "Cinematic Narrator"; Gunning); and the motivations and effects of perspective as studied in psychology and other human sciences prove that narratorial points of view have real pragmatic purposes and results (Gerrig). Advanced students might pursue these further implications and approaches, but any group will benefit at least from a concluding sketch of them. Such conclusions proceed from some final questions about "Sarah Cole: A Type of Love Story": Were you to make a film of the story, how might you reproduce its perspectival structure, and what might you learn in the process about point of view in film? What seem to be the psychological—or even therapeutic—effects of the story's peculiar perspectives on the story's narrator, and to what extent do these effects translate into the reading experience? On the basis of those effects, can we draw any conclusions about the psychological effects of variations in narratorial perspective? Finally, does Banks's portrait of perspectival difference tell us anything about the use of narrative in contemporary culture? Does his version of perspectival complexity compare in telling ways to (for example) versions produced by Austen and Woolf?

If indeed students think they value literature for its other points of view, theories of perspective can enrich their fundamental interest in literary study. Discovering just how complex it is to "show other points of view," students not only enhance their appreciation of literary form but learn to question simple correlations between literary representations and ethical issues. Most important, they might cease to consider narrative a transparent window into the experience of others, registering more fully how the content of what is shown depends on the formal manner in which it is shown. Students who have long ago made such discoveries might find themselves energized to learn that no consensus currently unites scholars on these questions: as we have seen, the concept of focalization only incompletely satisfies narrative theorists, who are still searching for the best way to describe the perspectives our stories can take.

Works Cited

Auerbach, Erich. *Mimesis: The Representation of Reality in Western Literature.* 1946. Trans. Willard R. Trask. Princeton: Princeton UP, 1953. Print.

Austen, Jane. *Pride and Prejudice.* 1813. London: Penguin, 1972. Print.

Bal, Mieke. "Narration and Focalization." *On Storytelling: Essays in Narratology.* Sonoma: Polebridge, 1991. 75–108. Print.

Banks, Russell. "Sarah Cole: A Type of Love Story." Williford and Martone 53–72.

Booth, Wayne C. *The Rhetoric of Fiction.* Chicago: U of Chicago P, 1961. Print.

Braudy, Leo, and Marshall Cohen, eds. *Film Theory and Criticism: Introductory Readings.* New York: Oxford UP, 1999. Print.

Brooks, Cleanth, and Robert Penn Warren. *Understanding Fiction.* 2nd ed. Englewood Cliffs: Prentice, 1959. Print.

Chatman, Seymour. "Characters and Narrators: Filter, Center, Slant, and Interest-Focus." *Poetics Today* 7.2 (1986): 189–204. Print.

———. "The Cinematic Narrator." Braudy and Cohen 473–86.

Cohn, Dorrit. *Transparent Minds: Narrative Modes for Representing Consciousness in Fiction.* Princeton: Princeton UP, 1978. Print.

Eliot, George. *Middlemarch.* 1871–72. London: Penguin, 1994. Print.

Fludernik, Monika. *Towards a "Natural" Narratology.* London: Routledge, 1996. Print.

Friedman, Norman. "Point of View in Fiction: The Development of a Critical Concept." 1955. *The Theory of the Novel.* Ed. Philip Stevick. New York: Free, 1967. 109–37. Print.

Genette, Gérard. *Narrative Discourse: An Essay in Method.* Trans. Jane E. Lewin. Ithaca: Cornell UP, 1980. Print.

Gerrig, Richard. "Perspective as Participation." Peer and Chatman 303–24.

Gunning, Tom. "Narrative Discourse and the Narrator System." Braudy and Cohen 461–72.

James, Henry. "The Art of Fiction." 1884. *The Art of Criticism: Henry James on the Theory and Practice of Fiction.* Ed. William Veeder and Susan M. Griffin. Chicago: U of Chicago P, 1986. Print.

———. *The Art of the Novel: Critical Prefaces.* Ed. Richard P. Blackmur. New York: Scribner's, 1947. Print.

Martin, Wallace. *Recent Theories of Narrative.* Ithaca: Cornell UP, 1986. Print.

McHale, Brian. "Free Indirect Discourse: A Survey of Recent Accounts." *Poetics and Theory of Literature* 3 (1978): 249–88. Print.

Nelles, William. *Frameworks: Narrative Levels and Embedded Narrative.* New York: Lang, 1997. Print.

Oates, Joyce Carol. "Ghost Girls." Williford and Martone 488–500.

Peer, Willie van, and Seymour Chatman, eds. *New Perspectives on Narrative Perspective.* Albany: State U of New York P, 2001. Print.

Phelan, James. *Living to Tell about It: A Rhetoric and Ethics of Character Narration.* Ithaca: Cornell UP, 2005. Print.

———. "Why Narrators Can Be Focalizers—and Why It Matters." Peer and Chatman 51–64.

Prince, Gerald. "A Point of View on Point of View or Refocusing Focalization." Peer and Chatman 43–50.

Proulx, Annie. "Brokeback Mountain." Williford and Martone 521–41.

Rimmon-Kenan, Shlomith. *Narrative Fiction: Contemporary Poetics.* 2nd ed. New York: Routledge, 2002. Print.

Stanzel, F. K. *A Theory of Narrative.* 1979. Trans. Charlotte Goedsche. Cambridge: Cambridge UP, 1984. Print.

Timecode. Dir. Mike Figgis. Screen Gems, 2000. Film.

Watt, Ian. *The Rise of the Novel.* Berkeley: U of California P, 1957. Print.

Williford, Lex, and Michael Martone, eds. *The Scribner Anthology of Contemporary Short Fiction.* New York: Simon, 1999. Print.

Further Reading

Culler, Jonathan. "Omniscience." *Narrative* 12.1 (2004): 22–34. Print.

Herman, David. "Beyond Voice and Vision: Cognitive Grammar and Focalization Theory." *Point of View, Perspective, Focalization: Modeling Mediacy.* Ed. Peter Hühn, Wolf Schmid, and Jörg Schönert. Berlin: de Gruyter, 2009. 119–42. Print.

———. "Hypothetical Focalization." *Narrative* 2.3 (1994): 230–53. Print.

Jahn, Manfred. "Focalization." *The Cambridge Companion to Narrative.* Ed. David Herman. Cambridge: Cambridge UP, 2007. 94–108. Print.

Lanser, Susan Snaider. *The Narrative Act: Point of View in Fiction.* Princeton: Princeton UP, 1981. Print.

David Gorman

Character and Characterization

At the very beginning of literary study, everyone learns a set of terms having to do with narrative, which always includes *plot*, *character*, *theme*, and *setting*, and usually also *imagery*, *atmosphere*, and *symbolism*. Among these terms, *character* is one of the most intuitive. A middle-school student may struggle to grasp the concept of theme or symbol, but character, never. And it remains indispensable as a category of narrative analysis and discussion at any level. Yet character has proved a problematic notion for theorists of narrative. Teachers should view this situation as an opportunity for their students to explore the aspects of one of the field's fundamental concepts. In what follows, I begin by reviewing the influential work of the formalist-structuralist tradition on character. Then I outline some of the recurrent issues that have arisen about character as a category of literary analysis, while the third part of this essay goes on to deal with techniques of characterization, a topic that lies closer to the border between narrative theory and the actual practices of reading and writing narrative. I conclude with some cautionary remarks on the pedagogical unsoundness of treating the notion of character as a given rather than as something that has varied historically. Except perhaps for a very specialized doctoral seminar, I do not envision character as a primary topic for a course in what follows.

165

Since my fundamental assumption about literary character is that it is interwoven with other components in the production and comprehension of narrative, I think that it is best taught in connection with other notions.

Character and Modern Narrative Theory

By "modern narrative theory" I refer primarily to the work of formalist or structuralist theorists—beginning in Russia during the 1910s and 1920s and culminating in France during the 1960s and 1970s—and secondarily to all the research on narrative that has followed, which has departed in many ways from the formalist-structuralist paradigm, though without being able to leave it behind.

A major target of the Russian and French theorists was impressionistic criticism of the kind that, with respect to narrative, inclined to treat literary characters as self-subsistent beings. The European theorists would have found a perfect example of what they rejected in A. C. Bradley's lectures on Shakespeare, which discuss Hamlet, Othello, Lear, and Macbeth not only in the context of the plays in which they appear but also, extensively, as if they were actual persons. The category of character does not figure in formalist-structuralist work on narrative, which proposes two kinds of reductions or transformations.

One, articulated most fully by the folklorist Vladimir Propp, begins from the observation that, in fairy tales, different figures can fulfill the same function: for example, the hero's opponent may be a troll, a witch, or a dragon; the goal of his quest can be a pot of gold, a beautiful princess, or a throne; and so on. In Propp's analysis of fairy tales, then, the category of functional role replaces that of character. Theorists like Claude Bremond, A. J. Greimas, and Tzvetan Todorov suggested extensions of this kind of analysis as well as applications to literary narratives. Greimas's theory of actantial roles represents the broadest development of this model (for exposition, critique, and applications, see Herman, ch. 4). A second way in which formalists like Viktor Shklovsky and Boris Tomashevsky eliminated character from narrative analysis was by pursuing the hypothesis that a narrative can be completely accounted for in terms of device and motivation, where the story events and their bare sequence count as devices while motivation includes whatever connects them so as to suggest reasons and causes. In E. M. Forster's example of a plot, "The king died and then the queen died of grief" (86), the queen's grief is not a consequence of her character but rather of the plot maker's need to link the two events. The upshot is that character is dissolved into an aspect of motivation.

An extension along these lines, formulated by Roland Barthes, treats literary characters as "transitory" by-products of a narrative (94). Specifically, Barthes claims that "when identical semes [i.e., predicates] traverse the same proper name [in a narrative] and appear to settle on it, a character is created" (67; cf. 191). In the system of five codes he uses in *S/Z*, Barthes ostentatiously omits a code for character; he subsumes many of the predicates that, in traditional analysis, would be called characterizing elements, along with much else, under one code (the semic), and disperses others across other codes.

In undergraduate courses, no more than a good summary of formalist and structuralist work is needed. Graduate students can be asked to wrestle with some of the source texts. How an instructor chooses to handle this material matters less than the decision it calls for, namely, where it leaves us with regard to character. In hindsight, formalist and structuralist proposals can appear misguided. In practice, character remains a basic concept in discussing narrative. The best pedagogical approach might be to present the ideas of Propp, Barthes, and others as so many thought experiments, which, if they have failed to dissolve a category dear to belletristic criticism, did succeed in giving theorists a much more sophisticated sense of the complexities involved in the elaboration of literary characters.

Of course other work has been done on character during the past century, notably by scholars in the German tradition of narrative study, that has only recently begun to have a wide impact; in addition there is an Anglo-American tradition that takes its point of departure from Henry James, some of whose ideas about character come up later in this essay. Though it may seem absurd to ignore the huge mass of modern psychological criticism, I have decided not to discuss it because so much of it deals with authors and readers rather than characters. Finally, one character in particular has been subject to intense scrutiny in recent years, by many theorists and critics—the narrator. But because this work has focused exclusively on the narrator's position in the narrative (and because disagreement persists as to whether all narrators should count as characters), I have decided to bypass it as well.

Character: Issues

Among the issues raised by this undertheorized but highly intuitive notion, four stand out. The first two come up routinely in modern discussions of literary character. If only because such issues have become standard topics, instructors should not neglect them; however, they also deserve to be taken seriously because they can be used to bring out important aspects of character.

One near cliché about character in narrative theory involves a disagreement (real or not: see below) between Aristotle and Henry James. In chapter 6 of the *Poetics*, Aristotle categorically states that, among the elements of narrative, *ethos* (character) must be subordinate to *muthos* (plot structure). "It is not . . . the function of the agents' actions to allow the portrayal of their characters; it is, rather, for the sake of their actions that characterisation is included" (37). In a well-known passage of his essay "The Art of Fiction," however, James directly implies that action and personality have an equal status in narrative: "What is character but the determination of incident? What is incident but the illustration of character?" (55). Staged as a debate over the importance of characterization, these comments offer teachers a useful opening. Aristotle's remarks can be presented as anticipating the formalist-structuralist line that the significance of each element of narrative depends on its functional contribution. James's questions, meanwhile, can be framed as a rejection of theoretical purity or neatness. In the end, most contemporary critics would probably endorse the compromise position attributable to James. Indeed, its lack of theoretical purity is what most recommends it to critics who recognize the diversity of narratives and the variability of the positions that characters occupy in them. This outlook is already manifest in the 1920s, when Edwin Muir noted that there are not only novels of action and novels of character but also novels that focus on intensely dramatic situations involving small character sets as well as novels that offer panoramic chronicles with large casts. Sixty years later James Phelan offered a parallel analysis of characters, noting that each is describable in terms of components—personlike ("mimetic"), structural ("synthetic"), and "thematic"—that can be mixed in any number of ratios. Alex Woloch in *The One and the Many* has recently proposed an intriguing twist to the Muir-Phelan line by viewing the personlike and structural components as inherently in conflict: he suggests that minor characters are "the proletariat of the novel" (27) because their personlike components are always sacrificed to their structural ones.

The other commonplace in discussions of character is the contrast established by Forster between flat and round characters. Forster explained the former as simple, static figures and the latter as complex and dynamic (ch. 4). Students can easily be brought to recognize the problem with these definitions, which is that they conflate two different criteria (simple versus complex, static versus dynamic), two axes along which characters can be typed. These distinctions suggest many pedagogical questions and exercises. One is to identify characters who mix Forster's criteria, either those who exhibit few personality traits but who also change or those with complicated personalities that stay the same throughout a narrative. Another is to focus on the static-dynamic axis and ask how common characters who change really are in literature—and whether it is easy to identify them. (In *Heart of Darkness*, does Kurtz change, or do circumstances bring out qualities that he always had, though they were repressed?) Part of the lesson here may involve historical or generic factors. For instance, drama may turn out to have outpaced the novel, in that the kind of change that Shakespeare's protagonists regularly undergo (Hal, Lear, Prospero) does not find a parallel in recounted fiction until the end of the neoclassical period (Mr. Darcy, Julien Sorel, and protagonists of the bildungsroman). Or again, tragedy may be more accommodating of character change than comedy (as in Shakespeare, overall—though Jane Austen provides a counterexample). One more lesson might suggest that Forster's criteria, though logically distinct, are not unconnected. While major characters can be complex, dynamic, or both, minor characters, introduced for contrast or other kinds of support, must be, precisely, "flat" (see Galef). Like other background elements, they must be static in order to provide a fixed ground against which to perceive the main characters, as well as simple, so as not to distract from the main action. The terminology would probably be improved by calling characters who play this role in narrative "schematic" rather than "flat," and those in the contrasting class "full" rather than "round" (Margolin).

Forster attempted no more than a limited venture into character typology; but other critics have made more extended lists (the fullest to date being the one developed along eight axes by Hochman). Taxonomy has been a third salient issue in the study of character and remains a project worth pursuing, so long as investigators recognize in advance that no complete typology is feasible. The reason is that taxonomy, like other concepts (e.g., theme), extends from literature out into the world. On the one hand, the pertinent question for narrative study is, How do we discriminate different kinds of literary characters? On the other hand, we also use the notion of character to identify and to judge real people. The question then becomes, Are there any strictly literary criteria for typologizing characters? Aside from the very familiar distinction invoked just previously, between major and minor characters, there may not be many.

If we accept stylization as one axis along which to classify characters, the scale can only run from more stylized (or conventionalized) to less: the alternative would involve contrasting stylization with realism, naturalism, or some other theoretical dead end. Whether characters are fully knowable or not may also provide a criterion of classification, or rather two: the degree of breadth (the amount of narrative time it takes readers to learn what is encompassed by a particular trait or set of traits—for example, how long it takes to learn just how eccentric Tristram Shandy's family is) and the degree of depth (e.g., Jay Gatsby appears opaque and therefore deep until the revelation of his secret renders him transparent). Many other criteria have been proposed: simplicity, consistency, completeness, predictability, openness, and their counterparts. Since we use these criteria to describe actual people, they would not qualify as "strictly literary." Nevertheless, it is arguable that "breadth" and "depth" cannot be confined wholly to the literary realm, and the frequent proposals of other nonliterary criteria provide the basis for posing the question of whether we can, as Forster put it, fully distinguish *Homo fictus* from *Homo sapiens* (55–56).

This question can be further developed by returning to the literary measure of a character's degree of functionality. At one extreme, a character may be nothing more than what James calls Maria Gostrey, a *ficelle* (Preface 1317); but what lies at the other extreme? Is a literary character that stands completely independent of the narrative in which it appears even conceivable? Many narrative theorists would say no, and thus they endorse the view that literary characters are essentially textual features, semiotic mechanisms, or, as it is sometimes put, "people made of paper." But others—most obviously, traditional critics like Bradley—would contend that some literary characters have a life of their own, an integrity and an impact on readers that, though it begins with a text, transcends it. These positions can provide the starting point for a productive debate in the classroom. On the one hand, it appears to be an undeniable fact that a fictional character has no existence outside the narrative in which it appears. But critics who want to recognize some characters as in effect transcending the works in which they originate—Hamlet, Anna Karenina, Holden Caulfield—can point to an equally undeniable fact: readers respond to literary characters as intensely as they do to real people. (Empathetic response to fictional characters has long been recognized as a problem in aesthetics: for a good summary, see ch. 4 of New.) Of course not all characters qualify; proponents of this view must conditionalize it by saying that only *successful* characters can evoke emotional response; but they can claim that, in addition, this gives them an evaluative criterion for narratives. Finding symbols in characters is a closely related phenomenon: because action is specific but agency is general, anything an agent in a narrative does will suggest more than is needed to explain that particular action. In the extreme case, this phenomenon underpins the claim that a character represents an archetype.

Obviously I have presented this last issue in a drastically oversimplified way. Many intermediate positions are imaginable. An instructor might initiate discussion, however, by putting the matter starkly as this, contrasting the implications of textual analysis to those of reader reaction. At the beginning of *Huckleberry Finn*, Jim is presented as a collection of verbal and behavioral mannerisms, with entirely predictable responses in each episode; by the end he has taken on emotional depth and moral stature. Readers can remember Jim long after they have forgotten the details of Twain's story and think about him in relation to situations completely separate from those in the novel. Where classroom conversation goes from there, like so much else having to do with the topic of character, remains open.

Characterization: Techniques

Because the strength of modern narrative theory lies in the analysis of textual and technical specifics rather than in broad reflection on concepts, characterization is a much better understood area of narrative study than character. In fiction, there are three basic means available for characterizing the figures in a story: behavioral, reported, and associative. To each of these sources of characterization belong particular techniques, at least nine of which have been identified in various analyses and surveys.

Narrative agents are characterized behaviorally by what they do (by "showing," to use the traditional, catchall phrase). The things that characters do include their (1) actions, (2) words, and (3) thoughts. In addition, an agent can also be characterized by report ("telling"), through comments made about him or her that can come from (4) the agent, (5) other characters, or (6) the narrative. There is also another, rather miscellaneous—and typically literary—means by which to characterize persons in a story, namely by things associated with them. These include (7) what they are called, (8) their appearance, and (9) any other item or motif with which the figure is recurrently connected in the narrative.

Of course this is only a bare list. An instructor outlining any of these techniques should emphasize first that they are nonexclusive, in the sense not only that all of them can be used in a given narrative but also that there may be considerable overlap between them in practice: for example, what the characters say (number 2 in the list above) necessarily includes anything they say about themselves (4) or each other (5); likewise, no sharp line divides characters' actions (1) from their appearance (8). Overlap will be particularly obvious in narrative situations involving a first-person narrator, but the pedagogical value of an abstract typology of devices lies in the gap between it and the specific practices that actual narratives exhibit. How, for example, do readers come to understand the character of Emma Woodhouse? While the narrative states immediately that she is "handsome, clever, and rich" and provides much other information as well, it does so with an ironic inflection suggesting that there is more to Emma than what it overtly states. Readers also observe Emma's interactions with other characters and are able to compare her manipulative treatment of Harriet with her circumspect handling of her father and to realize—before Emma herself does—what her feelings are for Knightley. The action of the novel turns on Emma's almost complete misjudgment of Frank Churchill in a way that reveals both their characters and is the result of Austen's dazzling orchestration of many kinds of evidence, including all the techniques on the list. The bareness of the list also conceals many questions and problems that an instructor might raise about any given technique. Consider the highly ingenuous statement that a narrative agent can be characterized by what the narrative says (number 6 above). Can a narrative speak? If we do not accept this idea, then we have to restate the technique as involving what the narrator says about the agent; but this raises another question as to whether, even in third-person narration, we count a narrator as a character. If we do, then technique (6) should be assimilated into (5). Another issue: what if the narrative voice or position varies in the course of a narrative—what if there are many narrators or shifts between first- and third-person narration, or some other such possibility? It is the range and variety of possibilities here that teachers should emphasize, the potential breadth of the palette available to narrative artists.

Another way in which an instructor might organize a list of devices for characterization would be to begin by asking students to consider the means available to a dramatist for characterizing the persons in an enacted narrative and then to think about the wider spectrum of techniques that can be used by a writer telling the same story in the format of, say, a novel or tale. While the most obvious device peculiar to recounted fiction is narrative discourse (6), its unavailability in drama limits the ways in which characters' thoughts (3) can be expressed and affects the way their appearance (8) can be described. The possibilities might also differ for using associated motifs to characterize persons (9)—which, incidentally, remains a completely miscellaneous category that might subsume all the others. Something else that makes recounted narrative a completely different language game is the ability to summarize actions (1) and words (2) in the discourse.

In addition to these techniques for qualifying agents in narrative, another device is available to storytellers: they can use stereotypes. Stock characters need no detailed introduction or explanation. Everyone familiar with the relevant narrative conventions recognizes figures like the tricky slave and the naive shepherdess, the dopey neighbor and the soap-opera bitch. Standard as the device of stock or type characterization may be, teaching the conventions involved faces resistance from contemporary students, who have been warned incessantly against the evils of stereotyping. But this warning relates to actual people; literature, by contrast, thrives on typecasting, for good technical reasons. If every agent in a narrative had to be characterized from scratch, storylines would either be very hard to get going or very mysterious. Instructors might turn this problem to advantage by using it to illustrate the *Homo sapiens-Homo fictus* contrast. Or they might use it to open up a historical perspective on how narratives bring out cultural assumptions through what goes without saying about character types—the principles of decorum, verisimilitude, or "likeness" accepted by Christopher Marlowe, say, or Daniel Defoe, or Charles Dickens. Beyond these lies the theoretical question of whether stock characters represent a sharply delimited subset or whether conventionalization plays a much larger or less dispensable part in the creation of any literary character.

Positioning is yet another way to characterize agents. One pertinent technique consists of placing the characters in significant relation to each other to provide telling parallels and contrasts (much of Austen criticism concerns her mastery of the use of what are sometimes called "flanking characters," such as Lizzy Bennet's sisters). Another technique of this kind involves the characters' placement relative to their fictional world, with each character having a greater or lesser autonomy, or "power of action," in Northrop Frye's words (in the classic first essay of his *Anatomy of Criticism*).

The Genealogy of a Category

While character may be a basic notion in literary study, that is no reason
to treat it as a fixed notion. On the contrary, the working pedagogical
assumption should be that it has both a history and a prehistory. The
history of the category of character includes the changes that it can be
presumed to have undergone since it first emerged as a nameable feature of narrative. For example, what Aristotle means by *ethos* in the *Poetics*
has to do with generic ethical qualities and lacks the psychological nu-
ance and the presumption of individual uniqueness associated with the
concept of character in the novelistic age (see Halliwell 94–95, 139–40).
The prehistory of the category includes literary and critical practice from
periods before its explicit appearance, as well as—if we extend the idea of
"prehistory" slightly—practices in traditions with no equivalent term. *The
Tale of Genji* (Japan, eleventh century), *Njal's Saga* (Iceland, thirteenth
century), and *The Story of the Stone* (China, eighteenth century) all feature
characters and use techniques of characterization whether or not there
was, in the cultures to which these narratives belong, an answerable term
available.

Granted the importance of historicizing the concept of character, the
fact is that contemporary theorists tend wildly to overrate historical variability. Therefore we need to recognize that thinking about character historically requires us to do justice to two principles. First, what does not
change is that actions in narratives need agents. Although stories can be
told without agents—about the origin of the planets, say, or the extinction
of the dinosaurs—these are narratives of events, not actions. What differentiates actions from events, mere happenings, is agency (see Davidson),
which in turn opens the door to considerations about intention, motive,
and characterization in the broad sense (keeping it in mind, obviously, that
action includes reactions to what befalls, since these also manifest agency).
But, second, what does change is how the notion of character relates to
others, particularly ethical and psychological notions, with which it remains bound up, in ever-shifting constellations: person and personality;
identity; agent and agency; responsibility; subject and subjectivity; desire;
self and selfhood; protagonist; consciousness, the subconscious, and the
unconscious; maturity and immaturity; actor, role, and performance; behavior; soul; and so on, quite open-endedly. And, as Amélie Oksenberg
Rorty's indispensable discussion brings home, these historical changes affect the way that agents are figured in narratives.

An illustration familiar to all teachers of Renaissance literature would be the way in which the psychology of the humors provides a background against which characters in the drama and narrative of the period must be understood. A less obvious illustration might lie in how much fiction in the twentieth century was composed by writers who took psychoanalysis seriously. Even in the unlikely circumstance that some variant of Freudian theory proves to reveal the absolute truth about the human psyche, students need to think about its influence on the novelists they read, particularly in cases of authors who rejected psychoanalysis, like Vladimir Nabokov, or who developed alternative theories, like D. H. Lawrence.

Large shifts in literary convention and assumptions about narrative composition also have a potential impact here. Consider once again what I previously described as the controversy between Aristotle and James over the status of character and plot. Only by assimilating Aristotle to the framework of assumptions that James shared with modern writers can the two writers be said to disagree, strictly speaking. Something very simple explains Aristotle's seemingly mysterious demotion of character: the epic and tragic poems he analyzes usually took their plots from myth and legend. Given that the storyline is set (at least broadly), obviously all other elements must follow: the poet can endow the figure of Oedipus with varying personal traits, but it remains a given that Oedipus kills his father and marries his mother. The idea that writers of fiction should *invent* their stories, which at some point became the default assumption that it was for James (though it was not for, e.g., Shakespeare or Racine) entails that the novelist, dramatist, or narrative writer can begin with character elements as easily as with story elements—and that it is probably best to begin with some of both kinds.

At the other extreme from ahistoricism lies the idea that concepts like that of literary character are merely factitious (the buzzword is "contingent"), which I reject. As I have stressed repeatedly, we seem unable to dispense with this concept, despite the bracing reductionism of formalist and structuralist theory. As a practical matter, reading and writing narrative seems to presuppose the recognition of something like character. I have only suggested that instructors might emphasize how the content of this category—not to mention its connection to other categories—is subject to change over time. Instructors can go on to add that this feature of the category shows that narrative study involves more than microanalysis and technicalities, that potentially there is a historical and conceptual depth to it.

Works Cited

Aristotle. *Poetics.* Halliwell 31–65.

Barthes, Roland. *S/Z: An Essay.* Trans. Richard Miller. New York: Hill, 1974. Print.

Bradley, A. C. *Shakespearean Tragedy: Lectures on* Hamlet, Othello, King Lear, Macbeth. 1904. 4th ed. New York: Palgrave, 2006. Print.

Davidson, Donald. *Essays on Actions and Events.* 1980. New and enl. ed. Oxford: Clarendon, 2001. Print.

Forster, E. M. *Aspects of the Novel.* New York: Harcourt, 1927. Print.

Frye, Northrop. *Anatomy of Criticism: Four Essays.* Princeton: Princeton UP, 1957. Print.

Galef, David. *The Supporting Cast: A Study of Flat and Minor Characters.* University Park: Pennsylvania State UP, 1993. Print.

Halliwell, Stephen. *The* Poetics *of Aristotle: Translation and Commentary.* Chapel Hill: U of North Carolina P, 1987. Print.

Herman, David. *Story Logic: Problems and Possibilities of Narrative.* Lincoln: U of Nebraska P, 2002. Print.

Hochman, Baruch. *Character in Literature.* Ithaca: Cornell UP, 1985. Print.

James, Henry. "The Art of Fiction." 1884. *Literary Criticism: Essays on Literature, American Writers, English Writers.* Ed. Leon Edel. New York: Lib. of Amer., 1984. 44–65. Print.

———. Preface to *The Ambassadors.* 1909. *Literary Criticism: French Writers, Other European Writers, the Prefaces to the New York Edition.* Ed. Leon Edel. New York: Lib. of Amer., 1984. 1304–21. Print.

Margolin, Uri. "Character: Types of Characters and Theories about Characters in Novels." *Encyclopedia of the Novel.* Ed. Paul Schellinger. Vol. 1. Chicago: Fitzroy-Dearborn, 1998. 197–201. 2 vols.

Muir, Edwin. *The Structure of the Novel.* 1928. New York: Harcourt, N.d. Print.

New, Christopher. *Philosophy of Literature: An Introduction.* New York: Routledge, 1999. Print.

Phelan, James. *Reading People, Reading Plots: Character, Progression, and the Interpretation of Narrative.* Chicago: U of Chicago P, 1989. Print.

Propp, Vladimir. *The Morphology of the Folktale.* 1928. Trans. Laurence Scott. Rev. Louis A. Wagner. Austin: U of Texas P, 1968. Print.

Rorty, Amélie Oksenberg. "Characters, Persons, Selves, Individuals." 1976. *Theory of the Novel: A Historical Approach.* Ed. Michael McKeon. Baltimore: Johns Hopkins UP, 2000. 537–53. Print.

Woloch, Alex. *The One and the Many.* Princeton: Princeton UP, 2003. Print.

Further Reading

Bremond, Claude. *Logique du récit.* Paris: Éditions de Seuil, 1973. Print.

Frye, Northrop. *The Secular Scripture: A Study of the Structure of Romance.* Cambridge: Harvard UP, 1976. Print.

Genette, Gérard. "Vraisemblance and Motivation." Trans. David Gorman. *Narrative* 9 (2001): 239–58. Print.

Greimas, A. J. *Structural Semantics: An Attempt at a Method.* Trans. Danielle McDowell, Ronald Schleifer, and Alan Velie. Lincoln: U of Nebraska P, 1983. Print.

Knapp, John V., ed. *Literary Character.* Spec. issue of *Style* 24.3 (1990): 349–497. Rpt. as *Literary Character.* Lanham: UP of America, 1993. Print.

Margolin, Uri. "Character." *The Cambridge Companion to Narrative.* Ed. David Herman. Cambridge: Cambridge UP, 2007. 66–79. Print.

Palmer, Alan. *Fictional Minds.* Lincoln: U of Nebraska P, 2004. Print.

Schneider, Ralf. "Toward a Cognitive Theory of Literary Character: The Dynamics of Mental-Model Construction." *Style* 35.4 (2001): 607–40. Print.

Scholes, Robert, James Phelan, and Robert Kellogg. *The Nature of Narrative.* 2nd ed. Oxford: Oxford UP, 2006. Print.

Shklovsky, Viktor. *Theory of Prose.* Trans. Benjamin Sher. Normal: Dalkey, 1991. Print.

Todorov, Tzvetan. *The Fantastic: A Structural Approach to a Literary Genre.* Trans. Richard Howard. Ithaca: Cornell UP, 1975. Print.

Tomashevsky, Boris. "Thematics." *Russian Formalist Criticism: Four Essays.* Ed. and trans. Lee T. Lemon and Marion J. Reis. Lincoln: U of Nebraska P, 1965. 61–95. Print.

Part III

Genres and Media

Brian McHale

Popular Genres

Narrative theory and popular fiction exist in a symbiotic relation. Much of what one might study or teach under the rubric of "popular culture" is narrative in form. Thriller, situation comedy, soap opera, crime, science fiction, horror, Harlequin romance, superhero comics, even reality television: these and many other popular genres and subgenres are narratively organized and are amenable to narratological analysis. Conversely, many aspects of narrative theory and poetics can profitably be explored and illuminated through examples drawn from popular genres, each of which tends to stake a claim to a particular aspect of narrative form as its own special province, in part to differentiate itself from competing genres. Historically, narrative theorists have often developed their basic theoretical insights by turning to "formula fiction" for models and examples, using popular genres such as the detective story or the thriller as farm clubs wherein to hone the tools and methods that could then be applied in the major leagues of canonical literature.

Given their symbiosis, it is hardly surprising that narrative theory and popular fiction prove to be a formidable pedagogical team. Popular fiction can be useful in teaching basic narrative theory, not least because it is likely to be familiar and accessible to students in ways that more aesthetically ambitious high-literary narratives might not be. Conversely, narrative analysis comes in handy when teaching popular fiction, shedding light on the formal distinguishing marks of different genres and supplementing or substantiating historicist and cultural studies approaches.

The discussion that follows reflects my experience of both kinds of pedagogical setting: the use of popular fiction in narrative theory courses and the use of narrative theory in popular fiction courses, both single-genre courses (e.g., courses on science fiction) and omnibus popular fiction courses featuring units on several different genres. I also teach units on popular genres in courses on postmodernism because of the well-known rapprochement between high-art and low-art strata in postmodernist culture, which manifests itself (among other ways) in postmodernist fiction's piggybacking on the genre conventions of popular fiction. Even in "straight" genre courses, I often juxtapose "classic" examples of a genre with one or more postmodernist parodies, pastiches, or appropriations of the genre, because postmodernist versions "lay bare" genre conventions in pedagogically useful ways.

My teaching of this material differs between the undergraduate and graduate levels mainly with respect to two variables: first, the means of making key theoretical tools and categories available to students and, second, the means of filling in indispensable historical, cultural, and scholarly background. With undergraduates, I am more likely to rely on lectures, supplemented by handouts and readings chosen for their reader friendliness, to deliver both kinds of foundational material, whereas with graduate students I am more likely to assign classic theoretical texts and background readings, perhaps supplemented by student presentations (e.g., oral reviews of relevant books or articles on literary and cultural history). Small-group research projects are an option at both levels, especially with respect to the historical backgrounds and sociological milieus of genres.

The three sections that follow, then, reflect three possible units, or three possible courses, each devoted to one particularly conspicuous and durable genre of contemporary popular fiction: the Western, detective fiction, and science fiction. Each of these genres foregrounds a different dimension of narrative form, and each can be instantiated across a range of media—prose, film, television, graphic novel, video games, and other digital forms—presenting multiple opportunities for cross-media comparisons. These are hardly the only popular genres that one might teach, needless to say, and I invite the reader to imagine parallel units or courses on the thriller, romance, horror, fantasy, popular historical fiction, and so forth or for that matter on popular fiction of earlier periods (the domestic novel, the dime novel, Victorian pornography, turn-of-the-century imperial romance, etc.).

The Western; or, Functions

Texts of popular fiction are invaluable when it comes to introducing and illustrating the deep structure of story (also called fabula or *histoire*). This is the level at which narrative analysis identifies not only actants, that is, characters' roles as defined by the actions they perform in the story, but also functions, or the actions these actants perform, viewed in the light of their significance to the story as a whole. (For a different approach to teaching actantial analysis, see Keen's essay in this volume.) The formulaic nature of popular fiction means that actantial roles are literally generic—they recur across many instances of the genre—and that characters are more fully defined by their roles than might be the case in literary fictions. To a certain extent, characters in formula fiction are identical to their roles, with relatively little left over for "characterization." So it is no accident that when Umberto Eco undertakes to describe the poetics of the James Bond cycle, he uses a modified version of A. J. Greimas's actantial analysis or that when Luc Herman and Bart Vervaeck need to illustrate actantial analysis, they use a Bond story, "From a View to a Kill" (no relation, happily, to the execrable Bond movie that echoes its name). Actantial analysis fits thrillers pretty snugly.

Surprisingly, though, an analysis in the spirit of Vladimir Propp's functional analysis of the Russian fairy tale yields even a snugger fit. This is surprising because, if the structuralists' critique of Propp is to be credited, he failed to analyze the actants and functions of his fairy-tale corpus into their simplest and most universal components, thereby limiting the range of their applicability. Greimas's analysis, on this account, is more universally applicable because more abstract. (A comparison of Propp and Greimas might be an appropriate exercise for a graduate-level course.) Nevertheless, Propp's reduction of the fairy-tale corpus to a relatively fixed sequence of some thirty-one functions proves to be applicable to a wide range of popular genres, not just thrillers of the James Bond type but also fantasy narratives (*The Wizard of Oz*, *The Lord of the Rings*), some science fiction (*Star Wars*), and certain types of Westerns. Propp's model works as well as it does because of the genealogy of these genres: they all descend historically from earlier forms of quest romance, and the fairy tales that Propp analyzed were essentially folk versions of quest romances.

Many Westerns, though not all of them, conform to the generic template of quest romance and so are amenable to a functional analysis modeled on Propp's. Thus, for example, the John Ford Western *The Searchers* will yield to a Proppian analysis but probably not Ford's *My Darling Clementine*, the television miniseries *Broken Trail* will but probably not *Deadwood*, and so on. To approach the Western from this angle—or, conversely, to use the Western to illustrate the deep structure of story—one needs first to introduce students to Propp's method of analysis. Graduate students might be asked to read key chapters of *The Morphology of the Folktale* for themselves; undergraduates might instead receive a "cheat sheet," listing and illustrating Propp's thirty-one functions. Students at both levels would work through Propp's example of a fairy-tale analysis (Propp 96–98) and perhaps bring in fairy-tale analyses of their own, imitating Propp's, for "show and tell." The object of these preliminary exercises is to familiarize students with the gross outlines of the quest story as analyzed by Propp: the initial condition of lack, or the act of villainy that inflicts damage; the dispatching of the hero to remedy the lack, or combat the villain; the hero's departure to some "other" place; his difficult negotiations with one or more donors for the acquisition of a magical agent; his struggle with the villain, perhaps repeated; his liquidation of the lack and return home followed by a sort of epilogue involving a struggle with a false hero or sometimes by a second quest.

With these instruments in hand, one is ready to begin anatomizing Westerns. (Background readings at both graduate and undergraduate levels could include Tompkins and selections from Slotkin.) In a course devoted exclusively to the Western genre, one might consider screening several Western movies to compare them in the light of Propp. Cattle-drive Westerns are a rich source for this type of quest structure: *Red River*, *The Cowboys*, television's *Lonesome Dove* and *Broken Trail*. So are the "Mexico Westerns" of the cold war era: *The Magnificent Seven*, *The Professionals*, *The Wild Bunch*, even, belatedly, *All the Pretty Horses*. Highly stylized, revisionist, and even parodic varieties of Western can yield good examples: Sergio Leone's *The Good, the Bad, and the Ugly*, Peter Fonda's *The Hired Hand*, the John Wayne vehicle *True Grit*, maybe even Mel Brooks's *Blazing Saddles*. In discussing films such as these, one might begin by trying to map them onto Propp's sequence of functions, which is certain to provoke productive controversies over competing mappings. One might ask, which mapping seems to offer the best fit? What insights does each mapping give rise to that others do not? Conversely, what features does each mapping obscure? Just how good *is* the fit in each case, anyway? Where the match up is less than perfect, what explains the divergence? How could Propp's model be modified to improve the fit and accommodate anomalous features of these films? Does Propp's model capture salient *differences* among these films, or does it reduce them to one-size-fits-all sameness? And so on.

In a narrative-theory course, or a popular-genre course with multiple units, one might not have the time to screen more than one film and might choose instead to compare a film with one or more Western novels. Candidates abound, of course, not all of them equally amenable to Proppian analysis. My own preference would be to use one of the volumes of Cormac McCarthy's *Border Trilogy* (1993, 1994, 1998). Despite being high-literary "upgrades" of the Western genre, all three volumes belong to the Mexico Western subgenre, and all three involve multiple quests. The first volume, *All the Pretty Horses*, has the advantage, for our purposes, of having been adapted as a film (albeit a mediocre one).

Postmodernist Westerns, in common with postmodernist appropriations of other genres, lay bare the conventions of the genre in one of two ways. Either they remain faithful to certain key genre formulas as a backdrop or foil to their flagrant deviations on other fronts or they outright sabotage the genre by abusing its indispensable, genre-defining conventions (see D'Haen). Texts such as E. L. Doctorow's *Welcome to Hard Times*, Ishmael Reed's *Yellow Back Radio Broke-Down*, Donald Barthelme's "Daumier," Robert Coover's *Ghost Town*, Gilbert Sorrentino's *Gold Fools*, and even Ed Dorn's postmodernist narrative poem *Gunslinger* all belong to the first type of Western; for all the liberties they take with the genre, they preserve its quest-narrative form more or less intact. More problematic in this respect is Michael Ondaatje's fragmentary fictional "dossier," *The Collected Works of Billy the Kid*. More problematic still is Barthelme's "The Indian Uprising," which wreaks havoc on actantial analysis—as I have reason to know, having undertaken, in collaboration with Moshe Ron, just such an (abortive) analysis of this text. I have sometimes assigned our essay to graduate students as a case study of how a postmodernist text can evoke genre formulas while at the same time sabotage the narrative logic of the genre.

Detective Fiction; or, Gaps

Of the three or four landmark narratological discoveries of the Russian formalists, the most consequential of all must be their findings about the displacement of discourse relative to story—or, in their own terminology, of *sjužet* relative to fabula. It is not too much of an exaggeration to call the disparity between fabula and *sjužet* the cornerstone of all narrative poetics. The paradigmatic instance of such disparity is the systematic chronological disorder that defines the detective-story genre. The classic account here, faithful to the spirit of formalist theory, is Tzvetan Todorov's essay on the "double story" of the whodunit—an essay suitable for graduate students and undergraduates alike.

Todorov's essay can be the occasion for a useful chalkboard exercise (which can be enlivened for undergraduates by making one or more volunteers responsible for the chalking up, with coaching and kibitzing from their classmates). Instructors should choose a relatively conventional detective story, for instance one of Sherlock Holmes's cases. Chalk up a timeline capturing the main steps in what Todorov calls the story of the investigation, starting from the point where Holmes accepts the case and ending when he reveals "who done it"; this, roughly, corresponds to the *sjužet*. Then, to the left of the beginning point (assuming that time's arrow in this exercise proceeds conventionally from left to right), chalk up the sequence that precedes Holmes's intervention—the story of the crime. Then indicate with an arrow where, in the course of the story of the investigation, the story of the crime is told—namely, just before the end, when Holmes explains everything. There on the board one has illustrated just what the displacement of *sjužet* relative to fabula means in a conventional detective story: the occlusion of part of the fabula (the backstory of the crime itself) and the backstory's withholding until the latest possible moment of the *sjužet*. Of course, the story of the investigation, which functions to withhold and reveal the backstory of the crime, constitutes a fabula of its own—in fact, a continuation of the fabula of the crime, so that the reconstructed fabula of the story as a whole extends from the preliminaries to the crime through the crime itself and its investigation down to the final revelation (and maybe beyond, if the revelation has an aftermath).

Next, instructors might consider stepping up to a more complex example, one where subsidiary mysteries arise and are solved (or not) in the course of the story of the investigation rather than one where all the solutions are withheld until the conventional wrap-up. My own preference would be to use Raymond Chandler's first novel, *The Big Sleep*, which illustrates the double story structure but also features multiple informational gaps and gap filling as it unfolds. (My preferred theoretical model of gaps and gap filling is that of the Tel Aviv school, and I sometimes have graduate students read Perry and Sternberg's classic essay on informational gaps in the biblical episode of David and Bathsheba—a crime story, if not quite a detective story.) Chandler's detective, Philip Marlowe, begins by investigating the mystery of who is blackmailing Carmen Sternwood and why, but this quickly ramifies into a number of subsidiary mysteries: What is Arthur Geiger's racket? Who killed Geiger? Who killed Geiger's killer, the chauffeur Owen Taylor? How is the gangster Eddie Mars involved in all this? Where is Eddie Mars's wife? And so on. Gaps open and are closed (some of them) in the course of Marlowe's investigation, so that the chalkboard timeline sprouts a number of arrows indicating segments of fabula withheld and belatedly supplied. Characteristically for a Chandler novel, a deeper mystery emerges behind or beneath the one Marlowe has accepted as a case: What has become of Rusty Regan? It is the solution to this mystery, appearing at first tangential to the "official" case, that is withheld to the end and given pride of place in the detective's final revelations. (Carmen did it.)

The Big Sleep has been filmed, of course, and in this case the film, directed by Howard Hawks and starring Humphrey Bogart and Lauren Bacall, is at least as memorable and influential as the novel on which it is based. Comparison of the two treatments of the same story allows for further reflection on gaps and gap filling, since the film is not, after all, identical to the novel in this respect. (Carmen didn't do it; Eddie Mars did.) Screening the film gives the instructor the opportunity to retell the famous anecdote about an incident during its production, when no one on the script-writing team (which included William Faulkner) could explain to the director's and the leading man's satisfaction who killed Owen Taylor, the homicidal chauffer. So they consulted Chandler himself—and he didn't know either (Phillips 56). This comic anecdote actually yields a distinction worth pondering between gaps at the *sjužet* level, which are in principle capable of being filled, and gaps at the fabula level, which are permanently irreparable.

Chandler's novel and the film based on it belong to the subgenre of hard-boiled detective fiction that begins with Dashiell Hammett and includes Mickey Spillane, Ross Macdonald, James Ellroy, and many others. One could imagine organizing a course around the novels of this hard-boiled tradition and the films associated with it, both adaptations and originals, perhaps including earlier films such as John Huston's *The Maltese Falcon* (based on a Hammett novel) and later ones such as Roman Polanski's *Chinatown*, Robert Altman's *The Long Goodbye* (another one based on Chandler), Arthur Penn's *Night Moves*, Curtis Hanson's *L.A. Confidential* (based on Ellroy), and so forth. Alternatively, one could branch out and sample a wider range of the generic diversity of detective fiction. Todorov, in the essay on the whodunit I mention above, conveniently distinguishes among three subgenres (for more details, graduate students could be referred to Malmgren's *Anatomy of Murder*): the whodunit proper, or mystery story, exemplified by Conan Doyle's Sherlock Holmes stories, Agatha Christie, Dorothy Sayers, and many others; the hard-boiled detective story; and what we might call the crime story, which is animated not by curiosity (the desire to discover what happened in the past) but by suspense (the desire to learn what happens next). Crime fictions—for instance, Patricia Highsmith's Ripley novels, but also many police procedurals, serial-killer fictions, and so forth—do not *necessarily* (i.e., not generically) involve disparity between fabula and *sjužet*, so examples of crime fiction could function as a foil to the subgenres that do.

Diversity of gender, of ethnicity, and of sexual orientation is a conspicuous feature of the contemporary detective genre, as it is not of Westerns, so that one could easily illustrate the poetics of gaps and gap filling using detective novels by and about women, people of color, and gays or lesbians. Moreover, one could customize one's syllabus to reflect almost any region one chose, since by now nearly every major metropolitan area has at least one fictional detective of its own, from Jerusalem to Edinburgh to New Orleans, as do even some rural areas. Detective fiction is in many respects the contemporary version of regional or local-color fiction.

The detective genre is affiliated with the poetics of modernism, since both detective fiction and modernist fiction are animated by epistemological quests. Think of the many modernist novels that are organized around central mysteries, from Henry James and Joseph Conrad through F. Scott Fitzgerald and William Faulkner to Vladimir Nabokov and beyond. No surprise, then, that postmodernist fiction has mounted a determined assault on the narrative logic of mystery and detection, introducing irreparable gaps at the fabula level, evacuating or collapsing key roles in the genre's structure (detective, criminal, crime, victim), and wrecking the genre's necessary closure (see Merivale and Sweeney). Examples that might prove useful in a course or unit on detective fiction include

Jorge Luis Borges's "Death and the Compass," Alain Robbe-Grillet's *The Erasers*, Thomas Pynchon's *The Crying of Lot 49*, Ishmael Reed's *Mumbo Jumbo*, Eco's *The Name of the Rose*, Steve Katz's "Death of the Band," and Paul Auster's *New York Trilogy*. (My all-time favorite deconstructed detective story, Clarence Major's *Reflex and Bone Structure*, has been scandalously out of print for some time.) One might sample graphic novels such as the one by Paul Karasik and David Mazzucchelli based on Auster's *City of Glass*. Graduate students (though maybe not undergraduates) might be intrigued by Martin Rowson's graphic-novel adaptation of *The Waste Land* (!) as a hard-boiled detective story modeled on Hammett and Chandler. (Phlebas the Phoenician, a fortnight dead in the front seat of a car, is dredged up from the Pacific in a scene modeled on the one from the film version of *The Big Sleep* in which Owen Taylor's body is recovered. No one knows who killed either of them.)

Science Fiction; or, Worlds

At the beginning of a unit or course on science fiction, I ask two trick questions. The first is, What type of plot distinguishes science fiction from other genres? The answer is, none. Unlike detective fiction, which *is* defined by plot type, science fiction makes use of all kinds of plots, opportunistically as it were; there are science fiction–detective stories (*Neuromancer*, *Blade Runner*), science fiction–quest romances, and so on. Science fiction must be defined by something other than characteristic plots. Next I ask, What gives pleasure in science fiction? Someone usually volunteers, "Ideas," in which case I counter that science fiction ideas are at best secondhand when they're not half-baked and that anyone genuinely interested in the ideas of science fiction would be well advised to read the works of popularized science, sociology, philosophy, and so on where science fiction novelists typically find their "ideas." With any luck, someone will clarify, "Not ideas as such, but ideas *realized* in an imagined world," and then we are off and running, primed to identify what *really* attracts us readers of science fiction: worldbuilding.

Science fiction is distinguished from other genres by its foregrounding of worldbuilding, and science fiction criticism has accordingly developed its own tools for describing worldbuilding in science fiction. (For a different but compatible set of tools, see David Herman's essay in this volume.) The key concept is the *novum*, the "new thing" that a science fiction novel introduces into its model of the world and that is responsible for the difference between that world and the novel's world of contemporary reference. (For fuller details, graduate students could be directed to Malmgren's *Worlds Apart*.) Just like fiction of any other kind, science fiction observes the principle of minimal departure: whatever in the science fiction world is not specified as being in some way different or "new" (i.e., a *novum*) is assumed to be identical with the state of affairs in the contemporary world of reference. In addition, however, science fiction operates with a supplemental set of generic givens, which, like contemporary reality, can be taken for granted without having to be specified; these vary over time but might include, for example, faster-than-light space flight, laser-type weapons, and extrasensory perception. Now fantasy fiction also depends on the positing of *novums* against a background of minimal departure and generic givens (magic, medieval technology, etc.), so a crucial early exercise involves distinguishing science fiction from fantasy. I have sometimes assigned Shakespeare's *The Tempest* for this purpose, contrasting it with one or more of its many updated science fiction versions—say, *Brave New World* and the classic 1956 film *Forbidden Planet*. The difference emerges clearly enough: science fiction motivates its *novums* rationally and naturalistically—"scientifically," even if the science in question is pseudoscience—while fantasy is under no obligation to rationalize its *novums* in naturalistic terms.

A full-dress exercise in identifying *novums* and unpacking their consequences for worldbuilding is indispensable. For this purpose, I have sometimes used Stanislaw Lem's *Solaris*, which not only anatomizes the worldbuilding process in a particularly explicit way but offers two options for cross-media comparison, Andrei Tarkovsky's high-minded Soviet art film and Steven Soderbergh's Hollywood star vehicle. Other successful exercises have involved Samuel Delany's *Trouble on Triton* and *Dawn*, the first volume of Octavia Butler's Xenogenesis trilogy. But my favorite text for this purpose is Alfred Bester's *The Stars My Destination*, a superior pulp fiction, garish and inventive. The principal *novum* of Bester's twenty-fifth century is "jaunting," the capacity for human beings to transport themselves over distances telekinetically, merely by willing it. We write the word *jaunting* on the blackboard and then extend from it a tree of knock-on consequences that Bester posits for his world: consequences for personal security, for sexual mores, for housing and suburbanization, for commuting and migratory labor, for imprisonment, and so on. These are secondary *novums*, dependent on the primary one. Other *novums* are independent of jaunting and merit their own trees: the supplanting of nation-states by business dynasties as well as the colonization of the planets and moons of our solar system and the resulting interplanetary rivalries. Once these *novums* and their consequences are on the board, we are in a position to discuss the interactions among the various *novums* that create the texture of Bester's world.

We are also in a position to discuss the fundamental problem of science fiction poetics, namely, the presentation and distribution of information crucial to worldbuilding—in other words, the problem of exposition. (Graduate students could be directed to Sternberg's landmark book on expositional modes.) *The Stars My Destination* opens with an expositional prologue, detailing the history and practice of jaunting, and other blocks of exposition are distributed throughout the text where needed. Not all science fiction novels are so accommodating. Bruce Sterling's *Schismatrix*, an outer-space picaresque novel deeply indebted to Bester, opens this way: "Painted aircraft flew through the core of the world. Lindsay stood in knee-high grass, staring upward to follow their flight" (Sterling 3). Students unfamiliar with science fiction poetics might be disposed to interpret "core of the world" metaphorically; those who do so may be surprised to discover, a couple of pages later, that the expression is to be taken literally. The "world" in question, it turns out, is an artificial habitat orbiting the moon, cylindrical in shape, so that these painted ultralight aircraft literally are flying through its core. This is an instance, in other words, of realized metaphor, a major device of science-fiction worldbuilding (see Stockwell); but it is also an instance of deferred exposition.

Alternatively, worldbuilding information may be presented not through exposition but by inference, a particularly powerful device because it engages the reader so intimately in the worldbuilding process. Delany writes, in an appendix to *Trouble on Triton*, about the potent effect produced by Robert Heinlein's withholding his hero's racial identity as an African American until two-thirds of the way through *Starship Troopers*, allowing us to infer for ourselves the withering away of racial discrimination in Heinlein's future world (Delany 287). To illustrate the operation of inference in worldbuilding, I often screen the chase sequence from Ridley Scott's *Blade Runner*, when Deckard pursues the female replicant through the crowded streets of a future Los Angeles. The film makes extensive use of explicit exposition, including a scroll-up prefatory text and (in the theatrical release, though not in the director's cut) voice-over narration. Nevertheless, there is an enormous volume of information about this world that is not presented expositionally but may be inferred from the glimpses of punks, Hasids, Hare Krishnas, women's fashions, mass transit, and street furniture (including a neon Atari sign that comically dates the film) afforded the viewer in the visually cluttered background of the chase.

In choosing films to screen in a unit or course on science fiction, I stay away from blockbusters such as the *Star Wars* and *Star Trek* franchises because their worlds are too familiar, not to say fetishized, so that the actual apparatus of exposition and inference in these films might be preempted by prior knowledge. I prefer instead films like *Blade Runner* that are no longer as generally familiar as they once were, or superior B movies like *Forbidden Planet*, *Colossus: The Forbin Project*, or *Screamers* (like *Blade Runner*, an adaptation of a Philip K. Dick text, though less well known). For purposes of laying bare the conventions of science fiction cinema, I have tended to favor art films or "cult" movies, such as Tarkovsky's *Solaris*, Nicolas Roeg's *The Man Who Fell to Earth*, Jean-Luc Godard's *Alphaville*, or Slava Tsukerman's over-the-top *Liquid Sky* (universally despised by undergraduates).

Detective stories are defined by their plot type, so postmodernist parodies and pastiches target plot conventions of detective fiction; but science fiction is defined by worldbuilding, so postmodernist fictions counter by deconstructing science fiction worlds, sometimes literally cutting them up and shuffling them, as in William Burroughs's *Nova Express* or J. G. Ballard's *The Atrocity Exhibition*. A favorite example of mine is Sterling's "Twenty Evocations" (1984), a story set in the same world as *Schismatrix*, in which dense paragraphs of worldbuilding, calling on readers' most sophisticated inferential skills, alternate with paragraphs of cutup prose—worldbuilding and unbuilding in intimate proximity. However, there is really no need to resort to the avant-garde fringe for instances of world unbuilding. One need look no further than Dick, by now all but synonymous with the science fiction mainstream. Dick's fiction, including novels such as *Ubik* or *A Scanner Darkly* (basis for another recent film), illustrates and thematizes the deconstruction of worlds, perhaps confirming what some of us have suspected all along—that science fiction has always already been postmodern.

In fact, however, something similar could be said of other popular genres. Formula fiction almost always displays some degree of self-consciousness, often laying bare its own devices and reflecting critically on its own conventions—in effect, preempting and outflanking postmodern parody and deconstruction. Part of the pleasure and profit in reading—and teaching—formula fiction lies in recognizing the ways it *almost* performs its own narrative analysis on itself, right before our eyes. Almost, but not quite; it needs a little help from its friends.

Works Cited

Bester, Alfred. *The Stars My Destination.* 1956. New York: Random, 1996. Print.

Blade Runner. Dir. Ridley Scott. Warner Bros., 1982. Film.

Chandler, Raymond. *The Big Sleep.* 1939. New York: Random, 1992. Print.

Delany, Samuel R. *Trouble on Triton.* 1976. Hanover: Wesleyan UP, 1996. Print.

D'Haen, Theo. "The Western." *International Postmodernism: Theory and Literary Practice.* Ed. Hans Bertens and Douwe Fokkema. Amsterdam: Benjamins, 1997. 183–93. Print.

Eco, Umberto. "Narrative Structures in Fleming." *The Role of the Reader: Explorations in the Semiotics of Texts.* Trans. R. A. Downie. Bloomington: Indiana UP, 1979. 144–72. Print.

Greimas, A. J. *Structural Semantics: An Attempt at a Method.* Trans. Danielle McDowell, Ronald Schleifer, and Alan Velie. Lincoln: U of Nebraska P, 1983. Print.

Herman, Luc, and Bart Vervaeck. *Handbook of Narrative Analysis.* Lincoln: U of Nebraska P, 2005. Print.

Malmgren, Carl. *Anatomy of Murder: Mystery, Detective, and Crime Fiction.* Bowling Green: Bowling Green State U Popular P, 2001. Print.

———. *Worlds Apart: Narratology of Science Fiction.* Bloomington: Indiana UP, 1991. Print.

McHale, Brian, and Moshe Ron. "On Not-Knowing How to Read Barthelme's 'The Indian Uprising.'" *Review of Contemporary Fiction* 11.2 (1991): 50–68. Print.

Merivale, Patricia, and Susan Elizabeth Sweeney, eds. *Detecting Texts: The Metaphysical Detective Story from Poe to Postmodernism.* Philadelphia: U of Pennsylvania P, 1999. Print.

Perry, Menakhem, and Meir Sternberg. "The King through Ironic Eyes: Biblical Narrative and the Literary Reading Process." *Poetics Today* 7.2 (1986): 275–322. Print.

Phillips, Gene D. *Creature of Darkness: Raymond Chandler, Detective Fiction, and Film Noir.* Lexington: UP of Kentucky, 2000. *Google Book Search.* Web. 6 Apr. 2010.

Propp, Vladimir. *Morphology of the Folktale.* 1928. Trans. Laurence Scott. 2nd ed. Austin: U of Texas P, 1968. Print.

Slotkin, Richard. *Gunfighter Nation: The Myth of the Frontier in Twentieth-Century America.* New York: Atheneum, 1992. Print.

Sterling, Bruce. *Schismatrix.* Sterling, *Schismatrix Plus* 3–236.

———. *Schismatrix Plus.* New York: Ace, 1996. Print.

———. "Twenty Evocations." Sterling, *Schismatrix Plus* 313–19.

Sternberg, Meir. *Expositional Modes and Temporal Ordering in Fiction.* Baltimore: Johns Hopkins UP, 1978. Print.

Stockwell, Peter. *The Poetics of Science Fiction.* Harlow: Pearson, 2000. Print.

Todorov, Tzvetan. "The Typology of Detective Fiction." *The Poetics of Prose.* Trans. Richard Howard. Ithaca: Cornell UP, 1977. 42–52. Print.

Tompkins, Jane. *West of Everything: The Inner Life of Westerns.* New York: Oxford UP, 1992. Print.

Further Reading

Cawelti, John G. *Adventure, Mystery, and Romance: Formula Stories as Art and Popular Culture.* Chicago: U of Chicago P, 1976. Print.

Freedman, Carl. *Critical Theory and Science Fiction.* Hanover: Wesleyan UP-UP of New England, 2000. Print.

Kearns, Michael. "Genre Theory in Narrative Studies." *Routledge Encyclopedia of Narrative Theory.* Ed. David Herman, Manfred Jahn, and Marie-Laure Ryan. London: Routledge, 2005. 201–05. Print.

Radway, Janice A. *Reading the Romance: Women, Patriarchy, and Popular Culture.* Chapel Hill: U of North Carolina P, 1984. Print.

Suvin, Darko. *Metamorphoses of Science Fiction.* New Haven: Yale UP, 1979. Print.

Todorov, Tzvetan. *The Fantastic: A Structural Approach to a Literary Genre.* 1970. Trans. Richard Howard. Ithaca: Cornell UP, 1975. Print.

James Morrison

Film

Old Movies and the New Disorder

Because for many students the story is their principal entrée into the cinematic text, narrative theory remains an invaluable tool for teaching American film. Its basic concepts help students give names to what they have registered cognitively, an exercise that enables them to model theoretical practice in a way that can lead them to broaden the scope of their intellectual inquiry. Christian Metz argued that film is essentially narrative because it is temporal, and this may be why narrative theory can illuminate even key concepts in film not immediately related to narrative, from the formal to the ideological—from the role of editing in mapping space and time to the feminist critique of Hollywood patriarchy.

Perhaps most striking in the classroom is how attuned students are to differences between classical narratives from the studio era and the styles of storytelling of the contemporary films they love and think of as uniquely their own. Narrative theory provides categories through which these contrasts, recognized instinctively, may be understood more fully—not just as the divide between "slow" "old" movies and "fast" new ones, but as the bridge between two kinds of films: those that tend to closely identify fabula and *sjužet*, sternly monitor style, and firmly control frequency, order, and duration and those that casually play with story and discourse, render style overt and intrusive, broach interruptions (in the form of special-effects set-pieces or chase sequences, for example), and welcome fragmentation. Such shifting assumptions about narrative coherence have often been said to define the history of American film—and of American culture more generally—since World War II. If that is so, then narrative theory, despite its long-standing association with formalism, can provide important points of access not only to text-based phenomena but to questions of film and cultural history.

Though narrative theory has in practice explicated stories of every type or cultural affiliation, its modernist heritage makes it especially attuned to unconventional narratives that revise, modify, or challenge conceptions of what stories are, what they do, what they can do. In teaching American popular film, such basic theoretical questions are often difficult to raise in the classroom without adverting to the modernist or postmodern traditions that can seem so distant from the transparency or accessibility of mainstream movies. Yet these films do raise such questions, and my own teaching, among other things, is an effort to investigate how this is the case. As modernist or postmodern models increasingly influence this putative mainstream, such investigations become both more complicated and more directly available. In a *New Yorker* piece of 2007, David Denby surveys what he calls "the new disorder" in film narrative. Denby admits the possibility that the "dislocations and disruptions" of modern film arose from simple "boredom" with the "conventional 'story arc,'" and he declares that "the majority of narratives . . . are still constructed in the traditional way." Yet he notes a novel feature of this trend, its extension beyond the "radical aesthetics" of "the political and artistic avant-garde" into the domain of mainstream cinema (82).

Several of the films Denby mentions form something like an unofficial canon among my recent students, including examples like *Magnolia* (1999), *Fight Club* (1999), *Memento* (2000), *Requiem for a Dream* (2000), *Twenty-One Grams* (2003), the series of films scripted by Charlie Kaufman—*Being John Malkovich* (1999), *Adaptation* (2001), and *Eternal Sunshine of the Spotless Mind* (2004)—and, preeminently, *Pulp Fiction* (1994). For the years that I have been teaching, such current frames of reference have served as touchstones, defining the field of the "contemporary," against which to measure prior instances and therefore to some extent conditioning responses to the films under discussion in a given course. What distinguishes this group, however, is its rangy commitment to narrative experimentation—rearranging chronology, broaching extreme ellipses, slowing down or speeding up narrative time, and generally deriding the norms of traditional storytelling (as in the satirical treatment in *Adaptation* of Robert McKee, the guru of the conventional "story arc").

This cycle of films reflects a widening consciousness about the nature of narrative, unprecedented in popular cinema, that has lent new excitement to the study of the field. On the one hand, among my own students, this development has produced an increasing impatience with the conventional practices of "old" movies. Often, initially, such impatience is articulated in sweeping terms and is based on conceptions of how particular mores of past times are represented in given films or on surface stylistic traits as general as the difference between black-and-white and color cinematography. On further discussion, however, a deeper suspicion emerges of the unities of the classical text, combined with a growing preference for narrative ambiguities, enigmas, gaps, and unresolved contradictions. On the other hand, this awareness of narration itself as a complex act makes the aims and concepts of narrative theory less foreign or "academic" even to beginning students, and it can be harnessed for many pedagogical aims, including that of teaching the complexities of the allegedly "closed" text of classical narration.

Fabula and *Sjužet*, Female Agency, and Closure in *Stella Dallas* and *Erin Brockovich*

I often begin my undergraduate course, American Film Narrative, with pairings of movies from classical and contemporary Hollywood, so as to define and contrast the conventions of these traditions and examine viewers' responses to them. In the first weeks of the course, I introduce through lecture and coordinated readings the two main lines of approach to narrative theory in film studies, which were strictly opposed throughout the 1990s in a so-called paradigm war.[1] Though the sense of contention between these approaches has diminished in the field in the following years, it remains a useful comparative framework for presenting the differing accounts of film narrative provided by these models, with the added benefit of a built-in argument that enables one to "teach the conflicts."

These two lines may broadly be divided between a reconstructed structuralism or self-styled neoformalism (David Bordwell, Kristin Thompson,

Edward Branigan, and others) and an increasingly orthodox poststructuralism (Christian Metz, Raymond Bellour, Colin MacCabe, Laura Mulvey,
and others).[2] The first traces dynamic interactions between the levels of
fabula and *sjužet* in film narration, geared to control temporal dimensions
(frequency, order, duration) and to produce maximum intelligibility. A
key reading here is David Bordwell's "Classical Hollywood Cinema: Narrational Principles and Procedures," in which all the elements Bordwell
attributes to classical Hollywood narration as the dominant paradigm—
clearly defined narrative goals, linear construction, tight causation, stable
character identification, and full plot resolution—are predicated on these
interactions.

The second takes shape around recurrent—indeed, determining—it-
erations of an "oedipal narrative" maintained by "signifying chains" that
operate at symbolic levels (usually with specific reference to Lacan's "symbolic order"), where they elude precise explanation. Though this proposition suggests a structuralist heritage, the attendant conception of the
signifying chain as mercurial and elusive explains why this tradition abandoned the search for localized narrative units (Metz's *grande syntagma-
tique*) in favor of an essentially deductive approach, deriving from overarching narrative infrastructures. As defined, this oedipal narrative inheres
at the level of content, in repeated stories of men's ascension to states of
patriarchal authority, a trajectory successively blocked—by conflicts with
real or symbolic father figures and by the appearance of female figures
encoded as threatening harbingers of sexual difference—but ultimately
achieved, at least in the most typical presumed ur-cases. Formal vectors,
such as the "male gaze" at the level of narrative focalization, are taken to
be hardwired, as it were, into this narrative system, as it in turn subtends
them. In the first weeks of the class, Laura Mulvey's "Visual Pleasure and
Narrative Cinema" provides an introduction—an admittedly heady one
for undergraduates—to the approaches of this second model.

Pairings of sample film texts work best when these are broadly representative and bear clear intertextual resonances, as in *Stella Dallas* and
Erin Brockovich. The first is a classic Hollywood "woman's melodrama,"
and the second a film that may broadly be seen as its contemporary counterpart. Both center on their title characters, women from the working
class who find themselves in middle- or upper-class milieus in which they
are viewed as outsiders, and both turn on conflicts between the women's
maternal status and their desires for kinds of fulfillment beyond that role.
Stella marries a rich businessman and gives birth to a daughter, but her

marriage disintegrates because of her fun-loving and irresponsible ways and her "vulgar" demeanor, both traits linked fairly explicitly to her class origins. Her love of her daughter is shown to be deep and steadfast, but she ultimately decides that she must withdraw so that her daughter may enjoy a happy life among the aristocracy, unburdened by her mother's embarrassing presence, and the film duly ends with a famous scene in which Stella stands outside in the rain watching through a window as her daughter is wed. In *Erin Brockovich*, Erin is a single mother who serendipitously lands a job in a law firm, where she investigates a powerful corporation's pollution of the drinking water of a working-class neighborhood, a breach thought to have caused cancer among the residents. Though her dedication to this case leads to accusations concerning her neglect of her children, she perseveres and is ultimately rewarded with a large settlement for the residents and an enormous bonus for herself.

Since neither film conforms readily to the patterns of oedipal narrative, both enable discussion of the sway or the influence of that model as a contextual point of departure. For those who view *Stella Dallas* as an archetypal tale of female dependency and maternal self-sacrifice and *Erin Brockovich* as a postfeminist chronicle of women's empowerment, the films broadly establish a trajectory from regressive to progressive representations. Even among those who initially reject both as two sides of the same insufficient coin—negative images from the Hollywood stable, "then" and "now"—there is usually little doubt that *Erin Brockovich* represents some progress, however meager.

Closer analysis of the film's narrative structures complicates these positions, and in discussion I ask students to consider questions about the validity of a progressivist historical model of Hollywood storytelling and cinematic style. With its swift cutting, handheld camera work, vibrant colors and film stocks that shift according to mood, changing visual textures from scene to scene without clear plot motivation, *Erin Brockovich* has all the earmarks of "contemporariness." Yet it conforms almost exactly to the Hollywood narrative template as Bordwell defines it. Erin's goal of incriminating the corporation and aiding the townsfolk is intertwined with events of her domestic life as she juggles the warring demands of career and home. This dual plotting determines the interaction of *sjužet* and fabula, dictating the selection and exclusion of plot elements, and the story is resolved in a forceful gesture of closure.

Covering a much longer time period, *Stella Dallas* follows its characters over twenty years, necessitating intricate *sjužet*-fabula negotiations. At first the film seems to be about Stella's quest for a husband, but that goal is achieved early on, flying in the face of Hollywood conventions that tend to identify the process of courtship with *sjužet* time, with the plot culminating in marriage. Afterward, the film seems to lose interest in the dynamics of heterosexual romance except as something of a red herring—that is, the plot does culminate in marriage, but in the light of the events leading up to it, it is difficult to see the concluding wedding as an unqualified triumph. Following this turn, it seems as if the plot will pursue a concern with Stella as a "bad" mother, but that too proves to be a false lead. Moreover, amid these turns and a few stray digressions, the film thwarts easy identification with its main character and resolves in a conclusion that no student in my experience has ever been able to accept as a "happy ending," despite its surface rhetoric of uplift.

My pedagogical goal here is not to arrive at conclusions about the relative "progressiveness" of these individual texts but to underline how appeals to particular frames of reference condition individual acts of interpretation. In the course of discussion, it is not unusual for students to shift positions, discovering more parallels than differences between the two texts—noting, for instance, that both Stella and Erin are positioned according to discourses of fashion and that both films include scenes in which the women "use" their sexuality to achieve short-term goals (Stella to charm the minions of a swank resort, Erin to persuade a bureaucrat to release secret documents). For some, such observations lead them to claim that both films continue to objectify their protagonists despite the agency they appear to grant them in driving the narrative, thus preserving certain elements of the oedipal narrative.

A key question I raise throughout is that of narrative's ideological functions—how it promotes identification, what (if anything) this has to do with cinema as a vehicle of identity formation, how (if at all) film "interpellates" viewers, and so forth. The poststructuralists proceed from the assumption that film's potential as a vehicle for ideology, especially in popular cinema, constantly constricts its spontaneity and threatens or overwhelms the spectator's sense of agency. The viewer in this model emerges as a subject produced in and by chains of signification that do not so much manipulate at some local level—though they can do that too—as they participate in an interlocked cultural system of institutions of which the cinema is one. For his part, Bordwell flatly denies to texts the capacity for this sort of interpellation, arguing that viewers are active agents who take "cues" from the narrative that are then collated in various ways with their own preexisting standpoints. One of the first assignments in this course is for students to write about this point of contention, pro or con, using our test cases to bolster their claims.

The issue of resolution tends to figure prominently in these discussions. Erin's concluding triumph is frequently seen as a powerful gesture of fore-closure, displacing or evading concerns the film seems to have raised about class, corporate power, and ecological crime with the reassuring sugges-tion that Erin's newfound wealth handily resolves any lingering problems. The "happy ending" of *Stella Dallas*, meanwhile, produces an effect of ir-resolution frequently glossed in class discussion along two main lines: it is really "intended" to be a happy ending, but it cannot possibly be felt that way, considering both the events of the story and certain given sociopoliti-cal realities, and the obtuseness of the filmmakers is thus confirmed; or, it is not meant to be seen as a happy ending at all but must gesture ironically in that direction because of the constricting nature of Hollywood conven-tions, and it therefore serves as something of a narrative figure for Stella's own entrapment in oppressive systems of gender positioning. Either way, such schisms in interpretation, especially when considered with the plot's unusual deferral or sidetracking of viewers' inferences, can lead students back into the text with a new sense of the interpretive possibilities of its increasingly visible ruptures and contradictions, making room for various "readings against the grain"—or, at least, suggesting that the "grain" is seldom quite as smooth as it might initially appear.

Technique, Character Motivation, and Ideology in *Touch of Evil* and *Training Day*

Another pairing that has worked well is *Touch of Evil* and *Training Day*. Both are crime narratives concerned with drug trafficking and comment on the dynamics of race in America, turn on a quintessential conflict of "good cop / bad cop," and are shaded with the styles of film noir. Both are also relatively linear narratives—*Touch of Evil* about the investigation of a bombing shown in the first scene, and *Training Day* about a drug deal established early on. For many, *Training Day* exposes depths of corrup-tion in the modern police force and "tells it like it is" in presenting con-temporary racial conflicts, while *Touch of Evil* shows one bad cop amid an otherwise virtuous police force and seems racist in portraying its Chicano characters—one of whom, to make matters worse, is played by the white actor Charlton Heston. Such arguments are buttressed by the claim that

Training Day is, by comparison, *less* "linear." In defining this difference, students sometimes point to strategies of causation, development, or resolution in the narrative, contrasting, for instance, portrayals of the "bad cop" in the two films. In *Touch of Evil*, this character frames suspects because, as many references to anterior action make clear, his wife was murdered many years before the plot commences and her killer was never brought to justice, driving the cop to compensatory illicit tactics to ensure convictions. In *Training Day*, the bad cop's corruption is something of a given, supplied with no parallel motivations beyond those of simple greed—a pattern often seen to depart from the Hollywood tendency toward neat explanation.

Stephen Heath's treatment of *Touch of Evil* in "Film, System, Narrative" is a useful reading in this regard, providing a model for the synthesis of formalist and psychoanalytic-ideological analysis.[3] Heath views the murder of the bad cop's wife as a gap in the fabula that swathes the event in ambiguity, leaving open the possibility that the cop himself is the murderer and motoring the vexed dialectic of order and disorder that, for Heath, drives the textual system. In turn, this dialectic points to more complex motivations, such as the character's racism, since those he frames are Mexican—an issue complicated still further by the fact that his victims are shown to be, in fact, criminals, thus potentially justifying his vigilantism. Yet these debates, useful as they may be in modeling approaches, seem somewhat beside the point, because they do not answer a larger issue that partisans of *Training Day* typically argue: that it is, at base, working according to a different narrative template from that of *Touch of Evil*, from an altered conception of "coherence" itself, indicating, essentially, a postclassical model of narration. Even if *Training Day* can be brought back under the sway of classicism at a "global" narrative level, this does not account for a microlevel—a stylistic current that modifies everything—in the syntactic relation between shots.

Training Day incorporates a pattern of ellipsis, not in the form that ellipsis is usually apprehended in narrative theory—from scene to scene—but *within* scenes, snipping a subliminal second or two here or there to move action along more quickly and generally foregoing the careful shot matching, stabilizing uses of establishing or master shots, painstaking sequences of shots/reverse shots, or deliberate tempo of a "slow" film like *Stella Dallas* or, for that matter, *Touch of Evil*. The film's first few shots illustrate the pattern: a close-up of a digital alarm clock, a shot of the main character staring at the clock from his bed, and a cut to the main character turning the alarm off. The shots are spatially disorienting because the first close-up is really the character's reflection in the clockface, brought into view through a shift of focus so sharp that it is perceived as a cut. We thus move, in successive shots, from a reflection of the character to a direct view; although we are looking at the character from the same angle in the third shot of the sequence as in the second, the visual effect is that of an odd spatial shift. Such spatial dislocations at a formal microlevel define a consistent pattern across the film. Except for a number of scenes that use a dynamic Steadicam, *Training Day* features fast elliptical cuts throughout, approximately matching the current average shot length of Hollywood films—about four seconds.

By contrast, though key sequences of *Touch of Evil*, especially the last, make use of rapid cutting, its dominant formal technique is the long take, as in the famous three-minute opening shot. Orson Welles's movie significantly exceeds the average shot length of its day, which was about nine seconds. It is not uncommon, in discussion of Welles's film, for some students to acknowledge that they had not noticed the absence of cuts in the first shot. If this technique has a marked effect on narrative transmission, it does not impinge on narrative comprehension, since all watchers of the sequence, even those unconscious of the long take, remained cognizant of the basic story information the sequence delivers. Welles's style here offers opportunities for discussion of the role of point of view in cinematic narrative since, once registered, it is frequently seen as indicating the presence of a more overt narrator, one who is identified with the camera itself, than the strategies of continuity editing provide. In these long takes, Welles's sinuously mobile camera retains temporal unity for protracted periods, refusing to make the impossible "leaps" in space or time enabled by classical cutting and thus forfeiting the attendant sense of omniscience. Examining the dynamics of the long take, students become increasingly aware of how cinematic technique controls the presentation of narrative information. Some—especially those influenced by poststructuralist models of analysis—conclude that Welles's long-take style, in making the limitations of the camera's vantage point obvious, exposes by contrast the manipulative mechanisms concealed in traditional Hollywood patterns of omniscience with their assertions of an optimal perspective on narrative events.

If Welles's long-take style is accepted as a radical departure from the contemporary conventions "of its day," it is not unusual for students to rethink their own initial interpretations of the films' respective narratives or ideological implications. Some are consequently inclined to see *Touch of Evil* less as a thoughtless reproduction of discredited stereotypes of the past than as a self-conscious critique of them—subtly mocking Heston's persona, "laying bare" his performance as a camp artifact, and exposing the absurdity of his casting in the role, itself indicative of a thankfully waning convention of the classical era. By contrast, far from marking a departure from convention, the stylistic procedures of *Training Day* are, as an examination of any handful of contemporary films confirms, much in keeping with the conventions "of its day"—even if its day happens to be understood as "the present." It is always useful to ask students to see current, familiar conventions in the larger context afforded by film history; yet this exercise rarely dissuades those who argue that the very fact of this pervasiveness of formal ellipsis, even in the most "ordinary" examples, suggests something new afoot, with which theories of film narrative will have to contend. In either case, whether or not students alter their initial conclusions about the relative value of these examples, exercises of this kind can raise significant questions about the function of norms and the role of style in narrative comprehension.

Linearity and Ideology: The Case of *Pulp Fiction*

Whether a "classical" theory of narration like Bordwell's remains applicable to postclassical storytelling in the mainstream cinema is another question. As part of their definitions of the classical, both neoformalist and poststructuralist approaches to film narrative depend on a notion of linearity: for Bordwell, it is what the hypothetical spectator brings to bear on each and every text—whether classical or radical—while for the poststructuralist, it is what the classical text tries to impose on the passive spectator. In teaching these lines of thinking, I have recently encouraged students to ask what happens if the paradigm shifts, if our notions of the "classical" undergo redefinition. *Pulp Fiction* is an exemplary test case for these questions, not only because it stands as a sort of mythic point of origin for "the new disorder" in contemporary film narrative but also because it deranges story and discourse so drastically that it could have sprung from remedial readings in narratology. Mixed in with several brief and spirited digressions, the story parses three lines of action that are, in the discourse, placed with so little regard for traditional sequence that the film gives the sense of a high degree of self-consciousness.

Students are usually willing to consider the possibility that their "activity" as spectators as they watch this film is essentially to bring the freewheeling *sjužet* back into congruence with the wayward fabula. Less eagerly, they take up the question of whether the film can be seen as an instance of the "denarrativization" called for (or already diagnosed) in poststructuralism. Yet in the latter case, almost nobody seems inclined to argue that the textual self-consciousness of an example like *Pulp Fiction* brings about the thought reforms that seem to be the object of such calls or diagnoses; few would suggest that the film marks any kind of ideological "advance." For some, the film is a parody or pastiche that makes reference to multiple sources, including ideas about patriarchy and the male gaze, but neutralizes them in a manner that makes it "postideological." For others, it is, if anything—and despite its outright rejection of linearity—seen to shore up the power of the male gaze (as in a scene, to name one instance, in which a comatose woman's body is thrown around violently) and the oedipal narrative, concerned as the film is with fathers and sons. For these viewers, the film ultimately illustrates how these currents are fully compatible with a convulsively sophisticated, self-conscious narration. In either case, it is not clear that prevailing theories are responsive to what is most distinctive in this film's narrative construction: its strange rhythms of alternating shock and boredom, its whimsical, passive-aggressive explosions of accidental brutality amid a pervasive atmosphere of violence. Drawing on the material of these discussions, students are assigned late in the course to consider the more advanced question of the relation between self-conscious narration and ideology.

Despite the self-consciousness about narrative found in *Pulp Fiction* and other recent movies, the field of film studies has moved further and further from narrative theory in the last ten years. This is, in part, a response to some of the same concerns with the aleatory and the contingent, some of the same suspicions of traditional causality, reflected in the "new disorder." At the graduate level, to connect students with currents in the field, I ask them to consider how these developments have the potential effect of turning narrative form simultaneously into a version of the "already known" or the "unconscious" of the discipline and—at just the moment that narrative could be studied with a new vigor—robbing the field of this opportunity to explore a creative dialogue between conceptual programming and aesthetic dislocation or reconfiguration. Where the discipline has not turned to a cultural studies infused with historicism or a concern with "the body," it has renewed interest in the kind of nonnarrative poetics Roland Barthes championed in his work on "the third meaning" (52–68)—in, for instance, revivals of the surrealist concept of *photogénie* (Ray 3–13) or of the notion of cinephilia (Keathley 96–102) or reconceptualizations of the "figural" in the visual (Rodowick 202–32), prompted in each case by an overt hostility to narrative and an impulse to "rescue" the image as an aesthetic-ideological category from narrative's enduring grasp. Faced with similar concerns, literary narratology has continued to contend with new developments along these lines, often to show that narration remains a compelling answer to such skepticism. Thus, despite shifting concerns in the field, narrative theory remains a necessary element to an understanding of many of the discipline's guiding assumptions.

At both the graduate and undergraduate levels—further reflecting the new awareness of time-honored problems in narrative theory—students have typically ended recent semesters by calling for a theory of film narrative geared to the age of digital and electronic media, in which, as in *Pulp Fiction*, the accidental and the random play a significant role and in which it is not assumed that all contingencies will or can be accounted for. My own sense of my students' skepticism about classical narration (however much this may be mitigated in the course of our studies) is that it is not at all a trivial one but rooted in a genuinely philosophical skepticism, based on growing concerns about our collective capacity to explain, to discover causal connection through empirical perception. The "new disorder" in film narrative allows these questions, which have been basic to narratology from the start, to take on a new resonance in the film studies classroom.

Notes

1. See Gaines (2). At the undergraduate level, I use Gaines's lucid introduction as a summary of the conflicts between formalist and poststructuralist approaches to narrative in film. At the graduate level, I have used the book as a whole in my course Film and Narrative Theory with some success.

2. A sampling of work from both traditions is usefully collected in Rosen (see Bordwell; Metz; Bellour, "Segmenting" and "Obvious"; Browne; Wollen; Thompson; Linderman). Readings from this collection are assigned throughout the course.

3. Heath's essay exists in two versions, a short one collected in *Questions of Cinema* (131–44) and an extended treatment that includes some of the same material, "Terms of Analysis." The first of these is a workable introduction for undergraduates to a critical practice that combines structuralist and poststructuralist approaches; the second is an excellent introduction for graduate students.

Works Cited

Adaptation. Dir. Spike Jonze. Columbia, 2001. Film.
Barthes, Roland. "The Third Meaning." *Image-Music-Text*. Trans. Stephen Heath. New York: Hill, 1978. 52–68. Print.

Bellour, Raymond. "The Obvious and the Code." Rosen 93–101.

———. "Segmenting/Analyzing." Rosen 66–92.

Bordwell, David. "Classical Hollywood Cinema: Narrational Principles and Procedures." Rosen 17–34.

Browne, Nick. "The Spectator-in-the-Text: The Rhetoric of *Stagecoach*." Rosen 102–19.

Denby, David. "The New Disorder." *New Yorker* 5 Mar. 2007: 80–85. Print.

Erin Brockovich. Dir. Steven Soderbergh. Universal, 2000. Film.

Gaines, Jane. *Classical Hollywood Narrative: The Paradigm Wars*. Durham: Duke UP, 1993. Print.

Heath, Stephen. *Questions of Cinema*. Bloomington: Indiana UP, 1981. Print.

———. "Terms of Analysis." *Screen* 16 (1975): 7–77. Print.

Keathley, Christian. *Cinephilia and History; or, The Wind in the Trees*. Bloomington: Indiana UP, 2005. Print.

Linderman, Deborah. "Uncoded Images in the Heterogeneous Text." Rosen 143–54.

Metz, Christian. "Problems of Denotation in the Fiction Film." Rosen 35–65.

Mulvey, Laura. "Visual Pleasure and Narrative Cinema." *Screen* 16.3 (1975): 6–18. Print. Rpt. in Rosen 198–209.

Pulp Fiction. Dir. Quentin Tarantino. Miramax, 1994. Film.

Ray, Robert. *How a Film Theory Got Lost*. Bloomington: Indiana UP, 2001. Print.

Rodowick, D. N. *Reading the Figural; or, Philosophy after the New Media*. Durham: Duke UP, 2001. Print.

Rosen, Philip, ed. *Narrative, Apparatus, Ideology: A Film Theory Reader*. New York: Columbia UP, 1986. Print.

Stella Dallas. Dir. King Vidor. United Artists, 1937. Film.

Thompson, Kristin. "The Concept of Cinematic Excess." Rosen 130–42.

Touch of Evil. Dir. Orson Welles. Universal, 1958. Film.

Training Day. Dir. Antoine Fuqua. Warner, 2001. Film.

Wollen, Peter. "Godard and Counter-cinema: *Vent d'est*." Rosen 120–29.

Further Reading

Bordwell, David. *Narration in the Fiction Film*. London: Routledge, 1987. Print.

Branigan, Edward. *Narrative Comprehension and Film*. London: Routledge, 1992. Print.

Braudy, Leo, and Marshall Cohen, eds. *Film Theory and Criticism: Introductory Readings*. 6th ed. New York: Oxford UP, 2004. Print.

Chatman, Seymour. *Coming to Terms: The Rhetoric of Narrative in Fiction and Film*. Ithaca: Cornell UP, 1990. Print.

———. *Story and Discourse: Narrative Structure in Fiction and Film*. Ithaca: Cornell UP, 1978. Print.

Kozloff, Sarah. *Invisible Storytellers: Voice-Over Narration in American Fiction Film*. Berkeley: U of California P, 1988. Print.

Plantinga, Carl, and Greg M. Smith, eds. *Passionate Views: Film, Cognition, and Emotion*. Baltimore: Johns Hopkins UP, 1999. Print.

Marianne Hirsch

Visual Culture

Ever—the Human Document to keep
the present and the future in touch with the past.

—Lewis Hine[1]

Teaching Visual Literacy

I have been using images in my teaching of literature for the last twenty
years, at least. Gradually, I came to rely on images, particularly photographs, in my introductory literature and literary theory courses and in
my courses on the novel to teach basic literary and narrative concepts:
perspective, focalization, and audience (who took the picture? how is it
framed? what is the angle from which it is taken? for whom is it taken?);
time and plot (what is the instant in which the picture was snapped? what
happened before and after?); space (where was the picture taken? what lies
outside the frame?); representation and mediation (how does the presence
of the camera inflect the scene? what aspects of the picture signal its distance from the "real?"); ideology and power (whose point of view dominates? whose is submerged? who or what remains invisible?); and so on.

As I incorporated the teaching of images into my literature classes, I realized something about students' relation to the visual that significantly altered my pedagogy: although our students are products of a world that is oversaturated with visual images and although the visual dominates their generation's conception of itself and its world, students actually lack a vocabulary and the tools with which to analyze images and their relation to words. Students can describe the power of private and media images, but they typically have not learned to articulate how pictures, as opposed to and in conjunction with words, produce meaning. In teaching the narrative dimension of images and the visual dimensions of narrative, I realized that I had to teach not just theoretical concepts from narrative theory and art history but also some basic concepts from semiotics, psychoanalysis, media studies, performance studies, and film theory to cultivate some amount of what we might call "visual literacy" in my students. Doing so, however, also produced something else—an acute sensitivity, through relation and through contrast, to words and to how they mean and, particularly, to their narrative dimensions.

In *What Do Pictures Want: The Lives and Loves of Images*, W. J. T. Mitchell identifies visual culture as the object of "visual studies," an emergent field that is a "dangerous supplement" to art history (336–37). The notion of "visual culture" assumes that vision is a cultural construction and invites the critical scrutiny not just of images but of vision itself and of all that exceeds vision and remains invisible. For example, visual studies looks critically at the conjunction of knowing and seeing and locates that conjunction historically and geographically in the modern West. It looks at the impulse to power and mastery that pervades the domain of the visual and at how power circulates through the gaze and the look. If we follow Stuart Hall and his cultural studies group and define culture as a set of assumptions and practices shared among and defining a social group, then visual culture comprises those cultural elements, those media, that take a visual form, as well as the processes of producing and receiving them. Images circulate in newspapers and magazines; in painting and drawing; in film, video, television, advertising, and fashion; in photographs; on the Web; in science and technology; in games and sports; on e-mail and cell phones. Visual culture traces shifts in the production and consumption of images, in their mediation and remediation.

Teaching literature and visual culture, then, requires a way of talking about hybrid, visual/verbal texts like advertisements, comics, visual artworks that include words and verbal texts that include images. How do words and images interact to produce meaning; how can images be read as words and words be looked at as images? How do we negotiate reading and looking as we receive texts and images of this kind? These hybrid, "biocular" texts, to use Peggy Phelan's term, demand not just a visual but a visual-verbal literacy (1286). It is here that theories of visual culture necessarily intersect with narrative theory.

In what follows, I discuss four kinds of texts I have used to teach visual-verbal literacy on the undergraduate and graduate levels: novels and memoirs that describe visual images without reproducing them, novels and memoirs that reproduce visual images, visual images that imply narratives, and truly hybrid works that privilege neither the verbal nor the visual but focus equally on both. Each of these kinds of works can form the basis of a course unit on visual culture and narrative or on narrative theory or, indeed, on just about any unit in which visual-verbal literacy is a relevant issue. (For a discussion of related issues, see Kafalenos's essay on "image-text studies" in this volume.)

In the first three units, I use photographs because they put the relation between visuality and narrative into especially sharp focus. To explain the phenomenology of photography, I begin with Charles Sanders Peirce's tripartite definition of the sign: symbol, icon, and index. The photograph, for Peirce, is both an icon based on the similarity or physical resemblance between the image and the object it represents and an index based on a relation of cause and effect, or of contiguity, like a footprint or a trace. Symbols, in contrast, signal a purely arbitrary relation between a sign and its referent. It is precisely what we understand as the closer referential relation between the photographic image and its object that also brings out its narrative dimensions: every picture has a story of origins behind it—signaling, in particular, both the possibilities and the limits of invention or fabulation. In addition, the photograph's inherent temporality and its framing also place it into a narrative context: the instant that was captured by the image is one among many and thus each still image implies the temporal sequence from which it was selected. Every picture tells a story. But, as Victor Burgin has written, "To look at a photograph beyond a certain period of time is to court a frustration; the image which on first looking gave pleasure has by degrees become a veil beyond which we now desire to see" (152). When I ask students to look in the way Burgin suggests, they find that the frustration and the desire Burgin evokes is precisely a desire for a narrative that would place the image back into a temporal progression.

To flesh out the discussion of photographic reference, I supplement Peirce's semiotic approach with Roland Barthes's discussion of photography in *Camera Lucida: Reflections on Photography*. For Barthes the relation of the image and its referent is more than indexical: the photograph (and Barthes, of course, is writing about analog photography) is a physical, material "emanation" of a past event whose reality it authenticates and to which it provides a direct evidentiary link; it is "a *magic* not an art" (88). At the beginning of my courses I use Barthes's assertion that the "'photographic referent' [is] not the *optionally* real thing to which an image or sign refers but the *necessarily* real thing which has been placed before the lens, without which there would be no photograph" (Barthes 76–77) to open a productive discussion about representation and mediation.

More than indexical, Barthes asserts, the relation of the image and its object is palpable, carnal: it goes beyond the limits of representation to a level of incarnation. In his terms, it is a skin I (the viewer) share with anyone who has been photographed (81). Its materiality, moreover, leads us to think about the medium itself, about the photograph as an object—its look and feel, its size and texture—expanding the discussion of representation to mediation that focuses less on a relation of image to referent than on the qualities of the medium itself. But Barthes's belief in the "it has been" of the photographic object also, necessarily, initiates a discussion of digital media and the capacity we now have to construct images that have no direct relation to a prior referent. And still, students tend to agree that the idea of reference "adheres," in Barthes's terms (6), to photography, and that agreement provides the basis for a valuable discussion of why and how it does so.

Prose Pictures

When Marguerite Duras describes the photograph that is such an integral part of her narrative in *The Lover*, she insists that it is a photograph that might have been taken but never actually was. What function does this hypothetical, imagined photograph play in the progression of the novel, in its construction of character, the setting of its scene, its focalization, and its plot? The "prose picture" Duras describes "might have existed, it might have been taken, just like any other, somewhere else. But it wasn't" (10). This failure to be taken is, in fact, its "virtue," and it is this particular formulation that provokes a broader class discussion of the function of "prose images."

The prose picture is, of course, an old and established genre. Usually referred to as ekphrasis, it can be traced back to Homer's description of the shield of Achilles in *The Iliad*. But ekphrastic verbal descriptions of visual forms usually evoke images that exist, or at least are meant to exist within the fictional framework. Why, then, does Duras invent a photograph if it was "not taken"? Does the absent invented image undermine the authenticity of the plot, its autobiographical dimensions? Does it underscore a level of ambiguity? I suggest to my students that the image that was not taken helps define particular generic conventions of the adolescent narrative by contesting them. The novel of adolescence is a story of becoming, of *Bildung*. This picture, not taken, of the fifteen-and-a-half-year-old narrator, enables her to figure the fluidity of adolescence, the threshold between childhood and adulthood also announced by the "half" in her age. The shape of the photograph, albeit an invented one, can freeze an instant in this process of becoming but not solidify it so much as to grant it determinative or predictive value. It enables the narrator to present several temporalities and perspectives at once: of herself as a fifteen-and-a-half year old and of herself looking back retrospectively and remembering the moment as though it were a photo; of herself as both actor and spectator of the scene, as both subject and object of the look. The invented photo helps clarify a distinctive detail of the novel's narrative voice and focalization—its occasional shift from first to third person and back. This simultaneous internal and external view, evident in the narrator's photographic performance, further develops the adolescent scene. But the photo itself also shows the subversive aspects of this transitional life moment.

In the scene that the narrator remembers and misremembers as a picture, she is on a boat crossing the Mekong River, the only white person in the midst of a Vietnamese crowd. Her strange and hybrid outfit consists of an old, almost transparent silk dress, unsuitable for school; a large manly leather belt, probably borrowed; shoes she cannot remember but presumes to have been gold lamé sandals; and a man's pink, flat-brimmed felt hat with a black ribbon. The rebellious outfit, now "captured" in the imaginary photograph, constructs adolescence as subversive. But if the picture had been taken, it would have been to mark an important transition in her life, the moment she meets the Chinese man who would, inappropriately again, become her lover and usher her out of adolescence into a premature adulthood. It is only in retrospect that such a moment stands out enough to warrant a photo, and thus the imaginary picture reveals a great deal about narrative temporality.

Is a "prose picture" the same whether, in the novel's diegesis, it was or was not ever taken? Do we not imagine it equally whether we are told that it did or did not exist? With this absent and, as she says, "absolute" photograph (10), Duras points to the indexicality and hyperreferentiality of photography only to attenuate its force. She demonstrates the predominance of the visual in the process of memory and life writing in the second half of the twentieth century. And she finds in the prose picture a medium through which to figure the plot of adolescence—the many possible paths that might lead out of it into adulthood and the one that emerged as inevitable in retrospect.

I begin my teaching of narrative and visual culture with prose pictures such as the ones in Duras's novel or with Marcel Proust's description of the photo of Monsieur Vinteuil or with Jamaica Kincaid's many descriptions of photographs in *Annie John* or *Lucy* or with Rachel Seiffert's important post-Holocaust novel about photography, *The Dark Room*. Each of these examples facilitates a discussion of the semiotics of photography and its referential, indexical function. As an assignment in this course unit, I ask students to compare the "prose pictures" that are assumed to exist in the world of the narrative and those that, like Duras's, are said to be imagined and to reflect on the referential force of photography on the basis of this comparison. The prompt asks the students to use this comparison to reflect in particular on the referential force of photography.

Reading and Looking: Beyond Illustration

I next turn in class to fictional works that reproduce photos—Carol Shields's *Stone Diaries*, for example, or the novels of W. G. Sebald. One need only leaf through Sebald's *Austerlitz*, for example, to be struck by the placement of numerous images, some blurry, none well reproduced, throughout its pages. On the second and third pages of the work, we readers are confronted by four pairs of eyes staring out at us from the page. I start my discussion with these images of the eyes that depict, the narrator tells us, two nocturnal animals from the zoo in Brussels and two unidentified human heads. The eyes looking out are an invitation to look back, to look as well as to read. What does this looking entail? How does the work ask us to negotiate looking and reading? What is the function of the images: are they to be read as illustrations of the figures and scenes evoked in the narrative, or is more at stake in their placement and presence? Do they support the narrative? undermine it? Or are they on a parallel track altogether? And how, most disturbingly, are we to view the photographic depiction of fictional characters like Austerlitz?

This discussion invites students to focus on the reception of images both in themselves and in relation to narrative. The images in the novel, on the most superficial level, provide information; they enable the reader to visualize the plan of Fort Breendonk as it is described in the text, for example, or the layout of the Terezín ghetto, and they thus undergird the historical dimension of the novel. We see photographs of British and Welsh landscapes described in the text, of the gardens in Paris's new Bibliothèque Nationale, and of that city's Austerlitz train station. These function as illustrations. On this level, the images also help support and flesh out the character of Austerlitz, who is an architectural historian: we imagine him as the collector of this visual archive. But there is another set of images that complicate our ideas about reference and fictionality. Some images do not seem to relate to the narrative at all and others depict characters and scenes that are clearly invented: Austerlitz, his mother Agáta, the theater performance in which she supposedly performed, and so on. But who is the curly blond boy on the cover of the book? If, as Barthes says, the photograph is evidence for someone's presence in front of the lens, who was in front of the lens and what is his relationship to the fictional Austerlitz? This question can lead to a fruitful discussion of the self-referentiality and the intertextuality of the novel. Jacques Austerlitz, after all, is named after a train station that figures in the text, and that station refers to a famous Napoleonic battle. And, of course, Austerlitz also recalls the name of the most infamous Nazi death camp. We are in the midst of a play of signifiers. And yet the novel insists on its historical authenticity and uses photos to solidify it.

These reflections on photographic evidence are intricately related to the plot in which Austerlitz searches for traces of his parents' history during the Holocaust. He tries desperately to trace his mother to Terezín and searches through a documentary film about the ghetto to find her presence in its images. Here, again, a documentary film is used to try to identify the fate of a fictional character. What I most want students to understand is how lines between fiction and history are blurred and how the indexical nature of the photograph actually helps blur them.

Such a discussion of the reception of images in relation to narrative can be enlarged by using Barthes's distinction between what he calls the *studium*—the historical and contextual information provided by the photograph—and the *punctum*, that aspect of the image that touches the viewer emotionally, grabbing, piercing, and puncturing us. The *punctum* is a detail in the picture that jumps out of the frame and demands our focus. It is subjective, "what I add to the photograph and *what is nonetheless already there*" (Barthes 55). While the *studium* is coded, Barthes says, the *punctum* is not. Do some of the images in Sebald's novel perform the function of the *punctum* for the reader?

Barthes's discussion of the *punctum* reveals not the conjunction but the conflict between visuality and narrative: it reveals the antinarrative dimensions of visual images, those dimensions that, in their affective power, stop the temporal development that mobilizes narrative. The effect of the *punctum* is to render the photo static, repetitive, akin to a haiku. The *punctum* does not facilitate the recollection of the past in narrative form but instead occasions the return of past fragments that cannot be integrated into the present. (See James Morrison's essay in this volume for a discussion of arguments concerning the non- or antinarrative dimensions of images in cinema.)

A larger point of this unit is that the work of looking at images, of looking as well as reading, consists in learning a "foreign language" in order to respond to the summons of photographs of the past and to allow them to sit inside the narrative, if not to be integrated into its progression. It is to allow them their performative force, to ask what they do, or, in Mitchell's terms, what they "want" rather than what they tell.

One effective assignment asks students to reflect on the idea of the *punctum*: I assign one image drawn from an archive that would have personal meaning to a group of students and ask them to identify the detail or the circumstance that for them would constitute a *punctum*. Within the group, they read one another's analyses and discuss the subjective nature of the *punctum* and also its relation to affect, to narrative, and to their interrelation.

Narrative Pictures

Even if some of the images in Sebald's novels arrest the narrative rather than advance it, they only gain their meaning from the context in which they are placed. But what of images that we encounter without such a context: anonymous images whose provenance is not provided? Can a photograph mean without a context and the narrative dimensions it provides? What, if anything, can it, in itself, do?

To explore these questions in class, I tend to use various image archives and collections, extracting individual images without their labels. A very useful such archive is *Collected Visions* (http://cvisions.nyu.edu), a Web-based archive of family pictures donated by hundreds of individuals from places around the globe to the photographer Lorie Novak, who cataloged and organized the images according to a number of categories—historical, thematic, generic. The fact that family pictures are, in fact, so generic, so coded and similar to one another, could lead one to conclude that these images do not need any particularized narrative and can rely on the more generalized narrative of family life to which they gesture or allude. The assumption that all we need to know about such a picture is that it is of a birthday party or a family vacation or a school play can be tested by studying *Collected Visions.* Its images are cataloged according to common, almost stereotyped aspects of family life that are usually photographed: who is in the photograph (e.g., "girl or woman alone," "mother and children," "brothers," "pets," "friends"), the genre of the photograph (e.g., "graduation," "on vacation," "school picture," "birthday party," "family reunion," "crying or pouting"), and the period to which the image belongs.

One of the most distinctive aspects of this site is the invitation for visitors to submit images and also "photo-essays" and thus to become part of the exhibition. Images need not be labeled with any particular disclosing information and that makes the photo-essays that have been submitted all the more interesting. Through these essays, the site becomes a collective autobiographical-narrative project, using projection, identification, and imagination to recount or to invent narratives that particularize the genres and themes revealed by the categories under which they are collected. While some people write photo-essays about their own images, it turns out that most of the essays submitted are about the photographs of others, about which most people write as though they were of themselves. As Novak writes on the site, "maybe writing about the resonant images of others frees authors from the personal baggage surrounding their own photographs and allows them to be more revealing." But are photographs really as anonymous and interchangeable as all that? Can they be so easily adopted by others? In collecting these ordinary images and inviting visitors to create narratives around them, Novak's site invites us to reflect on the relation of images and narrative, on the genre of family photos and the conventional and unconventional narratives of family. It both affirms and subverts the aura of the family and the snapshot as its technology of representation. Pedagogically, the best way to approach these issues is to ask students to write their own photo-essays in response to photos on the site and to analyze the visual and narrative dimensions of their contributions.

I ask students to search through the archive by general categories and then to look at images that are accompanied by essays that offer a verbal narrative to contextualize and situate them. I ask them to select several images that they might submit to such an archive and to think about how, through them, they might tell the story of their lives. I then invite them to write a narrative about images of others and to compare these stories for conventional versus particularized plots, for the myths of family they invoke and the variety of plot details that each image is able to spur. These exercises allow us to reflect on the dependence of images on narrative contextualization and also their openness to narrative invention and elaboration. But they also reveal the limits to this invention—limits set by the codes and conventions of the photographic genre in which they are cast.

Biocularity

The photo-essays on the *Collected Visions* site are good examples of hybrid "biocular" texts that require the visual-verbal literacy my courses try to cultivate. The photo-essay is another well-known genre, most famously exemplified by James Agee and Walker Evans's *Let Us Now Praise Famous Men*; by Edward Said and Jean Mohr's *After the Last Sky*, by Mikael Levin's *War Story*, and by Barthes's *Camera Lucida*. A more graphic instance of "biocularity" can be found in comics. I tend to use the work of Art Spiegelman, Marjane Satrapi, and Alison Bechdel because of their self-conscious exploitation of the interaction of images and words. Meaning, in comics, resides not just in the images or in the words or in their interaction: it resides as much in the gutters between the frames as in the frames themselves. ·

Spiegelman's *Maus* and *In the Shadow of No Towers* offer numerous examples of the visuality of words and the narrativity and antinarrativity of images. In Spiegelman's work, visual images both create narrative and impede it, both compete with the words and illustrate them. The work forces us to look *and* to read; meaning is dependent on both. But by making each page a visual tableau, Spiegelman also points to the limit of biocularity and allows the visual to dominate. He exposes what Tobin Siebers usefully refers to as the "excessive expressivity" of visual images and allows us to examine the source of such excess (1316). His work demands that we consider in particular the relation between visuality and trauma.

Peggy Phelan cites Samuel Beckett's description of seeing: "For it is not at all about a sudden awareness, but a sudden visual grasp, a sudden shot of the eye. Just that" (1286). This suddenness that is akin to wounding, this shot, is profoundly antinarrative: it is the cut of the *punctum*. The art historian Jill Bennett, building on Charlotte Delbo's notion of "sense memory"—the memory residing in the body of the Auschwitz survivor and remaining split off from the "ordinary memory" that produces narratives about life in the camp—argues that

> although words can clearly serve sense memory, vision has a very different relationship to affective experience. . . . The eye can often function as a mute witness through which events register as eidetic memory images imprinted with sensation. (35)

Spiegelman's work is a meditation on such traumatic seeing—its wounding impact, its repetition, its resistance to narrative elaboration, its "excessive expressivity." *In the Shadow of No Towers*, for example, is dominated by one image that recurs obsessively throughout its pages—the image of the burning tower that the narrator saw and tries to reproduce for the reader. That image cannot be described; it must be shown even though, paradoxically, it does not exist as an image. It is like a photograph that, amid the thousands taken on September 11, 2001, was not, in fact, taken. And because it was not taken, it recurs in the background of some of the pages, behind other images, blurred, at times receding, but always obsessively present, like the image that was not taken in *The Lover*.

Spiegelman writes that the burning tower was "burned into the inside of my eyelids," and he is haunted by it. At the same time, he is "haunted now by the images he didn't witness" (*No Towers* 5), like the image of the falling man that he saw only as a series of photographs. "What he actually saw," he insists, "got seared into his skull forever," and in *No Towers*, he draws a series of photographs that have become as powerful and as wounding as seeing it all "unmediated" had been for his character on the morning of September 11 (4).

Traumatic seeing makes time stand still. It provokes repetition, not progression. "Images," Bennett writes,

> have the capacity to address the spectator's own bodily memory; to *touch* the viewer who *feels* rather than simply sees the event, drawn into the image through a process of affective contagion. . . . Bodily

response thus precedes the inscription of narrative, of moral emotion or empathy. (36)

As we get to this point in a class discussion of Spiegelman's *Maus* or *In the Shadow of No Towers*, we come to the limits of "biocularity," to consider carefully how the "excessive expressivity" of visual images works. Spiegelman and Bennett provide a vocabulary with which to discuss the performative power of the image and the limits of narrative and representation. They enable us to analyze how images produce affect in the viewer-reader rather than how they represent, describe, or narrate the traumatic circumstances that motivate the plot and progression of these works. At the end of the course, I hope that students will have learned that what the images do in these circumstances, they do outside and in excess of the temporal progression basic to narrative. John Berger and Jean Mohr write that "when we find a photograph meaningful we are lending it a past and a future" (89). Berger and Mohr's book is called *Another Way of Telling*. But what if images refuse to "tell"? What if they resist, defy, or exceed such meaning production? As a final writing exercise, I ask students to select an image that, in their eyes, performs such an antinarrative act of refusal and to write about their experience of looking at it and their attempts to make it "tell."

Note

1. Hine is quoted in Knauer 25.

Works Cited

Barthes, Roland. *Camera Lucida: Reflections on Photography*. Trans. Richard Howard. New York: Hill, 1981. Print.

Bennett, Jill. *Empathic Vision: Affect, Trauma, and Contemporary Art*. Stanford: Stanford UP, 2005. Print.

Berger, John. *Ways of Seeing*. New York: Penguin, 1972. Print.

Berger, John, and Jean Mohr. *Another Way of Telling*. London: Writers and Readers Cooperative Soc., 1982. Print.

Burgin, Victor. *Thinking Photography*. London: Macmillan, 1982. Print.

Collected Visions. Comp. Lorie Novak. NYU Center for Advanced Technology–Media Research Laboratory, 1996–2007. Web. 16 Oct. 2009.

Duras, Marguerite. *The Lover*. Trans. Barbara Bay. New York: Pantheon, 1985. Print.

Hall, Stuart, ed. *Representation: Cultural Representations and Signifying Practices*. Thousand Oaks: Sage, 1997. Print.

Knauer, Kelly, ed. *Great Images of the Twentieth Century: The Photographs That Define Our Times*. New York: Time-Life Books, 2001. Print.

Mitchell, W. J. T. *What Do Pictures Want? The Lives and Loves of Images.* Chicago: U of Chicago P, 2004. Print.

Peirce, Charles Sanders. *Collected Papers.* Ed. Charles Hartshorne and Paul Weiss. Vol. 2. Cambridge: Belknap–Harvard UP, 1960. Print.

Phelan, Peggy. "Lessons in Blindness from Samuel Beckett." *PMLA* 119 (2004): 1279–88. Print.

Sebald, W. G. *Austerlitz.* Trans. Anthea Bell. New York: Modern Lib., 2004. Print.

Siebers, Tobin. "Words Stare like a Glass Eye: From Literary to Visual to Disability Studies and Back Again." *PMLA* 119.5 (2004): 1315–24. Print.

Sontag, Susan. *On Photography.* New York: Anchor, 1973. Print.

Spiegelman, Art. *In the Shadow of No Towers.* New York: Pantheon, 2004. Print.

———. *Maus: A Survivor's Tale.* New York: Pantheon, 1986. 2 vols. Print.

Further Reading

Bal, Mieke. *Double Exposures: The Subject of Cultural Analysis.* New York: Routledge, 1996. Print.

Chute, Hillary, and Marianne Dekoven, eds. *Graphic Narrative.* Spec. issue of *Modern Fiction Studies* 52.4 (2006): 767–1030. Print.

Groensteen, Thierry. *The System of Comics.* Trans. Bart Beaty and Nick Nguyen. Jackson: U of Mississippi P, 2007. Print.

Hughes, Alex, and Andrea Noble. *Phototextualities: Intersections of Photography and Narrative.* Albuquerque: U of New Mexico P, 2003. Print.

Sturken, Marita, and Lisa Cartwright. *Practices of Looking: An Introduction to Visual Culture.* Oxford: Oxford UP, 2009. Print.

Trachtenberg, Alan, ed. *Classic Essays on Photography.* New Haven: Leete's Island Books, 1980. Print.

Scott Rettberg and Jill Walker Rettberg

Digital Media

A New Cultural Paradigm

We live in an age of ubiquitous digital textuality. We are teaching the first generation of digital-native students, who are more accustomed to writing and reading e-mail than they are to writing and reading letters, more inclined to send an instant message to a classmate than to pass a note, and more likely to read their news online than to pick up a newspaper. Yet almost all these students come to our classes having had no specifically literary experience on their computer screens, and they are not accustomed to considering electronic environments as spaces for narrative literature.

A great deal of the work involved in teaching digital narrative is encouraging students to rethink their cultural assumptions about the nature of literary forms on the one hand and the nature of computer programs and network writing on the other. In a course that surveys contemporary digital narrative, we keep several objectives in mind. We need to teach our students to understand digital narratives in formal ways, as text machines, what Espen Aarseth describes as "cybertexts." But, once they have a handle on that, we need to return them to the interpretive mode, to encourage them to read these works in social, ideological, and historical contexts.

Digital narratives are both formally innovative literary forms, which necessitate effort on the part of the reader simply to "operate," and literary forms intended to reflect and comment on human experience in the same manner as other kinds of literature. Digital narratives furthermore require new conceptualizations of the relations among reader, writer, and media. The reader is often required to participate and make decisions that influence the outcome of the narrative, and the computer itself plays a role that N. Katherine Hayles describes as one of "active cognition" ("Print" 84), interpreting and processing information in a feedback loop with the reader and with the text.

This essay presents a rough outline for a course in digital narrative. We provide a brief overview of some important critical activity in electronic literature, introduce works of electronic literature that have proved fruitful as subjects of classroom discussion, and identify issues that digital narratives raise for our students. While for reasons of space we neglect important theories and entire genres of electronic literature, our hope is that our essay will guide other teachers toward deeper pedagogical experiments with these unruly literary objects. This is a new field, without an established canon. What we are teaching is not literature that has "stood the test of time" but rather literary experiments of the present and recent past, which may yield a rich harvest of born-digital literature in the future.

Origins and Theories of Digital Narrative

Electronic literature emerges both from the culture of networked computing and from contemporary literary and artistic practices. From the sixties to the present, there have been a number of narrative experiments in print where the order of reading may vary according to the reader's choices. Julio Cortázar's *Rayuela* or *Hopscotch*, Italo Calvino's *If on a Winter's Night a Traveler*, and Vladimir Nabokov's *Pale Fire* are among the most well known. American literary postmodernism is replete with examples of works by authors who broke down and reconfigured narrative structures, including Robert Coover, John Barth, Kathy Acker, Ron Sukenick, and Carole Maso. The Paris-centered Oulipo writers practiced and popularized the idea of writing under constraints, using rule-based processes and combinatorial procedures in the creation of potential literature.

Digital narratives are a form of literature that largely evolved as the personal computer became common in homes from the eighties and onward. Early computers used a command-line interface, which gave birth to early forms of digital narrative such as the sixties chatbot ELIZA, a simulated Rogerian psychologist that responds in brief, humanlike sentences to words or sentences you type in, or *Adventure* (1976), a text-based adventure game where the reader types instructions such as "go north" or "kill troll" into a parser that responds with descriptions of what happens next. Although these works and many of those that followed are clearly narrative and literary, the genres were rarely considered literary at the time. It was with the introduction of hypertext that explicitly literary works began to be made for the computer. The idea of "trails" connecting different types of knowledge in a "memex" was proposed by Vannevar Bush in 1945, but it was Ted Nelson who coined the term *hypertext* in the midsixties, sketching a vision of a system he called Xanadu that would in many ways have been similar to the World Wide Web today but that was never completed. Nelson also saw hypertext as a creative, authored form of writing: "Hypertext," he wrote, "means forms of writing which branch or perform on request; they are best presented on computer screens" (19). Hypertext requires a graphical user interface with a mouse that can be used to click links, and when these features became available on personal computers in the eighties, authors began to write hypertext literature for the computer.

In parallel with the development of hypertext fiction and electronic literature in the nineties, theorists engaged with the new media available to narrative. Early, influential theorists include George Landow and Jay David Bolter, whose book *Writing Space* theorized the transition from print to screen in a variety of contexts ranging from word processing to hypertext. Landow's *Hypertext* is heavily influenced by poststructuralism. Landow writes about hypertext being writerly text in Barthes's sense, arguing that the reader participates and almost becomes a coauthor. Much poststructuralist theory describes literature in metaphors that Landow argues have become actualized in hypertext and digital narratives. For instance, where intertextuality in print literature is a reference to another text that remains within the writer's and reader's minds, hypertext can include a link that leads the reader straight to the other text.

Aarseth's *Cybertext* aims to describe more accurately the differences and similarities between digital texts and print texts. *Cybertext* is a neologism Aarseth derives from Norbert Weiner's theory of cybernetics, which encompasses systems that include information on feedback loops. He describes cybertexts as "ergodic," a word he creates from the Greek *ergos*, meaning "work." "In ergodic literature," Aarseth writes, "non-trivial effort is required to allow the reader to traverse the text" (1). To clarify what this nontrivial effort might consist of, Aarseth proposes a typology with seven dimensions: dynamics, determinability, transiency, perspective, access, linking, and user functions, arguing that these dimensions can describe all texts, whether digital or print based. *Cybertext* provides a way of understanding digital texts that builds on the methods of structuralist narratology but that refuses to simply apply narratological tools and terms to new genres. Cybertext is a useful concept in classroom discussion of digital narratives because it provides students with a systematic method of describing the way that a given textual machine works. Advanced students may find Marie-Laure Ryan's extension of and challenge to Aarseth's theory in *Avatars of Story* a useful counterpoint, since Ryan argues that narratology itself is more pliable than Aarseth's theory assumes (97).

For her part, Hayles has encouraged a shift in critical attention in electronic literature and other artistic digital artifacts toward a focus on their materiality as digital objects. Hayles elaborates on the idea that while some early dismissals of electronic literature were based on the idea that these texts were ephemeral or immaterial, in fact they are coded objects that result in embodied reading experiences. Hayles encourages critics of electronic literature to engage in "media-specific analysis," to consider each work in the context of the specific affordances of the media in which it is produced, distributed, and read. There are some effects an author can achieve in a printed book that are impossible in any computer-based medium and many multimedia effects that are conversely impossible in print. Each type of software used to compose digital narratives furthermore has its own specific constraints and affordances. Just as someone authoring a work intended to be read in a codex book faces different constraints from someone writing a poem for a broadsheet or a scroll or note cards, someone authoring a work in *Storyspace* software has different opportunities and limitations than someone authoring a work in HTML/XML, Flash, or Inform. Students need to understand how the specific platform a work is created in can have a profound impact on the work.

These historical and theoretical underpinnings help establish a framework for the course that encourages students to consider which aspects of the digital narratives we study challenge previous understandings of narrative and which aspects fit within conventional understandings of story. While essential aspects of narrative such as plot, character, and temporality are still important elements of digital narrative, they are often radically re-configured. Our students are encouraged to critically examine these recon-figurations and to contemplate the extent to which the nature of narrativ-ity itself might be changing as the nature of storytelling media changes.

Digital Narratives

After giving students a historical and theoretical overview of digital nar-rative, we move to the genre of interactive fiction because it provides a useful entrance into closely reading digital narratives, particularly given the form's close relation to computer games, a genre with which most contemporary students are familiar. *Adventure*, the text adventure game mentioned above, was the first of a series of popular text-based narrative games in the eighties. While these games disappeared from the commer-cial market as graphical games took over, interactive fiction has remained a vibrant literary genre sustained by a community of independent writ-ers and programmers. Among the works that have proved most useful in classroom explorations of the form is Emily Short's *Galatea*, an interactive retelling of the Pygmalion myth, in which the player questions a talking statue to find out about her origins. *Galatea* forces us to reconsider our understanding of how characters can be presented in digital narratives and also the role of the first-person interactor. The player-character must work both to unveil the non-player-character's story and to discover his or her own story as a participant in the narrative. Close readings of interactive fiction can be usefully framed by Aarseth's conception of the ergodic and by Hayles's description of the computer as an active cognizer ("Print" 84), and Nick Montfort provides a comprehensive introduction to the history of the form. Unlike hypertext fictions, which require the reader to simply choose links in order to select new portions of the narrative, works of interactive fiction require the reader to type responses into a parser. The text machine then responds in a feedback loop with the reader-player. The community of interactive fiction developers often use the words *game* and *interactive fiction* interchangeably, and class discussion of interactive fiction inevitably comes around to questions about the relation between those two general forms.

Michael Joyce's *Afternoon, a Story* is one of the first hypertext fictions and also one of the most critically examined digital narratives. This pre-Web work was written in *Storyspace* software and must be installed on the computer from a disk or CD-ROM. *Afternoon* is told in paragraph-length screens of text connected by hyperlinks, but these links are more complicated than most Web links are: they are unmarked, and some links are conditional, so that clicking a particular word might lead you to one place if you have already read a certain part of the work and to another place if you have not. Peter, the narrator of *Afternoon*, has driven past an accident on his way to work, and he is worried that his ex-wife and son were involved in the accident. He attempts to find out whether this is so by calling his son's school and the hospital, but he also avoids thinking about the accident by calling other people and drinking coffee with a colleague. As you read on and return to certain scenes, you begin to wonder whether Peter himself may have been more involved in the accident than first seemed the case. The most common interpretation of *Afternoon* is that the digressive structure of the nodes, forcing the reader through detours without coming to a clear end, mirrors the way that Peter himself attempts to avoid looking the truth in the face (Douglas 105). Of course, the digressive structure of the work is also the root of much student frustration.

While students tend to accept that it takes time to read novels, it can be difficult to coax them into realizing that reading a hypertext fiction like *Afternoon* requires more sustained effort than surfing *Facebook*. One strategy is to read the work aloud together, discussing how we accrue layers of meaning differently when reading a hypertext than we do reading a print narrative. Another is to instruct students to read for a specific measure of time (an hour) rather than simply to "read *Afternoon*." Then, when students have all read some of the work, ask them to begin again at the beginning and consider how a second reading changes their experience. Building on work by reader-response theorists that emphasizes how texts in general are experienced differently when they are reread, a number of scholars have focused on ways in which rereading shapes interpreters' understanding of hypertext fiction in particular (Joyce, "Nonce"; Walker). For its part, *Afternoon* not only invites rereading but also thematizes recursivity, suggesting the need to view events from multiple perspectives—even if no final, authoritative synthesis of those perspectives is possible.

While *Afternoon* serves as a kind of narrative shock therapy, forcing students to consider how they might go about piecing together a story from a scattered field of narrative shards the author has left them with, Shelley Jackson's 1995 *Storyspace* hypertext novel *Patchwork Girl* is intimately tied to print culture and in particular to Mary Shelley's classic novel *Franken-*

stein. Jackson's novel thus provides an opportunity to reground students' assumptions about narrative structures in hypertext. One good approach to teaching *Patchwork Girl* is to begin by closely reading Shelley's novel. Without this context, many students have a culturally received notion of Frankenstein's creature as a grunting green monster with bolts in his head rather than the eloquent Promethean figure of Shelley's novel. The complex nested narrative structure of *Frankenstein* serves as a good starting point to discuss how authors can manipulate chronology and use multiple points of view to demonstrate how different subject positions can frame the same series of events in radically different ways. The textual history of Mary Shelley's writing of *Frankenstein*, including Percy Shelley's revision of the novel, is also important in building an understanding of *Patchwork Girl*. Among the topics of *Frankenstein* that are important to discuss in setting up a reading of *Patchwork Girl* are the abuse and objectification of women throughout the novel, the portrayal of the creative act as destructive hubris, and the idea that texts actively shape identities. While the body of Frankenstein's monster is pieced together from body parts stolen from a graveyard, the books that Frankenstein reads in his abandoned isolation, a list of which the author provides, form the monster's worldview. In *Frankenstein*, Shelley gives us the monster as an intertextual identity. In the absence of the human contact that he craves, the monster develops an ethical system based primarily on the texts he has read.

While *Afternoon* is a modernist hypertext, *Patchwork Girl* has more in common with postmodernist metafiction. *Patchwork Girl* is an acutely self-conscious text that includes five subsections: the journal, story, graveyard, crazy quilt, and the body of the text. The story section includes a narrative of the monster's creation, escape to America on a ship, and relationship with another woman and her eventual dissolution. The graveyard section of the hypertext includes image-maps of different parts of the body. When the reader selects each individual body part, she or he learns the story of the woman from whom the part came. Each donor has some strong defining character trait. Jackson uses this patchwork body as a metaphor for the idea that women's identities are always multiple and that personalities are always pastiches of various and sometimes conflicting drives. The crazy quilt section of the hypertext takes this notion of pastiche further still, stitching together quotations from Jacques Derrida's *Disseminations*, Donna Haraway's "A Cyborg Manifesto," Mary Shelley's *Frankenstein*, L. Frank Baum's *The Patchwork Girl of Oz*, Barbara Maria Stafford's *Body Criticism*, and the *Storyspace* user's manual, creating mashed-up quotations that comment on the text itself. The journal section of the hypertext focuses on the monster's relationship with her author, Mary Shelley, by stringing together appropriated bits of *Frankenstein* with responses from the monster herself. The section devoted to the body of the text is the most explicitly metafictional part of the novel, including a variety of authorial asides on the writing process and on the nature of authorship. *Patchwork Girl* is a rich teaching text both because it is so intimately thematically related to several canonical works of print literature and because each of its sections is a formally distinct narrative experiment in its own right.

Patchwork Girl is a much more spatially oriented hypertext than *Afternoon*. While Joyce's work presents us with single screens of text with "words that yield" (hidden links), Jackson presents the reader with the same boxes-and-lines interface as the one that authors write *Storyspace* hypertexts in. *Patchwork Girl* is not intended to look like or to be read in the same manner as a codex book but is instead a textual landscape the reader navigates through. The work was also innovative at the time for its integration of images into the text. An important aspect of teaching this work in the same course as *Afternoon* is that students become very aware of the media-specific properties of *Storyspace* software in comparison with other reading technologies they are generally more familiar with, such as the codex book or the Web browser. By reading the two texts together, students also see how authors can exploit the technical affordances of the same software platform in radically different ways.

After addressing the important early work in hypertext fiction, our study of digital narrative turns toward the more contemporary digital narratives found on the Web. With the Web's development in the early nineties and its subsequent adoption by people worldwide, there was also a shift in electronic literature toward network-based narratives, including networked hypertext novels. In this part of the course, instructors can further sensitize students to the different constraints and affordances associated with various kinds of computer-mediated narratives, and "defamiliarize" reading practices that may have become more or less automatic. The Web differs in some fundamental ways from the *Storyspace* platform in which the earliest hypertext fictions were produced and distributed. While the *Storyspace Reader*, like the book, is a single-use technology, intended for reading, a contemporary Web browser is a multiple-use technology, which readers use for activities ranging from socializing in online communities to trading stocks to purchasing collectibles to checking news. The Web is a fundamentally distractive reading environment. While *Storyspace* politely tracked our reading, keeping our place and showing us where we had been in a given text, links on the Web go one direction: forward. We always have hundreds, if not an infinite number, numbers of options at our disposal, and as readers we have an expectation that we will be able to progress interactively through Web texts, not by turning pages but by choosing links. Web reading behaviors tend toward skimming and fragmentation. The Web is extensible, so authors can integrate a variety of other platforms and multimedia artifacts into an HTML document. While the early hypertext fictions were distributed by the publisher Eastgate Systems on floppy disk or CD-ROM and were thus fixed "editions" in the same manner as any printed text, network narratives are available on the Internet, accessible anywhere. Network documents are also tranformational in ways that books or hypertexts distributed on discs are not. When an author makes a change in a network document, the change is made across the entire network simultaneously. Every network copy is an exact replication of a dynamic original.

Robert Arellano's 1996 network hypertext *Sunshine '69!* is a novel about the sixties that centers on the Rolling Stones' Altamont Free Concert held in December 1969. The novel serves well as a case study that students can use to compare networked digital narratives with their standalone precursors. In comparison with the austere interfaces of *Storyspace* hypertexts, *Sunshine '69!* is a positively psychedelic mess of a novel, full of color and interactive choices everywhere the reader turns. In focusing on Altamont, Arellano presents the reader with a transition from idealism to cynicism. The main characters of the novel are either archetypes, such as the Glimmer Twins (The Rolling Stones) or Tim (Timothy Leary), or stereotypes, such as Norm (a veteran returned from Vietnam) or Ali (a CIA infiltrator). Arellano presents the reader with multiple means of navigating the text, including links within the text, a calendar allowing the reader to navigate through the novel chronologically, a map that the reader can use to navigate the novel geographically, and a people index that allows the reader to take the story one character at a time by following links to objects in their pockets. Presented with this array of choices, many readers first attempt to navigate the novel by the calendar, reasoning that chronological narration usually works best for print novels. Ultimately, however, the calendar method is less effective at accomplishing a sensible arrangement of episodes than reading through each character's pockets one at a time. Arellano's novel provides a useful example of how authors deal with the problem of presenting characters and a plot within a hypertext novel that the reader can read in any order. Arellano avoids the problem of character development by using stereotypes, archetypes, and "flat" postmodern characterization. Characters are presented not as "fully rounded" psychological entities in the Jamesian sense but as stand-ins for cultural types. By presenting the story in an episodic, picaresque style, Arellano presents a work that can be read in short bursts, suitable to the attention-deficient Internet reader. By providing the reader with character- and geography-based systems of navigation, Arellano points beyond chronological plot development, representing characters and events according to other types of logic.

While interactive fiction and hypertexts are narrative forms that are native to the digital environment, sometimes students wonder at the gap between these forms and the types of writing and reading they regularly engage in on the Web, in e-mail, chat rooms, and social networks. Contemporary authors of digital narratives have begun to incorporate network-specific communication technologies into their work, both formally and thematically. If most contemporary readers spend more time writing and reading e-mail, for example, than they do writing and reading traditional mail, doesn't it make sense to write fiction that explores the styles and narrative potentialities of e-mail? Rob Wittig's 2001 *Blue Company* is one example of this genre of e-mail fiction. Readers subscribed to Wittig's novel, and dispatches from the narrator, "Berto Alto," appeared in their in-boxes daily or sometimes multiple times a day as the narrative unfolded. The premise of the work was that a marketing executive had been sent back through space and time to Renaissance Italy and was using a smuggled laptop to send messages back to the present to a woman he admired, quite literally, from afar. Wittig plays with conventions of courtier poetry, the nineteenth-century epistolary novel, and the graphic novel in telling this distinctly twenty-first-century tale. Although the work is now archived on the Web in a version that readers can tackle in one sitting, original subscribers had the sense of experiencing the events of the novel as they were unfolding, reading the e-mails in the same in-box as they received their regular business and personal correspondence. *Blue Company* demonstrates how authors on the network can use serial publishing differently than they can in print. While many of Dickens's novels were published in monthly installments in magazines, Wittig was able to send hourly updates on a joust tournament as it occurred, in the time scale of the novel. Further, whereas the reader of a hypertext narrative has to engage in a good deal of "ergodic" activity to piece the bits of narrative into a coherent fiction, readers of e-mail novels find themselves reading in a state of anticipation, wondering when the next letter will arrive and what it will contain. As a time-based art form, e-mail narrative is a kind of performance art—as is evidenced in the work of Alan Sondheim, who publishes most of his work in daily postings on e-mail lists.

Rob Bevan and Tim Wright's *Online Caroline* combines e-mail narrative with other popular genres like the personal home page, the online diary, and the webcam. The reader of *Online Caroline* takes the role of Caroline's online friend, who looks through Caroline's photos, watches her daily prerecorded webcam sequences, advises her on what clothes to wear or whether to leave her boyfriend, and answers questions Caroline asks: "What's your favorite color? Do you have children? Have you ever been unfaithful?" Caroline then sends the reader e-mails customized according to the reader's responses but always sticking to a clear plotline that develops in twenty-four short episodes, one episode every day. As the narrative progresses, through the e-mails and the changing Web site, the relationship between Caroline and her boyfriend, David, becomes more and more disturbing. And, as David begins to take over Caroline's life, he also takes over her Web site, so that finally he has taken over as the narrator. Although the reader has no real influence over the storyline, she or he becomes a character in the story and thus feels a strong sense of immersion and even guilt when things begin to go badly for Caroline. Indeed, many readers believed that *Online Caroline* was real and were furious when they found out that she was fictional.

Classroom discussions of *Online Caroline* and *Blue Company* frequently turn on issues related to the distinction between fiction and reality. Because these narratives mimic nonfictional, self-representational writing, the distance between the actual reader and the fictional narratee tends to collapse, leading to a sense of immersion, another concept frequently discussed in relation to digital narratives. Concluding the course with these types of network narratives, which focus on "network styles" of writing, brings our focus back around to the world of digital textuality our students are immersed in every day. These texts help us encourage our students to question how the changes they have experienced in their own daily textual practices are beginning to influence the ways that we will tell stories and contextualize narrative in the near future.

The course we have outlined here sketches but one of many paths to the study of contemporary digital narrative. As literature and language programs increasingly include the study of electronic literature within their curriculum, more scholarly work is being published on the topic. The

Electronic Literature Organization's Web site (www.eliterature.org) is another good source of material. The first volume of the *Electronic Literature Collection*, published in 2006, contains sixty works that might work well in the classroom to present the breadth and diversity of contemporary approaches to digital narrative (Hayles, Montfort, Rettberg, and Strickland).

While our culture's immersion in the global network might seem pervasive, we're still only at the beginning of the second decade of our engagement with the Web. Today's experiments in creating literature for the computer and for the network are but harbingers of things to come. English programs have traditionally served as a repository of cultural memory, preserving and teaching literary works that have marked periods of cultural change. While English may be a field unaccustomed to dealing with the present, one can argue that just such a conservatorial role is necessary now as we begin to frame an understanding of how digital textuality will shape the way we tell stories in the future. Furthermore, one aspect of our courses that we have not addressed here is that after our students develop an understanding of the specificities of digital narrative, they then go on to create their own digital narratives in further courses. It is our hope that, if digital narrative has yet to find its first Chaucer and Shakespeare, such authors might well be waiting in the wings or are perhaps hunched over in the back row of our classrooms, sending text messages from their mobile phones, notes to a dynamic future of electronic literature yet to be fulfilled.

Works Cited

Aarseth, Espen. *Cybertext: Perspectives on Ergodic Literature.* Baltimore: Johns Hopkins UP, 1997. Print.

Arellano, Robert. *Sunshine '69!* 1996. Web. 19 Oct. 2009.

Bevan, Rob, and Tim Wright. *Online Caroline.* 2000. Web. 14 Dec. 2007.

Bolter, Jay David. *Writing Space: Computers, Hypertext, and the Remediation of Print.* 2nd ed. Mahwah: Erlbaum, 2001. Print.

Bush, Vannevar. "As We May Think." *Atlantic Monthly* 176.1 (1945): 85–110. Print.

Douglas, J. Yellowlees. *The End of Books or Books without End? Reading Interactive Narratives.* Ann Arbor: U of Michigan P, 2000. Print.

Hayles, N. Katherine. *My Mother Was a Computer: Digital Subjects and Literary Texts.* Chicago: U of Chicago P, 2005. Print.

———. "Print Is Flat, Code Is Deep: The Importance of Media-Specific Analysis." *Poetics Today* 25.1 (2004): 67–90. Print.

Hayles, N. Katherine, Nick Montfort, Scott Rettberg, and Stephanie Strickland, eds. *Electronic Literature Collection 1.* 2006. Web. 19 Oct. 2009.

Jackson, Shelley. *Patchwork Girl.* Watertown: Eastgate, 1995. CD-ROM.

Joyce, Michael. *Afternoon, a Story.* Watertown: Eastgate, 1990. CD-ROM.

———. "Nonce upon Some Times: Rereading Hypertext Fiction." *Otherminded-ness: The Emergence of Network Culture.* Ann Arbor: U of Michigan P, 2000. 131–49. Print.

Landow, George P. *Hypertext: The Convergence of Contemporary Critical Theory and Technology.* Baltimore: Johns Hopkins UP, 1992. Print.

Montfort, Nick. *Twisty Little Passages.* Cambridge: MIT P, 2003. Print.

Murray, Janet. *Hamlet on the Holodeck: The Future of Narrative in Cyberspace.* Cambridge: MIT P, 1997. Print.

Nelson, Ted. *Computer Lib: You Can and Must Understand Computers Now / Dream Machine: New Freedoms through Computer Screens: A Minority Report.* 1974. N. p.: n.p., 1977. Print.

Ryan, Marie-Laure. *Avatars of Story.* Minneapolis: U of Minnesota P, 2006. Print.

———. *Narrative as Virtual Reality: Immersion and Interactivity in Literature and Electronic Media.* Baltimore: Johns Hopkins UP, 2001. Print.

Shelley, Mary. *Frankenstein.* 1818. New York: Penguin, 2003. Print.

Walker, Jill. "Piecing Together and Tearing Apart: Finding the Story in *Afternoon.*" *Hypertext '99.* Ed. Klaus Tochtermann et al. Darmstadt: ACM, 1999. 111–17. Print.

Wittig, Rob. *Blue Company.* N. pub., 2002. Web. 5 Mar. 2010.

Further Reading

Bolter, J. D., and R. Grusin. *Remediation: Understanding the New Media.* Cambridge: MIT P, 1999. Print.

Ciccoricco, David. *Reading Network Fiction.* Tuscaloosa: U of Alabama P, 2007. Print.

Hayles, N. Katherine. *Writing Machines.* Cambridge: MIT P, 2002. Print.

Ryan, Marie-Laure, ed. *Narrative across Media: The Languages of Storytelling.* Lincoln: U of Nebraska P, 2004. Print.

———. "Narrative and Digitality: Learning to Think with the Medium." *A Companion to Narrative Theory.* Ed. James Phelan and Peter J. Rabinowitz. Oxford: Blackwell, 2005. 515–28. Print.

Tabbi, Joseph, and Michael Wutz, eds. *Reading Matters: Narrative in the New Media Ecology.* Ithaca: Cornell UP, 1997. Print.

Walker, Jill. "How I Was Played by *Online Caroline.*" *First Person: New Media as Story, Performance, and Game.* Ed. Noah Wardrip-Fruin and Pat Harrigan. Cambridge: MIT P, 2004. 302–09. Print.

Wardrip-Fruin, Noah, and Nick Montfort, eds. *The New Media Reader.* Cambridge: MIT P, 2003. Print.

Part IV

Interfaces

Robyn Warhol

Gender

All too often, even in the twenty-first century, when students hear the word *gender* they think, "Now we're going to talk about women." Unless, that is, they are thinking, "Now we're going to talk about sex!" Studying gender means learning to detach the concept from women, sex, and sexuality, to recognize *gender* as an amalgamation of those gestures, styles, and ways of being that a particular dominant culture deems appropriate for women or for men. Gender is no more specific to women than is hair color or the placement of the nose on the face. Even where gender is ambiguous ("Is that a boy or a girl?"), every person bears signs of gender—and so does every narrative. In this essay I present feminist narratology as I do in my courses, first outlining the development of "gender" as a term for literary analysis, then giving examples of how gender affects key elements of narrative, and finally commenting briefly on how narratives not only reflect but reinforce gendered attitudes and behaviors in the reading audience.

Sex, Gender, and Narrative

I arrange this section in ascending order of complexity, beginning with topics I introduce in even the most basic courses and moving through

237

refinements of theory appropriate in courses for seniors and graduate students interested in narrative theory. I find that I need to explain the sex-gender distinction in virtually every introductory course I teach, from Introduction to Women's Studies to Nineteenth-Century British Novel to Critical Approaches, a sophomore-level theory course required for English majors. The first exercise I do in an introductory class is to ask aloud, "What are some things popularly attributed to feminists that you are pretty sure are *not* true?" Students find this more amusing and less intimidating than being asked what feminists *do* believe. "They burn their bras." "They hate all men." "They do not shave." "They never wear makeup." "They get mad if you open a door for them." I fill the board with clichés as students list them. It is easy to offer myself, as well as each of my feminist colleagues, as either contradictions to or variations on the stereotypes. Then we go down the list and discuss tenets of feminism that are behind the misconceptions each cliché represents. Fundamental to these tenets is the theoretical move of understanding sex as distinct from gender.

At every level I explain to students that feminist theory in the seventies and eighties adopted from structuralist anthropology the distinction between gender and sex. Sex refers to the biological markers of difference between women and men: ovaries and testicles, breasts and penises. The adjectives associated with sex are *female* and *male*. Gender, by contrast, refers to cultural notions of what it means to look or behave or feel "like a man" or "like a woman." In academic contexts (as opposed to forms like those you fill out for getting a driver's license) the answer to, Gender? is not "male" or "female" but "masculine" or "feminine." I write a list on the board and ask students to volunteer examples of gestures and styles considered masculine or feminine in our present culture.

The list thus presents the structuralist model of the sex-gender distinction:

Sex	Gender
biology	culture
male/female	masculine/feminine
body parts	gestures/styles

Students find this exercise easy and can readily supply an endless list of binary oppositions like aggressive/passive, rational/emotional, or dominant/nurturing.

Gender does not refer to sexual orientation, although many gendered gestures are associated with heterosexuality or homosexuality among women and men. No direct correspondence exists among sex, gender, and sexuality. For example, a hypermasculine male might be straight or gay; a feminine male (more commonly called effeminate) could be gay, as cultural stereotypes dictate, or he could just as easily be heterosexual. Until the rise of gender theory, though, the dominant model of gender and sexuality was strictly binary (see table 1).

Table 1 diagrams the heteronormative model (to borrow Adrienne Rich's term). It can only be read vertically: to be "normal," a man had to act masculine, be attracted to women, and be biologically male.

In the twenty-first century, the model has become much more complex, as a third gender identity, transgendered, enters the picture (see table 2). Now "Gender Expression" includes androgynous, as well as masculine and feminine; "Sexual Orientation" includes attraction not only to women and men but to both; and "Biological Sex" includes intersexed, to refer to those who are born hermaphroditic or undergo hormonal and/or surgical sex changes across a lifetime. Table 2 can be read vertically, diagonally, or in a zig-zag pattern. It is complicated enough to warrant duplication on a handout, since students may have trouble copying it from the board. I reproduce it on the same sheet as the binary model above, for contrast. This inclusive model of sex/gender/sexuality acknowledges that a woman whose biological sex is female could be androgynous or even masculine and nevertheless be attracted to men or that a transgendered person whose biological sex is male could express feminine gender traits and be attracted to women.

In an introductory course, this is as far as I would go with the theoretical model. The point, for feminist narrative theory, is that gender

Table I
The Binary Model of "Normal" Gender Identity

Gender Identity *"I am a ..."*	Man	Woman
Gender Expression *"My dress, posture, roles are ..."*	Masculine	Feminine
Sexual Orientation *"I am attracted to ..."*	Women	Men
Biological Sex "My hormones, genitalia, and secondary-sex characteristics are ..."	Male	Female

Table 2
An Inclusive Model of Gender Identity

Gender Identity *"I am a . . ."*	Man	Bigendered or Transgendered	Woman
Gender Expression *"My dress, posture, roles are . . ."*	Masculine	Androgynous	Feminine
Sexual Orientation *"I am attracted to . . ."*	Women	Both	Men
Biological Sex *"My hormones, genitalia, and secondary-sex characteristics are . . ."*	Male	Intersexed	Female

expression in something like writing styles is not tied to an author's biological sex or sexual preference: a male writer might write androgynously; a female writer might write in a masculine style; a transgendered author might express a gendered style that encompasses masculinity, femininity, and androgyny or might tend more toward one gendered style than another. What determines the "gender" of a writing style is literary-historical context. A style associated with male writers in any given period is a masculine style; ways of writing common among female writers in the period constitute a feminine style. In the eighteenth-century novel, for example, masculine style was authoritative, ironic, full of allusions to Greek and Latin classics, aggressive in its address to the reader; feminine style during the same period was more effusive, more likely to allude to biblical quotations than to the classics, more steeped in sentiment. If masculine eighteenth-century novelists include Henry Fielding and Tobias Smollett, a list of feminine novelists of the period might include Laurence Sterne as well as Ann Radcliffe and Fanny Burney. The introductory student needs to complete this sequence of the course with the understanding that there is no "natural" correspondence between the sex of an author and the gendering of his or her text.

Recognizing and Disrupting Binary Oppositions

With seniors or graduate students, I go on to link the models to the movement from structuralism to poststructuralism. I explain first that poststructuralist theorists of gender began in the mid eighties to question the either-or framework of the structuralist model of sex and gender. Inspired by deconstruction, feminists critiqued the binary structure not only of the gender system but also of traditional Western thought, showing how its distinctions and alignments disadvantaged women and feminine persons. The dominant Western style of thinking bases analysis on an infinite series of binary oppositions. When I am explaining this idea to students, I give them the first two or three of the oppositions below and ask them to supply more along the same lines while I write the pairs of oppositions on the board. This is an easy exercise for students at every level; they could go on supplying oppositions for a whole class period if I asked them to:

mind	body
reason	emotion
culture	nature
light	darkness
soul	body
good	evil
openness	secrets
civilization	savagery
self	other
whiteness	blackness
virility	effeminacy
man	woman

In writing this list on the blackboard, I am careful to keep the "positive" terms on one side—here, the left—and their "opposites" on the other and to finish with the opposition of "man" (which usually very clearly aligns with the positive terms) and "woman" (which is then revealed as the positive term's opposite). This alignment helps the students see the inequities implicit in the basic structure of Western thinking.

Students at all levels need to learn or be reminded of how structuralism made it possible to see how these pairings of "either/or" shaped traditional thought, while poststructuralism made it possible for feminists to show how this kind of categorical thinking reinforces patriarchy. For classroom purposes, I define *patriarchy* as the maintenance of a culture and society that systematically advantages First World, white, middle- and upper-class heterosexual men. Building on our analysis of the binaries underlining Western thought, I explain that in defining patriarchy in this way I am suggesting that our culture implicitly constructs privilege on one side and links among gender, race, class, and sexuality on the other. I also remind students that patriarchy reproduces itself in the power relations among members of nonelite groups. Black feminist theorists such as bell hooks, for instance, have shown that while African American men do not share the privilege of white men in the culture at large, within the African American community their relation to African American women can only be understood as patriarchal.

Students are usually surprised by my next move: making the point that men alone are not responsible for patriarchy. Women and men have colluded for centuries in maintaining the boundaries of either-or thinking as well as the patriarchal cultural and social arrangements that this kind of thinking has fostered. To break free from the hierarchical constraints of patriarchal thinking, poststructuralist feminists had to repudiate the structuralist model of gender.

They achieved this repudiation by moving from an either-or to a both-and model. I explain to more advanced students two other lessons from deconstruction. First, each term in a binary opposition can be shown to resemble its opposite as much as the two terms differ; J. Hillis Miller cleverly demonstrates such a resemblance between *host* and *parasite*. Second, each term depends on the other for its own meaning. There can be no notion of the self without a corresponding notion of the other; male depends for its meaning on its difference from female. Furthermore, even the category sex is not as straightforward as the either male–or female model would suggest, given the experience of transsexuals, hermaphrodites, and transgendered people. If the either-or model breaks down in the relatively simple category of the biological, the supposed differences between masculinity and femininity are even more problematic. What is understood as appropriate to men or to women is contingent on the time and place in which the masculinity and the femininity are found. Differences of race, social class, historical period, nationality, ability, and age always inflect any given culture's notions of gender.

At this point in the discussion, I remind my students of the driver's license question: "Gender: M or F?" and explain why this common elision of sex and gender matters. I ask them, If biology is destiny, how can we hope for political or cultural change? Change, I tell them, is the ultimate goal of gender studies.

The Impact of Gender on Narrative

Whether an author self-identifies as male or female is what determines the author's sex. The ways in which the author adopts styles, gestures, conventions, diction, and genres associated in a given culture with male writers or female writers add up to the masculinity or the femininity, the gender of the writing. I tell students that I believe the signs of gender show up on every level of narrative discourse but that feminist critics must keep in mind the cultural context in which they and the text are defining gender at all times. At their most basic, signs of gender manifest themselves at the level of story, where characters' actions, thoughts, and attitudes define their gender identities. At their most complex, signs of gender figure at the level of discourse, where the writing itself can be said to be gendered. I find that the most direct way to help students begin thinking about gender and narrative is to start with the familiar territory of character and plot and then to move into the more technically inflected discussions of narrative discourse.[1]

Character

The feminist analysis of characters in narrative traces back to the study of "images of woman" that began in the seventies. Analyzing female characters raises the question of the politics of representation. Students can ask, What indicates this character's gender identity, besides personal pronouns? In what ways do the character's actions and feelings conform to cultural stereotypes about what is appropriate for women or men, and in what ways do they deviate? How does the character's gendered behavior intersect or conflict with assumptions about the race, social class, and nationality attributed to her? What corresponding or contrasting portrayals of women does the novel juxtapose with this character? In what ways does she resemble, and in what ways differ from, male characters in the same text? Students can ask a parallel set of questions about each male character as well as other female characters (and, more interestingly, any transgendered characters) in the text.

Plot

Students very quickly catch on to the idea that certain plot formulas carry strongly gendered connotations, most notably "the marriage plot." As Nancy K. Miller observed in the late seventies, virtually all English and French novels with a woman character at their center written from the mid–eighteenth century through the mid–nineteenth century end in only one of two ways: the heroine can get married, or she can die. This convention holds equally strongly among male and female authors. It accounts for the comfortably predictable endings of all six of Jane Austen's comic novels, in addition to novels as different in tone from one another as Charlotte Brontë's *Jane Eyre*, Emily Brontë's *Wuthering Heights*, and even George Eliot's *Middlemarch*. The heroines whose nonconformity keeps them single (like the gender-rebel Maggie Tulliver in Eliot's *The Mill on the Floss*) or whose transgressions prohibit their becoming respectably married (like the unwed-mother heroine of Elizabeth Gaskell's *Ruth*) must die at the novel's end. The writing careers of Austen, both Brontës, and Eliot flatly contradict the idea that a nineteenth-century woman had nothing to do except die if she did not marry, and Elizabeth Gaskell's long productivity as a novelist and mother strikingly illustrates that a real woman's story, unlike a fictional heroine's, was not over once she did marry. I like to puzzle my students with this counterintuitive axiom: in the nineteenth century there were many more limits on what could happen to women in fiction than there were in real life. Feminist narratology provides a way to think about the persistent power of the marriage plot (which still governs such genres as chick lit and Hollywood romantic comedy) and to recognize those exceptional novels from the period that deviate from this norm—for example, Charlotte Brontë's *Villette*—for their subversive experimentation with plot.

Narration and Narrative Transmission

Gender can figure prominently at every level of the analysis of narrative voice and perspective. To introduce this idea, I ask students to consider the gendered implications of the narrative transaction itself. Following James Phelan's version of Seymour Chatman's diagram of the actual and virtual figures who participate in narrative transactions (Phelan 40), we can introduce it to students using figure 1.

Narrative Voice and Implied Author

Determining the gender of the narrative voice in novels narrated by characters is typically uncontroversial: Pip, a grown man looking back on his life's experience, narrates *Great Expectations*, just as Jane Eyre, a grown woman, narrates hers. With character narration, the gender of the implied author usually corresponds to the gender identity of the flesh-and-blood author. Framed novels can complicate the matter by presenting one narrator's story through the voice of another narrator, and frames in nineteenth-century novels often cross genders. The canonical example is Emily Brontë's

Flesh-and-Blood Author *Actual person who wrote the book*	Implied Author *Pseudonym or persona*	Narrator *Speaker of the text*	Narratee *Addressee in the text*	Implied Reader/ Authorial Audience *Ideal audience*	Flesh-and-Blood Reader *Actual person who is reading*
Charlotte Brontë	"Currer Bell"	Jane Eyre	"Reader"		
Emily Brontë	"Ellis Bell"	Nelly Dean	Lockwood		James Phelan, Robyn Warhol, Jane Student, Joe Student, Another Student
Charles Dickens	"Dickens"	Pip	Unnamed	Someone who "gets it"	
Anthony Trollope	"Trollope"	Unnamed	Unnamed		
Mary Ann Evans	"George Eliot"	Unnamed	"Reader"		

Figure 1. Contemporary narrative theory's model of the narrative transaction.

Wuthering Heights: the male narrator, Lockwood, reports on his own impressions of the Earnshaw and Linton families and their retainers and also repeats lengthy narrative passages spoken by Nelly Dean, the female housekeeper whose career has taken her back and forth between the two families' homes. Nelly's own narrative includes verbatim quotation from other characters' letters, just as Lockwood's includes a short piece of Catherine Earnshaw's childhood journal. In speaking to Lockwood, Nelly communicates across differences of gender as well as class and regional affiliation, a situation of enunciation likely to affect the way she narrates. Feminist narrative analysis invites comparisons and contrasts between Lockwood's and Nelly's voices, because it looks for differences that may carry gendered connotations that affect the actual reader's interpretation of the novel.

Traditionally, readers and critics have referred to unnamed narrators with the pronouns appropriate to the authors who created them, calling Jane Austen's narrator "she" and Anthony Trollope's "he." In this way, the unnamed narrators tend to be collapsed into the implied authors. Accordingly, the novelist's characteristic narrative styles come to be coded as feminine or masculine, depending on the actual author's gender expression. Authors adopting cross-gendered pseudonyms can play with these styles, so that the "George Eliot" of *Adam Bede* imitates the narrative gestures of Henry Fielding and the "Currer Bell" of *Shirley* strives more to resemble William Makepeace Thackeray's narrator than, for instance, Jane Austen's. In their anxiousness to be taken seriously on the literary market, women, of course, had more pressing reasons to use cross-gendered pseudonyms than men have ever had, so that instances of male authors' creating female implied authors and unnamed narrators who use a feminine style (for example, earnest, direct address to "you, Reader") stand out as unusual. Some contemporary novelists experiment with character-narrators who have no specified gender; one particularly well-executed example is *Written on the Body*, by Jeanette Winterson. A novel like Winterson's is useful in getting students to see what the signs of a narrator's gender usually are by noticing their absence.

Narratee and Implied Reader

Just as the narrative voice can carry signs of gender, so can the figure of the reader created in the text. The narratee (a figure of the reader invoked within a text) can in the same text sometimes be styled "sir" and sometimes "madam," as they often are in Sterne or in Fielding. Narratees can also be gendered in situations such as Nelly Dean's passages of *Wuthering Heights*, where her interlocutor, Lockwood, is always male, or in experimental novels such as Italo Calvino's *If on a Winter's Night a Traveler*, whose narratee evolves into a male character in the story. More often, the narratee's gender is unmarked. Whether the narratee is Jane Eyre's oft-invoked "Reader" or a version of the "You" that gender-ambiguously figures as a character in Jane Rule's *This Is Not for You*, students can look for gender cues in what the narrator says to the narratee and in how the narrator says it. Seeking information about the characteristics of an unmarked narratee is very much like doing a Bakhtinian analysis of dialogics. The critic postulates the attitudes, beliefs, feelings, and (sometimes) gender of the addressee by looking at the implicit assumptions that motivate the speaker's words. When students are asked to do this postulating, they become more conscious of the markers of gender they generally take for granted in narrative texts.

Flesh-and-Blood Author and Reader

While much narrative theory steers clear of the "intentional fallacy," preferring to analyze author functions over speculating about authorial intention, feminist narratology nevertheless takes an author's gender identity and gender expression into account. Feminist narratology's emphasis on historical context is the reason for this attention. In a culture where gender so profoundly influences individual people's life experiences, it is bound to affect authors' choices, strategies, and styles. Virginia Woolf's groundbreaking *A Room of One's Own* taught readers of English fiction to think about the differences between the lives of Shakespeare and his imaginary sister Judith, between the relative degrees of confidence felt by authors coming out of the Oxbridge tradition and those scrambling up through newly established colleges for women, between writers born into the authority that comes with gender privilege and the "authoresses" who were not. Feminist narratology follows Woolf in looking for textual signs of the gender consciousness or gender rebellion that might arise from the inequities of the history of the sexes.

Flesh-and-blood readers are of course gendered, and their identities or expressions of gender are likely to affect the ways they interpret or evaluate narratives. While individual reactions to texts are the subject matter of reader-response criticism, narrative theory focuses on the continuities or discontinuities between the narratee, the implied or authorial reader, and the flesh-and-blood person who holds the book and reads. It isn't easy to break students of the habit of flatly referring to "the reader" as knowing or feeling or suspecting something about a detail in any given text. I am continually asking them, Which reader? Are you talking about the narratee inscribed in the text? or the audience you imagine the author was trying to reach (the implied reader)? Or are you just talking about yourself? Being able to make these distinctions through narrative analysis is an important step the students can take toward critical thinking. Becoming conscious of the ways their own gender expression affects their understanding of a text moves them another step in the direction of responsibly owning their identity positions.

Focalization and the Gaze

Focalization, the narratological term for management of point of view, is similar to a concept developed in film studies, *the gaze*. The character who "sees" the events being recounted in a narrative is the "focal character." In first-person narration, the focal character is also the narrator, often at an earlier age. For example, Jane Eyre, who speaks, also sees: she tells her life story from the point of view of the younger self who experienced it. The ironies arising from the gap between the narrating self and the experiencing self add interesting interpretive possibilities to such texts. When there is an unnamed narrator, focalization can be consistently filtered through one person's perspective (as in most of James's fiction), or it can move among characters from chapter to chapter or scene to scene.

Sometimes perceptions may be attributed to a particular character, and sometimes—when they are not "tagged"—they come across through free indirect discourse. The focal character in all these instances becomes the eyes, ears, and conduit of knowledge for the authorial audience and the actual reader. In this respect, the focal character equals the bearer of the gaze, or the virtual person suggested by the point of view that frames the film camera's perspective. As Laura Mulvey influentially argued about classic Hollywood film, in dominant culture the gaze is usually coded as masculine. The male gaze in film dismembers and objectifies the female body as the camera pans up a woman's legs or across her hips or bosom before showing—or sometimes, instead of showing—her face as the sign of her subjectivity. Male bodies in Hollywood film are seldom subjected to the same directorial treatment.[2]

Recognizing the heteronormative male gaze is crucial to understanding the political dynamics of narrative discourse. For an example of how the male gaze operates in Victorian fiction, I show students this passage from Wilkie Collins's *The Woman in White*, in which Walter Hartright, the protagonist/narrator of this section, sees Marion Halcombe for the first time:

> I looked from the table to the window farthest from me, and saw a lady standing at it, with her back turned towards me. The instant my eyes rested on her, I was struck by the rare beauty of her form, and by the unaffected grace of her attitude. Her figure was tall, yet not too tall; comely and well-developed, yet not fat; her head set on her shoulders with an easy, pliant firmness; her waist, perfection in the eyes of a man, for it occupied its natural place, it filled out its natural circle, it was visibly and delightfully undeformed by stays. . . . She turned towards me immediately. The easy elegance of every movement of her limbs and body as soon as she began to advance from the far end of the room, set me in a flutter of expectation to see her face clearly. She left the window—and I said to myself, The lady is dark. She moved forward a few steps—and I said to myself, The lady is young. She approached nearer—and I said to myself (with a sense of surprise which words fail me to express), The lady is ugly! (58)

For a Victorian novel, this description is unusually sexual: Walter's gaze lingers on Marian's waist because he can tell that she is not wearing a corset under her dress, and his emphasis on her "well-developed" though "not fat" form indicates an explicit attention to female flesh that is not common in Victorian fiction, though it presages so well the way the Hollywood camera will take in the female body a century later. The passage also breaks the female body into its component pieces (form, figure, head, waist, limbs, body), thus representing the woman as an object without a subjectivity of its own. A gender-centered analysis of the novel's narrative structure would attend to the interpretive cues this passage provides. Introducing Marian into the fiction so literally through Walter's heterosexual eyes establishes her right away as not the heroine of the novel. Her personality turns out to be amiable, her character virtuous, her intelligence strong, but Marian's face disqualifies her from attracting the romantic attention of the novel's hero. Within the constraints of novelistic genres, an "ugly" face can only belong to what Marian in the end turns into, a superfluous woman devoting her life to the household of her prettier cousin and this man whose gaze has sealed her fictional fate.

As a counterexample to the aggressively masculine gaze of Collins's novel, I ask students to consider a passage of Edith Wharton's *The House of Mirth*, focalized through its doomed heroine, Lily Bart:

> To Lily, always inspirited by the prospect of showing her beauty in public, and conscious tonight of all the added enhancements of dress, the insistence of [Mr.] Trenor's gaze merged itself in the general stream of admiring looks of which she felt herself the centre. Ah, it was good to be young, to be radiant, to glow with the sense of slenderness, strength and elasticity, of well-poised lines and happy tints, to feel one's self lifted to a height apart by that incommunicable grace which is the bodily counterpart of genius! (123)

Wharton's text does not, as students might expect, reverse the gendering of the gaze by putting the heroine in the position of sizing up a male body. Instead, *The House of Mirth* turns the perspective of the gaze inside-out, showing the effect of the male gaze on its female object. Here Lily experiences the male gaze as inspiring; she relishes the sense of power her beauty and grace can command. Read in the context of the whole novel, however, the passage takes on a painfully ironic slant. Lily's belief in the power of her own beauty is naive, destined for disappointment. Her social class and lack of connections figure far more importantly in her marital future than her beauty can. The power she feels as the object of the male gaze is an illusion.

The Impact of Narrative on Gender

Not all male-written narratives use a male gaze in their focalized passages, nor do all female-written narratives represent the gaze from the perspective of its object. All the possible combinations of gender identity, gender expression, and sexual orientation suggested by table 2 can shape narrative focalization, and, in shaping the perspective from which the fiction is seen, can represent both blindness (as in Collins's text) and insights (as in Wharton's) about gender. Discussing the gender dynamics of focalization in a particular text provides an excellent bridge between talking about how gender affects narrative and talking about how gender can be constructed, constituted, or reinforced through narrative. As the actual reader takes in the text, he or she enacts the perspective of the focal character(s). This enactment results in a calisthenics of gender expression, putting actual readers through the motions of seeing the fictional world through a masculine, feminine, or androgynous narrative perspective. Every time a reader engages a narrative text, he or she entertains the possibility of revising his or her own gender expression to reflect the experience of that reading. In this way, I tell my students, not only does gender influence narrative but also reading narrative influences our own gender.

Notes

1. For complementary accounts of the issues of character, plot, narrative transmission, and perspective, see the essays by Kafalenos; Boehm and Journet; Shuman; and Kellner in this volume.

2. For more on issues of gender vis-à-vis focalization or the gaze in cinematic narratives, see Matz, in this volume.

Works Cited

Brontë, Emily. *Wuthering Heights*. 1847. Harmondsworth: Penguin, 2002. Print.

Collins, Wilkie. *The Woman in White*. 1859–60. Harmondsworth: Penguin, 2003. Print.

Miller, J. Hillis. "The Critic as Host." *Critical Inquiry* 3 (1977): 439–47. Print.

Miller, Nancy K. *The Heroine's Text: Readings in the French and English Novel, 1722–1782*. New York: Columbia UP, 1980. Print.

Mulvey, Laura. "Visual Pleasure in Narrative Cinema." *Screen* 16.3 (1975): 6–18. Print.

Phelan, James. *Living to Tell about It: A Rhetoric and Ethics of Character Narration*. Ithaca: Cornell UP, 2005. Print.

Rich, Adrienne. "Compulsory Heterosexuality and Lesbian Experience." 1980. *Blood, Bread, and Poetry*. New York: Norton, 1986. 23–75. Print.

Wharton, Edith. *The House of Mirth*. 1905. Boston: Bedford, 1994. Print.

Woolf, Virginia. *A Room of One's Own*. London: Hogarth, 1929. Print.

Further Reading

Allrath, Gaby, and Marion Gymnich. "Gender Studies." *Routledge Encyclopedia of Narrative Theory*. Ed. David Herman, Manfred Jahn, and Marie-Laure Ryan. London: Routledge, 2005. 194–98. Print.

Case, Alison. *Plotting Women: Gender and Narration in the Eighteenth- and Nineteenth-Century British Novel.* Charlottesville: UP of Virginia, 1999. Print.

Lanser, Susan S. *Fictions of Authority: Women Writers and Narrative Voice.* Ithaca: Cornell UP, 1992. Print.

Page, Ruth E. *Literary and Linguistic Approaches to Feminist Narratology.* New York: Palgrave, 2006. Print.

Salih, Sara, ed. With Judith Butler. *The Judith Butler Reader.* Malden: Blackwell, 2004. Print.

Warhol, Robyn R. *Having a Good Cry: Effeminate Feelings and Popular Forms.* Columbus: Ohio State UP, 2003. Print.

Frederick Luis Aldama

Ethnicity

To integrate effectively the teaching of narrative theory with the teaching of so-called ethnic literature, instructors need to take a multipronged approach. First, they must provide students accustomed generally to character- and theme-focused analyses with the more precise tools offered by narratology: character filter, narrator slant (first-, second-, third-, and multiperson), temporal play, and plot types, for instance. Second, they must teach the narrative texts with a double vision: from one perspective, as informed by their idiomatic cultural specificities (some more culturally inflected and marked by code switching than others), and from the other perspective, as an active participant within and shaper of world literature. Third, they must teach locally inflected narratives as contributing to the world's stock of stories. This suggests a pedagogical as well as a scholarly imperative to which I return at the end of my essay. Since "local" narratives are instantiations of the whole formed by world narrative literature, such narratives inevitably help us sharpen the tools of narratology.

With several slight adjustments, this general three-pronged approach can be applied to the teaching of both undergraduate- and graduate-level courses. In my graduate-level course on ethnic literature, we read and discuss selected fictional narratives in conjunction with a range of secondary materials, including some that offer quite specific narratological tools and others that present relevant historical, biographical, and cultural information. One strategy is to read Ana Castillo's short story "Loverboys" along with both an article dealing with point of view and gender, such as Susan Lanser's "Queering Narratology," and a piece furnishing contextual information, such as Marcial González's "A Marxist Critique of Borderlands Postmodernism." (This template is one I also use when teaching an undergraduate honors course.) In a nonhonors, undergraduate-level course, I have the students focus on the primary material (the narrative fiction), and I provide the narratological tools and contextual information through minilectures supplemented with handouts. When I teach an ethnic American literature survey course, I announce the first day that we will look at a number of different ethnic-identified literatures—Latino, Asian American, Native American, and African American—as they shape and at the same time are shaped by particularities of their cultures. In addition, I note that even as these literatures are inescapably inscribed in the American culture as a whole, they are simultaneously inscribed in the worldwide circulation and construction of fiction as a significant cultural object. It is this last dimension of inscription, I inform the students, that links one literature to all the rest and that makes it possible to develop and universally apply analytic tools such as those of narratology.

In all my course descriptions I therefore seek to establish a contract to be fulfilled with the students from beginning to end: that we will sidestep so-called identity politics and discussions of felicitous or infelicitous representation of "ethnicity" and the "ethnic experience" by the authors concerned. We will instead heighten the pleasure of reading our narratives by getting to know better what makes them tick and which procedures allow them to connect with our living realities, both here (locally and throughout North America) and elsewhere (in other parts of the globe). This contract also informs the writing assignments, in which I ask students to use various narratological tools in their analyses. By the first paper assignment, the students know enough about the difference between narrator slant and character filter to be able, for example, to write a paper prompted by a question such as, in Ana Castillo's "Loverboys" the story is sometimes "filtered" through the eyes of the character and sometimes presented through the narrator's slant. Do the two techniques create significant tensions in the story, or do they peacefully coexist? If there is a tension, is it a productive or a counterproductive one?

Teaching the Narrative-Ethnicity Interface:
Some Guiding Principles

This approach does not exclude value judgments or political and moral arguments from the ethnic literature classroom. On the contrary, both on my part and on the part of my students there is a great concern with value judgments of all sorts, particularly those concerning the worth of the narrative being analyzed. Nevertheless, as a teacher of ethnic literature, I appeal to the reason of the student—and not to his or her emotions (fears) and unfounded beliefs. I require that all of us check the baggage of political correctness at the door.

In all my courses that one way or another focus on ethnic narrative fiction—which can include not only novels and short stories but also comic books and films—I articulate five big-picture concepts and key principles to guide discussion and analysis. Their role is to contextualize our subject matter and help us avoid parochial views about it. While I do not devote a separate unit of the course to laying out these principles in detail, I do present or recall them whenever they are especially germane to the discussion. I draw on the principles to suggest the broader background of human abilities and practices in which ethnic-identified narratives need to be situated, in order for us to separate out what is distinctive about the structure, contexts, and meaning of such stories.

1. For all practical purposes, all human beings are endowed with the same biological and psychological equipment. One and the same anatomical, physiological, and neurological configuration accounts for shared human attributes, including our ability to acquire new skills and dispositions. For example, the bioneurological function of the sense of hearing is identical in all human beings not affected by a relevant disability, though the "education" of hearing varies between individuals and from one historic moment to another. If one's hearing has been educated by listening to Bach in late-twentieth-century Los Angeles, it will differ from that of a person who has never listened to Bach and has been educated instead by Mexican corridos, boleros, and pop music. However, from the biological point of view nothing would impede the corridos listener from becoming educated by Bach or, vice versa, the Bach listener from becoming educated by Mexican musical forms.

2. Narrative has been present in all human societies, presumably since the beginning. As a universal of human culture, narrative has been the

subject of intensive research from numerous perspectives; research attempts to discover and describe features shared by stories of all sorts. One approach, associated with structuralist or classical narratology, seeks a syntax of narrative; another approach attempts to identify a phonemics, that is, features of rhythm, metered speech, onomatopoeia, and prosody that persist across cultures; a third approach, promising though still somewhat inchoate, pursues a narrative semantics, that is, a thematics and a theory of genres; and a fourth approach addresses issues of pragmatics, involving the analysis of the relation between reader or audience and narrative. These approaches are all connected in myriad ways, but it helps to treat them as distinct to keep instruction and research manageable.

3. Recent neuroscience has given a solid basis to the hypothesis that emotions are also universal, and emotions, of course, are of central concern in the study of narrative. That is one reason why—as I never tire of discussing with my students—we must look closely at the most recent research in neurobiology, where the discovery of a mirror neuron system in human beings (after its discovery in macaque monkeys in 1996) has opened the door to many new explorations concerning the brain and our social behavior. The mirror neuron system in human beings is related to imitation, action observation, intention understanding, and understanding of the emotional states of others, to mention a few of the human faculties that are essential for the interpretation of fictional narratives and for the survival and the evolution of the human race. Moreover, the mirror neuron system, by providing us with an experiential (precognitive) insight into other minds, could provide the "first unifying perspective" of the neural basis of social cognition (Gallese, Keysers, and Rizzolatti 401). Might not art be a specialized activity aimed at firing the mirror neurons in a certain direction? Might not the will to style displayed by authors, composers, film directors, and artists involve the deliberate use of syntax, semantics, pragmatics, and phonemics to trigger the mirror neuron system in particular ways to elicit specific insights and emotions in the reader or the audience? In raising such questions, I aim to show my students the need to be always alert to new findings in science that might allow us to see our own discipline in a new and perhaps clearer light.

4. Nothing human is alien to ethnic narrative fiction: it deals with everything under the sun, by any means possible. Moreover, ever since *Gilgamesh* and *The Iliad*, narrative themes and procedures have been common property and, potentially at least, universal property. So I ask my students, can there be an exclusively ethnically identified literary tradition?

In undergraduate and graduate courses alike, lively discussions ensue that complicate the very basis of the concept of ethnic literature and of the academic disciplines founded on that concept. Do not ethnic narratives, in their tireless travels around the globe and their permanent interactions with other ethnic narratives from all corners of the world, participate in world literature? Is not world literature the outcome of thousands of years of ethnic narrative and the present sum of all ethnic literatures? Of course, there is ethnic and there is *ethnic*. I always remind my students of the subordination and decimation of other ethnicities by post-Renaissance Europeans, especially in the Americas. Under such circumstances, certain ethnic identities and their associated literatures survive today as endangered species, and the stakes of studying such literatures are correspondingly high.

Nevertheless, today narrative fiction in all its guises is a shared worldwide achievement, and local ethnic narrative fiction partakes of narrative fiction in the global village (to use Marshall McLuhan's expression). The world is one, the science describing and understanding it is one, and the arts representing and re-creating it are one. The divisions into branches of inquiry, professions, and academic disciplines are contingent, the result of our human limitations and our political, historical, economic, and other equally contingent circumstances that we should not hypostatize, turn into facts of nature, or consider as simply given. In particular, ethnic studies, the development of the very notion of ethnicity, and the identification of ethnic literatures are all politically and historically situated phenomena. They have all taken center stage since the sixties in the United States, one of the world's most massively diversified countries in ethnic and cultural origins. All European countries are present in the United States through emigration; so are most of the countries of Latin America, Asia, Africa, and the Middle East.

The writers and artists of such diverse origins who live and work in the United States are grouped according to ethnicity and studied as representative of their respective cultural backgrounds. But this is an exceptional situation. Writers of African, Middle Eastern, Asian, or Caribbean descent living in France or in Sweden, for instance, are not studied separately in different departments in French or Swedish universities. Nor do the authors themselves generally wish to be considered and evaluated in any way differently from their European counterparts living in France or Sweden. Albert Camus and Jacques Derrida were born in Algeria and lived there all their formative years; yet their mother tongue was French, and they wrote in French. They never asked to be considered ethnic writers in France, and they always considered themselves as innovative thinkers and narrative creators in the French language. The larger point is that, to understand the place of ethnic studies in American academia and the political and economic importance these studies have acquired in our country, we must study and know the particular circumstances that led to their conception and establishment.

5. Understanding ethnic narratives requires approaching them with appropriate and reliable theories and analytic tools. This principle requires the teacher to distinguish clearly—both for himself or herself and for the students—between well-founded and well-reasoned concepts and hypotheses, on the one hand, and mere preaching, on the other.

Modeling a Course That Uses the Narratological Toolkit

Narrative theory helps students find their footing when exploring how syntax, semantics, pragmatics, and phonemics—the resources of narrative expression and interpretation—come together as a unified whole in a work of narrative fiction. It furnishes the students means to identify structures in a given text that can be studied in comparison with literature by all sorts of authors in all parts of the world and in many different epochs. It can provide them with the tools and key ideas to understand better how all authors, including ethnic (or multicultural) authors, use techniques such as vision and voice; narrative speed; reported, transposed, and narrativized speech; and embedding to create engaging stories that move readers. Narrative theory also reminds the students of the artifice of the narratives—that stories are constructs represented verbally, in written form or else graphically or multimedially (by means of pictures, drawings, films, or live theatrical performances).

In a course focused on Chicano literature, I have the students read an autobiography (Oscar Zeta Acosta's *The Autobiography of a Brown Buffalo*), a novel (John Rechy's *The Miraculous Day of Amalia Gómez*), a play (Cherríe Moraga's *Giving Up the Ghost*), a short story (from Luis Rodriguez's *Republic of East L.A.*), and a graphic novel (Los Bros Hernandez's *Love and Rockets*). In this course, we move between considering the effects of specific textual details such as the use of particular syntactic structures or specific kinds of verbs and addressing more general questions such as what can Rodriguez do (and not do) when texturing the lives of a Chicana gang in the short story form as opposed to a novel. How does the length of Moraga's *Giving Up the Ghost* allow Moraga to engage her audience in ways that a short story cannot? How does the interplay of the visual with the verbal in *Love and Rockets* work to engage readers differently from the unbroken succession of black marks on the white pages of Rechy's novel *The Miraculous Day*?

In exploring these general questions, we consider a variety of narrative tools capable of enriching our understanding of these different forms of fictional narrative.

Story and discourse. At the outset, I teach graduate and undergraduate students the distinction between story and discourse—the different effects that authors produce by manipulating the relation between the what and the how of their narratives. I often create a diagram on a blackboard or overhead and lecture on this material to undergraduates; for graduate students, I provide copies of Seymour Chatman's discussion of the distinction in *Story and Discourse*. The *Autobiography of a Brown Buffalo* provides an amusing example because of the way Acosta plays with chronology (the account starts in medias res in a bedroom in front of a mirror).

Implied author and implied reader. Rechy's *The Miraculous Day* works well in helping the students understand how the text constructs a felt persona, the sense that someone is standing behind the scenes but is constituted by the narrative itself. This is not Rechy, the biographical author who has written many different kinds of novels, each with its own distinctive implied author, but the novel's constructed master of ceremonies—its grand conductor. The implied author is centrally concerned with constructing a world whereby the implied reader—that entity who responds to the implied author's communication as that author intends—fully grasps the subjective experience of an uncertain reality conveyed by the narrative in toto, a world characterized by the racist anti-immigrant xenophobia and gay-plague homophobia of late-twentieth-century America.

Narrator and the voyeur. These concepts and Castillo's short story "Loverboys" provide mutual illumination. As the students engage slowly, line by line, with the story, they are constantly faced with a narrator who is not only a voyeur but one whose voyeuristic acts call attention to the reader's own act of voyeuristic intrusion. Castillo uses a homodiegetic narrator, so I take the opportunity to identify the different possible ways of narrating: homodiegetic (narrator who also participates as a character in the story she or he recounts); autodiegetic (narrator as main character in the story he or she tells); and heterodiegetic (narrator not a character in the story he or she presents). (For more on these concepts see Phelan's contribution to this volume, as well as the glossary in the back of the volume.) She begins the story as follows: "Two boys are making out in the booth across from me. I ain't got nothing else to do, I watch them" (11). I ask the students to pause here and identify the narrator's gender and to take into consideration the voice and position of the narrator as well as the title of the story. The students typically identify the narrator as male. Soon after, however, the students discover the homodiegetic narrator to be a woman—a woman who desires both men and women. Tuned into narrator position and voice, the students can better comprehend the thematic focus of the story, its blurring of the boundaries between gender and sexual preference. Moreover, by understanding Castillo's choice to create a homodiegetic narrator who desires and objectifies, they also come to discern how the story subverts and resists a politically correct reading, demonstrating that to be queer and of color doesn't necessarily mean one is above reifying others.

Style and voice. I ask the students to pay attention to how the syntax, diction, pace, reiterations, imagery, and other textual features of the narrative crystallize in their minds as a particular, identifiable voice. For instance, when an author uses bilingual wordplay as an element of characterization, he or she gives the implied reader not only a sense of the character's cultural background—Chicano, say—but also an indication of the narrative's general tone and orientation. The students see this dramatically in "Babies," by Abraham Rodríguez, Jr. It begins: "It was good fuckenshit, not that second-rate stuff. It was really good shit, the kind you pay a lot for, so I stared at Smiley for a while cause I got real curious bout whea the money came from" (121). The style of the narration gives the reader a sense of the urban, gritty, and marginal. Style here also functions to set readers up for a surprise, when they discover that this hard-edged voice is that of a *female* autodiegetic narrator.

Duration. It is important for students to understand that the story-discourse configuration of narrative fiction allows for considerable play in how the story stretches, speeds up (elides), and summarizes scenes and events within the storyworld. These variations of rhythm and tempo are produced by the noncoincidence of story and discourse and can profoundly influence the overall feel of the narrative—for instance, serving the function of a dramatic buildup to a climax. Thus, in the penultimate paragraph of Cristina Garcia's "Inés in the Kitchen," we are provided with a descriptive shift to details of Inés's childhood, including a father who wanted to keep his daughter "dolled up in her starched Sunday dress, all to himself" and a mother who dressed her up for pageants and considers Inés's winning the Little Miss Latin New York to be her "greatest achievement" (156). The shift allows the reader to see more clearly that Inés's marriage to a controlling, starched-shirt-wearing gringo husband is less a sellout than something predetermined from childhood. And, equally important, the shift slows the narrative down just enough so that the final paragraph of the story can deliver a big bang even as it blurs the distinction between iterative and singulative narration, that is, between the condensed presentation of multiple repeated actions and single reports of actions that occur only once:

> Other times, mostly in the early afternoons, she feels like setting fire to the damask curtains that keep their living room in a perpetual dusk. She dreams about blowing up her herb garden with its basil leaves, then stealing a thoroughbred from the stable across the street and riding it as fast as she can. Inés finishes the last of her milk. She rinses the glass and leans against the kitchen sink. There is a jingling of keys at the front door. Richard is home. (157)

Palimpsest. It can be useful for students to understand just how a text overlays, gestures toward, and interweaves another world-literary text (or texts). For example, Rechy sets his novel *The Miraculous Day of Amalia Gómez* during a twenty-four-hour period and follows the journey of a racially marginalized protagonist, a middle-aged Chicana single mother of three living in East LA, in a way that immediately evokes James Joyce's *Ulysses* (and, by extension, *The Odyssey*). That Rechy uses stream-of-consciousness narration and free indirect discourse reinforces this intertextual relation. Rechy's overlaying of *The Miraculous Day* on *Ulysses* is neither ironic nor satiric, nor does it undermine Joyce's narrative in any other way. Its nonironic relation to its model is emphasized in Rechy's creation of a careful correspondence between Amalia's encounters during her journey around Los Angeles and Leopold Bloom's in Dublin. At the graduate level, I introduce Gérard Genette's concept of a "second-degree" (5) narrative in connection with Rechy's echoing of *Ulysses*, and I familiarize the students with two major types of allusion discussed by Genette, the parodic (the new narrative pokes fun at the original) and the ludic (the new narrative aims to engage the reader in gamelike play).

Genre. Awareness of genre conventions can help students begin to identify how individual ingredients in a given narrative function. For instance, in teaching Alfred Arteaga's story "Gun," I ask the students to read out loud the first line: "So when the police had my daughter in an assassination position, kneeling, gun to her head, I took care to choose and phrase my words precisely." I then ask, Does this text's technique identify it as a short story or a member of any other genre? More generally, can we move from the presence or absence of any technique to a reliable identification of genre? We discuss how techniques do not in and of themselves allow us to identify a work as a member of a genre. Instead, we identify genres on the basis of a wide range of textual and extratextual information. I then turn to the specific example of what has been identified in Latin America as the *crónica*, a hybrid of literary essay and urban reportage, focusing on its characteristic conventions and techniques. We then reread "Gun," attending to whether the knowledge of such a genre makes any difference in our understanding and appreciation of the text.

Filter and slant. Rechy's *Miraculous Day of Amalia Gómez* is also useful for teaching students how an event can be filtered by the character one way and slanted by the narrator in another way. For instance, what is described as a miracle by Amalia (her Catholic filter) is identified as a filmy cloud of smoke caused by "a sky writing airplane" by the narrator.

Flashback. I explain how this kind of anachrony (the narrative present interrupted by shift to narration of events in the past) is yet another technique that authors can use (or not) to different effects. Analepsis is a technique that Moraga employs in her play *Giving Up the Ghost* to impress a particular rhythm on the presentation of the story, while in novels such as Arturo Islas's *La Mollie and the King of Tears* and Rechy's *Miraculous Day of Amalia Gómez* it functions not only to stretch narrative time but also to provide backstory necessary for the implied reader to understand the characters and their motivations in the present.

Exposing the device. James Alan McPherson's short story "Elbow Room" surprises students in a cerebral, metatextual manner. Following the lives of an interracial couple, white Paul and African American Virginia, McPherson uses the device of frame breaking over and over again. The story opens:

> Narrator is unmanageable. Demonstrates a disregard for form bordering on the paranoid. . . . Flaunts an almost barbaric disregard for the moral mysteries, or integrities, of traditional narrative modes. This flaw in his discipline is well demonstrated here. In order to save this narration, editor felt compelled to clarify slightly, not to censor but to impose at least the illusion of order. (256)

I ask the students why McPherson would use such a device. Is this simply a way to draw attention to the story's own fictionality, or does it do something more, such as underscore the already fragile and quasifictional sense of identity of the story's African American characters? Or does it do both? McPherson's exposing of the device is an atypical technique in "ethnic" American literature; it pushes the boundaries not only of the ethnic narrative toward ethnography but also of the black vernacular coming-of-age narrative.

Cognition and emotion. Devices such as the intrusion of the editor in McPherson's "Elbow Room," the colloquial style in Alfred Arteaga's "Gun," and the filtering of events through the eyes of Rechy's Amalia aim to move the reader in specific ways. So too does Julio Cortázar's very short story "Continuity of Parks," which foregrounds issues of coherence and questions whether we can or should invest emotionally in the story as a result of (or despite) this (in)coherence.[1] "Continuity of Parks" raises the issue of what we actually do when reading narrative fiction: do we really suspend disbelief, or are we simultaneously aware of our environs and immersed in the fictional world? The story's protagonist

> tasted the almost perverse pleasure of disengaging himself line by line from the things around him, and at the same time feeling his head rest comfortably on the green velvet of the chair with its high back, sensing that cigarettes rested within reach of his hands, that beyond the great windows the air of afternoon danced under the oak trees in the park. (64)

At the story's end, the fictional world of the protagonist who is reading the novel fuses with that of the novel he is reading; ontological spaces mix, and the story suggests that he is about to be killed by the character he is reading about. I ask the students to explore whether and how this technique of metalepsis—the destabilizing of conventions of the story within a story and mixing of planes of reality—moves them.

Vice Versa; or, The Relevance of Narrative Dialects for Teaching Narrative Theory

These examples are a mere sampling of the ways narrative theory can enrich the study and teaching of ethnic literature. Indeed, they also steer the students back to the foundational concepts that inform all my courses on ethnic (or postcolonial) narrative fiction. Ultimately, I ask the students to return to the question of ethnic literature as a narrative "dialect" within world literature. Are these dialects finally more similar than they are different? This is the question that Gerald Prince also asks in his forthcoming essay "Reading Narratologically: Azouz Begag's *Le Gone du Chaâba*," where he points out that narratology is not equivalent to textual, literary, or cultural theory, reminding us that a narratological consideration of "any set of (multicultural) texts . . . should not aspire to say everything we would want to know about [them] and their infinitely many contexts but, more modestly and systematically, [it should try] to characterize (the functioning of) their narrativity." So in our teaching and research, we would do well to examine ethnic and postcolonial narrative dialects in the broader context of world narrative literature, thus contributing to "the coherence of the discipline and [facilitating] the systematic study of its object."

At the same time, however, focusing on such narrative dialects can deepen students' understanding and appreciation of what narrative is and the many ways it shapes our understandings of our own and other cultures. In other words, not only does the careful analysis of specific narrative dialects or textual traditions confirm the general applicability of narratological concepts and methods, but doing such analysis across different traditions teaches us that the structures specific to narrative can have vastly different meanings in different contexts. For example, though the basic structure of anachrony remains constant across all narrative dialects, nonchronological narration is put to strikingly different uses in Marcel Proust's *Recherche* and Rechy's *Miraculous Day of Amalia Gómez*. The same goes for the metaleptic structures of Cortázar's "Continuity of Parks" versus André Gide's *The Counterfeiters*. A useful analogy here is sociolinguistic research on vernacular language patterns, which focuses on the social meanings attached to universal linguistic structures. In much the same way, the study of narrative vernaculars illuminates both what makes for a story and the meanings that stories help us make.

Note

1. The case of Cortázar, a writer who was born in Belgium of Argentine parents and who spent much of his life in France, raises the question of who should be considered an ethnic writer in the first place. This question can be introduced at the beginning of the course and again as the class discusses specific aspects of Cortázar's text, as a way of reinforcing broader problems of definition and methodology through the study of narrative and ethnicity.

Works Cited

Acosta, Oscar Zeta. *Autobiography of a Brown Buffalo.* 1972. New York: Vintage, 1989. Print.

Arteaga, Alfred. "Gun." *House with the Blue Bed.* San Jose: Mercury, 1997. 57–58. Print.

Castillo, Ana. "Loverboys." *Loverboys: Stories.* New York: Plume, 1997. 11–22. Print.

Chatman, Seymour. *Story and Discourse: Narrative Structure in Fiction and Film.* Ithaca: Cornell UP, 1978. Print.

Cortázar, Julio. "Continuity of Parks." *"Blow-Up" and Other Stories.* Trans. Paul Blackburn. New York: Pantheon, 1985. 64–65. Print.

Gallese, Vittorio, Christian Keysers, and Giacomo Rizzolatti. "A Unifying View of the Basis of Social Cognition." *Trends in Cognitive Science* 8 (2004): 396–403. Print.

Garcia, Cristina. "Inés in the Kitchen." *Little Havana Blues: A Cuban-American Literature Anthology.* Ed. Virgil Suarez and Delia Poey. Houston: Arte Público, 1996. 152–57. Print.

Genette, Gérard. *Narrative Discourse: An Essay in Method.* Trans. Jane E. Lewin. Ithaca: Cornell UP, 1980. Print.

González, Marcial. "A Marxist Critique of Borderlands Postmodernism: Adorno's *Negative Dialectics* and Chicano Cultural Criticism." *Left of the Color Line: Race, Radicalism, and Modern Literatures of the United States.* Ed. Bill Mullen and Jim Smethurst. Chapel Hill: U of North Carolina P, 2003. 279–98. Print.

Hernandez, Los Bros. *Love and Rockets.* Vol. 10. Seattle: Fantagraphics, 1993. Print.

Islas, Arturo. *La Mollie and the King of Tears.* Albuquerque: U of New Mexico P, 1996. Print.

Lanser, Susan. "Queering Narratology." *Ambiguous Discourse: Feminist Narratology and British Women Writers.* Ed. Kathy Mezei. Chapel Hill: U of North Carolina P, 1996. 250–61. Print.

McPherson, James Alan. "Elbow Room." *Elbow Room.* New York: Fawcett, 1979. 256–86. Print.

Moraga, Cherríe. *Giving Up the Ghost: Teatro in Two Acts.* 1986. New York: West End, 1994. Print.

Prince, Gerald. "Reading Narratologically: Azouz Begag's *Le Gone du Chaâba.*" *New Horizons in the Analysis of World Fiction.* Ed. Frederick Luis Aldama. Austin: U of Texas P, forthcoming.

Rechy, John. *The Miraculous Day of Amalia Gómez.* 1991. New York: Grove, 2001. Print.

Rodríguez, Abraham, Jr. "Babies." 1992. *Latino Boom: An Anthology of U.S. Latino Literature.* Ed. John Christie and Jose Gonzalez. New York: Longman, 2005. 120–32. Print.

Rodriguez, Luis. *Republic of East L.A.: Stories.* New York: Harper, 2003. Print.

Further Reading

Aldama, Frederick Luis. *A User's Guide to Postcolonial and Latino Borderland Fiction.* Austin: U of Texas P, 2009. Print.

Hogan, Patrick Colm. *Empire and Poetic Voice: Cognitive and Cultural Studies of Literary Tradition and Colonialism.* Albany: State U of New York P, 2006. Print.

Saldívar, Ramón. *Chicano Narrative: The Dialectics of Difference.* Madison: U of Wisconsin P, 1990. Print.

Sollors, Werner. "Ethnicity." *Critical Terms for Literary Study.* Ed. Frank Lentricchia and Thomas McLaughlin. Chicago: U of Chicago P, 1995. 288–305. Print.

Treuer, David. *Native American Fiction: A User's Manual.* Saint Paul: Graywolf, 2006. Print.

Adam Zachary Newton

Ethics

I begin on a deceptively jocund note. There is a teasing anamorphic moment in an episode of *The Simpsons*, when, at a Renaissance fair, intrepid Lisa approaches the police chief dressed in friar's garb and standing at the entrance of a tent whose sign reads, "Friar Wiggum's Fantastical Beastarium."

[*Lisa walks up.*]
Wiggum. Alight your gaze on yonder fabled beasts of yore.
[*motions to chimera and manticore pictures*]
Behold, the rarest of the rare, the mythological two-headed hound born
  with only one head.
[*A regular dog wags its tail with a bored look.*]
Ooh, and here, out of the mists of history, the legendary esquilax, a horse
  with the head of a rabbit . . . and the body of a rabbit.
[*The rabbit hops out of its pen.*]
Oh, it's galloping away.
Lisa. [*chasing it*] Here, bunny bunny. Here, bunny.
Wiggum. [*correcting her*] Here, esquilax.

Comic fun like this always risks being spoiled if belabored. Yet it does have the advantage of offering a useful little allegory about compound entities (especially when theoretical) and the suspension of disbelief.[1] Given an academic twist—with a cautionary tale about fancy nomenclature into the bargain—*The Simpsons*'s joke about enchantment underscores the complex give-and-take, at once familiar and strange, between ethics and storytelling, from out of the mists of their own recent entangled history. Thus, the little tent exhibition above serves as a scene of instruction—in other words, it tells us that there's a story or myth behind this little animal, which we not only have to regard imaginatively but also address by its right name. Stories, that is invariably come to us attached with little morals. And this one, in some part at least, brings us back to pedagogy.

At another level, compared with a less fantastical beastie like, say, Ludwig Wittgenstein's duck-rabbit (which appears to the eye as one animal if one looks left and the other if one looks right),[2] everyday dogs and bunnies assume a legendary aspect (a second head, a horse disguised) by having to be reimagined as mythical creatures. This, of course, is the *Quixote* perplex: quotidian reality in a state of dogged enchantment. But transposed to the realm of narrative theory, Friar Wiggum's fable prompts questions such as these: What if the commerce of stories is always a two-headed affair, one head for narrative, one for ethics—even if one of them (but which?) may sometimes, and only accidentally, be missing? Or what if narrative discourse, denuded of the seeming interference of overt ethical statements, is actually ethics through and through—all the way from premise or point (head) to content, plot, and character (body)? As bunny renamed, esquilax is thus the familiar made other, strange to itself. And if we assume that narrative need not be assigned to correlate with ordinary rabbit, or ethics with the stuff of legend, when we flip the terms, it is ethics, regarded imaginatively, that becomes narrative through and through.

This was the deconstructive illusion J. Hillis Miller deftly performed in his chapter on Kant in his own beastarium called *The Ethics of Reading: Kant, de Man, Eliot, Trollope, James, and Benjamin*, when he asserted that "[e]ven when it is defined as pure practical reason, ethics involves narrative, as its subversive accomplice" (23). And it is in just this sense that Geoffrey Harpham more recently conjures the ethical as the province of what he calls "shadows." For, however else the precincts of narrative theory may be haunted (by, say, the political or the visual or even the nonnarrative), one constant companion would be ethics itself: a pressure on literary narrative from within and without, the exclusive property of neither theory nor practice, locatable but nonetheless elusive for all that.

Call this hybrid creature *narrethics*—hound or hare fused together with or enchanted into its "legendary" other. The little allegory from *The Simpsons* has its distinctive uses.

Here, however, on the more sober plane of critical discourse, my essay discusses how I convey to my students this larger conception of narrative and ethics as distinguishable albeit coefficient entities. I focus, first, on how Harpham provides a valuable overarching frame, including a helpful definition of ethics. I then turn to the ways in which shadow figures for narrative theory like the ethical theorists Mikhail Bakhtin, Emmanuel Levinas, and Stanley Cavell, in dialogue with specific kinds of literary narrative, can offer students a more reflexive understanding of this shadowed and intertwined relation between storytelling and the ethical. My overall pedagogical goal is to give my students a deeper understanding of how affinities as well as tensions between narrative and ethics need to be reflected in our efforts to bring narratological analysis and ethical criticism into a closer, more synergistic relation. A secondary goal is to show that understanding this synergistic relation also means that we newly envision the philosophical project of theorizing ethics. Indeed, it requires us to move from the abstractions of philosophical theory to the concreteness of narrative or to see them as codependent.

Preliminary Considerations: Theory as an Opening to Shadows

I use Harpham's *Shadows of Ethics* as gateway reading because it both carefully refines the word *ethics* and provides an excellent lead-in to the articulation of some more concrete applications. Although recent work in narrative ethics rehearses the term's genealogy, invoking first-generation theorists such as Martha Nussbaum, Miller, or Wayne Booth,[3] Harpham's introductory chapters lay a different foundation. His project is threefold: to pose and answer the crucial question, Why ethics?; to explain how the tripartite nature of literary transactions (writing, reading, and criticism) gets disturbed, both clarified and obscured, by ethical interpositions; and to co-implicate the first two aims.

Defining ethics as a "dynamic engagement with otherness" (x), Harpham advances two striking claims. The first is that ethics matters because it represents the point of intersection between literature and theory, "the point at which literature becomes conceptually interesting and theory becomes humanized," where "theory becomes literary and literature theoretical" (33, 35). Second, Harpham insists that ethics is "a hub or matrix from which various discourses, concepts, terms, energies fan out and at which they meet, crossing out of themselves to encounter the other, all the others" (37). The two claims are useful for highlighting a major consequence of seeing narrative and ethics as mutually shadowed: an exposure of the tension between narrative understood as the representation of moral character and content (the ends and effects of actions) and narrative conceived as relationality or encounter itself, that is, the "engagement with otherness." Ethics, in the latter sense, names the dynamic between one discourse and its other(s) over and above a set of possible dilemmas or situations or problematics. It is transitive rather than propositional. With Harpham's help, I alert students to this tension from the start, and we go on to discuss the many forms of its presence in our subsequent reading.

At a more specific level of pedagogical practice, I initially identify three goals for our discussions: being able to recognize the interconnection between formal elements of narrative (e.g., voice, place, randomness—elements I return to below) and the ethical as a matter of content; to distinguish but also to link the ethical and the political; and to ground our interpretations of texts in our open-ended encounters with them. In these encounters, we become subject to texts' claims on us as they engage us in torsions of proximity and distance in relation to the situations they name, the discourses they inscribe, and the voices in which they speak. Expressed another way, this third goal is to approach the act of reading as the opening to shadows—my answerablility for it, in Harpham's terminology, as this text's other.

These goals explain why I defer for extramural support to thinkers who in their theoretical work push off the literary but who nevertheless resist appropriating it in the name of moral philosophy—and who in turn suggest how the philosophical traditions at issue are reshaped by their own encounter with the literary. I "braid" Mikhail Bakhtin, Emmanuel Levinas, and Stanley Cavell (*Must We Mean?*) because all three enact a nonproprietary ethical criticism (an ethics *about* ethics, as it were). All three preserve the otherness of the literary discourse their respective ethical philosophies implicitly invoke. None make the case for the literary as supplement to moral reasoning (contrast Nussbaum and Booth), and none take up more strictly narratological categories in the manner of James Phelan's recent work on readers' ethical positioning and narrative judgments. But the three theorists can be triangulated given their common emphasis on solicitation or appeal (the text as *other*) and their call for a posture of responsive separateness, a readerly practice of proximity (Levinas) or acknowledgment (Cavell, *Must We Mean?*) or answerability (Bakhtin). These considerations lead to my fourth goal: demonstrating that the traditional shadowing of literary criticism by ethical philosophy—a twinning established as early as the Sophists and Plato—marks a point of departure, not arrival. Indeed, the portmanteau phrase *narrative ethics* invites students to open up conventionally static philosophical definitions of and approaches to the ethical by attending to the way it plays secret sharer to acts of narrative.

Voice and Spectacle in Classical Narrative

With this theoretical framework and these pedagogical goals established, we then devote our attention to the plane of textual "practicings" while sustaining the utility of the shadow metaphor as a teaching device. Depending on whether I'm teaching a whole course on narrative ethics or just a unit within another course, we read either four texts or two, but always two kinds of differently shadowed literary texts—first, a section from Saul Bellow's *Herzog* and perhaps chapters from *Autobiography*, by John Stuart Mill; then, an excerpt from W. G. Sebald's *Austerlitz* and perhaps a short story by Haruki Murakami, "The Kidney-Shaped Stone." The first pair can be considered classical, heir to nineteenth-century and modernist traditions alike, while the second pair is posttraditional in tone as well as theme.

The selection from Bellow describes Herzog's reactions to two courtroom dramas, one of which is a jury trial for a couple's murder of their child. As excluded third party, Herzog inserts himself into these scenes as a kind of moral therapy for his own confused psychic state. I begin by giving the students some context, noting that Bellow places Herzog, a scholar of Romanticism (his PhD thesis is entitled "The State of Nature in Seventeenth- and Eighteenth-Century English and French Political Philosophy"), in the position of Jean-Jacques Rousseau's arrested spectator in the *Discourse on Inequality,* who can only watch pityingly as a wild beast devours a child in front of its mother. "What horrible emotions must not such a spectator experience at the sight of an event which does not personally concern him?" asks Rousseau. "What anguish must he not suffer at his not being able to assist the fainting mother or the expiring infant?" (34). Our selection provides the parallel: "With all his might—mind and heart—he tried to obtain something for the murdered boy," says Bellow's narrator of his desolated witness protagonist. "And what did he feel?"

> Herzog experienced nothing but his own *human feelings*, in which he found nothing of use. . . . Why he felt himself—his own trembling hands, and eyes that stung. And what was there in modern, post . . . post-Christian America to pray for? Justice—justice and mercy? And pray away the monstrosities of life, the wicked dream it was? He opened his mouth to relieve the pressure he felt. He was wrung, and wrung again, and wrung again, again. (294)

I build on the comparison between Rousseau and Bellow by asking the students to discuss the following issues: each text's representation of mimetic desire—helplessness before the "real" spectacle of others that nevertheless offers itself as a tableau for projective identification; each text's pointed treatment of pity, first the Romanticist take and then the modern—and, in the case of *Herzog*, the relation of the ethics of that treatment to legal-political aspects of witnessing;[4] and how these treatments introduce a hermeneutical dilemma for Bellow's readers because his novel self-consciously foregrounds the problems of observing others through the lens of one's own interests. With this third point, we open out to broader questions about the ethics of reading: In what sense is our reading always interested? Are some interests more ethically sound than others? And then going back to Bellow, to what extent does the novel anticipate these questions? My goal is not to settle on answers to these questions but to leave them open precisely because doing so seems more ethically appropriate.

Bellow's attention to discourse (Herzog's toggling between rarified and vernacular registers, the novel's modulations of free indirect discourse) provides the opportunity for another set of questions, this time about an ethics of individualized speech and narrative fiction's peculiar responsiveness to the "grain of the voice." How does it either articulate or transgress the boundaries of personality to be an unidentified narratorial consciousness with privileged access to a character's interiority? That is, not just Who speaks? or Who sees? or Where does filter end and slant begin? but also How does any act of reading resist the ethical torsion of such focalized and vocalized trespass? Even at its most transparent and unvexed, the signal property of literary narrative to transmit not only another's story but also that other's proprietary thoughts and feelings is never wholly innocent. Indeed, that property might otherwise be specified as the permanent shadow falling between narrative and ethics in their dialectical linkage. As with the first set of questions, we move back and forth between the case of *Herzog* and these more general questions.

John Stuart Mill's *Autobiography* provides another valuable text for working through questions about the relation between voice and ethics. Mill's story accentuates the pathos of a split subject (in more than just the linguistic sense) whose voice keeps opening up crevices in expressive content through the very act of putatively zero-degree autobiography (whose title conspicuously lacks either definite article or possessive pronoun): "I do not for a moment imagine that any part of what I have to relate can be interesting to the public as a narrative or as being connected with myself"(1). I use Mill's narrative to advance the idea that many of narrative theory's purely formal considerations about person, voice, and rhetorical mode are revealed to be purely formal only through suppressing the ethical entailments that call not only for readers' judgment but also for their own play of desire and care. As part of this lesson, I bring in my braid of Bakhtin, Cavell, and Levinas.

I ask the students whether a responsible reading of Mill's text will somehow "rescue" Mill from, or at least reckon with, the double weight of paternity (the biological and the transferential in the figures of Bentham, Coleridge, Wordsworth, Harriet Taylor Mill) and thus require us to share with him somehow the task of what we might call auto-de-biography. Does his work thus beckon an act of what Cavell calls redemptive reading (*Themes* 27–59)? Does reading Mill ineluctably make us "responsible," and, if so, how exactly?

I also seek to take the discussion deeper by introducing Bakhtin's pre-dialogistic exploration of autobiography in the early "Author and Hero in Aesthetic Activity" (4–256). Bakhtin's concern with exteriority—the boundary between lived self and other—can be used to recast readers' stance toward a narrative text as the ethics of answerability. Adding Levinas's concept of facing, and its challenge to encounter the other as other, gives yet another dimension to the issue of what it means to read Mill—or any text—responsibly. As the students address these issues, I invite them to reflect on both their appeals to textual features of *Autobiography* and their own implicit ethical values and commitments, and in that way once again I stress the interrelations of formal and ethical analysis. This discussion then provides the groundwork for a writing assignment in which I ask the students to select another passage from Bellow or Mill and analyze within it the shadowy, enchanted relation between voice as formal feature and voice as a site for ethical response. Here, as in the following case studies, I either conclude or begin by stressing how the passages from Bellow and Mill do more than merely exemplify or concretize the abstract concept of "responsibility" (as if they were joining the narrative body to the ethical head). Rather, both novel and autobiography, through their special mimetic machinery of "motion capture," position readers as performers of observation, as witnesses and caretakers. Hence both texts make responsibility a direct consequence of participating in the narrative transaction.

Answerabilities in Reading and Criticism

The work of Sebald, which has attracted ever more attention since his death in 2001, provides the opportunity to explore another dimension of responsible, answerable reading. At two moments fairly close to each other in the text, the narrator of *Austerlitz* lays claim to contradictory experiences of unrest, noted in the act of moving and of standing still:

> Like a tightrope walker who has forgotten how to put one foot in front of the other, all I felt was the swaying of the precarious structure on which I stood, stricken with terror at the realization that the ends of the balancing pole gleaming far out on the edges of my field of vision were no longer my guiding lights, but malignant enticements to me to cast myself into the depths. (122)

> Minutes or even hours may have passed while I stood in that empty space beneath a ceiling which seemed to float at a vertiginous height, unable to move from the spot. (134)

Our previous work on Bellow or Mill prepares the students to recognize that the simile in the first passage, in addition to whatever else it may immediately signal, functions as an allegory of reading. I note that it is one of many reflexive nodes or clefts in the landscape of Sebald's narrative rhetoric and suggest that Sebald's writing proposes itself as a topography, a writing that traffics in surfaces, built on topoi in the twinned senses of subject and locality. One "keeps company" (Booth) with Sebald's narrators more properly by keeping pace (and place) with them. As we track what it means to keep pace, we necessarily encounter passages like the second one, which point more generally to what I have elsewhere called Sebald's "rhetoric of unrest" ("Mind the Gap"). His narratives repeatedly mime reiteration (a frame narrator embeds someone else's story, which is itself subject to internal divagations and interpolations of various kinds), and it is a mimesis designed to be gone over yet again in the reading. All of Sebald's books, I suggest, but especially *Austerlitz*, rehearse traversal, which ethically represents either a trespass of or pilgrimage across the boundaries separating self-contained text and the practice (ceremony?) of reading.

Yet I point out that a given act of reading can be recalcitrant and willful, keyed to an insinuating, productive movement that substitutes its own rhetoric for the one it finds. We are then ready for our main discussion of Sebald's narrative and ethics, which concentrate on this conflict between obligatory reiteration and creative substitution—on how the proprietary borders of someone else's story can be made to fit one's own modifying contours of critical reception and retelling. Does the rhetoric of unrest in Sebald actually encourage the reader's resistance to the obligation to stay within the boundaries of his characters' stories? Or is respecting that unrest itself part of the ethical challenge of Sebald's narratives? In other words, does Levinasian proximity or Cavellian acknowledgment call us to a reading in which we do much more than simply follow the lead of Sebald's spellbound narrator? But at what point in striking out on our own and willing to be dislodged do we cease to be answerable to Sebald's texts?

As we wrestle with these questions, we again repeatedly turn to formal features of Sebald's postmodern text. We note that Sebald redeploys temporality and focalization in the service of his ethical explorations of what it means to remember and what it means to transmit the past through narrative. Once again, the larger lesson is not any definitive answer to our specific questions but rather the recognition that narrative elements such as mood, aspect, level of diegesis, and temporality are more than merely structural.

"To search for a meaning is to bring to light a resemblance," Michel Foucault says decisively of the premodern *episteme* on display in Miguel Cervantes's *Don Quixote*; ever after, "the cruel reason of identities and differences make[s] endless sport of signs and similitudes" (29, 48). And while Sebald's tales of errancy are no less heir to its sixteenth-century progenitor than most others, the allegories of reading that his more somber postmodern texts perform reenchant the world through silhouettes of otherness and self-difference. Thus, the Sebaldian narrator of the earlier, 1992 novel, *The Emigrants*, remarks of one of its protagonists:

> The memoirs had seemed to him like one of those evil German fairy tales in which, once you are under the spell, you have to carry on to the finish, till your heart breaks, with whatever work you have begun—in this case, the remembering, writing, and reading. (193)

This is errancy in a different key, which indicates that the experience of such enchantment teaches a parallel lesson to Cervantes's: the transmission of stories, the commerce of producers and consumers, narrative transactions between those who address and those who are addressed (not to mention those who look on or listen in), always exact a price.

Thus, as with Bellow and Mill above, Sebald's work—or, more accurately, the experience of reading his work—challenges the view of literary narrative as supplement to or factotum of philosophy's ethical didacticism. Reading Sebald compels us not only to engage with the concepts of fidelity and trespass but also to experience them as the cost and consequence of literary enchantment and disenchantment alike. And to speak of enchantment and Cervantes, of course, recalls our cautionary fable of two-headed hounds and esquilaxes: to tell a story about something, and even to name it, is an act that never takes (its) place innocently in the world.

Murakami's prose fiction, especially his short stories, differs markedly from Sebald's. At its most successful, it is spare, aleatory, disjunctive yet hypnotic, a strange yet altogether distinctive coupling of realist and fictive elements. And yet, like Sebald's work, it is uncanny in a very deep and affecting sense. "The Kidney-Shaped Stone That Moves Every Day" is a story that aligns the pure gratuitousness of romantic love with the storytelling vocation: the protagonist is a young writer named Junpei who has the idea of a story dictated by his lover, who is also his reader. Murakami's text begins with the writer burdened with his father's fateful pronouncement that he will have only three chances in life to find a woman with real meaning for him. After speculating that he has met and lost the first of those three, his father's "three-women theory" becomes "a kind of obsession that clung tenaciously to his life" (293). Later on, he encounters a woman named Kirie, who appears to be his second chance, since she becomes a catalyst for both his literary and emotional life. She keeps her vocation mysteriously hidden from him and abruptly disappears one day entirely, until months later, purely by chance, he hears her voice on the radio and discovers that her profession all along has been tightrope walking between city high-rises.

In teaching this story, I focus first on the paradox of its relation to its readers. It seems absolutely *not* to involve its readers—the story is the romantic and narrative exchange between the two characters alone—and yet somehow to involve them centrally. As a first step in our analysis, we note that the ethical risk in encountering this narrative here does not conform to anything like the witnessing or tracking one finds in Bellow and Sebald or the custodianship inadvertently solicited by Mill. There is, in other words, no predicament, no problematic of readers' "positionality." The tangency between narrative and ethics in Murakami's text seems purely literary, wholly aesthetic.

Our second step is to explore the relation between Murakami's story and the story its hero is writing, which shares the same title: "The Kidney-Shaped Stone That Moves Every Day." (I use this word "hero" in Bakhtin's sense as laid out in "Author and Hero," because in that essay he insists, "I am not the hero of my own life" [112], a claim that comports well with the shifting interpersonal landscape of Murakami's story.)[5] We remark that its metaleptic plot of risky attachment—an internist conducts an affair with one of her male colleagues—has glinting reference to Junpei and Kirie's own tenuous cohabitation. But even more important, its subplot of uncanny transposition—a stone picked up by the doctor on vacation and deposited on her desk somehow alters its position in her office each night and reappears even when cast away—becomes a sliding trope for both Murakami's story of lovers as writers/readers and the story transacted by physicians within it (the stone is blood red and kidney shaped) and is thus a mobile specimen of elusiveness. In both lived story and told story, suspension becomes a migrating theme. We then pause over a question about responsible reading: Is this theme a modest rebuke of the grasping hand of interpretive appropriation?

I am content to leave the answer open as I then direct the students' attention to one two-page span in the text, during which Kirie asks Junpei to tell the story he's writing. He begins by starting to paraphrase it for her, but her interventions alter its ultimate direction. Murakami's narrator then takes over to "convey" further plot developments in the tale (which in its published form would, presumably, be indistinguishable from the narrator's partial representation of it as an inset narrative). As we trace the diegesis across persons and discursive levels in this short span of the text, we inevitably participate in the transitive method by which Murakami's fiction peculiarly and poignantly disperses itself. I bring in James Wood's evocative definition of criticism's "metaphorical" (not parasitical) relation to literature: "not to redescribe it but to describe it again, but for the first time; to share in making literature by not containing it but rather partaking of its impalpabilities" (109). In this sense, I suggest, "The Kidney-Shaped Stone That Moves Every Day" is a story in some artisanal, ideogrammatic sense *about* the literary. This suggestion then sets up our broader discussion about the way the story folds its ethical demand and narrative pragmatics into the text's freestanding quality as verbal art.[6] Again, my goal is not to arrive at a single, definitive account of that relation, but I do want the students to recognize that Murakami's story accommodates both hare and esquilax: on the one hand, it is answerable to its own aesthetic, text-immanent dictates, yet on the other hand, it solicits readers to become emotionally, affectively, and therefore in some indefinite but wholly defensible way, ethically answerable for the apparent autonomy of that aesthetic.

The discussion once again provides the groundwork for a writing assignment, this one deliberately more challenging. I ask students to confront the metaphor of "shadow" head-on as pivoted for them by Maurice Blanchot and Levinas. Blanchot's term for the uncanny workings of a work like Murakami's, a function of its ongoing self-difference, is "spectralité" (268). Levinas's phraseology is just as apropos: (literary) art, he says, involves a "commerce with shadows" (135). How might Murakami's story, as a specimen of narrative ethics, be addressed thus as a shadow text? If we grant that its textual economy reads out an ethics of proximity, of elusiveness, of thwarting, and of the near miss; if in reading it, we discover that it is a story (as Blanchot would say) *à venir* ("to come")—on the cusp but just short of being plumbed for full meaning; if we approach it as a friction of surfaces rather than a repository of depths, then what are our interpretive obligations to it? How do we read . . . in shadow? And that question returns us to Harpham's insight into ethics as "a kind of X-factor . . . exert[ing] whatever force it does by virtue of its singular capacity to adhere to, affiliate with, bury itself in, provoke, or dislodge other discourses" (xiii). Murakami's story tracks this X factor by making it adhere to, affiliate with, and bury itself in the shape of stories and their transmission while also provoking and dislodging the problem of "otherness" as something other than a philosophical abstraction. Murakami's story, in short, teaches the shadowing of narrative by ethics and of ethics by narrative.

The Ethics of Reading and the Ethics of Teaching

An ethics of reading in the light of these last two writers' narrative fiction is more the stuff of a reader placed off-kilter and dispossessed than in some totality of meaning legislated or owned. Being thus "delivered over to the work of difference" (Gibson, *Postmodernity* 192) or inducted/invited into a "certain living-through of the literary" (Attridge 3) is not an easy notion to teach, nor does it naturally line up with the analytic formulations and discursive categories specific to narratology. But it nicely parallels the "scene of teaching" as outlined by Bill Readings in *The University in Ruins*, where teaching and learning are identified as "sites of obligations, loci of ethical practices." "We must seek to do justice to teaching rather than to know what it is," writes Readings (154). All the texts or passages I enlist here make their own bid as sites of narrative obligations and loci of ethical practices. The virtues of Murakami's text, to take my last example, are its graceful postmodernism and the oblique, slightly shadowed way it illuminates Harpham's elective metaphor of relationality, which I use here as a generalizing trope for theorizing the codependent relation between ethics and narrative discourse. And to come full circle in this essay, I would suggest that another way of wording this shadow effect would be *allegoresis*. This term, like Don Quixote's or Friar Wiggum's way of putting things, signifies an altered reading enabling the scene of teaching to discover legendary beasts of yore—ethical shadows—amid the prose of the world.

Notes

1. In that spirit, I direct students' attention to Brian McHale's useful essay in the *Blackwell Companion to Narrative Theory* about the ghost-haunted and monster-plagued precincts of narrative theory itself. (However tempted, I stop just short of David Cronenberg's 1986 film *The Fly*, which extends our little allegory to the outer limits of the monstrous.)

2. Joseph Jastrow's famous "bistable" image was adopted by Wittgenstein as a lesson in "seeing an aspect" or "seeing *as*" in *Philosophical Investigations* (193–94), for which see James Guetti's explanation in *Wittgenstein and the Grammar of Literary Experience* (200–01).

3. See, for example, the special issue *Literature and Ethics* (Eskin); Gibson ("Ethics"); and the introduction to *Renegotiating Ethics in Literature, Philosophy, and Theory* (Adamson, Freadman, and Parker).

4. The publication of *Herzog* is roughly contemporaneous with the later F. R. Leavis and the early Wayne Booth, each of whom appealed to the juridical as an interpretive framework for reading and criticism. This section is also useful, therefore, for exploring the critical bias that stresses literary narrative's moral heft and its training effects on readers.

5. Bakhtin says in the same connection, "Just as the plot or story of my own personal life is created by other people—the heroes of my life, so the aesthetic vision of the world, its image, is created only by the consummated or consummatable lives of other people who are the heroes of this world" (11).

6. These issues also bear on the question of fictiveness as a play of rhetorical forces. See Richard Walsh's *The Rhetoric of Fictionality*, especially the first chapter, "The Pragmatics of Narrative Fictionality."

Works Cited

Adamson, Jane, Richard Freadman, and David Parker, eds. *Renegotiating Ethics in Literature, Philosophy, and Theory.* Cambridge: Cambridege UP, 1998. Print.

Attridge, Derek. *The Singularity of Literature.* New York: Routledge, 2004. Print.

Bakhtin, Mikhail M. *Art and Answerability: Early Philosophical Essays.* Trans. Vadim Liapunov. Austin: U of Texas P, 1990. Print.

Bellow, Saul. *Herzog.* New York: Fawcett, 1964. Print.

Blanchot, Maurice. *The Book to Come.* Trans. Charlotte Mandell. Stanford: Stanford UP, 2003. Print.

Booth, Wayne. *The Company We Keep: An Ethics of Fiction.* Berkeley: U of California P, 1988. Print.

Cavell, Stanley. *Must We Mean What We Say? A Book of Essays.* Cambridge: Harvard UP, 2002. Print.

———. *Themes Out of School.* San Francisco: Northpoint, 1984. Print.

Eskin, Michael, ed. *Literature and Ethics.* Spec. issue of *Poetics Today* 25.4 (2004): 557–794. Print.

Foucault, Michel. *The Order of Things.* New York: Vintage, 1970. Print.

Gibson, Andrew. "Ethics." *The Johns Hopkins Guide to Literary Theory and Criticism.* Ed. Michael Groden, Martin Kreiswirth, and Imre Szeman. Baltimore: Johns Hopkins UP, 2005. 287–96. Print.

———. *Postmodernity, Ethics, and the Novel: From Leavis to Levinas.* London: Routledge, 1999. Print.

Guetti, James. *Wittgenstein and the Grammar of Literary Experience.* Athens: U of Georgia P, 1993. Print.

Harpham, Geoffrey. *Shadows of Ethics: Criticism and the Just Society.* Durham: Duke UP, 1999. Print.

Levinas, Emmanuel. *Nine Talmudic Readings.* Trans. Annette Aronowicz. Bloomington: Indiana UP, 1994. Print.

McHale, Brian. "Ghosts and Monsters: On the (Im)possibility of Narrating the History of Narrative Theory." *Blackwell Companion to Narrative Theory.* Ed. James Phelan and Peter J. Rabinowitz. Oxford: Blackwell, 2005. 60–72. Print.

Mill, John Stuart. *Autobiography.* 1873. Boston: Houghton, 1969. Print.

Miller, J. Hillis. *The Ethics of Reading: Kant, de Man, Eliot, Trollope, James, and Benjamin.* New York: Columbia UP, 1987. Print.

Murakami, Haruki. "The Kidney-Shaped Stone That Moves Every Day." *Blind Willow, Sleeping Woman.* New York: Knopf, 2006. 291–308. Print.

Newton, Adam Zachary. "Mind the Gap: W. G. Sebald and the Rhetoric of Unrest." *A Companion to Rhetoric and Rhetorical Criticism.* Ed. Walter Jost and Wendy Olmstead. Oxford: Blackwell, 2006. 355–71. Print.

———. *Narrative Ethics.* Cambridge: Harvard UP, 1995. Print.

Nussbaum, Martha. *Love's Knowledge: Essays on Philosophy and Literature.* New York: Oxford UP, 1992. Print.

Phelan, James. *Living to Tell about It: A Rhetoric and Ethics of Character Narration.* Ithaca: Cornell UP, 2005. Print.

Readings, Bill. *The University in Ruins.* Cambridge: Harvard UP, 1996. Print.

Rousseau, Jean-Jacques. *A Discourse on Inequality*. Trans. Maurice Cranston. New York: Penguin, 1985. Print.

Sebald, W. G. *Austerlitz*. Trans. Anthea Bell. New York: Random, 2001. Print.

———. *The Emigrants*. Trans. Michael Hulse. New York: Random, 1996. Print.

Walsh, Richard. *The Rhetoric of Fictionality: Narrative Theory and the Idea of Fiction*. Columbus: Ohio State UP, 2007. Print.

Wittgenstein, Ludwig. *Philosophical Investigations*. Trans. G. E. M. Anscombe. Englewood Cliffs: Prentice, 1999. Print.

Wood, James. "Virginia Woolf's Mysticism." *The Broken Estate*. New York: Random, 2000. 105–18. Print.

Further Reading

Benjamin, Walter. "The Storyteller." *Illuminations*. Trans. Harry Zohn. New York: Schocken, 1968. 83–109. Print.

Davis, Todd F., and Kenneth Womack, eds. *Mapping the Ethical Turn: A Reader in Culture, Ethics, and Literary Theory*. Charlottesville: UP of Virginia, 2001. Print.

Leavis, F. R. *The Living Principle*. Oxford: Oxford UP, 1975. Print.

———. *Two Cultures? The Significance of C. P. Snow*. New York: Pantheon, 1961. Print.

Newton, Adam Zachary. "Versions of Ethics; or, The SARL of Criticism: Sonority, Arrogation, Letting-Be." *American Literary History* 13.3 (2001): 603–37. Print.

Parker, David. *Ethics, Theory, and the Novel*. Cambridge: Cambridge UP, 1994. Print.

Phelan, James. *Experiencing Fiction: Judgments, Progressions, and the Rhetorical Theory of Narrative*. Columbus: Ohio State UP, 2007. Print.

Robbins, Jill. *Altered Reading: Levinas and Literature*. Chicago: U of Chicago P, 1999. Print.

Scholes, Robert. *Textual Power: Literary Theory and the Teaching of English*. New Haven: Yale UP, 1986. Print.

Williams, Bernard. *Ethics and the Limits of Philosophy*. Cambridge: Harvard UP, 1985. Print.

Amy J. Elias

Ideology and Critique

In the Marxist tradition, ideological critique shows how superstructural productions such as literature operate in relation to capitalist economies and the attitudes of a class or social group. But redefined by cultural materialism, feminism, critical race studies, and postcolonial and cultural studies, ideological critique now also examines the ways in which subjects both incorporate and resist definitions of life-world and selfhood structured by hegemonic social powers. Upper-division undergraduate or graduate-level literature courses constructed on the assumptions of ideological theory present the narrative text as a palimpsest of cultural and political values; looking beneath the said reveals the political unsaid of both the text and the social conditions that produced it.

Ideological critique often opposes itself to formalist narrative analysis, and this opposition filters into university English classes, where formalisms are like the slightly odd cousin no one invites for the holidays. At my university, students have usually talked about race, class, and gender politics in some way through English department course offerings, but they never, ever, come to classes with a definition of *structuralism*, and few can give me a good definition of *narrative* or even of *novel*. A couple of them know the word *formalism* the way one knows a funny smell in the refrigerator or the presence of something gone fusty in the attic trunk, like grandma's old mink.

Somehow teachers have forgotten that the grand synthesizers of twentieth-century ideological criticism knew their formalisms intimately and never let them stray far. For example, Fredric Jameson's Marxist notion of the political unconscious depends on the structuralism of Vladimir Propp, Tzvetan Todorov, and Roman Jakobson—and Jameson's *A Singular Modernity: Essay on the Ontology of the Present* (2007) is dedicated to the narrative theorist Wayne Booth. The assumption of most ideological criticism is that culture is made up of stories, stories that power has constructed for its own perpetuation and that can be dismantled only by other stories more conducive to human flourishing. And so narrative theory can go hand in hand with ideological critique. Teaching Mikhail Bakhtin's theory of the carnivalesque introduces the complexity of cultural subversion as well as the interrelations between art forms and their sociopolitical contexts; teaching Hayden White's radically antipositivist theory of historiographic emplotment in relation to Northrop Frye's archetypes illustrates the potential ideological reach of plot typology; teaching Edward Said's concept of orientalism in relation to thematics and theories of realism (a topic also of interest to the Marxist Georg Lukács) illustrates how formalism is entwined with cultural criticism; teaching Stephen Greenblatt's new historicism as "cultural poetics" demonstrates that attention to tropes is often at the very heart of historical critique.

In my undergraduate courses in contemporary literature at the University of Tennessee, I have found the task of integrating narrative theory with ideological critique both challenging and rewarding. Such classes require, first, teaching narrative theory in a course primarily defined by historical period and literary genre; second, teaching interrelations between narrative theory and ideological theory; and third, teaching narrative theory to undergraduates, who generally are dismayed or bored by the unfamiliarity and technical nature of narratological analysis. I believe I have found some effective ways to meet this challenge in a course I call Worldmaking in Contemporary Literature.

The course premise is that narratology and ideological criticism can be put in productive relation through a critical focus on contemporary narrative fiction, broadly defined to include novels, short stories, hypertexts, and graphic novels. The concept of "worldmaking" ties together the narrative and cultural theory, as indicated by my course description:

The first unit examines how narrative theory says it is possible to create a language-based, fictional world that a reader can enter; the second unit examines how postmodern theory says it is possible for powerful political and cultural forces to create "real life" worlds that are equally fictional. The course explores the relationship between these two kinds of narrative worldmaking.

Course goals are to acquaint students with some important works of international contemporary fiction that are diverse in form, politics, and cultural representation; to introduce students to at least two discourses of literary criticism, that of narrative theory and that of postmodern ideological theory; and, most important, to explore how definitions of ideologically defined postmodernity are instantiated in contemporary narrative. The course relies heavily on Online-UT, the *Blackboard* course-management system (CMS) at the University of Tennessee and, in more recent versions, on Drupal.[1]

My course exploits the fact that there is an organic connection between theories of narrative and theories of postmodernity, often defined as the aestheticizing of the world through capitalist production. Postmodernist theory is an odd renarrativization of the world; according to Jean-François Lyotard, it is a movement from the utopian metanarratives of modernity to the antiutopian, contingent *petit récits* of resistance to globalized capitalism. Moreover, postmodernism is the turning of the real into simulation of one sort or another, the replacement of the real by the hyperreal, by signs. If this is the state of postmodernity, it is also the state of narrative fiction itself. The two were literally made for each other.

Worldmaking in Contemporary Literature is consequently broken into three learning modules that explore this connection. The first emphasizes worldmaking as text-making methodology and foregrounds the questions, What is a narrative world? How do we construct a world through language? The second module foregrounds the question, What is the relation between language worlds and actual worlds? The third, much longer, module foregrounds the question, Who controls the (narrative or real) world once it is constructed or identified?

Module 1: What Is a Narrative World?

The first course unit emphasizes worldmaking as textual method. Students learn terms of narrative theory and apply them to important works of contemporary short fiction and at least one novel. Key to this module are the ideas that writers do specific things with words, that there are complex narrative elements behind apparently transparent narrative constructions, and that many possible worlds are constructed by texts through the deployment of specific narrative techniques and devices.

Making the technical language of narrative theory interesting to undergraduates, who are accustomed to discussing literature emotively, is the central challenge of this unit. It helps that my Worldmaking course has numerous electronic components. I use the *Blackboard* CMS or Drupal to post announcements, homework assignments, test and study guides, and Web links important to course content and to run the team project (discussed below). Although I basically only use the electronic format as a text repository, doing so helps update the feel of the course.

Technology is part of my lectures in ways that are common now in all university classes. I begin the course with a *PowerPoint* introduction that is based on the first chapter, "Narrative and Life," of H. Porter Abbott's *Cambridge Introduction to Narrative*, a text I order for the class. (Another required text is Prince's *Dictionary*.) Important to the course introduction are Abbott's distinction between intentional, symptomatic, and adaptive readings and his definition of "masterplots"; both are central to the later course unit on ideological reading.[2] As we move to the first course unit on narrative theory, I continue to introduce terminology in *PowerPoint* format and post the slide presentations to our class *Blackboard* site. (Students can download or print the presentations from *Blackboard* as class notes.) Presenting narratological terms in *PowerPoint* is more effective than giving them out on printed handouts, and I have constructed presentations for "action frames," "existent frames," "idea frames," and "narrators and narration," using the *Routledge Encyclopedia of Narrative Theory* (Herman, Jahn, and Ryan) and work by Abbott, Prince, Seymour Chatman, Mieke Bal, James Phelan (*Narrative*), and others. This allows me to introduce terms related to character, plot, and theme early in the course. The definitions serve both as basis for a midterm exam and as a resource later for the team project.

I have learned two things about *PowerPoint* presentations, however. First, key to holding students' attention during such a presentation is interspersing short class exercises among the slides. After presenting the definition of *kernels* and *satellites*, I have students pull out a piece of paper and write down what they would understand to be the kernels of their own life stories if they were plotted comically; then I have them do it again, assuming their lives were plotted tragically. The exercise is fun, provokes discussion of how narrative and cognition may be intertwined, and leads into the story-discourse distinction. It also brings home the notion that genre and plot details are motivated, are more than just ways to move action forward in a story—another point important to our later unit on ideology.

Second, each *PowerPoint* presentation must be followed by a literary example and discussion; doing all the terms for the course and then moving on to literary examples is a deadly strategy. I've found it best to put the narrative theory into immediate relation to short fiction. Frontloading short fiction in the course allows me to introduce work by important contemporary writers and to set up homework "theory application exercises" in which students apply terms we've just covered in the *PowerPoint* presentations. I have paired discussion of story-discourse and action frames with Angela Carter's "The Tiger's Bride" and "The Courtship of Mr. Lyon" (1979); existent frames with Tim O'Brien's "The Things They Carried" (1987) and Italo Calvino's "Without Colors" or "All at One Point" (1968); idea frames with Ursula LeGuin's "The Ones Who Walked Away from Omelas"(1973) and Gabriel García Márquez's "A Very Old Man with Enormous Wings" (1955); discussion of narrators and narration with James Baldwin's "Sonny's Blues" (1948), David Foster Wallace's "Lyndon" (1989), and excerpts from Norman Mailer's *Armies of the Night* (1968). In a course attuned to ideological analysis, it is also possible to use short fiction that deals specifically with class issues. The study questions are short homework assignments and can address both narrative theory and story content. For instance, one may ask students to identify the different levels of diegesis in LeGuin's short story and how the idea frames—or thematic ideas—of the story are changed at each level.

It is useful to formulate questions that immediately encourage students to consider the relation between narrative form and ideological meaning. After I introduce master plot and intertextuality, we discuss Carter's "The Tiger's Bride" and "The Courtship of Mr. Lyon" and discuss the significant differences to their shared intertext, the Grimm brothers' fairy tale "Beauty and the Beast." But we cannot avoid asking how ideological meaning alters selection of actor, setting, and plot trajectory for each story, both based on a literary masterplot ("Beauty and the Beast") and cultural masterplot (the narrative of proper filiality and sexuality for women in patriarchal Western culture as well as the different class values criticized in each story).

This method of starting from narrative theory and working out to ideological context is centrally important to all the course reading. When students read Jamaica Kincaid's one-paragraph story "Girl," I ask first whether this is a narrative, given Phelan's definition of narrative as "somebody telling somebody else on a particular occasion for some purpose that something happened" (*Narrative* 218). This question opens the whole can of worms about who is speaking; to whom; on what occasion; and, most important, for what purpose. Students usually want to claim that the story presents a mother talking to a daughter in a traditional society in which women's roles and freedoms are narrowly defined and rigidly enforced and that the girl is so overcome by the power of this role that she speaks back only in her mind (the italics portion of the text). But I make them justify these claims using the terms of narrative theory we've discussed in class. How do you know who is speaking, and to whom? We hear a speaker but no narrator, but is there an implied author? From whose perspective is the narrative focalized? What do the italics signify about dialogue or monologue? How do we gain a sense of setting? What constitutes plot conflict in this "story"? Would some of the speaker's comments constitute analepsis? What are motifs in the text, and how do they indicate the mores of the girl's world?

I then initiate a class exercise: going around the room, each student in the class reads one sentence of the story out loud until the story's end. Since each sentence is an imperative, students quickly hear a different kind of narrative "voice" emerge from the new reading situation, one in which the speaker is "society" and is speaking to all women in the culture. The reading has a powerful effect: the social voice is many voiced and strong, and the pitiful little italic responses are no match for its overwhelming power, even though they offer a glimmer of hope that resistance is possible. The text becomes a cultural narrative, defined by Phelan (similarly to Abbott's "masterplot") as one

> that has a sufficiently wide circulation so that we can legitimately say that its author, rather than being a clearly identified individual, is a larger collective entity, perhaps a whole society or at least some significant subgroup of society. . . . Cultural narratives fulfill the important function of identifying key issues and values within the culture or subculture that tells them. (*Living* 8–9)

The exercise allows me to reinforce the importance of defining story elements and helps students practice applying the narrative terms they have just learned, but it also illustrates how narrative elements offer more than one reading of a text, that narrative theory can be used in the service of a cultural reading and that a political reading may in fact be encoded in subtle ways "beneath" another, more obvious reading of a text. I am convinced that this is different than hunting for feminist or proletarian themes in the text; the focus is on message through method.

By the end of module 1, students have been introduced to key terms in narrative theory as well as the concept that narrative structures many domains of human activity, and they have discussed a number of short stories by important contemporary writers.

Module 2: What Do Language Worlds and Actual Worlds Have in Common?

The second course unit emphasizes worldmaking as ontology, particularly in relation to mimesis. The class discusses some basic philosophical definitions of ontology as a hierarchical ordering of elements viewed as constitutive of what is real. We do so in order to examine the question, What does it mean to perceive a world *realistically*? Key to this module are the ideas that literature problematizes the relation between intrinsic and extrinsic worlds, however they are defined, and that there is no prerepresentational, unmotivated world that can be accessed outside language or perception.

In this short unit I usually present realism as a literary mode. We discuss general distinctions among actual, possible, and fictional worlds and a general definition of ontology as it is defined within philosophy; we then move to Thomas Pavel's distinction between internal and external approaches to fiction; mimesis in an Aristotelian sense; and philosophical definitions of realism (in philosophy the realist position is contrasted with antirealism, nominalism, and idealism). The idea is to convey how realism as a literary mode attempts to bridge the actual world–fictive world divide by evoking fictional worlds structured in accordance with more or less dominant conceptions of the real. Then we usually read an important contemporary novel that is realist in form—a text such as Ian McEwan's *Atonement* (2001), Kazuo Ishiguro's *An Artist of the Floating World* (1986), Cormac McCarthy's *Blood Meridian; or, The Evening Redness in the West* (1985), Muriel Spark's *The Driver's Seat* (1970), John Banville's *The Sea* (2005), or Andre Aciman's *Call Me by Your Name* (2007). The class uses the terms of narrative theory learned in the first module to guide our analysis of the novel as we explore the extent to which the story is "realistic" and what it says about the possibilities for truthfully accessing unmediated reality. The unit can also introduce students to literary terms that subdivide "realist novel" into generic or modal categories (psychological realism, stream-of-consciousness writing, domestic realism, sentimental novel, picaresque, the novel of manners, etc.). The short unit provides a segue between narrative theory and social theory, introduces terms on which postmodern theory builds, and introduces the idea that even something as seemingly simple as realism is incredibly complex both philosophically and narratologically.

Module 3: Who Controls Worlds?

The third, much longer, learning module of the course concerns world-making as an ideological formation. It foregrounds the questions, How is a social world the same as a fictive world? and Who controls a narrative world? Key to this unit are the ideas that culture is constructed through ideological narratives, that there is no preexisting or universally accepted model for a cultural world, and that prose fiction uniquely raises questions about the interrelatedness of textual and social worldmaking.

After going through the first two modules, students tend to see the assertion that ideology permeates culture less as a claim stemming from a hermeneutics of suspicion than as another facet of narrative constructivism. This naturalizing of ideology as narrative construction makes it easier to introduce students to key ideas about postmodernism as a sociocultural moment, an array of ideological theories such as those mentioned at the beginning of this essay, and a set of literary assumptions. I usually start with Brian McHale's definition of postmodernism as a literary and cultural formation in which ontological concerns are dominant; starting here resituates the idea of worldmaking presented in module 2 within postmodern theory and a contemporary sociopolitical context. We then read prose fiction texts that provoke discussion of different postmodernist literary techniques and different theories of postmodern culture as a moment in late capitalism.

In one version of the course, we began with McHale's notion of the postmodern ontological dominant and Jean Baudrillard's theory of the postmodern simulacra. We then read Don Delillo's *White Noise*, starting with narrative technique and using the terms of module 1 but then segueing into theory. We discussed how the text destabilizes the real and hence realism at the level both of narration (the narrating voice is not only unreliable but also derivative of the commercialized "voices" of its social surround) and of politicized idea frame (the story asserts that society is afloat in a sea of signs, cut off from referents by the values of consumer capitalism). In other versions of the course, I have paired Guy Debord's theory of the postmodern spectacle with Jessica Hagedorn's *Dogeaters* (1991); Jameson's theory of postmodern hyperspace with Steven Millhauser's *Martin Dressler* (1997); Jameson's theory of postmodern historical pastiche with Jeanette Winterson's *Sexing the Cherry* (1989); postcolonial theories of politicized border space with J. M. Coetzee's *Waiting for the Barbarians* (1980); and postmodern critical race theory with Colson Whitehead's *The Intuitionist* (1999). The possible pairings are, of course, myriad, referring to all kinds of postmodern theory and fiction.

What makes this course a little different from other courses in contemporary fiction, however, is that students are asked to bring ideas from narrative theory to bear on the workings of ideology in each of the texts we discuss. For example, as Percival Everett's *Erasure* tackles the problem of postmodern simulation, it demands that readers confront how literary form becomes ideological vehicle. We start with existents and events—characters and plot—and quickly move to diegetic levels and discussion of implied author, narrator, and embedded narrators, for the novel contains not only a hypodiegetic level (novel within a novel) but also (among other techniques) analepsis in the primary diegesis, epistolary writing, the narrator's notes for other novels, and retellings of classics in the African American literary canon (primarily Ralph Ellison's *Invisible Man* but also novels that depict passing and Sapphire's novel *Push*). The novel is difficult for most undergraduates to comprehend fully, but it helps that one of the main thematic ideas (that African American men in the United States must conform to media stereotypes of macho ghetto gangsterism to be seen as "black") directly links postmodern theory to ideological critique. We juxtapose the narrator's (and implied author's) many references to the rich artistic, cultural, and historical traditions of African American music, political culture, and literature (the name of *Erasure*'s narrator, for example, is Monk Ellison) with the media's flattening of identity and history into stereotype and ahistorical "blaxploitation" pastiche. We discuss why the middle-class, professorial African American narrator can only gain literary acclaim if his novels portray black men as illiterate, macho, historyless "boyz n the 'hood," but we have this discussion by contrasting the one-dimensional narrative techniques of the novel within the novel "My Pafology" (written under the nom de plume Stagg R. Leigh) to the multifaceted, layered techniques of the main narrative.

After the unit on realism, module 3 can present fiction that is formally experimental, and, given that the course is about postmodernism, students can read provocative weddings of form and ideological theme in this unit. Teaching a text such as Tomás Rivera's ... *Y no se lo tragó la tierra* (*And the Earth Did Not Devour Him*) introduces students to the historical fact of the Chicano Renaissance ("El Movimiento") and provokes discussion about how the hybrid and multivoiced form relates to ideological themes about migrant workers as underclass and about the debilitating alignment of religion with hegemonic power. In line with class analysis, Rivera's narration blurs the distinction between individual and collective experience. We discuss how disrupted plot and paratactic form in the text might be correlated to migrant or underclass psychology, subvert dominant Western literary techniques of realism, and interrupt the hegemonic cultural narratives legitimating the seamless reality of global capital.

Likewise, teaching graphic novels such as Art Spiegelman's *Maus* or Gene Luen Yang's *American Born Chinese* raises complex questions about textual politics as well as about diegetic levels, story-discourse divisions, characterization, and literary forms (such as the bildungsroman, *Künstlerroman*, frame tale, historical novel, or metafiction). Both texts portray people as animals in a kind of political and cultural iconography that isn't possible in prose narration and that seems to function differently than does film iconography. Spiegelman's text provokes discussion of postmodern literary forms ("historiographic metafiction," Holocaust trauma narrative) and questions about how appropriateness of form is itself a cultural and often politicized idea. Once students break out of the idea that graphic novels are "comic books," they can discuss how the frame breaks, paratactic narrative jumps, and gradations of iconographic layering work to fracture narrative and historical memory in ways similar to the fracturing of personal memory in trauma victims and the fracturing of community through war and exile. But Spiegelman is also working from Ashkenazi mythic iconography (as Yang's use of the trickster monkey works with Chinese myth), and this strategy offers an opportunity to discuss the politics of identity, hybridity, translation, and cosmopolitanism in relation to migrant history as well.

The relation of fractured and hypodiegetic forms to ideological critique can be further explored by assigning CD-Rom or online hypertexts such as Shelley Jackson's *Patchwork Girl*, an extremely complex hypertext feminist narrative that reworks Mary Shelley's *Frankenstein* (1818) and L. Frank Baum's *The Patchwork Girl of Oz* (1913). Jackson plays with the correlations between bodily, psychic, and narrative fracturing; the monstrosity of the feminine; cyborg identity; and deconstruction as critique. She simultaneously plays with the political nature of the visual gaze. Through her feminist poststructuralism, she refuses distinctions between the bodily and written text and thus forces students to confront the politics of form and the notion of "embodied" ideology.

Similarly, a cyberpunk text such as Neal Stephenson's *Snow Crash* raises formal questions with ideological implications. The novel allows me to introduce narrative theory about game worlds, but, because it embeds the libertarian politics often associated with digital cultures, it also raises questions about relations between postmodern simulation and liberal humanism. The novel has spawned a real-world counterpart, *Second Life*, an MMORPG (Massively Multiplayer Online Role-Playing Game) modeled on Stephenson's virtual world, the Metaverse. Putting the book and game world together produces a mind-bending discussion of narrative ontology: once inside *Second Life*, a virtual world within the "real" world but outlined in the hypodiegetic narrative of *Snow Crash*, also a text in the "real" world, Where are we? And is this corporate-owned virtual world something ontologically different from consensus reality?

The key to this unit is wedding form with ideological analysis to show that they depend mutually on each other.

The Team Project

The team project cements the connections among the three course units. Instead of doing a long research term paper, students work in groups and create a narrative analysis using a wiki. This assignment counts for thirty percent of the final grade for the course, split into a group-project grade (15%) and an individual grade (15%).

For the group-project grade, early in the term students are put in groups of four to five, choose a short story to work on (out of 5 or 6 options, each with little published criticism), and create a Wiki lesson about worldmaking at our *Blackboard* or Drupal site. Student teams must create full commentary about narrative and ideological worldmaking in these stories. They can do so by creating online versions with hyperlinks, adding informative endnotes concerning narrative form, writing an author biography or interview, or attaching original critical analyses. Their Wikis may include original *PowerPoint* presentations about techniques of narrative worldmaking, Weblogs, or any other kind of electronic or text-based information such as photo-essays. They can present this material in audio as well as visual form. Because the presentation may go online, I emphasize proper source citation and plagiarism penalties. Everyone in the group gets the same grade for this portion of the assignment, and grades are awarded on the basis of useful and correct analysis of narrative techniques, depth of teaching methods about worldmaking, scope of analysis, and creativity in correlating narrative elements to ideological meanings. Each group must clear its project with me well before deadline, do library research, and present its final Wiki project to the class in a fifteen-minute presentation at the end of the term.

For the individual-grade portion of the assignment, short response essays (5–7 pages) explain what work each student did on the group project; how this work reflects his or her understanding of worldmaking in the group's story; and how his or her own readings of the story compare or contrast with the author's intentions (if an interview was conducted) or against other works we've read in the class.

Because the group is working on a Wiki, there are none of the usual problems with assigning a group project, such as students not being able to find time or space outside class to meet; anyone on the team can access the Wiki and work on it at any time, alone or with others online simultaneously. As instructor, I control who has access to each team Wiki, so there is no threat of malicious play; moreover, I can set *Blackboard* to track usage of every element of the site.

Students enjoy this assignment (even though there is initially a lot of griping about a group project). And they produce good work. One group researched Roland Barthes's definition of readerly versus writerly texts (which we hadn't discussed in class) because they thought it applied to their story, while another drove to the University of North Carolina to interview Randall Kenan about his worldmaking techniques as they worked on his short story "Things of This World." In another class, students worked up a presentation on magic realism and how it is modified by different cultural versions of magic realist writing. Students have given presentations on autodiegetic narration, nonlinear narrative, ekphrasis, remediation and the role of footnotes in narrative, the relation between diegesis and mimesis in illustrated short fiction, photographic ontology (a new coinage), and free indirect discourse. Students work hard to show how the narrative techniques of their story construct an ideological theme, provoke a dialectical reading, and are integral to the class politics of the text. One semester, three graduate students in the class who were creative writers supplied their own unpublished short fiction for the undergraduates to analyze and gave "author interviews" to the teams; the experience was mutually enlightening.

Teaching Worldmaking in Contemporary Literature has made clear to me that narrative theory has for too long been estranged from ideological critique. A fourteen-week undergraduate literature course can make both narrative analysis and ideological analysis richer and more complex, and technology may also help us enrich our teaching of narrative theory in new and exciting ways. By the time this essay is published, the technology discussed will be outdated. The idea, however, is to keep integrating a focus on ideology in narrative using updated teaching methods.

Notes

1. *Blackboard* is comparable to *WebCT*; Drupal is an open-source content management and discussion engine (drupal.org/). A course syllabus for World-making in Contemporary Literature is available at the author's Web site.

2. Abbott defines *adaptive reading* as one text's interpretation or adaptation of another's story; *intentional reading* as a reading that seeks to understand what the implied author intended the text to mean; and *symptomatic reading* as a reading that decodes an author's state of mind or unacknowledged cultural conditions. He defines *masterplots* as recurrent skeletal stories that belong to cultures and play powerful roles in formation of identity, values, and perceptions of reality—what cultural critics often term "ideology."

Works Cited

Abbott, H. Porter. *The Cambridge Introduction to Narrative*. Cambridge: Cambridge UP, 2002. Print.

Bakhtin, Mikhail. *Rabelais and His World*. Trans. Hélène Iswolsky. Bloomington: Indiana UP, 1984. Print.

Bal, Mieke. *Narratology: Introduction to the Theory of Narrative*. 2nd ed. Trans. Christine van Boheemen. Toronto: U of Toronto P, 1997. Print.

Chatman, Seymour. *Story and Discourse: Narrative Structure in Fiction and Film*. Ithaca: Cornell UP, 1978. Print.

Elias, Amy J., ed. Home page. U of Tennessee, Knoxville, n.d. Web. 26 Oct. 2009.

Everett, Percival. *Erasure*. New York: Hyperion, 2002. Print.

Frye, Northrop. *Anatomy of Criticism: Four Essays*. Princeton: Princeton UP, 1957. Print.

Greenblatt, Stephen Jay. *Shakespearean Negotiations: The Circulation of Social Energy in Renaissance England*. Berkeley: U of California P, 1988. Print.

Herman, David, Manfred Jahn, and Marie-Laure Ryan, eds. *Routledge Encyclopedia of Narrative Theory*. London: Routledge, 2005. Print.

Jackson, Shelley. *Patchwork Girl*. 1995. Watertown: Eastgate, 2001. CD-ROM.

Jameson, Fredric. *The Political Unconscious: Narrative as a Socially Symbolic Act.* Ithaca: Cornell UP, 1981. Print.

Kincaid, Jamaica. "Girl." 1983. *American Short Stories since 1945.* Ed. John G. Parks. Oxford: Oxford UP, 2002. 419. Print.

Lukács, Georg. *The Theory of the Novel: A Historio-Philosophical Essay on the Forms of Great Epic Literature.* Trans. Anna Bostock. Cambridge: MIT P, 1971. Print.

Lyotard, Jean-François. *The Postmodern Condition: A Report on Knowledge.* Trans. Geoff Bennington and Brian Massumi. Fwd. Fredric Jameson. Minneapolis: U of Minnesota P, 1984. Print.

McHale, Brian. *Postmodernist Fiction.* New York: Routledge, 1987. Print.

Pavel, Thomas. *Fictional Worlds.* Cambridge: Harvard UP, 1986. Print.

Phelan, James. *Living to Tell about It: A Rhetoric and Ethics of Character Narration.* Ithaca: Cornell UP, 2005. Print.

———. *Narrative as Rhetoric: Technique, Audiences, Ethics, Ideology.* Columbus: Ohio State UP, 1996. Print.

Prince, Gerald. *A Dictionary of Narratology.* 2nd ed. Lincoln: U of Nebraska P, 2003. Print.

Said, Edward. *Orientalism.* New York: Pantheon, 1978. Print.

Spiegelman, Art. *The Complete Maus.* New York: Pantheon, 1997. Print.

Stephenson, Neal. *Snow Crash.* New York: Bantam, 2000. Print.

White, Hayden V. *Metahistory: The Historical Imagination in Nineteenth-Century Europe.* Baltimore: Johns Hopkins UP, 1973. Print.

Yang, Gene Luen. *American Born Chinese.* New York: First Second Books, 2006. Print.

Further Reading

Bottomore, Tom, et al. *A Dictionary of Marxist Thought.* Oxford: Blackwell, 1983. Print.

Eagleton, Terry. *Ideology: An Introduction.* London: Verso, 1991. Print.

Herman, Luc, and Bart Vervaeck. "Ideology." *The Cambridge Companion to Narrative.* Ed. David Herman. Cambridge: Cambridge UP, 2007. 217–30. Print.

Hutcheon, Linda. *The Politics of Postmodernism.* 2nd ed. New York: Routledge, 2002. Print.

Williams, Patrick. "Marxist Approaches to Narrative." *Routledge Encyclopedia of Narrative Theory.* Ed. David Herman, Manfred Jahn, and Marie-Laure Ryan. London: Routledge, 2005. 283–87. Print.

Glossary

Terms set in small caps have their own glossary entries.

Actant   A. J. Greimas's term ("Actants"; *Structural Semantics*) for a general role fulfilled by a particularized actor or CHARACTER, or even a setting. One such role is Opponent, exemplified by Satan in *Paradise Lost* or the sea in Stephen Crane's "The Open Boat."

Agency   At the level of the STORY, agency concerns CHARACTERS' ability to bring about deliberately initiated EVENTS, or actions, within a STORYWORLD. At the level of NARRATION, agency affects who gets to tell what kind of story in what contexts.

Anachrony   Gérard Genette's term for nonchronological NARRATION, where EVENTS are told in an ORDER other than that in which they can be presumed to have occurred in the STORYWORLD.[1]

Analepsis   Flashback. In Gérard Genette's account, analepsis occurs when EVENTS that occur in the ORDER *ABC* are told in the order *BCA, BAC,* or *CBA*.

Answerability   Mikhail Bakhtin's term (*Art*) for the ethical imperative to listen and respond to the communication of another, including a narrative text.

Audience   In the narrative-communication model developed by structuralist NARRATOLOGISTS and refined by RHETORICAL theorists of narrative, the audience can be defined as real or imagined addressees of (multilayered) acts of NARRATION. This model distinguishes among actual authors, IMPLIED AUTHORS, and NARRATORS on the production side of the storytelling process. On the reception (or interpretation) side, it distinguishes among the corresponding roles of actual readers, (types of) IMPLIED READERS, and NARRATEES (the audience implicitly or explicitly addressed by the narrator in the text). In the multitiered process of narrative communication, an implied author might use a narrator's communication to a narratee as a means by which to communicate something else to the implied reader—as happens in UNRELIABLE NARRATION.

Author   The biographical individual who produces a text or a discourse. See also IMPLIED AUTHOR; NARRATION; NARRATOR.

Autodiegetic Narration   Gérard Genette's term for first-person, or HOMODIEGETIC, narration, in which the NARRATOR is also the main character in the STORYWORLD.

Biocularity   The double seeing required by texts such as graphic novels whose meanings arise from the interaction of verbal and visual signs. (See Hirsch's contribution to this volume.)

Carnivalesque   Mikhail Bakhtin's term for the subversive, antiauthoritarian elements of literature, including events (anarchic behavior of all kinds) and how they're told—for example, by means of parody or satire or with the use of socially unacceptable language (*Rabelais*).

Character   The entity who acts or is acted on in narrative. E. M. Forster distinguishes between round characters who are capable of surprising the audience and flat characters who are not. In the RHETORICAL account pioneered by James Phelan in *Reading People, Reading Plots*, characters can be analyzed into three components: mimetic (like a person); thematic (representative of a larger group or set of ideas); and synthetic (a construct that performs a role in the larger construction of the narrative). See also ACTANT; CODES FOR READING.

Chronicle   A record of events in chronological sequence without an EMPLOTMENT. See also STORY.

Chronotope   Mikhail Bakhtin defined the chronotope as "a formally constitutive category of literature . . . [in which] spatial and temporal indicators are fused" into a gestalt representational structure that is originally associated with a particular genre (e.g., novels of the road) but that is subsequently taken up in later texts in ways that lead to generic intermixing and the copresence of phenomena hailing from different phases of "the historico-literary process" ("Forms" 84–85).

Closure   The sense of an ending and the textual elements that convey or reinforce that sense.

Codes for Reading   In *S/Z*, Roland Barthes identified five codes (or systems for signification) from which narrative texts are woven and by means of which readers can in turn navigate those texts. The proairetic code governs the interconnection of actions within an unfolding PLOT. The hermeneutic code, which also relates to plot structure, bears on questions or enigmas that function as a source of suspense and that are answered or resolved (or are not) over the course of the text. The referential code links the text to surrounding scientific, cultural, and other bodies of knowledge, allowing readers to draw on their understanding of storytelling genres, received truths about the natural world, and other repertoires to make sense of a narrative. The semic code, which concerns how semantic features are categorized as information relevant for understanding persons, governs the process by which readers identify and interpret CHARACTERS and their attributes. Finally, the symbolic code enables readers to make sense of stories in terms of underlying thematic contrasts or oppositions (good versus evil, naive versus sophisticated, etc.). See also SEME.

Cognitive Narratology   A strand within POSTCLASSICAL NARRATOLOGY that focuses on mind-relevant dimensions of storytelling practices, wherever—and by whatever means—those practices occur. See also CONSCIOUSNESS REPRESENTATION; DEICTIC SHIFT; EXPERIENTIALITY; NARRATIVE WORLDMAKING; SPEECH AND THOUGHT REPRESENTATION.

Consciousness Representation   The representation of characters' (or narrators') minds in narrative discourse. Topics of study in this area include the structural possibilities for representing conscious experience—that is, the system of available mind-revealing techniques; the evolution or emergence of such techniques over time; and the interconnections among these techniques and broader conceptions of mind circulating in the culture or in more-specialized discourses. See also EXPERIENTIALITY; SPEECH AND THOUGHT REPRESENTATION.

Consonant Narration   Dorrit Cohn's term for a mode of NARRATION in which a narrator's presentation of events in the storyworld merges with a character's vantage point on those events. In the case of first-person, or HOMODIEGETIC, narration, Cohn refers to consonant self-narration. In the case of third-person, or HETERODIEGETIC, narration, consonant narration is the equivalent of what Franz K. Stanzel calls the figural NARRATIVE SITUATION. In either case, it corresponds to what Gérard Genette terms internal FOCALIZATION. See also DISSONANT NARRATION.

Conversational Storytelling   See FACE-TO-FACE STORYTELLING.

Cultural Narrative   A story that circulates widely within a given culture whose AUTHOR is not an individual but a larger collective entity constituting a significant subgroup within that culture.

Cultural Poetics   The study of the distinctive literary practices of a given culture, the forces that influence those practices, and the relations among them.

Cyberpunk   A school or period style of science fiction, flourishing from the eighties through the present, characterized thematically by a focus on the impact of digital technologies and virtual reality on human identity and associated with such writers as William Gibson, Bruce Sterling, Neal Stephenson, and Pat Cadigan.

Cybertext (Ergodic Literature)   Coined by Espen Aarseth for texts requiring nontrivial effort on the reader's or user's part to produce not only the STORYWORLD but also the text itself (or one version of it). Examples include texts designed in and for digital environments, such as HYPERTEXT fictions, as well as some print-based texts, including some POSTMODERN NARRATIVES.

Defamiliarization   Associated with RUSSIAN FORMALISM and later, in a slightly different form, with Prague school STRUCTURALISM, the idea that the ultimate function of literary art is to refresh reality for us and "make it strange," and that it does so by violating literature's own conventions (or deviating from its norms). Also called estrangement or *enstrangement* (translating the Russian neologism *ostranenie*).

Deictic Shift   Elaborated in the 1995 volume *Deixis in Narrative* (Duchan, Bruder, and Hewitt), deictic-shift theory holds that in order to comprehend a NARRATIVE, interpreters must take up a cognitive stance in the world evoked by a narrative, or STORYWORLD. In other words, readers, viewers, or listeners must shift from the world of the here and now to a different orienting frame of reference in order to be able to parse deictic expressions such as "I, at that time," and "over there"—and build up on the basis of such cues a global mental representation of the world in which CHARACTERS exist and interact. See also NARRATIVE WORLDMAKING.

Dialogism   Mikhail Bakhtin's term for a text's exploitation of the dialogic or multivoiced nature of language (*Dialogic Imagination*), as in the case of an ironic statement or, even more richly, in the "polyphony" of novelistic discourse.

Diegesis / Diegetic Level   Originating from Genettean narratology as well as structuralist film theory, the term *diegesis* designates the primary or matrix narrative that serves as a point of reference for determining the relation among narrative levels (and the location of NARRATORS on different levels) as well as for identifying the degree to which narrators participate in the events they recount. A narrative embedded within the primary level, for example, Nelly Dean's story in *Wuthering Heights*, told to Lockwood, another character at the primary diegetic level, is a hypodiegetic narrative, and its narrator is intradiegetic. By the same logic, Isabella Linton's letter to Nelly contains a hypo-hypodiegetic narrative, and Isabella is an intra-intradiegetic narrator. Since Lockwood, Nelly, and Isabella are all characters who participate in the action being narrated, they are also HOMODIEGETIC narrators. By contrast, the level occupied by any retrospective narrator of the events at the primary level is extradiegetic. Thus, a retrospective narrator who tells of events that he participated in, such as the elder Pip in Charles Dickens's *Great Expectations*, is extradiegetic-homodiegetic. A retrospective narrator who recounts events he or she did not participate in, such as the narrator of Hemingway's "Hills like White Elephants," is extradiegetic-heterodiegetic. Prospective telling can likewise be extra-, intra-, or hypodiegetic and can involve homo- and heterodiegetic tellers. For example, a character narrator who uses the future tense to predict what will happen to others is intradiegetic-heterodiegetic; if that narrator predicts her or his own fate, she or he is intradiegetic-homodiegetic. In the case of simultaneous narration, instances of first-person, or homodiegetic, telling (Robbe-Grillet's *La jalousie*, Beckett's *The Unnamable*, Coetzee's *Waiting for the Barbarians*) would seem to collapse this system of levels, since the narrators would be, at least in principle, both the producers and the product of their acts of telling. See also METALEPSIS; NARRATION.

Direct Discourse   See SPEECH AND THOUGHT REPRESENTATION

Discourse   In NARRATOLOGY, the "discourse" level of narrative (in French, *discours*) corresponds to what the Russian formalist theorists called the *sjužet*; it contrasts with the "story" (*histoire*) level. In this usage, *discourse* refers to the disposition of the SEMIOTIC cues used by interpreters to reconstruct a STORYWORLD.

Dissonant Narration   Dorrit Cohn's term for a mode of NARRATION in which a narrator's presentation of events in the storyworld differs from a character's vantage point on those events. In the case of first-person, or HOMODIEGETIC, narration, Cohn refers to dissonant self-narration. In the case of third-person or HETERODIEGETIC narration, dissonant narration is the equivalent of what Franz K. Stanzel calls the authorial NARRATIVE SITUATION and what Gérard Genette calls zero focalization. See also CONSONANT NARRATION.

Distancing Narrator   Robyn Warhol's term for a teller whose direct addresses to a NARRATEE emphasize the distance between them and, in that way, encourage the actual reader also to remain distant from the narratee. See also ENGAGING NARRATOR; NARRATOR.

Dominant   Roman Jakobson's term for the focusing component of a given literary work—the component in the light of which all of its other components are subordinated, coordinated, and integrated. For instance, according to Brian McHale, modernist novels are dominated by epistemological issues, while POSTMODERN NARRATIVES have an ontological dominant.

Duration   Gérard Genette's term for the ratio between how long situations and events take to unfold in the STORYWORLD and how much text is devoted to their NARRATION. Variations in this ratio correspond to different narrative speeds; in order of increasing speed, these are PAUSE, STRETCH, SCENE, SUMMARY, and ELLIPSIS.

Ekphrasis   The representation in a literary work of a visual composition.

Ellipsis   Gérard Genette's term for the omission of STORYWORLD events during the process of NARRATION; in ellipsis, narrative speed reaches infinity. See also DURATION; GAPS.

Emplotment   Hayden White's term for the process by which situations and events are linked together to produce a PLOT.

Engaging Narrator   Robyn Warhol's term for a teller whose direct addresses to a NARRATEE close the distance between them and, in that way, also encourage the actual reader to close that distance. See also DISTANCING NARRATOR; NARRATOR.

Equilibrium/Disequilibrium   In Tzvetan Todorov's account of narrative structure, the prototypical story follows a trajectory leading from an initial state of equilibrium, through a phase of disequilibrium, to an end point at which equilibrium is restored (on a different footing) because of intermediary events—though not every narrative traces the entirety of this path. See also NARRATIVE PROGRESSION; NARRATOLOGY; PLOT; STRUCTURALISM.

Ethnic-Identified Fictions   Fictional narratives interpreted as originating from or giving a plausible representation of the experiences of a particular ethnic group. (See Aldama's chapter in this volume.)

Ethnography   The study of cultural practices of all sorts, nonverbal as well as verbal. Ethnographic approaches to narrative focus on how storytelling both reflects understandings of cultural situations and also helps create such understandings by emplotting events in mutually intelligible ways and by affording a mode of communication in which cultural practices can be "worked out" at a microinteractional level. See also CULTURAL NARRATIVE; FACE-TO-FACE STORYTELLING.

Event   A change of state, creating a more or less salient and lasting alteration in the STORYWORLD. Events can be subdivided into temporally extended processes, deliberately initiated actions, and happenings not brought about intentionally by any agent.

Experientiality   Monika Fludernik's term for the dimension of narrative, by means of which it conveys what philosophers of mind refer to as qualia, or the sense of "what it is like" for an embodied human being or human-like consciousness to experience the situations and EVENTS recounted in the story.

Exposition   A presentation, sometimes given in the form of backstory, of the circumstances (such as time and place) and EVENTS that form a context or background for understanding the main action in a narrative.

Extradiegetic Narrator   See DIEGESIS / DIEGETIC LEVEL.

Fabula   See STORY.

Face/Facing   Emmanuel Levinas's terms to designate the ethical responsibility of one individual toward another. As one faces the other, one must recognize and respond to that otherness.

Face-to-Face Storytelling   The range of narrative practices conducted in contexts of face-to-face interaction, including not just stories elicited during interviews but also informal conversations between peers, he-said, she-said gossip, and conversations among family members at the dinner table. See also ETHNOGRAPHY.

Feminist Narratology   A strand of POSTCLASSICAL NARRATOLOGY that explores how issues of gender bear on the production, transmission, and interpretation of stories.

Fiction   Negatively, fiction can be defined as a type of discourse or communicative practice for which questions of truth-value do not apply in the way that they do for factual discourse. Positively, fiction is a type of discourse, or communicative practice, that suspends questions of truth-value to explore possible events, characters, scenarios, and worlds.

Fictional Recentering   The process by which authors and readers move from their actual world to a STORYWORLD assumed to be imaginary. See also DEICTIC SHIFT.

Filter   Seymour Chatman's term (*Coming*) for the perspectival bias, or vantage point, of a CHARACTER in the storyworld as opposed to the attitudes of a NARRATOR reporting events from a position outside that world. See also FOCALIZATION; SLANT.

Flat versus Round Character   See CHARACTER.

Focalization   Gérard Genette's term for modes of perspective taking in narrative discourse. In internal focalization, the viewpoint is restricted to a particular observer, or REFLECTOR, whereas in zero focalization the viewpoint is not anchored in a localized position and in external focalization the viewpoint is "objective," always perceiving a character from the outside. Further, internal focalization can be fixed, variable, or multiple. In Ernest Hemingway's "Hills like White Elephants," the focalization is variable, shifting between the vantage points of Jig and the male character.

Formalism   An approach to literary works that emphasizes the synthesis of their parts into a larger whole. Also the tendency in some varieties of literary research and theory to focus more on the way works organize their materials (or content) than on the materials that are so organized—or, for that matter, on the contexts in which those works are produced and interpreted. Often associated with RUSSIAN FORMALISM, STRUCTURALISM, Anglo-American New Criticism, and the Chicago school of neo-Aristotelianism.

Formula Fiction   See GENRE FICTION.

Free Indirect Discourse   See SPEECH AND THOUGHT REPRESENTATION.

Frequency   Gérard Genette's term for the ratio between the number of times something is told and the number of times it can be assumed to have occurred in the STORYWORLD. In singulative NARRATION, there is a one-to-one match between how many times an EVENT occurred and how many times it is told; in iterative narration, something that happened more than once is told once; and in repetitive narration, the number of times something is told exceeds the frequency with which it occurred in the STORYWORLD.

Function   An act of a CHARACTER defined in terms of its significance for the overall course of the narrative's action—for example, "hero acquires magical agent." Vladimir Propp identified thirty-one such functions in a typical fairy tale, occurring in a fixed sequence (though not every function occurs in every tale). See also CODES FOR READING; ACTANT.

Gaps   Lacunae or omissions in what is told or in the process of telling. Omissions in the telling constitute ELLIPSIS; those in the told underscore the radical incompleteness of fictional worlds (in *Heart of Darkness*, how many siblings did Marlow have, and exactly how old and how large is *The Nellie*, the ship on which Marlow tells the story of his encounter with Kurtz in the Congo?).

Gaze   In film theory, the term for the perspective provided by the way the camera frames a shot. Laura Mulvey argues that in Hollywood film the dominant gaze is coded as masculine and that women are typically the object of the male gaze rather than the ones doing the gazing. The term has migrated from film theory to narrative theory more generally and refers to who is doing the looking and the degree of power implied by that looking. See also FOCALIZATION.

Gender/Sex   Sex is biology's way of distinguishing between male and female through different reproductive organs, different degrees and kinds of hormones, and other such anatomical and physiological matters. Gender is culture's way of labeling certain behaviors as masculine or feminine.

Genre Fiction   Mass-market entertainment fiction, more overtly dependent on shared convections than so-called "literary" or "serious" fiction, and catering more openly to the expectations of readers familiar with these conventions. It includes genres and subgenres such as detective, mystery, and crime fiction; thrillers; science fiction and fantasy; horror; romance; Westerns; popular historical fiction; erotica; and so on. Also called formula fiction.

Hegemony   Term coined by Antonio Gramsci to refer to the dominance of a particular view or group over other views or groups, often through a process of manufactured consent. In hegemonic power structures, those in a subordinate role are induced to participate in their own domination. In turn, NARRATIVE can be used either to shore up or to subvert hegemony. See also IDEOLOGY; POLITICAL UNCONSCIOUS.

Heterodiegetic Narrator   Gérard Genette's term for a NARRATOR who has not participated in the circumstances and events about which he or she tells a story. See also DIEGESIS / DIEGETIC LEVEL.

Heteroglossia   Mikhail Bakhtin's term ("Discourse") for the interplay of different sociolects within a society. He valued the novel as the genre that reflected—even required—such heteroglossia. See also DIALOGISM.

Homodiegetic Narrator   Gérard Genette's term for a NARRATOR who has participated (more or less centrally) in the circumstances and events about which he or she tells a story. At the limit, homodiegetic narration shades off into AUTODIEGETIC narration. See also DIEGESIS / DIEGETIC LEVEL.

Hypodiegetic Narrative   See DIEGESIS / DIEGETIC LEVEL.

Hypertext   An assemblage of texts connected by links that afford multiple navigational pathways.

Icon   See SEMIOTICS.

Ideology   In Marxist accounts, ideology is the process by which a particular, historically contingent state of affairs is constructed as natural, immutable, simply built into the structure of things. From this perspective, narrative can serve ideological as well as counterideological functions, depending on whether a given story shores up or undercuts dominant accounts of the way the world is. See also HEGEMONY; POLITICAL UNCONSCIOUS.

Immersivity versus Interactivity   These two terms refer to two dimensions of narrative experience, which are sometimes characterized as contrasting or dichotomous but which can also be complementary and mutually reinforcing. *Immersivity* denotes the process by which interpreters get caught up in STORYWORLDS, living out complex blends of emotional and intellectual response as they engage with CHARACTERS involved in unfolding situations and EVENTS. *Interactivity* refers to recipients' ability to shape the telling of a story. For example, in FACE-TO-FACE STORYTELLING a listener can request that a narrator customize her or his account, and in HYPERTEXT fiction a recipient can influence the telling by clicking on one link rather than another.

Implied Author   A term coined by Wayne C. Booth to refer to the "second self" who writes the text and who reveals his or her traits and values through the construction of that text. More recently, James Phelan (*Living*) defines the implied author as a streamlined version of the actual author, a real or purported subset of the actual author's traits, beliefs, values, and abilities. The implied author is responsible for the choices that create the text as "these words in this order" and that imbue the text with his or her values.

Implied Reader   The intended addressee or AUDIENCE of the IMPLIED AU-THOR; another term for what RHETORICAL THEORISTS of narrative, following Peter J. Rabinowitz's coinage ("Truth"; *Before Reading*), call the authorial audience. The implied reader of Ernest Hemingway's "Hills like White Elephants" will know, for example, that Madrid is a city in Spain—though an actual reader unschooled in geography may not know these details.

Index   See SEMIOTICS.

Indirect Discourse   See SPEECH AND THOUGHT REPRESENTATION.

Intentional, Symptomatic, and Adaptive Reading   H. Porter Abbott's way of distinguishing between three kinds of interpretation (*Cambridge Introduction*). Intentional interpretation seeks to understand the text as it was designed by its author. Symptomatic reading seeks to identify problematic communications in the text that escape the author's control. Adaptive reading leaves intention behind entirely and uses the text in the service of the reader's own interests.

Interactive Fiction   A digitally produced narrative that involves textual exchange between a user or interactor and a computer program. The computer generates a text that situates existents and events in the simulated world, while input from the user (commands to a character or avatar) influences the unfolding of those events.

Intradiegetic Narrator   See DIEGESIS / DIEGETIC LEVEL.

Kernel   Seymour Chatman's term for an event that cannot be deleted from the paraphrase of a narrative without altering the story itself (*Story*). Roland Barthes called such events *nuclei* ("Introduction"). See also SATELLITE.

Langue/Parole   Ferdinand de Saussure distinguished between the system of language (*langue*) and the individual communicative acts made possible and intelligible by that system (*parole*). The STRUCTURALIST narratologists drew on this distinction, focusing on the system supporting narrative production and interpretation rather than on individual narratives.

Marriage Plot   One kind of MASTER PLOT in which the events are organized around the quest of the female protagonist to find a suitable man to marry.

Master Narrative   See HEGEMONY.

Master Plot   A general pattern of events shared by many individual narratives, such as the MARRIAGE PLOT. The master plots of a culture reveal a lot about that culture's common concerns and the way it prefers to address them.

Metalepsis   The confusion or entanglement of narrative levels, as when characters situated in a story within a story (or hypodiegetic narrative) migrate into the DIEGESIS or main narrative level. In Flann O'Brien's *At Swim-Two-Birds*, for example, the protagonist writes a novel whose characters then jump up one narrative level and attack the novelist who created them.

Minimal Departure, Principle of   Marie-Laure Ryan's idea that, unless cued to do otherwise, readers can assume that the STORYWORLD evoked by a NARRATIVE obeys the same physical laws and contains the same kinds of entities, situations, and EVENTS as those found in the actual world. Genres such as science fiction regularly suspend this principle by prompting readers to alter their default assumptions about the structure and inhabitants of more or less exotic storyworlds. See also NOVUM.

Mirror Neuron System   The part of the nervous system activated both when a creature (human or animal) acts and when it observes another creature acting. COGNITIVE NARRATOLOGY is interested in the mirror neuron system for what it may suggest about such matters as how we can understand and empathize with CHARACTERS portrayed in narratives.

Mood   Gérard Genette's term for the control of information in narrative discourse. *Mood* encompasses the ratio of knowledge between NARRATORS and CHARACTERS, as well as issues of vision or PERSPECTIVE (who sees or perceives) versus NARRATION (who speaks)—in Genette's terms, FOCALIZATION versus VOICE.

Narract   Term used by Antoine Volodine to question the boundary between the real and the imaginary and between narrative viewed as representation and narrative seen as creation.

Narrated Monologue   See SPEECH AND THOUGHT REPRESENTATION.

Narratee   The AUDIENCE of the NARRATOR, like the emissary of the count in Robert Browning's "My Last Duchess." Insofar as the narratee is an AUDIENCE role more or less explicitly inscribed in a narrative text, it is distinct from both the actual reader and the IMPLIED READER. See also UNRELIABLE NARRATION.

Narration   The process by which a NARRATIVE is conveyed; depending on the SEMIOTIC medium used, this process can involve complex combinations of cues in different channels (visual, auditory, tactile, etc.), yielding multimodal versus monomodal narration. Also, some theorists of narrative make narration the third term in a tripartite model that includes the STORY level; the DISCOURSE or text level, on the basis of which the story can be reconstructed; and the narration as the communicative act that produces the discourse. Other relevant parameters include the modes of narration identified by Gérard Genette, including AUTODIEGETIC, extradiegetic, HETERODIEGETIC, HOMODIEGETIC, hypodiegetic, and intradiegetic narration, as well as Dorrit

Cohn's distinction between CONSONANT and DISSONANT narration. See also
DIEGESIS / DIEGETIC LEVEL.

Narrative   In informal usage, *narrative* is a synonym for STORY. Analysts
developing various frameworks for narrative study, however, have proposed
more technical definitions. Gerald Prince (*Dictionary*) defines narrative as
"[t]he representation . . . of one or more real or fictive events communicated
by one, two, or several (more or less overt) narrators to one, two, or several
(more or less overt) narratees" (59). James Phelan has developed a rhetorical definition of narrative as the act of someone telling someone else on a
particular occasion for some purpose that something happened (*Narrative*).
For his part David Herman characterizes narrative as a mode of representation that must be interpreted in the light of a specific discourse context or
occasion for telling; that focuses on a structured course of particularized
EVENTS; that concerns itself with some kind of disruption or disequilibrium
in a STORYWORLD; and that conveys what it is like to live through this storyworld in flux.

Narrative Progression   The movement of a narrative from beginning to
end and the principles governing that movement. James Phelan's RHETORI-
CAL THEORY describes these principles as governing the synthesis of textual
dynamics and readerly dynamics (see esp. *Experiencing Fiction*). Textual dynamics refer to the introduction, complication, and resolution (often only
partial) of a set of unstable relationships among CHARACTERS or between
tellers and AUDIENCES, and readerly dynamics refer to the trajectory of the
authorial audience's response to those textual dynamics.

Narrative Situations   The Austrian narrative theorist Franz Karl Stanzel,
developing a nomenclature that has been especially influential in German
language traditions of narrative inquiry, distinguished among three main
narrative situations: first-person; third-person, or authorial; and figural,
which combines a third-person narrative voice with a REFLECTOR figure, or
particularized center of consciousness. See also CONSONANT NARRATION and
DISSONANT NARRATION.

Narrative Universals   Dimensions of narrative structure or content that
can be found across the world's narrative traditions, as well as across different storytelling media. Though the scope and nature of narrative universals
remain a matter of debate, a candidate for inclusion in the category is the
representation of EVENTS in a structured course of time (whereby earlier situations are transformed into later ones by intervening actions or events). See
also NARRATIVE; TRANSMEDIAL NARRATOLOGY.

Narrative Worldmaking   As characterized in David Herman's contribution to this volume, the process by which (1) storytellers use the SEMIOTIC
cues available in a given narrative medium to design blueprints for creating
and updating STORYWORLDS and (2) interpreters draw on such medium-

specific cues to build models of the worlds evoked through these narrative designs. (See also Elias's essay in this volume.)

Narrativity   That which makes a story a story; a property that a text or discourse will have in greater proportion the more readily it lends itself to being NARRATIVIZED or interpreted in narrative terms—in other words, the more prototypically NARRATIVE it is. What constitutes an expected or proto-typical form of narrative practice can vary, however, depending on the com-municative circumstances involved. See also TELLABILITY.

Narrativize   To present a set of situations and events in narrative terms—in other words, to produce a representation that possesses at least some degree of NARRATIVITY. Alternatively, to make sense of a text or discourse by interpreting it as a STORY—a process sometimes purposely impeded by post-modern or avant-garde literary texts.

Narratology   Originally, an approach to narrative inquiry developed dur-ing the heyday of STRUCTURALISM in France. Instead of working to develop interpretations of individual narratives, narratologists focused on how to describe narrative viewed as a SEMIOTIC system—that is, as a system by virtue of which people are able to produce and understand stories. In recent years the term has widened its meaning, and it is now often used as a synonym for narrative theory more generally. See also LANGUE/PAROLE.

Narrator   The agent who produces a NARRATIVE. Some story analysts distinguish among AUTODIEGETIC, extradiegetic, HETERODIEGETIC, HOMODI-EGETIC, and intradiegetic narrators. See also AUTHOR; DIEGESIS / DIEGETIC LEVEL; NARRATION.

Novum   Darko Suvin's term for the key novelty (technological innova-tion, utopian or dystopian social order, alien being or place, etc.) that distin-guishes a science fiction world from the world of contemporary reference. See also NARRATIVE WORLDMAKING; REALIZED METAPHOR; STORYWORLD.

Oedipal Narrative   A MASTER PLOT in our culture based on Sophocles's *Oedipus the King* as interpreted by Sigmund Freud. While Freud used the term *Oedipus complex* to refer to the unconscious desire of a son to murder his father and to sleep with his mother, the master plot tells of a male sub-ject's desire for a female and violent attitudes toward a rival and the eventual working out of those emotions (or not) in a socially acceptable way or not.

Omniscience   A quality attributed to some extradiegetic-HETERODIEGETIC narrators, referring not only to their total knowledge of the CHARACTERS and STORYWORLD but also to their capacity to locate themselves anywhere in that world. See also DIEGESIS / DIEGETIC LEVEL; FOCALIZATION.

Order   In Gérard Genette's model, a way of describing the relation be-tween two temporal sequences: the sequence of events that can be assumed to have unfolded in the STORYWORLD, and the unfolding of the DISCOURSE used to recount that sequence. When these two sequences are aligned, the result is chronological narration. ANACHRONY results when the sequences are disaligned, yielding ANALEPSES (or flashbacks), PROLEPSES (or flash-forwards), and sometimes complex combinations and embeddings of the two.

Oulipo Group   Abbreviation for Ouvroir de Littérature Potentielle (Workshop for Potential Literature), a Paris-based circle of literary experimentalists, flourishing from 1960 to the present, dedicated to producing literary works through the operation of preestablished procedures or constraints and associated with such figures as Raymond Queneau, Georges Perec, Italo Calvino, and Harry Mathews.

Palimpsest   Literally, writing in layers, where the inscription on one layer covers but does not obliterate those on previous layers. Metaphorically, a term used to refer to meanings that arise from the relation between surface and subsurface levels of a text.

Paralepsis   Gérard Genette's term for a technique in which more information is provided about the STORYWORLD than one would expect, given the dominant code of FOCALIZATION used in the text. In a text that scrupulously limits itself to presenting events in the way in which they appear while unfolding, a paraleptic moment would be one in which there is a sudden revelation of details that could only have been learned about later in time.

Paralipsis   Gérard Genette's term for a technique in which less information is provided about the STORYWORLD than one would expect, given the dominant code of FOCALIZATION used in the text. In a text that freely draws on information gained in the future to evaluate the significance of present events, a paraliptic moment would be one in which details are withheld about an occurrence that subsequently prove fateful.

Paratext   Term coined by Gérard Genette to refer to materials accompanying a text, such as a title, authorial attribution, date of publication, preface, epigram, afterword, and so forth (*Paratexts*). These materials afford resources for interpretation, allowing readers to channel and delimit their inferential activities by situating texts within generic categories, historical epochs, authors' oeuvres, sociopolitical controversies, and so on.

Pause   Gérard Genette's term for the slowest possible narrative speed; a type of DURATION in which the DISCOURSE of the NARRATOR continues to unfold, even though the action has come to a standstill.

Perspective/Point of View   As noted in Jesse Matz's contribtion to this volume, issues of perspective and point of view are now most often treated under the heading of FOCALIZATION. Gérard Genette drew a distinction between focalization, which pertains to who sees or perceives, and NARRATION, which pertains to who speaks in a narrative. See also VOICE.

Plot   H. Porter Abbott ("Story") has distinguished between three senses of the term *plot*: a type of story (as in MARRIAGE PLOT); the combination and sequencing of EVENTS that make a story a story and not just an assemblage of events; and a sense similar to that of DISCOURSE, by which theorists emphasize how the plot rearranges and otherwise manipulates the events of the STORY. See also EMPLOTMENT; NARRATIVE PROGRESSION.

Political Unconscious   Frederic Jameson's term for how narratives are necessarily embedded in broader sociopolitical contexts, which exert, sometimes in subterranean ways, a shaping pressure on narrative structure. The workings of the political unconscious in a given text can be recovered through a three-stage hermeneutical process based on three concentrically arranged interpretive horizons. In the first horizon, the text can be read in Lévi-Straussian terms as a symbolic act, in other words, an imaginary resolution of underlying social contradictions. In the second, wider horizon, the text functions as an ideologeme, or smallest intelligible unit of ideology; in this horizon, the text can be read as a symptom of the antagonism among class discourses. Finally, when interpreted within the third and widest horizon, the text reflects recessive, dominant, or emergent modes of production, in the Marxist sense of that term.

Possible World   See NARRATIVE WORLDMAKING; STORYWORLD.

Postclassical Narratology   Frameworks for narrative research (e.g., COGNITIVE NARRATOLOGY, FEMINIST NARRATOLOGY, and TRANSMEDIAL NARRATOLOGY) that build on the work of classical, structuralist NARRATOLOGISTS but supplement that earlier work with concepts and methods that were unavailable to story analysts such as Roland Barthes, Gérard Genette, A. J. Greimas, and Tzvetan Todorov during the heyday of STRUCTURALISM.

Postmodern Narrative   Innovative narrative forms practiced in Europe and the Americas (and maybe farther afield) since about 1960, in the aftermath of modernism; characterized by a playful and gamelike (ludic) quality; by parody, pastiche, and the rewriting of earlier texts; by the conflation of serious literature with popular culture, including GENRE FICTION; by self-reflection and metafiction; by critical reflection on the historical past and its representations; by neofantastic and other antirealistic forms; and by various strategies for pluralizing, problematizing, and destabilizing STORYWORLDS. See also CYBERTEXT; OULIPO GROUP.

Poststructuralism   A cover term for a variety of different positions that, building on but also reacting against STRUCTURALISM, question the stability and certainty of knowledge. In the strand of poststructuralism most influenced by the work of Michel Foucault, knowledge is never disinterested or objective because of its inextricable connection with power. In the strand most influenced by the work of Jacques Derrida, the quest for secure knowledge is bound up with a metaphysics of presence, which is in turn premised on a quixotic attempt to overcome the inevitable instability of language. In the strand most influenced by the work of Jacques Lacan, knowledge is understood as unstable because the subjectivity of the knower is grounded in signifying systems that are, again, irreducibly unstable. Generally speaking, poststructuralists regard classical NARRATOLOGY as a movement that fails to recognize the instability of narrative and the structures that it purports to depend on.

Progression   See NARRATIVE PROGRESSION.

Prolepsis   In Gérard Genette's model, the equivalent of a flash-forward in film. Prolepsis occurs when events that occur in the order *ABC* are told in the order *ACB, CAB,* or *BAC.*

Psychonarration   See SPEECH AND THOUGHT REPRESENTATION.

Public versus Private Voice   Susan Lanser's distinction between NARRATION addressed to a NARRATEE external to the storyworld (public) and narration addressed to a narratee internal to the storyworld (private). See also VOICE.

Punctum   Roland Barthes's term for that element of a photograph that touches the viewer emotionally, that element that has the power to "puncture" the viewer (*Camera Lucida*).

Quoted Monologue   See SPEECH AND THOUGHT REPRESENTATION.

Reader   See AUDIENCE.

Realized Metaphor   A procedure, widespread in poetry but also typical of science fiction and some POSTMODERN NARRATIVES, whereby a metaphorical expression is converted into a literal reality in some STORYWORLD. For instance, "His world exploded" would be understood as metaphorical in most contexts but could be realized in a science fiction context where exploding worlds are literally possible. See also NOVUM.

Reflector   A term coined by the novelist Henry James to designate the center of consciousness through whose perceptions events are FILTERED in a narrative using third-person, or HETERODIEGETIC, narration. A paradigm case would be Gregor Samsa in Franz Kafka's *Metamorphosis.*

Remediation   The interadaptation of sign systems, whereby an artifact or representation originally produced in one medium is transposed into another. Remediation is thus a more general process than, say, film adaptation, since it encompasses everything from plastic action figures based on television series or comic books to video games based on movies (or vice versa) to transcriptions based on audiorecorded or videorecorded communicative interactions.

Rhetorical Theories of Narrative   Rhetorical theories emphasize narrative as an act of communication from AUTHOR to AUDIENCE by means of the narrative text, but different theorists emphasize different elements and effects of that communication. Deconstructionists such as Paul de Man focus on the rhetorical figures of the narrative text to reveal the divided logic or unreadability of those figures and of the larger communication. Wolfgang Iser emphasizes the inevitable gaps in the narrative text and the activity of the IMPLIED READER in filling in those gaps (*Act; Implied Reader*). Meir Sternberg also focuses on textual gaps, linking them to effects of suspense, curiosity, and surprise. Mikhail Bakhtin examines the author's orchestration of the dialogic interplay among different sociolects in the narrative text ("Discourse"). Wayne C. Booth, Peter J. Rabinowitz, and James Phelan emphasize narrative as an act designed by an author for an implied audience in the service of a particular purpose. Their approach regards the text as a multilayered communication, and they are especially interested in the cognitive, affective, and ethical dimensions of that communication. See also DIALOGISM; NARRATIVE PROGRESSION; UNRELIABLE NARRATION.

Russian Formalists   A group of literary scholars and theorists, based in Saint Petersburg and Moscow in the years just before and after the 1917 revolution, until their suppression by the Bolshevik regime in the late twenties, and including Viktor Shklovsky, Roman Jakobson, Boris Eikhenbaum, Boris Tomashevsky, Yury Tynyanov, and (more tangentially) the folklorist Vladimir Propp. They were responsible for breakthrough insights into literary language, versification, literary history, and, not least, the poetics of narrative prose.

Satellite   Seymour Chatman's term (*Story*) for an EVENT that can be deleted from the paraphrase of a narrative without altering the STORY itself. Roland Barthes ("Introduction") called such events catalyzers. See also KERNEL.

Scene   In Gérard Genette's model, scenic presentation is a narrative speed or mode of DURATION in which one can assume a direct equivalence between how long it takes for things to happen in the STORYWORLD and how long it takes the NARRATOR to recount those happenings.

Seme   In semantics, a minimal unit of meaning—for example, the lexical item *bachelor* (in one of its senses) might be analyzed into the semes "not married" and "male." In Roland Barthes's *S/Z*, it is a connoted meaning, the basic unit of what Barthes calls the semic code. See also CODES FOR READING; SEMIOTICS; STRUCTURALISM.

Semiotics   The study of signs and, thus, of the codes that regulate their use and interpretation. Such CODES FOR READING, as Roland Barthes called them (*S/Z*), link signifying expressions with what they are standardly taken to signify, as when a loud, angry remark signifies a character's aggressiveness or a large estate signifies someone's wealth. For Ferdinand de Saussure, language is only one of multiple sign systems, and hence linguistics is a subset of semiotics—or "semiology," as Saussure called it. For C. S. Peirce, signs can be divided into three main types: icon, where there is a resemblance between signifier and signified (as when big eyeglasses are placed in front of an optometrist's office); index, where there is a causal relation between signifier and signified (as when smoke signifies fire); and symbol, where there is a conventional relation between signifier and signified (as with verbal language). See also SEME.

Situation of Enunciation   All those features of the context in which a narrative DISCOURSE is produced that shape that discourse, including features of the spatial and temporal context, the medium or channel involved, and so on, and especially the relationships among the parties to the act of enunciation (differences of gender, race, class, or seniority, relative power or authority, etc.).

Sjužet   See DISCOURSE.

Slant   Seymour Chatman's term (*Coming to Terms*) for the dispositions and attitudes of a NARRATOR reporting events from a position outside the STORYWORLD, as opposed to the perspectival bias or vantage point of a CHARACTER in that narrated world. See also FILTER; FOCALIZATION.

Speech and Thought Representation   The representation in narrative discourse of characters' utterances and thoughts. In the speech-category approach critiqued by Alan Palmer in *Fictional Minds*, theorists assume a basic parallelism, or homology, between modes of speech representation and strategies for representing characters' minds. Thus, indirect speech is mapped onto indirect thought, or what Dorrit Cohn terms psychonarration (cf. "Bob said that he was hungry and needed to eat" and "Feeling hungry, Bob realized that he needed to eat"); free indirect speech gets mapped onto free indirect thought, or Cohn's narrated monologue (cf. "Bob was hungry; he was damn sure going to eat"); and direct speech gets mapped onto direct thought, or quoted monologue ("Bob said/thought, 'I'm hungry, and I need to eat'"). Palmer and other COGNITIVE NARRATOLOGISTS have argued for the need to move beyond this speech-category approach and its focus on inner speech—to be able to capture other aspects of CONSCIOUSNESS REPRESENTATION in narrative contexts. See also EXPERIENTIALITY.

Story   In informal usage, *story* is a synonym for NARRATIVE. In NARRATOLOGY, the "story" level of narrative (in French, *histoire*) corresponds to what Russian formalist theorists called the fabula; it contrasts with the DISCOURSE (*discours*) level. In this sense, *story* refers to the chronological sequence of situations and EVENTS that can be reconstructed on the basis of cues provided in a narrative text.

Storyworld   The world evoked by a NARRATIVE text or DISCOURSE; a global mental model of the situations and events being recounted. Reciprocally, narrative artifacts (texts, films, etc.) provide blueprints for the creation and modification of such mentally configured storyworlds. See also DEICTIC SHIFT; NARRATIVE WORLDMAKING.

Stretch   Gérard Genette's term for a narrative speed or mode of DURATION faster than PAUSE but slower than SCENE, in which both NARRATION and action progress but what is told transpires more rapidly than the telling.

Structuralism   An approach to literary and cultural analysis, especially prominent in the sixties and seventies, that used linguistics as a "pilot-science" to study diverse forms of cultural expression as rule-governed signifying practices, or "languages," in their own right. NARRATOLOGY was an outgrowth of this general approach. See also LANGUE/PAROLE.

Summary   Gérard Genette's term for a narrative speed or mode of DURATION faster than SCENE but slower than ELLIPSIS; summaries are more or less compressed accounts of STORYWORLD occurrences.

Tellability   To be tellable, situations and EVENTS must in some way stand out against the backdrop formed by everyday expectations and norms, and thus be worth reporting. See also NARRATIVITY.

Transmedial Narratology   A strand of POSTCLASSICAL NARRATOLOGY premised on the assumption that, although storytelling practices in different media share common features insofar as they are all instances of the narrative text type, those practices are nonetheless inflected by the constraints and affordances associated with a given medium. Unlike classical NARRATOLOGY, transmedial narratology disputes the notion that the STORY level of a narrative remains wholly invariant across shifts of medium. However, it also assumes that stories do have "gists" that can be REMEDIATED more or less fully and recognizably—depending in part on the SEMIOTIC properties of the source and target media.

Transmission   (1) The process by which narratives circulate in a culture or across cultures. (2) The process by which narrative communication flows from an actual AUTHOR to an actual reader. Different approaches to narrative describe this transmission in somewhat different ways, but the most widespread model is a symmetrical one with three agents on each side of the communicative act. On the sending side there is an actual AUTHOR who creates an implied version of himself or herself who in turn creates a NARRATOR. On the receiving side, there is the AUDIENCE addressed by the narrator (the NARRATEE), the one addressed by the author (the IMPLIED READER or the authorial audience), and the actual reader. See also IMPLIED AUTHOR.

Unnatural Narrative   A narrative whose effects depend on its violation of the principles of mimesis, either in its elements of discourse (e.g., by employing nonhuman narrators) or in its elements of story (e.g., by depicting a STORYWORLD in which the law of noncontradiction does not apply).

Unreliable Narration   A mode of NARRATION in which the teller of a story cannot be taken at his or her word, compelling the AUDIENCE to "read between the lines"—in other words, to scan the text for clues about how the STORYWORLD really is, as opposed to how the NARRATOR says it is. There is much debate about whether unreliability is a consequence of an IMPLIED AUTHOR's signals or a reader's inferences. James Phelan's rhetorical approach (*Living*; "Estranging") identifies three main kinds of unreliability—misreporting about facts and events, misinterpreting characters' behavior or events, and misevaluating characters' ethical qualities—and two main effects of it, estranging (in which the unreliability increases the distance between the narrator and the authorial audience) and bonding (in which the unreliability closes that distance).

Vision   See FOCALIZATION; PERSPECTIVE / POINT OF VIEW.

Visual Culture   The various representations of a society that take a visual form and the processes by which they are produced, circulated, and interpreted.

Visual Literacy   The ability to encode and decode visual signs according to the norms of one's visual culture.

Voice   In classical narratology, the answer to the question, Who is speaking? In ideological criticism, the power to speak and to be heard (as in Gayatri Spivak's question, "Can the subaltern speak?"). In rhetorical theory, the synthesis of style, tone, and values. See also FOCALIZATION; NARRATION.

Worldmaking   See NARRATIVE WORLDMAKING.

Note

1. References to Genette cite *Narrative Discourse* unless otherwise indicated.

Works Cited

Aarseth, Espen. *Cybertexts: Perspectives on Ergodic Literature*. Baltimore: Johns Hopkins UP, 1997. Print.

Abbott, H. Porter. *The Cambridge Introduction to Narrative*. 2nd ed. Cambridge: Cambridge UP, 2008. Print.

———. "Story, Plot, and Narration." *The Cambridge Companion to Narrative*. Ed. David Herman. Cambridge: Cambridge UP, 2007. 39–51. Print.

Bakhtin, Mikhail. *Art and Answerability*. Ed. Michael Holquist. Trans. Vadim Liapunov and Kenneth Bostrom. Austin: U of Texas P, 1990. Print.

———. *The Dialogic Imagination: Four Essays by Bakhtin*. Ed. Michael Holquist. Trans. Caryl Emerson and Holquist. Austin: U of Texas P, 1981. Print.

———. "Discourse in the Novel." Bakhtin, *Dialogic Imagination* 259–423.

———. "Forms of Time and of the Chronotope in the Novel." Bakhtin, *Dialogic Imagination* 84–258.

———. *Rabelais and His World*. Trans. Hélène Iswolsky. Bloomington: Indiana UP, 1984. Print.

Barthes, Roland. *Camera Lucida*. Trans. Richard Howard. 2nd ed. New York: Hill, 1982. Print.

———. "An Introduction to Structural Analysis of Narrative." 1966. *New Literary History* 6.2 (1975): 237–72. Print.

———. *S/Z*. Trans. Richard Miller. New York: Hill, 1974. Print.

Booth, Wayne C. *The Rhetoric of Fiction*. 2nd ed. Chicago: U of Chicago P, 1983. Print.

Chatman, Seymour. *Coming to Terms: The Rhetoric of Narrative in Fiction and Film*. Ithaca: Cornell UP, 1990. Print.

———. *Story and Discourse: Narrative Structure in Fiction and Film*. Ithaca: Cornell UP, 1978. Print.

Cohn, Dorrit. *Transparent Minds: Narrative Modes for Presenting Consciousness in Fiction*. Princeton: Princeton UP, 1978. Print.

de Man, Paul. *Allegories of Reading*. New Haven: Yale UP, 1979. Print.

Duchan, Judith F., Gail A. Bruder, and Lynne E. Hewitt, eds. *Deixis in Narrative: A Cognitive Science Perspective*. Hillsdale: Erlbaum, 1995. Print.

Fludernik, Monika. *Towards a "Natural" Narratology*. New York: Routledge, 1996. Print.

Forster, E. M. *Aspects of the Novel*. 1927. New York: Harcourt, 1964. Print.

Genette, Gérard. *Narrative Discourse*. Trans. Jane E. Lewin. Ithaca: Cornell UP, 1980. Print.

———. *Paratexts: Thresholds of Interpretation*. Trans. Jane E. Lewin. New York: Cambridge UP, 1997. Print.

Gramsci, Antonio. *Selections from The Prison Notebooks*. Trans. and ed. Quinton Hoare and Geoffrey Nowell-Smith. New York: International, 1971. Print.

Greimas, Algirdas Julien. "Actants, Actors, and Figures." *On Meaning: Selected Writings in Semiotic Theory*. Trans. Paul J. Perron and Frank H. Collins. Minneapolis: U of Minnesota P, 1987. 106–20. Print.

———. *Structural Semantics: An Attempt at a Method*. Trans. Danielle McDowell and Alan Velie. Lincoln: U of Nebraska P, 1983. Print.

Herman, David. *Basic Elements of Narrative*. Oxford: Wiley-Blackwell, 2009. Print.

Iser, Wolfgang. *The Act of Reading*. Baltimore: Johns Hopkins UP, 1978. Print.

———. *The Implied Reader*. Baltimore: Johns Hopkins UP, 1974. Print.

Jakobson, Roman. "The Dominant." *Readings in Russian Poetics: Formalist and Structuralist Views*. Ed. Ladislav Matejka and Krystyna Pomorska. Cambridge: MIT P, 1971. 105–10. Print.

James, Henry. *The Art of the Novel: Critical Prefaces*. New York: Scribner's, 1962. Print.

Lanser, Susan. *Fictions of Authority: Women Writers and Narrative Voice*. Ithaca: Cornell UP, 1992. Print.

Levinas, Emmanuel. *Entre Nous: Essays on Thinking-of-the-Other*. Trans. Michael B. Smith and Barbara Harshav. New York: Columbia UP, 1998. Print.

McHale, Brian. *Postmodernist Fiction*. New York: Methuen, 1987. Print.

Mulvey, Laura. "Visual Pleasure and Narrative Cinema." *Screen* 16.3 (1975): 6–18. Print.

Palmer, Alan. *Fictional Minds*. Lincoln: U of Nebraska P, 2004. Print.

Peirce, Charles Sanders. *Collected Papers*. Ed. Charles Hartshorne and Paul Weiss. Vol. 2. Cambridge: Harvard UP, 1960. Print.

Phelan, James. "Estranging Unreliability, Bonding Unreliability, and the Ethics of *Lolita*." *Narrative* 15 (2007): 222–38. Print.

———. *Experiencing Fiction: Judgments, Progressions, and the Rhetorical Theory of Narrative*. Columbus: Ohio State UP, 2007. Print.

———. *Living to Tell about It: A Rhetoric and Ethics of Character Narration*. Ithaca: Cornell UP, 2005. Print.

———. *Narrative as Rhetoric: Technique, Audiences, Ethics, Ideology*. Columbus: Ohio State UP, 1996. Print.

———. *Reading People, Reading Plots: Character, Progression, and the Interpretation of Narrative*. Chicago: U of Chicago P, 1989. Print.

Phelan, James, and Peter J. Rabinowitz, eds. *A Companion to Narrative Theory*. Oxford: Blackwell, 2005. Print.

Prince, Gerald. *A Dictionary of Narratology*. 2nd ed. Lincoln: U of Nebraska P, 2003. Print.

Propp, Vladimir. *The Morphology of the Folktale*. Trans. Laurence Scott and Svatava Pirkova-Jakobson. Austin: U of Texas P, 1968. Print.

Rabinowitz, Peter J. *Before Reading: Narrative Conventions and the Politics of Interpretation*. Columbus: Ohio State UP, 1987. Print.

———. "Truth in Fiction: A Reexamination of Audiences." *Critical Inquiry* 4 (1977): 121–41. Print.

Saussure, Ferdinand de. *Course in General Linguistics*. Ed. Charles Bally and Albert Sechehaye. Trans. Roy Harris. London: Duckworth, 1983. Print.

Spivak, Gayatri. "Can the Subaltern Speak?" *Marxism and the Interpretation of Culture*. Ed. Cary Nelson and Lawrence Grossberg. Urbana: U of Illinois P, 1988. 271–313. Print.

Stanzel, Franz K. *A Theory of Narrative*. Trans. Charlotte Goedsche. New York: Cambridge UP, 1984. Print.

Sternberg, Meir. "Telling in Time (II): Chronology, Teleology, Narrativity." *Poetics Today* 13.3 (1992): 463–541. Print.

Suvin, Darko. *Metamorphoses of Science Fiction*. New Haven: Yale UP, 1979. Print.

Todorov, Tzvetan. *The Poetics of Prose*. Trans. Richard Howard. Ithaca: Cornell UP, 1977. Print.

Volodine, Antoine. *Minor Angels*. Trans. Jordan Stump. Lincoln: U of Nebraska P, 2004. Print.

Warhol, Robyn. *Gendered Interventions: Narrative Discourse and the Victorian Novel*. New Brunswick: Rutgers UP, 1989. Print.

White, Hayden. *Metahistory*. Baltimore: Johns Hopkins UP, 1973. Print.

Notes on Contributors

Frederick Luis Aldama is Arts and Humanities Distinguished Professor of English at Ohio State University, where he uses the tools of narratology and research in the cognitive and neuro-sciences in his teaching and scholarship on Latino and postcolonial literature, film, and comic books. He is the editor of five collections of essays and author of seven books, including most recently *A User's Guide to Postcolonial and Latino Borderland Fiction*.

Robert F. Barsky is professor of French at Vanderbilt University. He is the author of *Constructing a Productive Other*; *Arguing and Justifying*; *The Chomsky Effect*; *Noam Chomsky*; and *Introduction à la théorie littéraire*. He edited Panne-koek's *Workers Councils* and *Marc Angenot and the Scandal of History* and coedited *Bakhtin and Otherness* (with Michael Holquist) and *The Production of French Theory* (with Eric Méchoulan). He founded the journals *AmeriQuests*, *415 South Street*, and *Social Discourse*. His book "Zellig Harris: From American Linguistics to Socialist Zionism" is forthcoming from MIT Press.

Beth Boehm is professor of English and interim dean of the School of Interdisciplinary and Graduate Studies at the University of Louisville. Her research and teaching cross three areas of English studies: modern British literature; narrative studies; and rhetoric, composition, and pedagogy. She is coeditor, with Debra Journet and Cynthia Britt, of *Narrative Acts: Rhetoric, Race and Identity, Knowledge*.

Amy J. Elias is associate professor of English at the University of Tennessee, Knoxville. Her publications include articles on contemporary narrative and theory, history, and aesthetics and the book *Sublime Desire: History and Post-1960s Fiction*, winner of the ISSN's Perkins Prize. She is founder and serves on the executive committee of the Association for the Study of Arts of the Present. Her book in progress concerns dialogue and the contemporary arts.

Brian Evenson is the author of *Understanding Robert Coover* and of nine books of fiction, including *Altmann's Tongue*, *The Open Curtain*, *Last Days*, and *Fugue State*. He serves as the director of Brown University's Literary Arts Program.

David Gorman is associate professor of English at Northern Illinois University. He has published in various formats on the history and theory of literary criticism, including essays, reviews, bibliographies, translations, and entries in reference works. He is primarily concerned with the history of the study of literature. A book on narrative is in progress.

David Herman teaches in the English department at Ohio State University. He has published widely in the areas of interdisciplinary narrative theory, modern and postmodern fiction, and storytelling across media. He is the editor of the book series Frontiers of Narrative and the journal *Storyworlds*.

Marianne Hirsch is William Peterfield Trent Professor of English and Comparative Literature at Columbia University and codirector of the Center for the Critical Analysis of Social Difference. She is coauthor, with Leo Spitzer, of *Ghosts of Home: The Afterlife of Czernowitz in Jewish Memory* and the author of *Family Frames: Photography, Narrative, and Postmemory* and *The Mother-Daughter-Plot: Narrative Psychoanalysis, Feminism*. She has edited *The Familial Gaze* and coedited *Teaching the Representation of the Holocaust*, with Irene Kacandes, and the forthcoming *Rites of Return*, with Nancy K. Miller. A volume of her essays, *The Generation of Postmemory: Gender and Visuality after the Holocaust* is forthcoming.

Debra Journet is professor of English at the University of Louisville. Her research focuses on the role of narrative in evolutionary biology, composition research, and new digital genres. Her work has appeared in *Written Communication, Journal of Business and Technical Communication, Social Epistemology, Computers and Composition,* and *Mosaic*. She is coeditor, with Beth Boehm and Cynthia Britt, of *Narrative Acts: Rhetoric, Race and Identity, Knowledge*.

Emma Kafalenos teaches comparative literature at Washington University in Saint Louis. She is the author of *Narrative Causalities* and served as guest editor of *Contemporary Narratology*, a special issue of *Narrative*. She has published articles on narratives, narrative theory, and interrelations among media in journals including *Comparative Literature, 19th-Century Music, Narrative,* and *Poetics Today*.

Suzanne Keen is Thomas Broadus Professor of English at Washington and Lee University, where she teaches undergraduates narrative and the novel. She is on the faculty of the Bread Loaf School of English of Middlebury College. Her most recent books are *Empathy and the Novel* and *Narrative Form*.

Hans Kellner is professor of English at North Carolina State University. He is the author of *Language and Historical Representation*, and coeditor, with Frank Ankersmit, of *A New Philosophy of History* and, with Ewa Domanska, of *Re-figuring Hayden White*. Among his essays are " 'However Imperceptibly': From the Historical to the Sublime" and "Ankersmit's Proposal: Let's Keep in Touch."

Jesse Matz is associate professor of English at Kenyon College. He is the author of *Literary Impressionism and Modernist Aesthetics, The Modern Novel:*

A Short Introduction, and articles on modernist narrative. His current project is a book on the cultural uses of narrative temporality.

Brian McHale is Humanities Distinguished Professor of English at Ohio State University. He is the author of books and articles on modernist and postmodernist fiction and poetry, narrative theory, and science fiction, and coeditor, with Randall Stevenson, of *The Edinburgh Companion to Twentieth-Century Literatures in English*.

Susan Mooney is associate professor of comparative literature at the University of South Florida. She is the author of *The Artistic Censoring of Sexuality: Fantasy and Judgment in the Twentieth-Century Novel*. She is working on a study entitled "Writing Resistance: Censorship and the Novel, Theater, and Film in Franco's Spain" and a monograph on the relation between masculinity and ethics in the modern novel.

James Morrison is professor of film and literature at Claremont McKenna College. He is the author, coauthor, or editor of books on film and culture, including *Roman Polanski*.

Adam Zachary Newton is University Professor and Ronald P. Stanton Chair in Literature and the Humanities at Yeshiva University and chair of the Yeshiva College English department. He is the author of *Narrative Ethics; Facing Black and Jew: Literature as Public Space in Twentieth-Century America; The Fence and the Neighbor: Emmanuel Levinas, Yeshayahu Leibowitz, and Israel among the Nations;* and *The Elsewhere: On Belonging at a Near Distance*. His new project is called "To Make the Hands Impure: Art and Ethical Adventure, the Difficult and the Sacred."

James Phelan is Distinguished University Professor of English at Ohio State University. He is the editor of the journal *Narrative* and coeditor, with Peter J. Rabinowitz, of the series Theory and Interpretation of Narrative. His most recent books are *Living to Tell about It: A Rhetoric and Ethics of Character Narration* and *Experiencing Fiction: Judgments, Progressions, and the Rhetorical Theory of Narrative*.

Jill Walker Rettberg is associate professor of digital culture at the University of Bergen. Her research centers on the ways narrative is evolving online, and she has published articles and books on blogs, social media, games, and electronic literature. Her recent publications include the book *Blogging* and the anthology *Digital Culture, Play, and Identity: A World of Warcraft Reader*, coedited with Hilde Corneliussen.

Scott Rettberg is associate professor of digital culture at the University of Bergen. He is the author or coauthor of works of electronic literature, including *The Unknown; Kind of Blue; Implementation;* and *Frequency*. He founded the Electronic Literature Organization. He is working on a book about contemporary electronic literature in the context of the twentieth-century avant-garde.

Brian Richardson is professor of English at the University of Maryland. He is the author of *Unlikely Stories: Causality and the Nature of Modern Narrative* and *Unnatural Voices: Extreme Narration in Modern and Contemporary Fiction*. He is the editor of *Narrative Dynamics: Essays on Time, Plot, Closure, and Frames* and *Narrative Beginnings: Theories and Practices*. He is working on the theory of antimimetic narratives.

Amy Shuman is professor of English at Ohio State University. She is the author of *Storytelling Rights: The Uses of Oral and Written Texts by Urban Adolescents*; *Other People's Stories: Entitlement Claims and the Critique of Empathy*; and, with Carol Bohmer, *Rejecting Refugees: Political Asylum in the Twenty-First Century*. She is working on theories of empathy in conversational narrative.

Robyn Warhol is Arts and Humanities Distinguished Professor of English at Ohio State University. Her books include *Having a Good Cry: Effeminate Tears and Popular Forms*; *Gendered Interventions: Narrative Discourse in the Victorian Novel*; and *Feminisms Redux*, coedited with Diane Price Herndl.

Index

Modern Language Association of America
Options for Teaching

Teaching Narrative Theory. Ed. David Herman, Brian McHale, and James Phelan. 2010.

Teaching British Women Playwrights of the Restoration and Eighteenth Century. Ed. Bonnie Nelson and Catherine Burroughs. 2010.

Teaching Early Modern English Prose. Ed. Susannah Brietz Monta and Margaret W. Ferguson. 2010.

Teaching Italian American Literature, Film, and Popular Culture. Ed. Edvige Giunta and Kathleen Zamboni McCormick. 2010.

Teaching the Graphic Novel. Ed. Stephen E. Tabachnick. 2009.

Teaching Literature and Language Online. Ed. Ian Lancashire. 2009.

Teaching the African Novel. Ed. Gaurav Desai. 2009.

Teaching World Literature. Ed. David Damrosch. 2009.

Teaching North American Environmental Literature. Ed. Laird Christensen, Mark C. Long, and Fred Waage. 2008.

Teaching Life Writing Texts. Ed. Miriam Fuchs and Craig Howes. 2007.

Teaching Nineteenth-Century American Poetry. Ed. Paula Bernat Bennett, Karen L. Kilcup, and Philipp Schweighauser. 2007.

Teaching Representations of the Spanish Civil War. Ed. Noël Valis. 2006.

Teaching the Representation of the Holocaust. Ed. Marianne Hirsch and Irene Kacandes. 2004.

Teaching Tudor and Stuart Women Writers. Ed. Susanne Woods and Margaret P. Hannay. 2000.

Teaching Literature and Medicine. Ed. Anne Hunsaker Hawkins and Marilyn Chandler McEntyre. 1999.

Teaching the Literatures of Early America. Ed. Carla Mulford. 1999.

Teaching Shakespeare through Performance. Ed. Milla C. Riggio. 1999.

Teaching Oral Traditions. Ed. John Miles Foley. 1998.

Teaching Contemporary Theory to Undergraduates. Ed. Dianne F. Sadoff and William E. Cain. 1994.

Teaching Children's Literature: Issues, Pedagogy, Resources. Ed. Glenn Edward Sadler. 1992.

Teaching Literature and Other Arts. Ed. Jean-Pierre Barricelli, Joseph Gibaldi, and Estella Lauter. 1990.

New Methods in College Writing Programs: Theories in Practice. Ed. Paul Connolly and Teresa Vilardi. 1986.

School-College Collaborative Programs in English. Ed. Ron Fortune. 1986.

Teaching Environmental Literature: Materials, Methods, Resources. Ed. Frederick O. Waage. 1985.

Part-Time Academic Employment in the Humanities: A Sourcebook for Just Policy. Ed. Elizabeth M. Wallace. 1984.

Film Study in the Undergraduate Curriculum. Ed. Barry K. Grant. 1983.

The Teaching Apprentice Program in Language and Literature. Ed. Joseph Gibaldi and James V. Mirollo. 1981.

Options for Undergraduate Foreign Language Programs: Four-Year and Two-Year Colleges. Ed. Renate A. Schulz. 1979.

Options for the Teaching of English: Freshman Composition. Ed. Jasper P. Neel. 1978.

Options for the Teaching of English: The Undergraduate Curriculum. Ed. Elizabeth Wooten Cowan. 1975.